Virginia Commonwealth University

Frontispiece: Dr. Edmund F. Ackell, president of Virginia Commonwealth University.

VIRGINIA COMMONWEALTH UNIVERSITY

A Sesquicentennial History

VIRGINIUS DABNEY

University Press of Virginia
Charlottesville

THE UNIVERSITY PRESS OF VIRGINIA

First published 1987

Library of Congress Cataloging-in-Publication Data

Dabney, Virginius, 1901–
Virginia Commonwealth University : a sesquicentennial history.

Bibliography: p.
Includes index.
1. Virginia Commonwealth University—History.
I. Title.
LD5651.V85D33 1987 378.755'451 87-1982
ISBN 0-8139-1138-9

Printed in the United States of America

This book is affectionately dedicated to
ALEXANDER PIERSON LEVERTY II, M.D.
A graduate of the Medical College of Virginia
who became an excellent physician
and having married my daughter is the father
of three of my beloved grandchildren

Contents

APPENDIXES

Illustrations

Preface

VIRGINIA COMMONWEALTH UNIVERSITY, on the one hundred and fiftieth anniversary of its founding, is a thriving, nationally recognized urban institution, with some twenty thousand students. It has come a vast distance since its parent component, the Medical College of Virginia, opened its doors on November 5, 1838, as a branch of Hampden-Sydney College, in what had been Richmond's Union Hotel at Nineteenth and Main streets.

The founding date of the college, according to one version, is December 1, 1837, since that was the day on which the Hampden-Sydney trustees accepted a petition of physicians requesting the college to establish a medical department in Richmond. However, the official seal of Virginia Commonwealth University, incorporating the Medical College, uses the year 1838 for the founding.

The Medical College of Virginia (MCV) functioned alone until 1968, when it came together with the Richmond Professional Institute (RPI) to form Virginia Commonwealth University (VCU).

RPI, originally known as the Richmond School of Social Work and Public Health, came into existence in 1917, shortly after this country entered World War I. It was domiciled in three former bedrooms on the third floor of a converted residence at 1112 Capitol Street, on the site of the present Virginia State Library. The scantily furnished rooms were heated by wood-burning stoves and lighted by gas. There was only one full-time teacher, and he, a human dynamo, was also the sole administrator, janitor, and general handyman.

Both segments of Virginia Commonwealth University have come to their present state after surviving stresses and strains of various kinds, financial and otherwise, that would have daunted less-determined educators.

The medical department of Hampden-Sydney survived until 1854, but in that year a bitter controversy broke out between two medical factions. It ended with the department breaking away from Hampden-Sydney and constituting itself as the Medical College of Virginia. This was the first of a long series of internecine and acrimonious brawls between medical groups in Richmond lasting, off and on, for about a century. These confrontations between leading medical factions and individuals in the city were almost unbelievable in their intensity. At least one duel was narrowly averted, police were called out on two occasions, and there was a suicide.

It is to be doubted whether such conditions prevailed in any other American city. The establishment of several private hospitals here, each with an eminent surgeon at its head, served to polarize the profession. Today there is much rivalry among the various groups, and healthy competition prevails. The hospitals strive with each other for patients, and there may be a fair degree of undercover hostility, but it is not carried on openly in the press, as was the case formerly. The year 1914 was apparently the last during which two groups of eminent medical men exchanged personal insults in the Richmond newspapers.

Indeed, the behavior of some physicians in days gone by, as described by one of them, was well-nigh incredible. Dr. William H. Taylor, for decades a distinguished member of the Medical College faculty, wrote in his book, *De Quibus,* published in 1908:

> Some of the famous physicians and surgeons of former days were notorious for their ill-temper and rudeness . . . Domineering insolence was by no means unknown among the old-time doctors of Richmond. It was not a very strange thing for the doctor to take possession of the patient's home, to go storming through it, to demolish with his own hands obnoxious articles of food and drink, plates, dishes, cups and saucers, and even beds, and to make himself such a portent and such a terror that when he hove in sight consternation fell upon the habitation, the women rolled themselves together as a scroll and the children fled into a back alley. This sort of thing is no longer tolerated, as it had to be when only one or two practitioners in a community possessed preeminent talent.

The Stethoscope, a medical journal published in Richmond before the Civil War, sought to deride those who said doctors were a contentious lot. Its editor wrote in 1854: "We have heard but one objection urged against the formation of medical societies: that is that they do not promote harmony. Doctors are proverbial for disagreement. Such sentiments are often proclaimed by gentle, meek, peace-loving, seedy newspaper editors, fruitless lawyers, and *pothouse* politicians, when they wish to discredit our profession, and who intermeddle in our politics."

But other doctors admitted, in their more candid moments, that there was truth in the allegation that they were wont to denounce one another to an excessive degree. For example, the *Virginia Clinical Record* declared in 1871: "The absence of union among medical men, as indicated by their jealousies, their enmities, and bickerings, has long been a source of painful regret to all good men in and out of the profession."

Also during these early days there was protest against so-called medical schools that promised to turn out a finished physician in sixteen weeks for $35. This led Dr. Claiborne Gooch, a prominent medical man of the antebellum era, to write:

> Doctors, how sorry they are made
> With locomotive speed!
> The College drives a thriving trade,
> The faculty are fee-ed.
>
> A Roman emperor, it is said,
> Once of his horse a consul made
> But things now come to pass—
> They make a doctor of an Ass.

While the medical profession in Richmond was guilty of decidedly raucous behavior at times, it is important to note that some of those involved were among the most distinguished physicians and surgeons in the United States. One finds it a bit difficult to understand how men of such exceptional attainments, high character, fine instincts, and attractive personality managed to work themselves up into so belligerent a state of mind vis-à-vis their fellow practitioners. Yet this happened over and over again.

In spite of, or because of, these confrontations, Richmond has long been recognized as an important medical center. A Medical College graduate won the Nobel Prize, and other graduates or faculty members have distinguished themselves with significant advances in research, in surgical or medical techniques, and in other ways. Richmond doctors who graduated elsewhere also have achieved much distinction. It is arguable that the rivalries, and even the enmities, in the city were in part responsible for some of these notable achievements, since intense competiton is often conducive to superior performance.

Richmond Professional Institute, now the Academic Division of VCU, has had its struggles and discouragements. Following its establishment in 1917, it operated for years on the merest shoestring, and was able to go forward only because certain Richmond businessmen raised funds to keep it alive. Not until 1940 did the state appropriate one cent to the hard-pressed school, and then only a minuscule amount. This despite the fact that the school was taken over in 1925 by the College of William and Mary, a state institution, and became the Richmond Professional Institute of the college. It remained so until 1962, when it was divorced from William and Mary to become a separate state institution, still under the name Richmond Professional Institute. A highly prestigious board of visitors was appointed at that time by the governor, and the General Assembly soon began making far more adequate appropriations. There was a rapid rise in the level of faculty, buildings, and equipment. In 1968, as already noted, the institute joined with the Medical College of Virginia to become Virginia Commonwealth University.

But before these things took place, RPI had a continuing battle for existence. Teachers were underpaid for many years, equipment was grossly inadequate, laboratories were inferior or nonexistent, and classes were held in lofts or converted stables, kitchens or former residences. It was hardly less than a miracle that the institute survived. Only by the use of the most amazing ingenuity and resourcefulness was this achieved.

Despite these vast discouragements, the institute performed an extremely important function in the educational life of Richmond and the state. At first its emphasis was on educating students to earn a living, and this was accomplished in innumerable instances. The problems of obtaining employment in an urban environment were stressed, and continued to be stressed thereafter. RPI and VCU were established as urban institutions, with constant efforts by faculty and students to solve problems growing out of an urban setting.

Courses taught at RPI in the 1920s included social work, public health nursing, recreational activities, and the fine arts. The evening school, which developed spectacularly in later years, opened at this time. In the 1930s departments of commercial art, interior decoration, costume design and fashion, and art education were added. Still other courses not offered elsewhere in Virginia were included in the curriculum. As time went on classes in the liberal arts and the humanities were introduced.

It should be noted that despite the many problems resulting from the tightest imaginable budgets, the recurring shortages of nearly everything, and the sorely underpaid teaching staff, there was often a good espirit de corps among both students and faculty. Members of both groups who survive from that era testify to this today.

The student body was unusually diverse, especially when the male matriculates arrived in force after World War II. Until then nearly all the undergraduates were women. Many different types of men were enrolled in the middle and late 1940s, from a great variety of age groups. There were regulations as to dress at mid-century, and these were violated at times, but in the late 1960s things got out of hand almost everywhere. As at many other institutions, boys and girls vied with one another in dressing in outlandish ways—the unkempt girls with patched, frayed, soiled blue jeans, and the boys with long, unruly hair, straggly beards, and dirty pants, often no shirts or shoes. At that particular period it was the same on nearly all campuses—Harvard, Yale, Princeton, the University of Virginia—there was no appreciable difference among them at this time. Since VCU's Academic Campus was right in the middle of town, and thousands of citizens passed through it daily, there was much criticism of the "tacky," "raffish," "frowzy," "hippie" students. The fact was that students were like that almost universally. In that era they were in revolt against established customs and mores. There were no riots at VCU, no tossing of deans downstairs, nor was mayhem committed on any professors, as happened elsewhere, but there was a distinct "bolshevist" trend, with "demands" for this and that. This "agin the government" attitude faded away gradually in the 1970s, with the result that the prevailing viewpoint everywhere became far more conservative.

As one contemplates the first one hundred and fifty years of Virginia Commonwealth University's history, it is obvious that many able and accomplished men and women have contributed to its success. Their roles will be examined in the pages that follow. But if one had to choose a single individual from each of the university's component parts whose contribution was greatest, indeed indispensable, the choice would have to be William T. Sanger from the Medical College and Henry H. Hibbs from Richmond Professional Institute.

Dr. Sanger took over the presidency of the Medical College when many feared that it was on its last legs. Efforts to merge with the University of Virginia Medical School had failed, and the college was almost bankrupt. Its future looked extremely bleak. There were problems galore, but Sanger tackled them with immense energy and insight. Within a year or two the trend was reversed, and the outlook was changed from one of near-hopelessness to one of optimism. While an enormous lot remained to be done, it was under Sanger that the Medical College came into its own and was finally recognized as a high-ranking medical school.

Henry H. Hibbs was the man who created RPI from virtually nothing. By means of astonishing ingenuity and drive, by scrounging funds here and there, converting stables and lofts into classrooms, and taking advantage of every conceivable opportunity, he slowly but surely built a unique institution.

VCU enjoys bright prospects today under Dr. Edmund F. Ackell, who came to the presidency in early 1978 from the University of Southern California, where he was special assistant for governmental affairs, and had served previously as vice president for health affairs. Holding both M.D. and D.M.D. degrees, with wide administrative experience at several institutions, Dr. Ackell has proved to be an excellent choice. A man of dynamic personality and marked executive ability, he has accomplished many of his goals for VCU, and he looks forward to accomplishing others. Under him the university has been strengthened in various directions.

When RPI and MCV were brought together in 1968, there was a decided lack of enthusiasm on the part of some MCV administrators, faculty, students, and alumni for joining with a younger and less prestigious school. MCV alumni were understandably proud of their college's ancient traditions. Some of them found it difficult to think of it as VCU rather than MCV. Others refused to contribute funds to anything but the medical school.

President Ackell has addressed these concerns effectively, and has stressed the importance of building a united university. His efforts have brought results. For example, he has persuaded the graduates of the Medical College to cooperate in the restructuring of their alumni association, in the interests of a more unified alumni operation. The overall result has been a better feeling all around, with closer cooperation between the Academic and Medical campuses.

Dr. Ackell has won a respected place in Richmond, and relations between VCU and the community have improved markedly. The west campus is no longer regarded as a haven for hippies, but rather as a valuable center of learning, contributing importantly to the academic, cultural, and material advancement of Richmond and Virginia, with particular emphasis on urban problems.

Virginia Commonwealth University's second century and a half promises to be even more productive than its first. Its place in Virginia history is secure.

Acknowledgments

I WISH FIRST to express my indebtedness to President Edmund F. Ackell, who has been completely cooperative and has facilitated my researches and writing in every way, leaving me complete freedom. Others who have read substantial portions, and to whom I am much obligated for their criticisms and suggestions, are Dr. Peter N. Pastore, Dr. Charles M. Caravati, Dr. Wyndham B. Blanton, Jr., Howard L. Sparks, and William O. Edwards. In addition, Herbert E. Teachey, Jr., Dr. Thomas W. Murrell, Jr., Dr. John P. Lynch, Dr. Lewis H. Bosher, Jr., Edwin R. Thomas, Lewis B. Mills, Earl McIntyre, George T. Crutchfield, and James L. Dunn have each read a portion, and have given me the benefit of their suggestions.

Dr. Harry M. Lyons, Dr. Kinloch Nelson, and Dr. Richard A. Michaux were gracious in assisting me with parts of the work. Dr. John Andrako was especially cooperative. And I cannot speak too highly of the total, and remarkably knowledgeble, helpfulness of the staffs of the Tompkins-McCaw and James Branch Cabell libraries. Jodi Koste and Melissa Irby Driver at the former institution went far beyond the call of duty, as did Katherine Bachman at the latter. I am vastly indebted to them. The library of Richmond Newspapers was the source of much material, and I am especially obligated to Kathy Albers there for her constant and informed assistance. Meg F. Price did much to facilitate the entire process at the VCU president's office, as did Kay Wood. The American Medical Association responded to my call for information.

Others to whom I owe thanks are Dr. Stephen M. Ayers, Daniel A. Yanchisin, Dr. Alexander P. Leverty II, Robert Archer Wilson, Col. John H. Heil, Richard A. Velz, Dr. Hunter H. McGuire, Jr., Dr. Russell V.

Bowers, Carole Roper, H. I. Willett, Samuel A. Anderson III, Dr. L. Benjamin Sheppard, John A. Mapp, Ashley Kistler, Anne Hobson Freeman, Dr. William H. Higgins, Jr., Dr. W. Taliaferro Thompson, Jr., Dr. Warren E. Weaver, Dr. Harry J. Warthen, Jr., Harold E. Greer, Jr., Robert J. Grey, Mary Sheffield Smith, Sara T. Morrow, Dr. H. St. George Tucker, Jr., Bruce Compton, Lois Washer, Helen Johnston Skinner, Dr. Alastair M. Connell, Ralph M. Ware, Jr., Anne P. Satterfield, Alden G. Bigelow, Charles Saunders, Thomas L. Dunn, Murry N. DePillars. Douglas H. Ludeman, Theresa Pollak, Arnold P. Fleshood, Beverly Orndorff, John Bryan, Martha Riis Moore, Alice Whiteside Jorg, Dr. Weir M. Tucker, Doris B. Yingling, Dr. John W. Lynn, Dr. DuPont Guerry III, David W. Brown, Dr. James W. Brooks, Rabbi Myron Berman, Franklin Stone, Richard I. Wilson, Bernard Martin, Elaine Z. Rothenberg, Wayne C. Hall, J. Curtis Hall, Jane Bell Gladding, Dr. John L. Patterson, Jr., W. Roy Smith, Lynda Moore, Alf Goodykoontz, Dr. Walter Lawrence, Jr., Dr. J. Shelton Horsley III, Bernard W. Woodahl, Dr. Dwain L. Eckberg, Dr. G. Watson James III, Bill Millsaps, Dr. Richard R. Lower, Edgar J. Fisher, Jr., Richard W. Wiltshire, Jack A. Duncan, Thomas V. McGovern, Thomas O. Hall, Jr., Dr. H. M. Lee, David Napier, William E. Blake, Jr., William H. Duvall, C. A. B. Foster, Dr. Leo J. Dunn, Carole Negus, Kenneth L. Ender, Louis C. Saksen, David E. Bagby, Jr., James R. Johnson, Clare M. Rosenbaum, Dr. John N. Pastore, Dr. Percy Wootton, David Mathis, Celia Barnes, and Fred Anderson.

It goes without saying that I am grateful for many things to the late Walker Cowen, director of the University Press of Virginia, who was wholly cooperative and helpful at all times. I also wish to express my sincere indebtedness to Gerald Trett, my editor at the Press, who saved me from errors of various kinds.

I have found six published works especially helpful, namely: William T. Sanger's *Medical College of Virginia before 1925 and University College of Medicine, 1893-1913,* and his memoir *As I Remember;* Henry H. Hibbs's *A History of the Richmond Professional Institute,* Dr. Wyndham B. Blanton's *Medicine in Virginia in the Nineteenth Century,* Dr. Charles M. Caravati's *Medicine in Richmond, 1900-1975,* and *The First 125 Years: 1838-1963,* MCV *Bulletin,* Fall 1963.

Such sins as I have committed in this book, whether of omission or commission, are my own, and not the responsibility of any of the numerous persons mentioned who were kind enough to give me a helping hand.

Virginia Commonwealth University

ONE

In the Beginning

A MIDDLE-AGED GENTLEMAN lecturing on surgery in a high silk hat and performing operations in the same stovepipe was a sensation at the Prince Edward Medical Institute, opened by him in 1837 near Hampden-Sydney College. He was Dr. John Peter Mettauer, whom Dr. Wyndham B. Blanton credits with "building a professional career unsurpassed in this country for originality and volume of work accomplished." When he died some decades later, and by his own direction was buried wearing his silk hat—his coffin had to be made eight feet long to accommodate it—Mettauer had made surgical history. He had also brought attention forcibly to the importance of improved medical instruction in Virginia. Such organized instruction had been offered at the University of Virginia since its opening in 1825, but elsewhere in the state the teaching of medicine consisted of apprenticeship under established physicians and surgeons.

As a part of the trend toward more effective medical training, four physicians petitioned Hampden-Sidney (it was spelled that way then) to establish a medical department of the college in their city of Richmond. It was argued that Richmond would provide a much wider selection of clinical material than rural Virginia or the village of Charlottesville. Another contention was that too many Virginians were going north for medical teaching—more of them from Virginia than from any other southern state.

Dr. Augustus L. Warner was the leader in organizing the petition to Hampden-Sydney for a medical department in Richmond. He was joined by three other Richmond physicians—John Cullen, Lewis Webb Chamberlayne, and Richard L. Bohannan. The college trustees granted the request, and the institution opened in the remodeled Union Hotel on November 5, 1838.

The faculty consisted of the four petitioners plus Drs. Socrates Maupin and Thomas Johnson. It was an impressive teaching staff. Medicine, of course, was in a relatively primitive state, and the epoch-making discoveries that have almost wiped out some of the most terrible scourges and greatly reduced mortality from others were far in the future.

Dr. Warner was chosen dean of the infant institution. He was an accomplished surgeon who came to the school from the University of Virginia faculty, and was a stunning lecturer. He is credited with important surgical advances. Dr. Cullen, an Irishman with a charming brogue, took snuff from a gold box before beginning his exceptionally attractive lectures. He built a handsome residence at the corner of Ross and Governor streets, which much later was the first home of St. Luke's Hospital. Dr. Chamberlayne, a great-grandson of William Byrd II of Westover, was the father of Mrs. George W. Bagby, the talented wife of the well-known writer. Chamberlayne's personality and character were widely admired. Dr. Maupin, whose entire adult life was given to teaching, succeeded Warner as dean when the latter died at age forty. Maupin headed two private academies in Richmond before joining the medical faculty in that city, and he retained the headmastership of one of them as long as he was in Richmond. He later was a distinguished member of the University of Virginia faculty, serving as its chairman for sixteen years and doing much to keep the institution in operation during the Civil War. Dr. Johnson served at the University of Virginia before joining the medical staff in Richmond. He had studied in Paris, and was said to be a competent teacher, but charges of some sort were preferred against him, and he resigned from the Richmond faculty in 1844. Dr. Bohannan, a pioneer in the field of obstetrics, was the only one of the six faculty members who had reached middle age when he joined the teaching staff, the others being much younger. Yet by 1855, when he died, the other five original members had all either died or resigned.

The former Union Hotel, which housed the medical school, was enthusiastically described as follows in 1839 by the *Southern Literary Messenger*, made famous by its recent editor, Edgar Allan Poe:

> The spacious and elegant building . . . could not have been better adapted to its various uses, if originally designed exclusively for such objects. The general lecture room has been fitted up in a style of superior taste, and is large enough, we should judge, to contain with ease two hundred students. There are, besides, two other

> lecture rooms for the chemical and anatomical students and we confess we were very agreeably surprised at the extent of the anatomical museum, and, so far as an unprofessional spectator could judge, the completeness and excellence of the chemical apparatus. That, however, which must give peculiar value to the institution, is the presence of an infirmary . . . in which the patients are provided with airy and comfortable rooms, attentive nurses, and constant medical attendance.

The nurses were members of the Sisters of Charity.

The college session began on November 1 of each year and lasted for five months. Any student who attended the lectures during that time, and the instruction in the dissecting room, and who also had "studied medicine with a respectable practitioner for two years" could take the examination for the M.D. degree. Professors were to receive $20 for each enrollee in their classes. Students were assured that "good boarding, including fuel, lights, servant's attendance, etc., can be obtained in this city for four dollars per week." Forty-six enrolled for the first session, all but six from Virginia, and fourteen graduated the following April.

Bodies of slaves were evidently used in the anatomical laboratory. The petitioners to Hampden-Sydney in 1837 for the establishment of a medical school pointed out that "the peculiarity of our institutions" would provide "material for dissection . . . in abundance."

Calomel was resorted to by physicians in that era for treatment of various ailments, ranging from mumps to delirium tremens. The famous Dr. Benjamin Rush was in part responsible for such widespread reliance on this drug, which he termed "the Sampson *[sic]* of medicine." If the doses of calomel became so effective that a halt had to be called, opium was given.

Southern doctors should be trained at southern institutions, Dr. Levin S. Joynes, dean of the Medical College, wrote in the catalogue for 1857–58. They are familiar with the particular types of diseases that occur in the South, he said, and on graduation "are at no loss in essaying the treatment which they have already *seen* successfully applied in similar cases."

Urging "a home medical education," Dr. Joynes went on to say: "Interest, honor and patriotism alike demand that the South shall throw off the intellectual vassalage which has so long degraded her; and the most important means for the accomplishment of so vital an end, is the bestowal of a liberal patronage on her own institutions. . . . She must stop the tide of southern youth and southern treasure which sets ever to the North."

Samuel Mordecai, writing in his sprightly chronicle *Richmond in By-Gone Days* (1856), contrasted the uses to which the Union Hotel was being put when it was converted to a medical school, with the happenings within its walls in previous years: "Limbs, instead of cutting capers, were cut in pieces in the ball-room—potions were mixed instead of punch—poultices supplanted puddings, and Seidlitz Water champagne.

After a few years in the reconditioned hotel, the board of the college concluded that improved and larger quarters were needed. Also, the school was being privately financed, and the burden was too great. Aid from the state was sought, and $25,000 was provided as a loan from the Literary Fund. The city also chipped in $2,000. A lot on Shockoe Hill, on the 1200 block of East Marshall Street, was accordingly purchased, and as architect the board chose Thomas W. Stewart of Philadelphia, a noted practitioner and designer of the new St. Paul's Episcopal Church. The Egyptian Building was the result—a remarkable example of exotic architecture, unique in its day. George Augustus Sala, a correspondent of the London *Telegraph*, declared that he was "more struck with the beauty of the Medical College of Virginia than any other building he had seen."

The college moved to this Egyptian Building upon its completion in 1845, and the catalogue of that year described the structure as "magnificent and commodious." Facilities were indeed more adequate, and the chemical lecture room seated 750 persons. The infirmary for patients was in the same building "embracing well-ventilated wards and private rooms for the accommodation of medical and surgical cases." Charges for board, medical attendance, surgical operations, nursing, medicines, and every necessary service were $5 per week for white patients and $4 for black. In a short time enrollment of students was doubled. Almost all the activities of the college would center in this building until the end of the century.

Despite the improved situation, there were hostile elements in the city's medical profession who assailed the school for giving inadequate courses. Some of this criticism was apparently justified. Twenty-two Richmond doctors, including some of the most prominent, issued a statement in 1853 attacking the school's teaching methods and curriculum in strong language. And when a vacancy arose on the faculty, the public was treated to a controversy in which, as one writer put it, there burst forth "the most venomous invective that printers would publish."

The reverberating uproar centered over the question whether the Medical School's faculty had the right to choose its own members. Since the opening of the college in 1838 the faculty had been allowed by the trustees to make those selections, with automatic ratification by the board. But the trustees decided that this had gone on long enough, and that since the charter gave them the right to name the professors, they were going to exercise that right on this occasion. The teaching staff had nominated Dr. Martin P. Scott, but the board rejected the nomination and elected Dr. Goodridge A. Wilson. Both men were well qualified. There followed a frightful row, the first in a long line of such that would continue for generations.

The faculty flatly refused to recognize Dr. Wilson, whom the trustees had elected. Not only so, they assailed the motives of the trustees in electing him. The embattled professors also let fly at the twenty-two local physicians who backed Wilson, and who had criticized them. They termed these doctors meddlers who were anxious to oust them from the faculty and get their teaching jobs, with accompanying income, for themselves.

The ruckus was continued before the General Assembly of 1854, when the faculty petitioned the lawmakers for an independent charter, entirely separate from Hampden-Sydney. There was accordingly waged before the Assembly "for weeks and weeks one of the bitterest fights ever before the legislature," W. Asbury Christian writes in his history of Richmond. It ended, strangely enough, with the legislators siding with the faculty by an overwhelming majority, although the college charter vested the right of appointment in the trustees. The General Assembly gave the faculty a charter of their own, severed the Medical Department from Hampden-Sydney, and the Medical College of Virginia came into existence.

This acrimonious controversy left many scars. The group that had backed Dr. Goodridge Wilson without success controlled the medical press, and they hammered on the Medical College for years, pinpointing its weaknesses and attacking its administration. Dr. Wilson became editor of the *Monthly Stethoscope and Medical Register*, and immediately began assailing the college, whereupon friends of that institution "tried to strangle" the publication that was attacking them. They sought an injunction to prevent it from publishing, but failed in that endeavor. The journal continued its assaults. "What chance have common sense, reason and sound argument when opposed to the more potent arguments afforded by champaigne *[sic]*, oysters and cigars?" said the paper. "For, with shame be it said, there are some few physicians in Virginia (monopolists), who from mistaken ideas of what is to their own advantage, oppose all practical measures for raising the standard of medical education, and who have hitherto defeated all legislation on the subject."

Dr. Beverley R. Wellford, former president of the American Medical

Association, served as spokesman for the college faculty in these vehement exchanges. His father was Dr. Robert Wellford, who came to this country from England with the First Royal Grenadiers, and became a prominent medical practitioner in Fredericksburg after the American Revolution. He and various other Wellfords have had distinguished careers as Virginia physicians.

Despite his high character and his standing in the profession, Dr. Beverley Wellford was abused unmercifully. The *Stethoscope* charged that as a trustee and professor at the college he had failed to put into effect the very reforms that he had advocated as president of the American Medical Association; that he was disloyal in sending his sons to a northern medical school, and that he was a partner in a Fredericksburg establishment "secretly engaged in the sale of quack medicines." Such allegations naturally brought forth indignant replies, and the controversy was carried on at immense length in the columns of the *Stethoscope.*

Criticism of MCV resulted in renewed but unsuccessful efforts to bring about amalgamation with the University of Virginia. Dr. James B. McCaw of the college faculty sought to achieve this in 1857. The *Virginia Medical and Surgical Journal* of which Dr. McCaw was co-editor, termed the university's school "the best medical school in America," though lacking in clinical material. A previous effort toward merger had been made in 1853.

A vacancy in the chair of Institutes of Medicine and Medical Jurisprudence at MCV brought to the staff a man who already was becoming widely known for his experiments in physiology and who would later become internationally famous as a neurologist and endocrinologist. He was Charles Edouard Brown-Séquard, the son of an American father and a French mother, born on the island of Mauritius in the Indian Ocean. His father, Charles Edward Brown, a captain in the U.S. merchant marine, sailed from Mauritius to get a cargo of rice for the suffering island, but did not return. Neither he nor his ship was ever found. His son was born after he disappeared.

By the early 1850s the son, then aged thirty-seven, had been lecturing to considerable acclaim at the University of Pennsylvania's medical school, and in New York and Boston. He had also married Ellen Fletcher, the niece of Mrs. Daniel Webster. Despite his rising fame, he was strapped for funds and without permanent employment. When he learned of the vacancy at the newly established Medical College of Virginia, he applied. There were six other applicants, but he got all votes except one on the first ballot.

Brown-Séquard joined the teaching staff in 1854, and his experiments were somewhat sensational. The inimitable William H. Taylor, then one of his students, and later a noted faculty member at the college, described Séquard's modus operandi in hilarious terms: "In studying the phenomena of digestion, he let down into his stomach pieces of food tied to the end of strings, and therewith fished up material for subjection to the processes of science. . . . At length the constant titillation of the organ turned him into a sort of cow, his food as fast as he got it down insisted on coming back into his mouth to be chewed over and over again. A disorder of this kind . . . would make any other man hang himself."

Séquard also "implanted a dog's tail in the comb of a rooster, and nurtured it until it took root and grew there," Taylor wrote. "The most touching passage in all his discourses was his sorrowful account of how the rooster, then magnificently embossed, had gone forth to do battle with an opposing rooster of the baser sort, and had his tail torn out of his head by his sanguinary adversary."

Séquard's account of this melancholy episode must have seemed somewhat inscrutable to his students, for his difficulties with the English language were great. Taylor says "his discourse . . . was not very unlike an attack of spasmodic asthma."

In what must have been an exceptionally hazardous enterprise, Taylor "held cats by the tail" while the professor "worked his way into their interiors." Another of Séquard's adventures in the more arcane mysteries of science was when, "in order to discover certain facts concerning human sweat" he "bedaubed himself from head to foot with waterproof varnish, and sitting down, notebook in hand, proposed to record the phenomena as they arose. . . . Among the first things he noted was that he was beginning to die." Fortunately, "assiduous scraping, rashing and sandpapering" saved the situation.

These and other experiments, strange as they may sound to the uninitiated, achieved spectacular results. "Little must the professors at the college have appreciated at the time that Brown-Séquard wrote here his great paper 'Experimental and Clinical Researches on Physiology of the Spinal Cord,' or that he was performing experiments in the basement that led the next year (1856) to the publication in Paris of probably the premiere paper of the world on endocrinology, 'Experimental Researches on the Physiology of the Superarenal Capsules," Dr. Beverley R. Tucker, an eminent member of a much later Medical College faculty, declared.

Brown-Séquard remained only one year at MCV. J. M. D. Olmsted, his biographer, explains: "His frankness was most displeasing when he used it to express the very great repulsion which he felt to the idea of slavery. . . . He felt so keenly and was so outspoken on this subject that it began to be whispered that coming from Mauritius, and having a dark complexion he must himself have Negro blood. In Virginia there could be no surer way of discrediting a man than to hint that he had tainted blood."

His outspokenness on the subject of human servitude, the suspicions as to his own ethnic makeup, the fact that he seems not to have been "socially inclined," and the further fact that he was disappointed in the lack of "original investigation" at the college all combined to cause him to leave for Paris in 1856. World fame was to follow. Long after his death, the MCV chapter of Alpha Omega Alpha national honorary medical fraternity was named for Brown-Séquard.

At about the same time that Séquard left the college faculty, the institution suffered another great loss in the death of thirty-two-year-old Carter Page Johnson. This brilliant young surgeon, one of the most promising and accomplished of his generation, had published no fewer than six articles in Smith's *System of Operative Surgery,* which recorded the most significant articles published by American surgeons. Among Virginia surgeons, only John Peter Mettauer, a much older man, had produced a larger number. Johnson, who had been elected president of the Medical Society of Virginia shortly before, went to Europe to rest and to visit various medical centers. He sailed for America on the SS *Arctic,* but it went down with all on board, in the worst sea disaster of the nineteenth century. Carter Johnson was the son of Chapman Johnson, the noted lawyer who was so conspicuous in the Virginia Constitutional Convention of 1829–30.

The Medical College had had no appropriation or endowment throughout its existence, and by 1860 financial problems became so acute that assistance again was sought from the state. It appropriated $30,000 on condition that the institution deed its buildings and appurtenances to the commonwealth. Thus the college became a state institution. This culmination came "after twenty-two years of self-sacrifice and loss by individual members of the faculty," the trustees declared, "and the faculty gave a release deed to all of the property and appurtenances held by them." Having appropriated $30,000, the state seemed to think that nothing additional was necessary for decades. "From 1866 to 1888 the munificent gift of $1,500 a year—

enough to poorly maintain a county cross-roads academy"—was forthcoming from the commonwealth.

The $30,000 appropriated by the state in 1860 made possible the construction of a new hospital at 1225 East Marshall Street, next to the Egyptian Building. "It was a plain, three-story brick building with approximately eighty beds and 'a bathroom with water closets adjacent' on each floor," Nancy G. Summers, of the MCV Library's Archives Department, wrote. "This building was the first separate hospital building at MCV. It had a turbulent history, housing five different hospital organizations before it finally became the Old Dominion Hospital in 1895." Upon its completion in 1860, the infirmary, library, and museum were moved to it from the Egyptian Building.

John Brown's raid at Harpers Ferry in 1859—which had as its object the launching of a slave uprising—and Brown's subsequent execution caused great excitement throughout the country. In Philadelphia, where hundreds of southern students were attending medical schools, fights broke out on the streets when Brown's coffin was carried through the city. The "rough element" injured several students and some of them were jailed. Young Drs., Hunter McGuire, later to become famous, and F. E. Luckett, who were conducting a private "quizzing class" there, rallied the southern students, and the group decided to leave Philadelphia en masse. McGuire and Luckett sent the following telegram to the Medical College of Virginia: "Upon what terms will your school receive 150 from this place first of January. . . . We anxiously await your reply. For God's sake let it be favorable."

The faculty answered that they would gladly admit to the lectures, without charge, for the remainder of the session, all students who had regularly matriculated and paid their tuition fees in Philadelphia. The result was a wholesale exodus from Jefferson Medical College and the University of Pennsylvania Medical School. The city of Richmond agreed to pay the cost of transporting the young men, and over $700 was raised by the Richmond business community. On December 22, 1859, 244 of them, nearly all from Philadelphia schools, but some from institutions in New York City and Albany, arrived. They were met at the railroad station by a brass band, and marched to Capitol Square. Governor Henry A. Wise and Dr. Charles Bell Gibson, a distinguished member of the Medical College faculty and pioneer surgeon, addressed the group. Later there was a dinner at the Columbian Hotel, attended by more than six hundred persons. A total of 144 students enrolled at the college, and fifty-six graduated the following March, together with 26 members of the original class.

The sudden departure of hundreds of students from the two medical schools in Philadelphia was a serious blow to them. Rumors were circulated in the northern press that the faculty in Virginia had bribed McGuire and Luckett to lead to revolt, with promises of preferment. All of this was indignantly denied by the Richmond faculty.

Arrival of the students on the campus of MCV imposed an extra burden on the teaching staff. They rose to the occasion. Perhaps in an effort to lessen the burden, the Board of Visitors decreed that there should be "no card-playing or any other vice . . . within the precincts of the college or the hospital."

The coming of the Civil War in 1861 brought much greater responsibilities for the hard-pressed teaching staff. Indeed, it is difficult to understand how they managed to carry on. To their great credit be it said that they made a salient contribution to the Confederate cause in various directions.

Dr. James B. McCaw, whose almost unparalleled services to MCV lasted for nearly half a century, planned and organized the great Chimborazo Hospital on Church Hill, the "largest single general hospital, civil or military, in the Western Hemisphere," according to Dr. Harry J. Warthen, Jr., who made a careful investigation of its relative standing. Dr. Charles Bell Gibson served as surgeon general of Virginia. Dr. David H. Tucker served as a surgeon at the extensive Winder Hospital in Richmond's West End, and was called in as a consultant in the illness and death of Stonewall Jackson. Drs. Arthur E. Peticolas and Isaiah H. White were surgeons in the armed forces, and Dr. Levin S. Joynes an assistant surgeon. Drs. Beverley R. Wellford and James H. Conway, the other members of the faculty during the war, also held posts in the Confederate service. The heavily burdened teaching staff was busily engaged in training doctors for the front. Two full sessions were conducted each year during the war.

On the outbreak of hostilities the facilities of the college were made available for the treatment of wounded and sick soldiers. The new hospital building became hopelessly overcrowded, so the hospital wards in the college building, which had been closed upon completion of the new structure, were thrown open. More than a thousand soldiers were admitted during 1861, and there were comparable figures for the ensuing years.

As the war went on, there was less and less of everything in Richmond. The Medical College was so short of funds that the horse which pulled the hospital's only ambulance had to be sold in early 1865, "bringing only three times the price of a bushel of corn." Funds were no longer available for operating the hospital, so the patients were transferred back to the Egyptian Building, and the hospital was turned into a rooming house. Part of the hospital's furnishing were sold in the desperate need for cash.

At Chimborazo Hospital a private wrote in 1864 that there was "very little to eat, and that of the roughest and coarsest sort, and not half enough wood to keep a comfortable fire." Rats were eaten at this time by the patients, Phoebe Pember records in her fascinating memoir, *A Southern Woman's Story.* "Epicures sometimes managed to trap them," she said, "and secure a nice broil for supper, declaring that their flesh was superior to squirrel meat."

Even after the South was worn down by the blockade and defeats on the battlefield, Chimborazo Hospital made a most extraordinary record, under the expert management of Surgeon-in-Chief and Commandant McCaw. Dr. Russell V. Bowers of the Medical College faculty wrote in the *Scarab* (August 1963) concerning the truly amazing thoroughness and efficiency with which the hospital was operated.

About 150 well-constructed, naturally ventilated whitewashed wooden buildings were erected. Each measured 100 feet by 30 feet, and accommodated forty to sixty patients. There were 100 Sibley tents, quartering 8 to 10 soldiers or convalescent patients. Total bed capacity was nearly 7,000. Wells were dug at the ends of the streets, and there was a sewage disposal system. Several hundred cows and 500 goats provided milk. The bakery turned out 10,000 loaves a day, and a brewer produced 400 kegs of beer at a time, the beer being stored in caves and five large icehouses. There were bakers, cooks, carpenters, shoemakers, dentists and, of course, surgeons and assistant surgeons.

Dr. Bowers writes that 76,000 patients passed through, of whom 17,000 were battle casualties, and 7,000 soldiers died. The overall deathrate was only 9 percent, an exceptionally good record. The figure is the more remarkable, in view of the relatively primitive state of medicine at that time. As Bowers puts it, "Medicine of that day bears a closer resemblance to medieval medicine than it does to the 1960s."

The Medical College faculty did its best to train its students for service in the field. The course was cut from five to four months, and there were other handicaps. Emergency situations required that the young men be sent to the front with hardly any medical experience. Dr. Simon Baruch, father of Bernard M. Baruch, and later eminent in his profession, remarked after the war that he had had to perform major surgery on Confederate soldiers when previously he had not even so much as lanced a boil.

With the end of the war, the college struggled back to something remotely approaching normal conditions. No other Southern medical school had managed to graduate at least one class each year during the conflict. The flames that destroyed most of Richmond's business district had not touched the college, but nearly everyone was impoverished, and many grieved over the death or maiming of loved ones. Along with the rest of the shattered South the teaching staff and students faced the ordeals of Reconstruction.

1. The Union Hotel at Nineteenth and Main streets, where the Medical College of Virginia began operations in 1838. It was then the medical department of Hampden-Sydney College.

2. Dr. Augustus L. Warner, first dean of the infant medical school.

3. Dr. Carter Page Johnson, brilliant young surgeon, drowned when the SS *Arctic* went down in the North Atlantic with all on board.

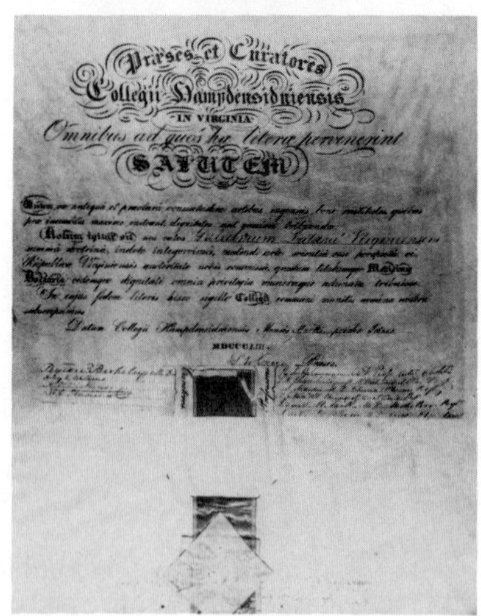
Praeses et Curatores
Collegii Hampdensidniensis
IN VIRGINIA
Omnibus ad quos hæ literæ pervenerint
SALUTEM

4. Dr. William Latané, with his medical diploma from Hampden-Sydney, 1853. He was the only Confederate killed in Stuart's famous ride around McClellan's army in 1862. "The Burial of Latané" still hangs in Virginia homes.

5. Dr. Simon Baruch, a graduate during the Civil War, whose son, Bernard M. Baruch, memorialized him with a handsome gift to the college.

6. Dr. James B. McCaw, longtime member of the MCV faculty, who planned and organized the great Chimborazo Hospital during the Civil War.

TWO

Postbellum Years and the Battling Doctors

ENROLLMENT AT THE MEDICAL COLLEGE dropped dramatically when it reopened after the close of hostilities in 1865. As late as 1870 there were only twenty students. The people of Richmond and Virginia were in a struggle for survival, and few had the resources with which to pursue a medical education.

Four members of the faculty served on a Commission on Artificial Limbs that convened in 1866 at the Spotswood Hotel in Richmond. The many Confederate soldiers who had lost an arm or a leg required this service. Reports were made on the latest prosthetic devices, such as they were. This was a continuing effort, and four years later the commission was still studying the subject and making recommendations.

In 1867 the faculty was increased from seven to eight, and the short course, which had been cut from five to four months during the war, was put back to five. In 1880 it went to nine months, but the following year dropped back to seven, and the year after to six.

Dr. Isaiah H. White returned to the faculty from Canada, apparently in the late 1860s. He seems to have gone there in apprehension, following the end of the war. Dr. White had been chief surgeon at the Andersonville prison in Georgia, and when Captain Henry Wirz, who had been in direct charge of the prison, was hanged by the federal authorities in November 1865, White is said to have felt it expedient to put himself out of range. Such was the statement of Dr. S. W. Dickinson of Marion, Va., one of his students at the college who greatly admired him, in the *Virginia Medical Semi-Monthly* for March 9, 1917.

Dr. Dickinson's assertion is assumed to be correct, although there is no substantiating evidence in the files of the college. There is a letter from Dean Joynes in May 1867, refusing to accept White's resignation from the teaching staff. He may have been attempting to leave for Canada then. That was when they were planning to try Jefferson Davis, and it is logical to assume that White was apprehensive. For be it noted that when Wirz was sentenced to hang, it was alleged that he conspired with Jefferson Davis, Howell Cobb, John H., Richard B., and W. S. Winder, Isaiah H. White, R. Randolph Stevenson, and others "to impair and injure the health and to destroy the lives . . . of large numbers of federal prisoners . . . at Andersonville."

Ovid L. Futch's *History of Andersonville Prison* is a scholarly and objective examination of conditions in that prison, and they were unspeakable. Tens of thousands of federal prisoners were crowded into a miasmic swampy area on starvation rations, with scarcely any shelter, virtually no sanitary arrangements, and totally inadequate facilities for treating the sick. The prisoners died in enormous numbers.

Yet the charge in the North that this was all a deliberate plot to kill Union prisoners was altogether unfounded. The hanging of Wirz was a "legal lynching," according to Futch, who admits that Wirz had faults. The fact is that neither Wirz nor White nor the others listed as responsible could cope with the appalling difficulties that confronted them and the entire South in 1864, when Andersonville opened. The whole region was being pinched unmercifully for supplies of all sorts, for the South was losing the war. The Confederacy's own wounded and sick soldiers didn't have enough hospitals and medicines either. Dr. White, as chief surgeon at Andersonville, made repeated requests for more doctors, more drugs, more everything. They were not to be had. There was undoubted mismanagement at Andersonville, for a small part of which Dr. White appears to have been responsible. It is stated in Ambrose Spencer's *A Narrative of Andersonville* that "visitors to Drs. White and Stevenson had all [the whiskey] that they did not drink themselves." A Dr. Thornburg, a surgeon assigned to the hospital, is quoted as saying that "the whiskey was drank by the medical director and his friends." How significant this was is anybody's guess. As will be seen later in this chapter, Dr. William H. Taylor of the Medical College faculty admitted freely after the war that he and his compatriots in the Confederate medical service drank up all the whiskey as soon as it arrived.

Blacks were congregating in large numbers at the college dispensary in 1867, and "certain exciting rumors were prevalent among the Negro population in relation to the college and its students, which made it desirable to prevent the daily congregation of Negroes about the college," the faculty minutes declared. The faculty directed Dr. J. J. DeLameter, chief surgeon of the Freedmen's Bureau, to discontinue "the system of issuing tickets for rations at the college," and requested the transfer of the dispensary to some other place in the city.

Another problem arose the following year when the faculty stated that "the welfare of MCV is seriously jeopardized by the apathy of a number of the visitors, who rarely or never heed a summons to attend a meeting of the board." It resolved to confer with the governor, and to request that future delinquents "forward their resignations."

An addition to the teaching staff in 1867 was Dr. Edwin S. Gaillard, a native of Charleston, S.C., who had lost an arm at the Battle of Seven Pines and who occupied the new chair of general pathology. In the previous year he had founded the *Richmond Medical Journal,* and as its co-editor proceeded, in its columns, to lambaste all and sundry—quacks, the American Medical Association, or anybody else whose behavior or tendencies he disliked. Possessed of a slashing polemical style and devastating humor, he skewered many victims, especially medical ones. In 1868 he accepted the deanship of the Kentucky Medical School, and moved to Louisville, where he reissued his publication as the *Richmond and Louisville Medical Journal.* He promptly took out after Dr. D. W. Yandell, a leading Louisville physician who had just been elected president of the American Medical Association, tossing at him such epithets as "extinguished surgeon," "base and notorious coward," "infamously treacherous," and "loudly braying animal." How a duel was avoided is difficult to understand. Many years later, in 1939, the new morgue and autopsy building at MCV was named for Gaillard, the college's first occupant of the chair of pathology as a separate and distinct department.

The perennial subject of "fusion" between the college and the University of Virginia Medical School came up again in 1867. The university issued a memorial to the General Assembly opposing the move, and implying—the MCV faculty charged—that the faculty had "attempted by unfair and secret means to force 'their bill' through" the legislature. The college faculty retorted that the idea "did not originate with them, but was a subject of discussion among members of both branches of the legislature, and added: "On the 14th of March . . . in the presence of the representatives of both faculties . . . the chairman of the committee [on schools and colleges] stated most emphatically that the whole movement had its origin in the legislature, and not with the faculty." The bill calling for union of the two schools was defeated.

Three years later there were overtures from Richmond College for a merger with the Medical College. The latter institution's faculty minutes state that the Rev. Dr. Jeremiah Bell Jeter, a member of the Richmond College Board of Trustees, had approached Dean Levin Joynes "with a request that the faculty of this college [MCV] would take into consideration the expediency of a union of the two institutions." The Medical College faculty passed the request along for future consideration, and that seems to have been the end of it.

The staff of the Medical College, along with all other medical men of the period, were seeking the cause and cure for such scourges as malaria, yellow fever typhoid fever, cholera, and tuberculosis, which were claiming their victims by the tens of thousands. There had been several virulent outbreaks of cholera in Richmond earlier in the century, and the MCV staff had endeavored to render assistance. Unfortunately, none of the doctors in Richmond or elsewhere had any idea how to treat the pestilence effectively. One theory was: "Wear a flannel shirt or jacket, flannel drawers and yarn stockings . . . never permit any fruit at all to be in your house, or any vegetable except rice and well-cooked potatoes." Watermelons were supposed to be especially dangerous.

One of the worst yellow fever epidemics in history struck Norfolk and Portsmouth in 1855, as devastating in its virulence as the Black Death of the Middle Ages. "Putrid and offensive bilgewater" from ships, and "filthy conditions" were advanced as causes of yellow fever. Walter Reed's discovery that a species of mosquito was the culprit would not be made until the turn of the century. Also, as a result of important bacteriological discoveries in the 1880s, the bacteria for cholera, tuberculosis, and typhoid fever were isolated, but it would be many decades before effective treatment of the last two diseases would be available.

Hostility between leading physicians flared at a meeting of the Richmond Academy of Medicine in 1875, and a duel apparently was narrowly averted. Drs. Hunter McGuire and John S. Wellford were both treating Mrs. Stephen Putney, whose attractive home stands today on the Medical College campus. Dr. McGuire gave Mrs. Putney, who was seven months pregnant, a hypodermic. She died a few days later, and Dr. Wellford stated freely in conversation on various occasions that Dr. McGuire was responsible for her death. The matter came to a head at a meeting of the Academy in June 1875, when McGuire denounced Wellford as "a liar and a trickster." Wellford threw a penknife at McGuire, and McGuire reached for his stick. In the ensuing uproar Dr. James Beale rushed out and summoned a policeman, who put both warring doctors under arrest. They were haled into Police Court next day and placed under bond of $2,500 each to keep the peace. This almost certainly prevented a duel, as in that era such words as had been passed meant a summons to "the field of honor." The affair received wide publicity, both locally and in the New York press. The overwhelming opinion in medical journals and among individual physicians was that Dr. McGuire was not responsible for Mrs. Putney's death.

The hostility between doctors in Richmond during these years, and especially among members of the Medical College faculty, was described by Dr. William H. Taylor in his reminiscences, published in 1913. Taylor was city coroner for many years, as well as professor at the college. He wrote of the "clawing and scratching, the rearing and snorting, figuratively speaking, when we got together." And he went on: "For the most part the proceedings were restricted to a graphic loquacity and a gentlemanly damning of one another." He said the position of faculty chairman "was created for my special behoof. . . . I was the only one with whom everybody was on speaking terms." The reason for this, he explained, was that "being a chemist, and not a practitioner of medicine, I was in no practitioner's way . . . while as coroner I meddled with no doctor's patients till he had finished with them himself."

The college was authorized in 1870 by the General Assembly to grant a degree in pharmacy. There was, however, no separate program of instruction leading to it. A student who passed examinations in chemistry and materia medica and who had had two years' practical experience in a drug store was eligible to be declared a Graduate in Pharmacy.

The hospital which was erected at 1225 East Marshall Street with $30,000 appropriated by the state in 1860 and housed the college infirmary had closed from 1864 to 1867 for lack of funds. It took the name of Church Institute in 1874, managed by a board of ladies, but closed two years later. At that time Dr. Hunter McGuire appealed to Mrs. Annabelle Ravenscroft Jenkins, a prominent Richmond woman, to cooperate with him in the organization of the Retreat for the Sick. It opened in 1877 at 1225 East Marshall. McGuire was the dominant figure in the Retreat, and the staff was composed of faculty members of the Medical College. Unfortunately, there were serious disagreements of various kinds among the faculty, and McGuire resigned from the college staff, after fifteen years as a member. His resignation was followed shortly thereafter by his termination of all connection with the Retreat, apparently because the management had failed to discipline a staff member in the manner that he thought necessary. The hospital received another blow the following year when the college ordered it, for unexplained reasons, to vacate the building it had been occupying. The Retreat opened in other quarters on Twelfth Street near Marshall, and for a decade the Medical College had no hospital of its own. Operations were carried out by college surgeons at the Retreat, at Dr. McGuire's recently organized St. Luke's, and in private homes.

The college now was heading into another crisis, brought about by the actions of Governor William E. Cameron, who had been elected by the Readjuster political faction. Cameron was engaged in a statewide effort to replace boards of visitors at the various state institutions, since these had all been appointed by previous governors allied with the opposition faction, the Funders. He did not encounter serious difficulties in carrying out this housecleaning until he attempted to oust the board of the Medical College.

The newly appointed members of the MCV board, all Readjusters, moved in a body from Ford's Hotel to the Egyptian Building on September 29, 1882, with a view to taking control. Among them were Lieutenant Governor John F. Lewis and several physicians active as Readjusters, including Dr. Lewis Wheat of Richmond, an instructor in anatomy at the college who had angered his colleagues there by lobbying before the legislature on behalf of a bill to replace the visitors and faculty. The measure had failed, which explains Governor Cameron's decision to fire the college board. There had been justifiable criticism of the college management on various grounds, including the failure of the incumbent visitors, throughout the previous decade, to file an annual report, as required by law. The visitors had also been extremely irregular in attending meetings, and were said to have left matters in the hands of the faculty to an excessive degree.

When the newly named board members approached the Egyptian Building, they found Dean James B. McCaw and Dr. John S. Wellford standing in front of it and barring the entrance.

"Do you mean to resist us by force?" Lieutenant Governor Lewis asked. "I do," said Dean McCaw, "and for this purpose the police of the City of Richmond are present."

Viewing the three uniformed policemen who were standing by, the putative board members decided to organize outside the building by electing a president and secretary. Lewis was chosen to the former post and Wheat to the latter. Whereupon Dr. Wellford instructed the police to "come here and stop this illegal organization." After some brief parleying back and forth, during which the Cameron-appointed visitors continued to insist on entry, McCaw directed the officers to arrest Lewis, who offered no resistance. A warrant had not been sworn out, which made the proceeding questionable, but the group headed for the police station.

On arrival, they saw that McCaw and Wellford had disappeared. The lack of a warrant had made the arrest illegal, and McCaw and Wellford had decided not to press the matter further. Chief of Police John Poe came to the police station and informed Lewis and his associates that they were free to leave.

This left McCaw and Wellford in possession of the college property. The embattled Readjuster visitors met that afternoon with Governor Cameron, and passed a resolution calling on the faculty to appear before them within twenty-four hours and state why they should not be removed from their respective positions because of their involvement in the "illegal proceedings" earlier in the day. Only one of the staff responded to the summons—Dr. Otis F. Manson, who was at odds with the other seven members of the faculty. He accepted the jurisdiction of the new board and resigned from the college teaching staff after many years as a member, and a fine record of original research, especially in the field of malaria.

The rest of the faculty remained adamant in its determination not to yield. The newly named visitors adjourned to meet again in three months, and things were temporarily at a standstill. The case was not taken immediately to the Virginia Supreme Court of Appeals, since that tribunal was composed entirely of members of the Funder Party. However, their terms would expire the following January, at which time they would be succeeded by Readjusters, elected by the Readjuster-dominated General Assembly.

During the intervening months there was agitation pro and con in the press. The Funder newspapers rallied to the support of the faculty, and assailed the "political machinations" of the Readjusters. The *Virginia Medical Monthly*, the state's foremost medical journal, edited by Dr. Landon B. Edwards, a Medical College graduate who had defended the college for a number of years, now turned against the institution's management as inefficient and ineffective. The *Richmond Whig*, organ of the Readjusters, attacked the faculty unsparingly for "shameful malpractice" and "dastardly and insolent" defiance of the state's official representatives. It also published the following amusing bit of verse:

His name is Doctor McCaw,
He's Professor of Cheek and Jaw,
And he won't admit Visitors,
Nor other inquisitors,
To see us cut and saw—
Haw, haw!

Yes, his name is Doctor McCaw,
And he cares not a drachm for the law,
For he's Dean of the Faculty,
Chief Quack of the Quackalty,
And he strikes all beholders with awe
Haw, haw!

When the Supreme Court convened in early January, the staff of the college viewed the solidly Readjuster bench with natural concern. Meanwhile the newly named visitors of the college decided to make another try at entry, but found the doors locked. It appeared that nothing could open them but a decree of the court.

Arguments were duly made by both sides before that tribunal, and it took the case under advisement. In April it handed down its surprising verdict—a unanimous finding in favor of the faculty and the Funders. With commendable integrity, the court had set aside all political considerations and ruled strictly on what it took to be the law of the case. It held that the governor had exceeded his authority in seeking to discharge the board.

This left the incumbent visitors and faculty triumphant, but the college was by no means out of the woods. The *Virginia Medical Monthly*, whose editor, Dr. Landon B. Edwards, was a steadfast advocate of higher medical standards, declared reluctantly in 1884 that in late years the college "has degenerated" and "become highly *notorious* in professional esteem." The publication listed medical journals in Paris, Chicago, New York, Philadelphia, and Baltimore "which have exposed some of the great wrongs done or attempted to be done the profession at large by this college, by its unexceptionable mismanagement."

The journal noted that the college had asked the General Assembly for an appropriation of $7,500, and

promised that it would annually receive, *free of tuition*, as many medical students from Virginia as there are members of the General Assembly—*one hundred and forty*. . . . Such a plan would have flooded the state with incompetent doctors. . . . Why has the college deteriorated? Professor [F. D.] Cunningham quit; [H. H.] McGuire left, [Otis F.] Manson abandoned it in despair. . . . Dr. [J. B.] McCaw's resignation leaves the chair of Practice vacant. . . . Dr. [M. L.] James, the late dean of the college, has resigned his position as professor of Anatomy. . . .

We fear that no man except a protege of the faculty will apply for any of the chairs. . . . Is the *faculty to control the board* or the *board the faculty?*

It is truly painful for us to write this regarding an institution on whose register we once felt proud to have our name enrolled as a student. . . . The Board of Visitors has not done its duty. . . . they have consulted the faculty, instead of finding out what was demanded.

The really astonishing resignation from the faculty was that of Dr. McCaw, who had led the defiance of the newly appointed board only two years before. No explanation for his action seems to be available. He was named to the Board of Visitors some years later. Dr. Christopher Tompkins gave up the chair of anatomy, but he was promptly appointed to the chair of obstetrics, and remained on the staff for many years.

Constant turmoil in the faculty would seem to account, at least in part, for the resignations of so many teachers. There was also the fact that the staff for the preceding two years had received no compensation. Dean M. L. James said in 1884: "Besides arduous personal toil, the faculty has, for the past two years, devoted the entire income of the college to the maintenance of its interests, and worked without pecuniary remuneration." Minutes of the visitors in 1885 show that with a faculty of about eight and seventy-one students, total receipts of the college for the precending year were the amazingly small sum of $7,277.16, and disbursements $5,847.64, leaving a balance on hand of $1,429.52. The annual state appropriation of $1,500 was included in the foregoing totals. Fees for each student came to $135, divided as follows: matriculation, $5; lectures of professors, $120; demonstrator of anatomy, $10. The state appropriation was increased to $5,000 a year in 1888.

The unremitting hostility of Dr. C. A. Bryce, editor of the *Southern Clinic,* a graduate of MCV but an inveterate foe, created other problems for the institution. In 1884, for example, he quoted a harsh appraisal of the college that appeared in *La France Medicale.* Bryce also assailed Dr. Hunter McGuire because McGuire had moved his expulsion from the Medical Society of Virginia on the ground that Bryce had publicly charged the society's publishing committee with misappropriation of funds. Bryce resigned, but in 1887 McGuire wrote him that he would vote for his readmission if he applied. Apparently he did not do so.

An amusing episode involving Billy, "the dear old black janitor" at MCV, was recounted by Bryce in recollections of his days at the college. He wrote that Billy was an excellent mimic, and could give imitations of the professors before they arrived in class. On one occasion, the students played a joke on him, pretending that a certain professor was greatly delayed, and that he would have plenty of time to go into his act. Bryce wrote:

> Billy came to the stand, made a low bow, and commenced making an almost exact imitation of the doctor's voice, subject and gesticulation, and was taken so with our applause that he was unaware of the entrance of the doctor, who stood behind him and listened attentively to old Billy's entertaining talk. When the old fellow made his closing bow and turned around, he was too much surprised to even offer an explanation or apology. He just wilted and told the doctor "I guess you wants another janitor after dis." But the doctor was a good sport, and said, "Billy, you have left off the most important thing. . . . pass the hat around, and if these boys don't all chip in for that lecture, they need not come before me for graduation." The old fellow wiped the beads of perspiration from his brow, said "Sure 'nough, boss?," gathered his old cap and called on every man in the class, realizing a nice little sum. As he was leaving, he asked the professor to permit him to address a few more words to the class, and leaning over the desk he put up a broad grin and said "Who is de laugh on now?"

Creation of the State Board of Medical Examiners in 1884 as a protection against quacks, of whom there were entirely too many, was an important forward step. All students from both the Medical College and the University of Virginia who took the examination in 1885 passed. The *Virginia Medical Monthly* pointed out that this was a far better showing than was made in the country as a whole, where only about 28 or 29 per cent of those taking "the very same exam" had passed.

Strangely enough, students at the Medical College petitioned the board in 1888 to exempt them from the test. The faculty minutes declare that they were "incensed at the action of the board at its last session when applicants from this college were rejected on account of what they believed was personal hostility of three members to the faculty."

A student committee sought the cooperation of the faculty in securing the exemption, but "were plainly and positively told that the college was committed to and believed in the principles of the law, and therefore could not aid them." The dean was instructed to appear before the legislature and "reaffirm the wish of the faculty that the law, unsatisfactory and imperfect as it was, should remain in its original form, rather than encounter the risk of defeat in contentions over amendments."

The *Journal* of the American Medical Association had criticized the college in connection with the action of the students. Dr. J. S. D. Cullen of the faculty declared that, contrary to the *Journal*'s argument, the college "had the smallest number of graduates rejected of any other college whose number of applicants was equal to it," or "about seven per cent." He added that students from Boston, Philadelphia and New York "show a rejection of 25 to 30 per cent." The attacks in the *Journal* of the AMA were said in the faculty minutes to reflect "an inimical partisanship in this city"; in other words, enemies of the college had misled the publication.

What may have been partisanship of another variety had appeared in 1880, when many members of the Richmond Academy of Medicine resigned and formed the rival Richmond Medical and Surgical Society. Members of the MCV faculty were to be found in both organizations. The *Virginia Medical Monthly*, whose editor, Dr. Landon B. Edwards, was chosen the first president of the newly formed organization, said that "there is no antagonism whatever between it and the older society." This may or may not have been correct. At all events the affairs of the younger society soon languished, and Dr. Moses D. Hoge, Jr., was credited with "rejuvenating" it. For a decade the two competing organizations continued to function, and it is noteworthy that the *Virginia Medical Monthly* never mentioned the Richmond Academy, while chronicling the affairs of the Richmond Medical and Surgical Society. In 1890 it was decided that this somewhat absurd situation with two rival academies in a small city the size of Richmond, had gone on long enough, and Dr. Hugh M. Taylor from the Academy and Dr. John N. Upshur from the Society brought the two back together, under the name of the Richmond Academy of Medicine and Surgery. In his reminiscences, published years later, Dr. Upshur said, in explaining the breaking away of so many members from the Academy in 1880: "The reason assigned was that too much prominence was given to discussion of the Code of Ethics, to the hurt of scientific and instructive subjects." Whether or not that explanation holds up, in light of the known hostility of the medical factions in Richmond, the split seemed to emphasize the existence of those warring groups of doctors.

A scandal erupted in the 1880s when wide publicity was given in the press to grave robbing by medical students, working with black janitors—known as resurrectionists—in order to provide cadavers for the Medical College and other similar institutions. Local operations were usually carried out in the Potter's Field, adjoining Oakwood Cemetery.

Grave robbing had been prevalent in England in the early 1800s; a biographer of the poet Keats, a medical student in his youth, wrote of the body snatching carried on at that time. Similarly, Augustus L. Warner, as a University of Virginia professor in the mid-1830s, organized groups of students "for anatomical expeditions." When Warner took the lead in founding the Medical Department of Hampden-Sydney College at Richmond in 1838, he had the assistance of "old Lewis" or "Uncle Lewis," a pioneer resurrectionist who functioned in this capacity at the institution for some forty-two years. He was succeeded by "Billy," another black major domo, and then by "Chris" Baker, who held sway for several decades.

These grave-robbing expeditions were carried out at medical schools throughout Virginia and various other areas of the United States in violation of law, and with the covert approval of eminent professors. It was the only means by which an adequate supply of cadavers could be obtained for anatomical instruction. The "sack-em-up-boys" operated under cover of darkness, and usually got away with it. But Dr. John F. Woodward of Ivanhoe, N.C., an MCV graduate, related in the *Scarab* how one expedition of which he was a part as a student was suddenly fired on, and "the diggers dropped their tools and fled to the wagon," terrified and badly shaken, and also annoyed that they had gotten only one "stiff." Dr. Charles R. Robins, an important member of the Medical College staff, related in 1939 how, on another occasion, "Chris" and the expedition of students he led were "caught redhanded" and tossed into jail. After a few days they were all pardoned by Governor Cameron. "That this would be done was definitely known to the dean of the college from the beginning," Dr. Robins related.

"Chris" Baker was viewed with dread by the blacks in the vicinity, who believed that he worked "black magic" and was in touch with the "spirit world." They were in constant fear that he would snatch one of them off the street for use in the dissecting laboratory. Dr. William T. Sanger wrote that when "Chris" was in his last illness for eight or nine months, it was impossible to get any black to substitute for him as the blacks feared "ghosts" in the building.

At the 1884 session of the General Assembly, legislation was passed to stop grave robbing and to provide unclaimed bodies "for the advancement of medical science." Thus the resurrectionists were permanently put out of business.

During the latter half of the nineteenth century there was no more admired or beloved member of the faculty than Dr. William H. Taylor, whom we have quoted several times. His lectures and writings were so delightful that it is difficult to refrain from citing them at length.

After his graduation from the college, he served in the Confederate medical corps and was severely wounded at Gettysburg. One phase of his experiences in the war was described by him as follows:

> Our most valued medicament was the alcoholic liquors, which were furnished to us sometimes in the form of whiskey, and at other times of apple brandy. These preparations were esteemed by the surgical staff very generally as a specific for malaria especially . . . to which the surgeons with whom I was associated believed themselves to be peculiarly susceptible. . . . By instituting a general soiree on the night of the day of which the supplies arrived in camp . . . we would tone up our systems and corroborate our constitutions by drinking up every drop of the prophylactic before morning.

Dr. Beverley R. Tucker, one of Taylor's many admirers, declared that "we students revere his memory as a teacher, as a man, and as a scientist for the inspiration that he gave us, for the example of tolerance that he set for us in the days of medical strife."

As to his appearance, "he wore spectacles with exceedingly thick lenses, and in addition always read with a reading glass in hand." He began his lectures "as was his custom, spitting a little tobacco juice and coughing."

His defective vision seems to have been no handicap, since he was widely read, and his literary style was graceful and attractive, with copious dashes of humor. The study of English grammar he considered "the sum of all villainies," since in his view reading the best literature was the important thing. His own writing was evidence of the soundness of his ideas on this subject.

A lifelong bachelor, Dr. Taylor was especially caustic and witty in his observations concerning the fair sex. His lecture on the subject was always widely attended, presumably mostly by males, since the ladies can hardly have relished his observations. "Woman is inferior physically, mentally and morally to man," said he, and "she has not succeeded in obscuring her descent from the ape to the extent that her brother has done." He went on to describe woman as "squatty and fatty, and built up with a variety of exaggerated spheres, cones and cylinders strung together." Furthermore, "a doctor who has collected a coterie of female worshipers, which can be done by cajolery, bamboozlement or insolence, each adroitly applied to the appropriate subject, has his fortune made."

Taylor detested lawyers. As city coroner for forty-five years, he was frequently cross-examined by attorneys, and their methods "drove him up the wall." He spoke of "the sophistries, the tricks, the cold-blooded villainies practiced in our court-rooms, where heaven, earth and hell are all pressed into service, alike to facilitate the escape of the criminal, and to obstruct the pursuit."

"No spread-eagle orator in the sublimest flight of effulgent exuberance has ever ventured to assault the understanding of his hearers with a suggestion of the hard lot of the noble lawyer," said Dr. Taylor, "but many and many an honest voice has uttered its commiserating word for the toil-worn doctor."

A fast man with a quip, Dr. Taylor was being cross-examined by an attorney on one occasion as to the precise height of a dead body. Asked how tall the victim was, he replied, "I don't know."

"Can't you give an approximate idea?" was the next query.

"I don't know," was the reply.

"Was the man as tall as I am?" said the lawyer.

"Well," said the witness, "I have never had the pleasure of seeing you dead."

The question was passed.

Dr. Taylor's religious views were unorthodox, in an age when such views were regarded in some quarters as atheism. A few of "the more pious members of the faculty—whose names have long since been forgotten—once agitated to have him dismissed." The undergraduates would not hear of it. "The student body rose to the last man and said they would leave with him. He was retained," an article in *The Messenger,* published by the Theta Kappa Psi medical fraternity, declared. Taylor's class in medical jurisprudence at the session of 1904–05 presented him with a silver loving cup "as a token of their esteem and appreciation of him as a man and as a professor." The faculty gave him another loving cup when he retired.

In his book *De Quibus,* Taylor paid tribute to the Medical College for the complete freedom that he enjoyed to express his views, "however violently the teaching may conflict with nonmedical opinion and creeds." He went on to declare: "Did I not feel thus, could I be assured that this college was only a kind of medical nucleus floating in a cytoplasm of orthodox theology, I would separate myself from it at once."

Dr. Taylor retired from the faculty in 1913 and died in 1917. Thus passed one of the unique personalities in Richmond's history.

7. Dr. Hunter H. McGuire, nationally famous surgeon, who founded the University College of Medicine in 1893 in competition with the Medical College.

8. Dr. John S. Wellford of the Medical College faculty, who almost fought a duel with Dr. Hunter McGuire.

9. Dr. George Ben Johnston, nationally famous surgeon, whose followers and those of Dr. Hunter McGuire carried on an intense rivalry for many years.

10. Dr. William H. Taylor, member of the MCV faculty for decades, whose witty lectures and literate writings were greatly admired.

THREE

Two Rival Medical Schools

THE BITTER ANIMOSITIES that prevailed between medical groups in Richmond in the late nineteenth century culminated in the founding in 1893 of the College of Physicians and Surgeons, with Dr. Hunter H. McGuire as president. The institution, which soon changed its name to the University College of Medicine, was located at Twelfth and Clay streets, almost around the corner from the Medical College of Virginia. Dr. George Ben Johnston was the dominant figure on the MCV faculty, and as Dr. Wyndham B. Blanton writes, from then on "it was a battle between these two superior men [McGuire and Johnston] and their respective faculties."

Dr. Stuart McGuire, Hunter McGuire's son, says in his memoir that he and Dr. Lewis Wheat, his father's assistant, made the suggestion that a new medical school be established in Richmond. He relates the facts as follows:

"A vacancy occurred in the professorship of surgery at the Medical College. Lewis Wheat applied for the appointment but it went to Dr. George Ben Johnston. Lewis and I talked a great deal about the advantages the position would give a doctor, and we finally determined to start a medical school ourselves." They went to see Dr. Hunter McGuire, and the latter "immediately caught fire" and agreed to head the new institution.

Hunter McGuire was a man of immense prestige, deservedly so. His service as Medical Director of Stonewall Jackson's Corps in the Civil War, and his subsequent notable achievements as a surgeon were enormous assets to the newly established school. He succeeded in putting together a large and prestigious faculty—much larger than that of MCV. He also instituted a superior curriculum.

One of the reasons given for establishing another school almost within a stone's throw of MCV was that it was needed to stem the flow of Virginia medical students to northern colleges. This had been going on since before the Civil War, as we have seen, but the flow was greatly slowed by the founding of the University College of Medicine. In one year the number of Virginia medical students in Virginia institutions jumped from 225 to 450.

The wartime residence of Confederate Vice President Alexander H. Stephens at Twelfth and Clay streets was converted into a college building, and the former mansion of Dr. John Brockenbrough, built in 1811 at the corner of Eleventh and Clay, became the hospital for the college, and was named the Virginia Hospital. The building was remodeled to provide 62 beds, and in 1895 an annex was added, bringing the total number of beds to 125.

The first faculty of the University College of Medicine, dominated by Hunter McGuire, who was not only president but chairman of the board, included the following: Drs. Stuart McGuire, Landon B. Edwards, Joseph A. White, John Dunn, J. Allison Hodges, Jacob Michaux, George Ross, Moses D. Hoge, Jr., William T. Oppenhimer, Thomas J. Moore, Lewis Wheat, Isaiah H. White, William S. Gordon, Lewis M. Cowardin, Edward McGuire, and Hugh M. Taylor. The school not only enrolled such men on its faculty, but it offered courses in dentistry, pharmacy, and nursing, which were not available at the Medical College of Virginia.

All of this put MCV very much on its mettle, and caused it to improve its curriculum, lengthen its course, reorganize the hospital, and add courses in dentistry, pharmacy, and nursing. It also caused great resentment at MCV, whose faculty was soon as dagger's points with the UCM staff.

The State of Virginia was appropriating the munificent sum of $5,000 per year to the Medical College. Dr. Hunter McGuire did not want the state to allot anything to the rival institution, and he wrote one of the senators in an effort to persuade the General Assembly to eliminate the appropriation. His action caused a furor in the ranks of the MCV faculty, who dispatched a long communication to the press, claiming that statements in McGuire's letter "are not only contrary to the fact, but, in our opinion, Dr. McGuire is in a condition to know that they are contrary to the fact."

The MCV staff went on to say: "We leave to McGuire himself to digest the mortification he feels as he realizes that he has done a most discreditable thing, and that he has done it so bunglingly as to be caught in the act." The letter was signed "The Faculty," with no names listed.

McGuire, of course, did not take all this lying down. The faculty's blast of several columns had gone into great detail, and McGuire's reply was of similar length. There was direct conflict of evidence on certain questions of fact, and in some instances it is difficult at this distance to tell who was right.

For example, there was the matter of the extent to which the MCV faculty had sought to have the students exempted from taking the examinations of the State Board—as McGuire claimed they had done. Reference was made to this matter in the preceding chapter, and the faculty appeared to make a good case in arguing that it had not supported the effort of the students to obtain exemption. In its communication the MCV faculty again denied that it had appealed to the legislature to exempt the students. It admitted that "two or three of the faculty agreed with the students, but one member appeared . . . in opposition," and "the action of the faculty as a body was also in opposition, as shown by an official letter." It offered to show the letter, if requested.

In reply, McGuire quoted the chairman of the legislative committee before whom the students asked for exemption as saying that his "recollection of the bitter and undignified fight made by the faculty and students . . . to have their graduates exempted from . . . the law . . . is very vivid." He also quoted the president of the Medical Examining Board as saying that faculty members addressed the committee as "very warmly opposed to any examination of their own students."

The MCV faculty referred to "the rage and humiliation" felt by McGuire "at his inability to divert the bounty of the state" and said he "displays much bitter hatred to our school." In his retort, the president of the University College of Medicine said: "I do not think this is exactly the way to state my feelings toward that institution. I have often felt ashamed of it, and . . . when its faculty appealed to the legislature to exempt their students from going before the State Examining Board . . . I felt the profoundest contempt for it." He went on to declare that "during the last few years . . . the college has slowly and gradually deteriorated . . . and has come to be regarded as a second-rate school." He also chided the faculty for not signing their names to their first communication to the press.

In their second communication they signed their names—Christopher Tompkins, William H. Taylor, Martin L. James, Henry H. Levy, John N. Upshur, Lewis C. Bosher, George Ben Johnston, Charles M. Shields, J. W. Long, and J. Page Massie—and said: "His affectation of not knowing who we are is . . . very childish. He has always known very well who we are when he has wished to injure us."

Repeated efforts were made by UCM to persuade the General Assembly to stop appropriating $5,000 a year to the Medical College, but without avail. After Hunter McGuire's death in 1900, his son, Dr. Stuart McGuire, carried on the fight. He also appeared before the State Constitutional Convention of 1901–2 in an effort to write into the constitution a clause "prohibiting the General Assembly from making appropriations for teaching theology, law, medicine, dentistry or pharmacy." In support of this thesis, McGuire declared:

> All admit the wisdom and necessity of the state making as liberal appropriations for the public free school system as her resources permit, but there is a question, both practical and theoretical, as to the grade to which the teaching should be carried. . . .
>
> If primary education taxes the financial ability of the state . . . then more advanced teaching is an unjust discrimination against the general masses in favor of the special classes. . . . It is not necessary that every individual should be a minister, a lawyer, a doctor, dentist or pharmacist; therefore the state should make no provision for free professional education.

Dr. McGuire stated that "a majority of the Committee on Education expressed personally their conviction that the appropriations were wrong," but said that "it was regarded as a matter for legislative consideration and action." The legislature did not go along with the McGuire thesis, and repeatedly turned down his recommendations on the point. Members of the Medical College faculty appeared regularly in opposition.

While the continued rancor between the two institutions had its deplorable aspects, there appears to be no doubt that the competition was good for both schools, especially the Medical College of Virginia. It instituted a three-year graded course in 1894 and stressed the importance of adequate preliminary education. The following year admissions were limited to high school and college graduates. A nurses' training school was launched at MCV in 1895, and two years later departments of dentistry and pharmacy were added. UCM had opened with a teaching staff of forty, including adjuncts, more than double that of MCV. By the end of the century the gap had not only been narrowed; it had almost been wiped out, with the two faculties very close to the same size. Hunter McGuire was the dominant figure at UCM until his death, while George Ben Johnston became preeminent at MCV. Surgery at the latter institution was divided for some years between Johnston and Lewis C. Bosher, another eminent man in the field.

In 1899 the Medical College set the pace for the other schools in Virginia by extending the course in medicine to four years, the most demanding requirement in the state. Not only so, but Dean Christopher Tompkins urged the adoption of this four-year course by all members of the Southern Medical College Association, and his proposal was approved unanimously.

Relations with the University College of Medicine during this period remained tense. In the words of Stuart McGuire, "Runners were sent by both colleges to meet incoming trains and try to secure students, and other undignified methods were resorted to." Another account says that "the rivalry was at fever heat," and "faculty members, class associates and even the freshmen passed each other while looking in opposite directions."

Questionable methods of attracting students were used elsewhere in that era. The *Richmond and Louisville Medical Journal* records that "students at the Louisville Medical College were enticed away to the Medical Department of the University of Louisville by offers of all tickets [courses] of that institution for the beggarly sum of $5. Resolutions adopted by the faculty of the University of Kentucky School of Medicine charge that 'the dean . . . of the Medical Department of the University of Louisville has been basely tampering with several members of their class, and by falsehoods and misrepresentation has endeavored to seduce students from their studies and their honor, and has succeeded by bribes and otherwise in enticing some.' "

The death of Hunter McGuire in 1900 removed the dominant figure from the University College of Medicine, but the school carried on. A firm foundation had been laid, to the extent that this was possible in a small city with two competing medical schools.

Hunter McGuire's passing was the occasion for an outpouring of sorrow, and expressions of admiration. On the day he died, the *Richmond News* said, "It may be doubted whether anyone has lived in Virginia since Lee and Jackson died who was loved by more people."

His career was an extraordinary one in several directions. After leading the exodus of hundreds of medical students from Philadelphia on the eve of the Civil War, he was assigned, on the outbreak of hostilities, as a medical officer to Stonewall Jackson's Army of the Shenandoah. His son, Dr. Stuart McGuire, recounted that his father was six feet three inches tall and very thin and pale from a recent illness, only twenty-six years old and looking younger than that. When Jackson saw him for the first time, he said: "Very good, Dr. McGuire, go to your quarters and wait until I send for you." He waited for three days, while Jackson sent a courier to Richmond to find out if a mistake had been made "in assigning him such a young and sickly-looking medical officer."

General Jackson soon found that there had been no mistake, and that he had acquired a man of extraordinary capacity. The two became fast friends, and remained so until Jackson's death after the battle of Chancellorsville, when McGuire attended him. Dr. James Power Smith, Jackson's chaplain, said that young McGuire developed remarkable administrative ability, and that "an extensive and immediate work of organization devolved upon him—appointments, instructions, supplies to be secured, medical and hospital trains to be arranged, hospitals to be established." He was the head of the medical department under Jackson, and "became a great favorite of his chief."

Young McGuire returned to Richmond after the war, joined the MCV faculty and entered private practice. But nearly everybody was "broke" and unable to pay medical bills. He said that he managed to make ends meet by serving as surgeon when Union officers fought duels with each other. He got $100 per duel, and remarked jokingly that an added bonus was witnessing "damn Yankees shooting one another."

Dr. W. Lowndes Peple said of him after his death: "What were the qualities of this tall, gaunt, angular man, without eloquence of speech or charm of voice or manner that made men listen to his every word? . . . It was not the clear intellect of the man that made this compelling appeal. It was a deep encompassing love of his fellow man; never expressed, but shown in a thousand ways that set him apart."

Hunter McGuire's statue by William Couper, a Virginia artist, stands in Capitol Square, in a rare testimonial to the admiration and affection felt for this president of the American Surgical Association and the American Medical Association. His bust by Dr. John W. Brodnax, of the faculties of UCM and MCV, occupies a niche at the Medical College, in McGuire Hall, which was named for him. Both bronzes are considered remarkable likenesses.

The McGuire family is without a peer in the annals of Virginia medicine.

Some fourteen members of the clan have ornamented the profession since the early years of the nineteenth century. The current generation is ably represented by Hunter H. McGuire, Jr., professor of surgery and assistant dean of medicine at MCV, first winner of the dean's award in the School of Medicine, and now chief of surgery at the McGuire Veterans Hospital in Richmond; and his brother, Lockart McGuire, professor of medicine and occupant of the Julian Beckwith chair of cardiology in the University of Virginia Medical School.

J. Allison Hodges, a member of the original University College faculty, who held the chairs of anatomy and of nervous and mental diseases, was chosen president of the institution, succeeding Hunter McGuire. He served five years, but resigned at the end of that time because of the press of affairs connected with Hygeia Hospital, which he had founded, and his private practice. Dr. Hodges was one of the founders of the Tri-State Medical Association and served as its president. He was also president of the Richmond Academy. Stuart McGuire succeeded him as president of UCM in 1905, and remained in that post until its consolidation with MCV in 1913.

The University College lost no time in organizing an alumni association. It was launched at the end of the first session in 1894, with Dr. Hugh McGuire as the first president. A distinguished alumnus was Dr. Hugh S. Cumming, an 1894 graduate who would be appointed U.S. surgeon general by President Woodrow Wilson.

An honor system for the students was put into effect in 1905. This had not been done previously, President J. Allison Hodges explained, "because of a want of a proper spirit among the students themselves to consistently maintain it." The students were in entire charge, any student seeing a violation was on his honor to report it, and pledges were signed that aid had been neither given nor received. A student was expelled in 1908 for cheating on an examination.

The students were anxious to have some sort of organized athletics, and they sought permission to field a baseball team. It was granted, and no less than $25 was made available for "fitting up" the team. In 1909 the undergraduates expressed a desire to play football, and to have an Athletic Association. The faculty acquiesced. Dr. Thomas W. Murrell, chairman of the faculty Committee on Athletics, reported in 1911 that the previous season had been most successful from a financial standpoint, and that the Athletic Association was out of debt. Obviously a schedule of games was being played, but the school publications are thunderously silent on the subject.

A woman applicant for admission to the school of medicine appeared in 1909. She was Miss Rachel Lovenstein, a B.A. and an M.A. of Richmond College, who had had her first year of medicine at Johns Hopkins University. "The faculty could not see its way clear to a change in its regulations concerning the attendance of women in the Department of Medicine," the faculty minutes declare.

Dissension reared its head in the Department of Dentistry. The trustees' minutes for 1909 reveal that the department was "in a most unhappy condition" and "must be either reorganized or abolished," as there was "friction between its professors and disquietude among its students," President Stuart McGuire stated. The cause of the trouble was a proposed law to require all dentists to graduate in medicine before becoming eligible to practice. The trustees' executive committee stood unanimously in opposition to this requirement, yet, according to Dr. McGuire, "several of the professors have worked actively for the measure." Not only so, but they "had a joint meeting with teachers from the Medical College, and passed resolutions beginning, "We, the faculties of the Dental Departments of the two Richmond schools, etc." McGuire lashed out at the UCM professors in question, saying that "such insubordination . . . is not to be tolerated." That apparently ended the matter.

President McGuire was conscious of the problems of his college, but he pointed out that those of the Medical College were "much worse." Its income he declared, despite its appropriation from the state, "is not as much as ours by a good many thousands of dollars, and its expenses, owing to the annual deficit of the Memorial Hospital [operated by MCV], are much greater." Furthermore, "its faculty is divided into two warring camps" and, "owing to this fact, it is not the time to open negotiations with it, as one faction would oppose whatever the other faction advocated." He was referring to a possible consolidation of the two institutions under one board and teaching staff. When the psychological moment for opening negotiations arrives, said he, "the faculties of the various institutions should not be considered, but the governing boards . . . should take such action as their wisdom dictates."

A stunning blow to UCM fell on January 6, 1910, when the college building burned and the Virginia Hospital was damaged. The college authorities were not too dismayed, and work was begun at once to raise funds for a new building. Dr. McGuire subscribed $10,000. There was some talk of merger with the Medical College, but the time was not felt to be propitious. Classes were held at the Mechanics Institute, and the following year the Millhiser tobacco factory was reconditioned and leased. Conversion of the factory cost $5,000, and $20,000 more was spent on equipment. When the college moved in, Dr. McGuire declared that "no college in the United States is better equipped than ours," a most extraordinary assertion. Virginia Hospital was said to be "in better physical condition than ever before in its history," with improvements and repairs costing $8,000. A very real asset was Miss Agnes D. Randolph, great-granddaughter of Thomas Jefferson, a graduate of the Virginia Hospital school of nursing, and its superintendent and director of nurses. Miss Randolph was one of the great pioneers in nursing education.

Two years after the fire McGuire Hall, the new home of the University College, opened on the site of the destroyed building. The Richmond community had raised sufficient funds to erect the structure, which cost over $200,000, and was excellently equipped.

Meanwhile there was additional talk concerning the desirability of merging the two medical schools. The Flexner Report, *Medical Education in the United States and Canada,* by Abraham Flexner, had appeared in 1910, and had given great impetus to the movement for consolidation. This landmark study, which went far toward revolutionizing the teaching of medicine in this country, was far from complimentary concerning the situation in Richmond.

"The destruction by fire of the University College of Medicine . . . should precipitate the consolidation of the two independent schools," the report declared. "Separately, neither of them can hope greatly to improve its present facilities, which, weak in respect to laboratories and laboratory teaching, are entirely inadequate on the clinical side. Their present hospitals utilized together, though still unsatisfactory, would at any rate be much more nearly adequate than is either hospital taken by itself."

The Flexner Report was much more favorable in its references to the University of Virginia medical school, saying that its "rapid improvement . . . in the last three years is one of the striking phenomena of recent medical education history." Perhaps with this in mind, Dr. McGuire released figures in 1912 on failures of graduates of the three Virginia medical schools on all state boards for the preceding twenty years. His statement was to the effect that 13.9 per cent of Medical College graduates failed, 10.6 per cent of University of Virginia graduates, and only 7.6 per cent of University College graduates.

A medical student at University College made history of a sort in the spring of 1912 by placing a bet with another student that he could steal a cadaver from the college's anatomical laboratory and drag it to a bar on Seventh Street. After imbibing freely, the young man purloined the corpse and made his way with his burden in the direction of the designated bar. The faculty minutes record that "he had gotten as far as the alley in the rear of the Sheltering Arms Hospital when he was overcome by a combination of the subject and the alcohol." As he and the cadaver lay side by side on the ground, "a passing Negro woman stumbled over the subject and promptly fainted." With three prostrate forms decorating the alley, the police were called. The student was dragged to his feet and taken to the police station, while the "stiff" was apparently returned to the anatomical laboratory, and the black woman regained consciousness and departed in haste. After the hearing in police court, the student "was sent in a carriage . . . to the Westbrook Sanitarium, and has been there straightening himself out." A month later, the faculty minutes record sadly that the student "was unable to remain straightened out, was taken away by his uncle and sent home."

A sad event of this period was the death of Dr. Landon B. Edwards, a member of the University College faculty from its inception until he resigned in 1907, and from 1898 to 1907 dean of medicine. But his contribution to medical education at UCM was only a fraction of what he accomplished. A graduate of the Medical College, he was a leader in organizing the revived Medical Society of Virginia in 1870, and he served as secretary from that time until his death, missing only one meeting in forty-one years. Dr. Edwards founded the *Virginia Medical Monthly* in 1874, and edited it for the rest of his life, exerting a far-reaching influence through its columns. Along with the foregoing, he carried on a large medical practice and served as president of the Richmond Academy of Medicine and Surgery, the American Medical Editors Association and the American Medical Publishers Association. And he did all this despite the fact that he suffered for many years with interstitial nephritis. Many medical societies passed resolutions of highest praise at his passing in 1910.

11. First faculty of the University College of Medicine, 1894. *Front row, left to right:* Dr. Thomas J. Moore, Dr. Hunter H. McGuire, president, Dr. L. M. Cowardin. *Second row:* Dr. William S. Gordon, Dr. J. Allison Hodges, Dr. Joseph A. White. *Third row:* T. Wilber Chelf, Dr. Landon B. Edwards, Dr. Moses D. Hoge, Jr., Dr. Jacob Michaux, Dr. Charles L. Steel, Dr. John F. Winn, Dr. Charles H. Chalkley. *Fourth row:* Dr. Paulus Irving, Dr. Stuart McGuire, Dr. W. T. Oppenhimer. *Fifth row:* Dr. Charles V. Carrington, Dr. James N. Ellis, Dr. Edward McGuire, Tom Haskins, morgue attendant, Dr. John Dunn.

12. Dr. Christopher Tompkins, dean of the Medical College, 1893–1913.

13. McGuire Hall, erected in 1912 to house the University College of Medicine when its home on the site burned.

14. Miss Agnes D. Randolph.

15. Miss Sadie Heath Cabaniss.

16. Miss Nannie J. Minor.

14–16. Three gentlewomen who entered the nursing profession in defiance of the prevailing custom, and became notable pioneers.

FOUR

The Feuding Schools Unite

THE MEDICAL COLLEGE OF VIRGINIA was organized in an unusual way in the latter years of the nineteenth century, according to Dr. Manfred Call, dean of medicine some decades later. He wrote in the college *Bulletin* in 1928 that "in the late nineties the members of the medical faculty had proprietary rights in the college, both professorial and financial," and he went on:

> The faculty was the dominating factor in shaping the policies of the school, educational, administrative and financial. Individual faculty leaders arose, assumed control, and with their followers constituted the majority which exercised authority. The college and its needs were apparently subordinate to the professional ambitions and political aspirations of the dominating faculty leaders. Political affiliations were at times more potent in gaining major and even minor faculty appointments than true worth and special fitness. . . . Members of the board of visitors were frequently pledged to the support of candidates before the full list of applicants . . . was known to such board members. Some years before consolidation was consummated, the board of visitors began to assume the real functions of a governing body, to the embarrassment, at times, of certain faculty members.

A more favorable picture was presented in 1898 in the *Medical Register*, published by the MCV alumni, which said:

> During the past five years the faculty has voluntarily expended in permanent improvement to the Medical College, which is the state's property, a larger sum than has been received from the state in the same length of time. . . . In spite of the fact that her appropriation is the smallest made to any state educational institution, the college has, by judicious management and the liberality of her faculty in devoting to the purpose almost the entire surplus of receipts from students' fees, contrived during the past five years so to improve her equipment that the growth and the advanced position she occupies today are matters of pride.

In 1893, for example, the Board of Visitors' minutes recorded that the faculty voted to advance $400 each to pay for repairs to the infirmary building as a hospital for clinical instruction. The General Assembly had reduced the state appropriation from $5,000 to $4,000 and then to $3,000, because of the nationwide depression. The faculty voted to advance $3,000 of its private funds, and urged the legislature to increase the amount provided by the commonwealth. The General Assembly complied, and put the appropriation back to $5,000. In 1898 it reduced the sum once more to $4,000, on account of the poor state of the economy.

Dean Christopher Tompkins remained cheerful, at least outwardly, in the face of competition from the newly formed University College of Medicine. In 1894, following the opening of the latter institution, he declared that the affairs of the Medical College were, in the opinion of the faculty, "far in advance of anything heretofore attained," and in 1901 he exulted: "We have 110 new students, an event never before realized in the history of the college. Attendance in the other classes has also been satisfactory, in spite of the fact the dean . . . declined to allow certain former students to again matriculate, who are unworthy of the high calling to which they had aspired."

Failure of professors to meet their classes was a cause of concern to the MCV administration, according to the minutes of the faculty in 1898. "Students are put to serious inconvenience," said the minutes, and the faculty recommended unanimously that "a register be kept in the faculty room wherein members of the faculty and adjunct faculty be required to register the time of their arrival." Certain unnamed faculty members also were rapped for not attending public functions of the college. There were similar complaints in 1902, 1903, 1904 and 1905.

"Secret organizations or fraternities" were banned by a unanimous vote of the MCV faculty in 1899. But by 1903 the teaching staff had reversed itself, for it announced that "the faculty has no objection to students forming any organizations or fraternities among themselves that they may see fit to." However, members of the teaching corps were discouraged from maintaining "active membership in any students organization or fraternity." There had been an upheaval in 1900, when eleven members of that class signed a petition to the faculty urging them "to remove from office at the end of the session all adjuncts [professors] who are members of Phi Mu fraternity." The petitioners said that some members of Phi Mu in the class made the "impudent claim" that they have " 'pull' with the faculty."

There was another stir in 1907 when Dr. W. Z. Beazley wrote from Richmond that he had been a guest of the faculty at a reception, and that as an alumnus he was protesting "the conduct of a great many young men." "When men lose control of themselves so that they overturn chairs, break dishes, tear table-cloths and forcibly place members of your faculty upon a table to afford fun for their beclouded brains, it seems time to call halt," Beazley wrote. "Some of the members of the adjunct faculty imbibed very freely." His letter was referred to a committee for consideration.

An applicant from a woman for admission to the dental school was received in 1905. The faculty voted "not to admit any females to the classes for next session."

The college had an honor system before 1898, but in that year it was abolished by vote of the students. Two sessions later the students petitioned for the system's restoration and the petition was granted. In 1905 five students were convicted of cheating and were expelled. The Board of Visitors expressed its pleasure at the manner in which the honor system was functioning.

The system continued to function after the consolidation of the University College and the Medical College in 1913, of which more anon. Two students were expelled in 1915, following an investigation by the student Honor Board. However, by the following year "dissatisfaction" with the system then in existence led to revisions, under which students were no longer required to report violations by others. Stuart McGuire stated that "during the early part of the session" of 1916–17, the system "was put to a severe test, but the students responded in a most creditable manner, and the principle of this form of government is now firmly established."

The erection at Twelfth and Broad streets of Memorial Hospital, with 200 beds "the largest hospital between Baltimore and New Orleans," was an important event just after the turn of the century. Ground was broken in 1901 "with an exquisitely wrought silver spade, fashioned by Tiffany," and used in all subsequent ground-breaking at the college. The handsome new edifice was opened with great fanfare and large crowds in 1903, and became the hospital of the college. It was a memorial to Charlotte Williams, daughter of John L. and Maria Ward Williams, who was drowned at Old Point Comfort in 1884. Williams was the principal contributor to the building fund, and George Ben Johnston, who had been instrumental in persuading Williams to make the contribution, was chairman of the building committee.

By 1905 the affairs of Memorial Hospital became "greatly embarrassed", and the faculty was notified that unless relief was forthcoming, the hospital would have to close, Dean Christopher Tompkins wrote the Board of Visitors. Certain faculty members agreed, in consequence, to be responsible for operating costs, and the faculty also pledged to work in their professional capacities without pay for at least two years, giving all the funds they received from tuition fees not needed for running expenses to the hospital. By these heroic means the hospital was kept functioning, and the MCV faculty had risen to another emergency.

With the consolidation of MCV and UCM in 1913, all patients in the latter institution's Virginia Hospital were transferred to Memorial, and Virginia Hospital became the property of the city for a ten-year period. It closed in 1922. Free treatment for white and black patients was provided there, and at the end of the decade it would become the Medical College's outpatient clinic until 1938. It would then be used as a teaching facility. Old Dominion Hospital, which had been dismantled in 1903 on the opening of Memorial and used as a teaching annex, was fitted up in 1914 as a nurses' home.

The Medical College Alumni Association had been organized in 1889, with the Rev. John B. Newton, who had graduated from the college with an M.D. in 1860, as the first president. He would become Episcopal bishop coadjutor of Virginia in 1894. The organization seems to have gotten off to an excellent start, since in 1905 the MCV *Bulletin* pronounced it "in flourishing condition, having over 500 members, more than one-fifth of whom attend the annual meetings." The foregoing statement was repeated in the *Bulletin* for each of the next three years.

But the organization seems to have become relatively inactive thereafter, for Dean Manfred Call said in a speech to the general faculty in 1923: "Until the last few years the alumni were never called upon for a concerted effort in any direction, and when called upon in time of crisis, so little organization was disclosed in their ranks and so retiring their leaders that only a small part of their influence could be brought to bear. Is any argument needed to prove that this alumni influence, so far as it concerns the Medical College of Virginia, is at present a very small asset to the parent institution? . . . They have been functionless for so long that atrophy from disuse has occurred."

Football and baseball teams were fielded by the Medical College at the session of 1907–8. Members of those teams were allowed by the faculty to be "absent from their work of the college for five or six days during the fall and again during the spring." It also was agreed by the faculty that "during the coming baseball session" they would "do what they can in excusing [the players] from college exercise for afternoon practice." The catalogue committee was urged "to arrange the schedule for next session so as to make a part of three afternoons a week available for athletics."

Information is sparse concerning the precise record made by the MCV teams for the next few years, but by 1912 their football eleven was "one of the strongest in the South that year," according to the MCV *Alumnus*. "It sported an all-American and a member of the mythical all-Southern team." The all-American was Jim Walker, who had been chosen by Walter Camp for that distinction when a student at the University of Minnesota, while Harry Hedgepeth, from the University of North Carolina, was the all-Southern player. The team captain was D. L. Elder, who had played two years at Chapel Hill. Frank S. Johns, previously a star at Hampden-Sydney, was in the backfield. Only twelve men were available for the team, the only extra being a guard. They were unable to scrimmage, said the *Alumnus*, as there was nobody to scrimmage with, and many had laboratories anyway. Yet these twelve men, with hardly any opportunity for practice, defeated William and Mary, Wake Forest, VPI, Hampden-Sydney, and University College of Medicine. They lost to Washington and Lee and the North Carolina Agricultural and Mechanical College, now N.C. State. The 1913 football team, the following year, was the last to represent MCV.

Efforts were made to have baseball and basketball teams in the immediately succeeding years, and spasmodic contests were held with a few colleges and local high schools, but this faded out on the eve of World War I.

During the 1920s, beginning in 1923, there was a revival of athletics in the college, and basketball, tennis, wrestling, and intramural sports were in vogue. The college was remarkably successful in some of these contests with other Virginia colleges and with a few from out of state.

Virginia's medical schools in the early 1900s were vulnerable to applications from students attending much-inferior medical institutions. The MCV *Bulletin* pointed out in 1910 that Virginia laws "require the State Board of Medical Examiners to admit, on equal terms, graduates of any legally chartered medical school, no matter how disreputable the school may be nor how low its standards for admission or graduation." This made Virginia a "dumping ground for physicians without either proper preliminary training or medical education."

The Medical College lost during this era one of its greatest figures when Dr. James B. McCaw died in 1906, aged eighty-three. The McCaw family had been eminent in medicine for several generations. James B. McCaw's great-grandfather, Dr. James McCaw, was a prominent physician in Norfolk; his grandfather, Dr. James D. McCaw, was a hero of Richmond's terrible theater fire of 1811, and narrowly escaped death; his father, Dr. William R. McCaw, also was prominent in the profession.

James B. McCaw was associated with the Medical College in one capacity or another from 1858 until his death forty-eight years later. He was chairman of the faculty, 1868–71, dean of the faculty, 1871–83, and chairman of the Board of Visitors, 1897–1906. His conspicuous service as surgeon-in-chief and commandant of the huge Chimborazo Hospital during the Civil War has been mentioned, together with his leadership in resisting successfully the firing of himself and the other members of the MCV faculty by Governor Cameron in 1882. McCaw was perhaps the leading military surgeon of the South during the Civil War. When he retired from active practice in 1901, the Richmond Academy of Medicine gave him a dinner and a loving cup. His versatility may be seen in the fact that he was for a considerable period president of the Mozart Association, which presented concerts, operas, and operettas in Richmond during the postbellum years.

The Tompkins-McCaw Library at the college is named for him and Dean Christopher Tompkins, as well as Brigadier General Walter Drew McCaw, chief surgeon of the American Expeditionary Force in World War I; Captain Sally Tompkins, head of the Robertson Confederate Hospital in Richmond during the Civil War, and Dr. James McCaw Tompkins, member of the faculty and Board of Visitors and editor of the *Old Dominion Journal of Medicine and Surgery.*

Reference has been made to the merger of UCM and MCV in 1913, but the precise steps that led up to that event have not been described. It was a difficult and tortuous process. In 1899, for example, the matter came up at an MCV faculty meeting, apropos of an intended union of that institution with the University of Virginia medical school. Dr. George Ben Johnston was instructed to "take whatever steps he thinks best, looking to a coalition" with the university, but he was "further instructed to state that under no circumstances will the Medical College of Virginia unite with the University College of Medicine."

By 1906, however, members of both faculties saw that a merger of the latter two institutions was becoming increasingly necessary, especially for financial reasons. Committees were appointed from both faculties, and discussions were held for months. The plans fell through, according to Dean Tompkins of MCV, "because of opposition of certain of their [UCM faculty] members."

When the UCM building burned in 1910, Dr. Stuart McGuire, who had led in seeking a coalition in 1906, declared that this disaster provided "an opportunity for effecting the amalgamation with MCV." The Flexner Report of that year, as already noted, had stressed the importance of such a step.

MCV offered its sympathy to UCM in the loss of its building and equipment, and made its own building and appliances available to the struggling institution. The *Virginia Medical Monthly* editorialized that it was "practically agreed" that there would be an amalgamation at the end of the session in 1910. But although the MCV faculty adopted a unanimous resolution favoring the move, and it was stated a few weeks later that the two faculties had "agreed on a general plan," the whole scheme fell through. This time the MCV faculty declined "to enter into amalgamation upon the terms proposed."

Two years later a bill was introduced in the General Assembly authorizing, but not requiring, the melding of MCV, UCM and UVA into a single institution. Dr. George Ben Johnston and Dr. Stuart McGuire favored the move, and both quoted President Edwin A. Alderman of the university as favoring it. Yet the bill was killed in committee by the legislature, without explanation.

Finally, after many vicissitudes, the consolidation of MCV and UCM was consummated in 1913. Dr. McGuire explained how it occurred:

> The reasons for the merger . . . were not numerical, physical or educational. To be plain, they were financial. The college [UCM] . . . had no income except from student fees. . . . The better it taught and the more students it got, the more money it lost. I am not of course in a position to speak for the Medical College, but I believe it found itself pretty much in the same position. . . .
>
> It was necessary for one school to sacrifice its name, and for the other to make concessions which, for various reasons, were almost equally difficult, but an agreement fair and honorable to both partners was effected.

The means by which this agreement was obtained were described by Dr. McGuire in his memoir. "After meetings of the two faculties had continued for some weeks," he wrote, "with apparently no progress being made, Dr. George Ben Johnston came to me and said he felt I was going about it in the wrong way, that I would never bring the rival faculties together, and there was no hope for it. He said the thing to do was to go to the respective governing boards, and win their approval; the boards could then dismiss their faculties and together appoint a faculty for the combined school. Dr. Johnston's suggestion was adopted."

Nine men from each board of trustees were named, and the nineteenth place was filled by Eppa Hunton, Jr., a prominent Richmond attorney. The two faculties were dismissed by their respective governing boards, and a new faculty appointed for the combined institution. "Their selection," according to Dr. McGuire, "was accorded general approbation." A new board of visitors for the institution was named, with Dr. Thomas H. Barnes of Nansemond, president of the MCV board from 1905 to 1913, and the school's oldest living graduate, as chairman. Dr. Barnes died a few months later, and Judge George L. Christian, former chairman of the UCM board, was named to succeed him.

The new college sorely needed a full-time president, and Dr. Samuel Chiles Mitchell, president of the University of South Carolina, was elected. He took office on May 27, 1913. Dr. Stuart McGuire was chosen dean of the faculty; Dr. A. L. Gray, chairman of the medical faculty; Dr. R. L. Simpson, chairman of the dental faculty, and A. L. Bolenbaugh, B.Sc., chairman of the pharmaceutical faculty. J. R. McCauley, former secretary of MCV, was made secretary of the college and the faculty.

Demagogic Governor Cole Blease of South Carolina claimed that he had "run Dr. S. C. Mitchell out of the state." This was nonsense, of course. As the *Newport News Daily Press* put it, "Dr. Mitchell is a complete gentleman and Governor Blease is his antithesis. Dr. Mitchell's position in South Carolina compelled him to associate with Governor Blease, and that was more than a gentleman of Dr. Mitchell's refinement and sense of decency could stand." The *Baltimore Evening Sun* opined that "Dr. Mitchell's inclination to return to his old home in Richmond . . . was no doubt intensified by the pitchforking to which he was subjected by Governor Blease and the South Carolina hillbillies." Many South Carolina papers praised Mitchell in the highest terms for his four progressive years as president of the state university. Blease had been expelled from the institution as a student.

In view of the long-held opinion that there was great personal animosity between Drs. Hunter McGuire and Stuart McGuire, on the one hand, and

Dr. George Ben Johnston on the other, Stuart McGuire's observations in his memoir are of special interest. He wrote:

> Dr. Johnston's cooperation and good judgment, and his sound advice, during this difficult period confirmed in me the good opinion my father had of him. Soon after my return from college I had gone to my father and told him that if I had to carry on the war between himself and Dr. Johnston I wanted to know how it started. My father replied that there had never been any trouble between Dr. Johnston and himself, and that they never had a quarrel. He said Dr. Johnston had come to Richmond not as an assistant, as did Hugh Taylor, Lewis Wheat and Ned McGuire, but as a competitor, and that the trouble had been made by their respective patients. He felt that his patients and Dr. Johnston's patients had by their loyalty really divided the city. My father ended our conversation with the statement that Dr. Johnston was an able surgeon and a good man, and that if I ever needed advice I should not hesitate to go to him.

The foregoing was written by Dr. McGuire in the last months of his life. He wished to be generous in his appraisal of Dr. Johnston, and there is no question of his sincerity on the point or that of his father. Undoubtedly there is much truth in his appraisal, yet both McGuires must have had one or two lapses of memory. Consider, for example, the bitter personal exchanges in 1894 between Hunter McGuire and the MCV faculty, the dominant member of which was Johnston. It should be remembered, however, that the competition between their followers, especially the rivalry between the two medical schools over a twenty-year period, kept both institutions on their toes and improved the quality of medicine in the city. In particular, let us not forget that the two McGuires and George Ben Johnston were magnificent citizens, each of whom made incalculably great contributions to their profession and their state.

Johnston led the campaign in 1913 that resulted in the city's acceptance of the Virginia Hospital, but the logical suggestion that he be named to the board of the new municipal institution led to another outburst of hostility toward him. He was also being mentioned for the University of Virginia Board of Visitors, and that too provoked animosity.

These matters came to public notice early in 1914 when the city's Administrative Board received a letter signed by Drs. Charles V. Carrington and Robert C. Bryan, protesting Johnston's proposed appointment to the Virginia Hospital Board. They declared that Johnston had been negligent in handling a surgical case involving a poor black with a head injury, that the patient had died, and that Johnston then misrepresented the facts. The letter referred to him as "a man who seems to have little regard for his duty, and who holds lightly the lives of the poor and humble who are entrusted to his care."

Enclosed with the letter containing these grave allegations was another, signed by Drs. Charles V. Carrington and J. Shelton Horsley, and directed to Armistead C. Gordon, rector of the University of Virginia. Johnston—who had accepted a post on the university faculty in 1905, but then had withdrawn his acceptance when certain stipulations as to additional facilities could not be met by the institution—was now being prominently mentioned for appointment to the university's Board of Visitors.

"Dr. Johnston is a most astute politician," the Carrington-Horsley letter declared, "and we know he will in every way endeavor to dominate and control any school with which he may be connected, regardless of the means by which he accomplishes his end."

The foregoing appeared in the *Richmond Times-Dispatch* of January 31, 1914, and Johnston lost no time in replying. In the same newspaper for February 2 he pronounced the charges a "vile slander" and set out his case at great length, giving his reasons why these three men were antagonistic toward him.

Johnston said he had refused Carrington's request for a recommendation for membership on the Medical College faculty, and this accounted for the latter's hostility. Horsley's request for a similar recommendation had been granted, and he had joined the faculty. But Johnston stated that he had found Horsley "to be unworthy and severed all professional and personal connection with him." No details were given in support of this disturbing allegation concerning one of the most distinguished and respected surgeons in Richmond's history. Johnston said that Bryan turned against him because Johnston had been unwilling to aid him "on the particular terms he proposed."

"I am not surprised that the malignancy and recklessness of Dr. Carrington will permit him to charge me with the responsibility for the death of a fellow man without a single fact to justify the charge," Johnston wrote, "but I am astonished that Dr. Bryan, whatever his personal feelings to me, could be induced to indorse this vile slander and libel."

As for his supposed neglect of the poor black who died, Dr. Johnston presented evidence that either he or his associate had visited the man daily in the hospital. He also gave a convincing account of his solicitude for the patient's well-being, and he presented a letter in full support of his version of the affair from Graham Hobson, chairman of the Committee on Relief for the Poor.

We have here another example of leaders in Richmond's medical community, men of high standards and impeccable principles, assailing each other with bewildering severity. A surprising aspect of these repeated attacks is that nobody seems ever to have sued for libel.

On another front, the North Carolina Medical College at Charlotte was closing its doors with the 1914–15 session, and it requested permission for its sophomore, junior, and senior classes to complete their education at MCV. The request was granted, and these students graduated with those from the Medical College in the next few years. The arrangement ended after these forty-nine students received their diplomas.

The amalgamation of MCV and UCM had created a much stronger school, but there were problems. President Samuel Chiles Mitchell performed well in getting the consolidated institution off to a good start, but he remained for only one year. In 1917 Dean Stuart McGuire urged that a committee be appointed to recommend a successor. Nearly two years later the committee named Dr. McGuire as its choice, and he was elected by the board. For all his merits, this was an impossible assignment, for Dr. McGuire could not devote anything like his full time to the position, since he also had to operate St. Luke's Hospital and carry on his large surgical practice.

A grievous loss to the college was the death of Dr. George Ben Johnston in 1916 at age sixty-three. It was the occasion for an outpouring of tributes such as had seldom accompanied the passing of a private citizen. Former animosities seemed to be forgotten as the Richmond Academy of Medicine, the Medical College faculty, the *Old Dominion Journal,* the Richmond press, various prominent physicians and many other Richmonders heaped unrestrained praise upon the former president of the American Surgical Association, the Southern Surgical and Gynecological Association, the Medical Society of Virginia, and the Richmond Academy of Medicine, who had contributed so much civic service along with his extensive surgical practice and his founding of Johnston-Willis Hospital.

Dr. Charles R. Robins pointed out that in 1879, the year after young Johnston came to Richmond, he performed the first operation in Virginia under Listerism, the foundation of antiseptic surgery. Dr. Frank S. Johns said this action "would shake the whole citadel of 'Confederate Medicine and Surgery' " and that acceptance of the theories of the not yet internationally famous Lister by a twenty-five-year-old "upstart from the provinces would not endear him to his established colleagues." W. Gordon McCabe paid tribute to Dr. Johnston in his annual report as president of the Virginia Historical Society. "He did an immense amount of what is called 'charity practice,' " said McCabe, "but he never remotely alluded to these constant benefactions." Along with others, the speaker noted Dr. Johnston's "thin, high-pitched voice" which "at once attracted the attention of his listeners . . . and held his audience as few so-called 'orators' can never do."

Dr. Beverley R. Tucker brought to light the fact that Dr. Johnston was extremely fastidious concerning his dress, and that the only shoes that suited him were made to order by a Richmond shoemaker. But the shoemaker died, and the last could not be found. Johnston tried a succession of thirty-five pairs of shoes, custom-made in New York, Boston, Philadelphia and Baltimore, and none of them fit. At this critical juncture, the missing last was located, and his requirements were cared for. In order to provide against future disasters, he had copies of the last made and deposited in three other cities.

Dr. Johnston's generosity in affording opportunities for other surgeons was touched upon by Dr. Tucker. "Time and time again, Johnston generously divided his surgical chair [at MCV] so as to give full professorships to other surgeons," Tucker wrote. "He brought specialist after specialist to Richmond, and gave them his support until they were firmly established. . . . Scores of physicians owe their successful start to this magnanimous man."

The George Ben Johnston Auditorium at the Medical College was named for him in 1949. It stands on the site of the historic building on Twelfth Street in which the Virginia convention of 1788 ratified the United States Constitution.

The MCV student YMCA, founded in 1898, was described in the 1920–21 catalogue as "the largest and most comprehensive of the student organizations." Jonah L. Larrick came in 1923 as full-time director and remained until 1969. During that period he was recognized as one of the most admired figures on the campus; and he entered into many colleges activities not directly related to the "Y." The high esteem in which Mr. Larrick was held is evidenced in the fact that the current Student Activities Center has been named for him.

Commencements at MCV have been "conspicuous farces," W. A. Simpson, editor of *Skull and Bones*, wrote in 1917. He urged a program that would attract seniors, alumni and undergraduates, none of which, he said, are now attracted. He suggested a College Night with several stunts; an Alumni Day; a Faculty Night, "when we could have a crack at these men," a dance, clinics, and demonstrations.

World War I was raging in Europe, and the United States was moving ever closer to involvement. A Puerto Rican student at MCV, Jorge Salvatore Vivo, embarked from Newport News in 1915 on the *Armenian,* "one of the horse-ships," as ship's surgeon. The vessel was torpedoed by a German submarine off Cornwall and Vivo drowned.

Thirty-two lectures by U.S. Army officers were given to the MCV seniors, beginning in February 1917, primarily for the purpose of making medical college graduates throughout the country eligible for commissions in the Medical Reserve Corps, in case the United States should be drawn into the war.

It was drawn in a few months later, in April, and the following month fifteen members of the senior medical class left college to enter the medical service of the navy.

That fall the student body voted by a small margin against setting up a system of military training on the campus. Dean Stuart McGuire urged second-, third-, and fourth-year medical students and second- and third-year dental students to join the Enlisted Reserve Corps. They would be detailed to attend college but would be subject to being called up at any time. Dr. McGuire and other faculty members were being called up.

A hospital unit came into being promptly, with Dr. Robert C. Bryan, who had been in the French service at the front, in charge. It was projected to be an "active, mobile hospital which operated in the field, and under gunfire, if necessary." But the plan was vetoed by the surgeon general, who said the War Department wanted "the much more pretentious base hospitals." Dr. Bryan was named chief medical adviser to the commission to Rumania.

The Medical College proceeded with plans to expand its unit "into a base hospital under Red Cross auspices," and an ambulance unit was organized. Major Stuart McGuire, a lifelong sufferer from tuberculosis of the spine, which made it necessary for him to wear a steel wire-mesh corset at all times, was deemed so essential to the war effort that he was exempted from physical examinations and placed in charge of Base Hospital 45, as it was known, and of creating the ambulance unit. Major McGuire announced that he would close St. Luke's Hospital, and accompany the hospital unit to France. St. Luke's became a dormitory for the women attending Westhampton College. Dr. Joseph F. Geisinger was named as aide to Dr. McGuire, and Dr. C. Howard Lewis was appointed to head the ambulance unit. More than forty MCV faculty members were in the hospital unit. Major J. Garnett Nelson was chief of medical service under McGuire, and Major W. Lowndes Peple chief of surgical service.

The War Department said that $40,000 would be needed for equipment for the hospital unit, but it turned out to be $140,000. The funds were raised by the Red Cross, under the leadership of Coleman Wortham. Equipment, fourteen carloads of it, was purchased by Richard Gwathmey. There was tremendous confusion in Washington during these early days, and this caused corresponding uncertainty and bafflement in Richmond.

Base Hospital 45 began moving to Camp Lee in February 1918, and by April was fairly well settled there, but then came what seemed an interminable wait. There were uncounted drills, exercises, lectures, inspections, and physical examinations. Finally, after numerous exasperating delays, with orders from Washington and counterorders, the unit sailed from New York on July 10 aboard the USS *Aeolus.* It was convoyed across the submarine-infested Atlantic and arrived at Le Havre on July 21.

Autun, a small town a couple of hundred miles southeast of Paris was the first stop. About two months later the unit moved to Toul, a much larger center of population, situated due east of Paris, and only a few miles from the German border. Here they occupied "a huge barracks, consisting of three large four-story main buildings and numerous smaller buildings."

The foregoing quotation is from *The History of Base Hospital No. 45 in the Great War,* edited by a committee of which Dr. Joseph F. Geisinger was chairman.

On arrival at Toul, the history declares, there "began to appear the consummate skill of our adjutant, Lt. [Thomas C.] Boushall, who had full opportunity to exhibit that personality and ability which soon won for him an affection and admiration that permeated the entire organization, and that persist to this day."

Six hundred and fifty patients were brought in and had to be cared for, despite utterly inadequate equipment and facilities. The nurses had not arrived, since they sailed later from New York. They reached Toul on September 9, to the relief of all. Ruth I. Robertson was the chief nurse; years later she would become Mrs. Stuart McGuire. Lieutenant Colonel Alex W. Williams, commanding officer of the unit, had a nervous breakdown and subsequently died. He was succeeded by Lieutenant Colonel H. C.

Maddux, who was in charge until Lieutenant Colonel McGuire took command.

The great Saint-Mihiel drive was launched by the Allies on September 12, and casualties began pouring into the hospital from the front—8,000 of them the first month. Previous patients had been mainly sick soldiers, but these were mostly battle casualties. There were often 2,000 beds, twice the number originally scheduled. Surgeons and nurses worked around the clock, almost until they dropped.

The situation was doubly complicated by the fact that equipment for the unit had arrived at Saint-Nazaire, but had not been forwarded to Toul. It was finally dislodged from that seaport by Lieutenant Charles Phillips, and reached the embattled members of Base Hospital 45 at the height of the overcrowding. The terrible influenza epidemic, devastating to soldiers and civilians on both sides of the Atlantic, added to the burdens. Students at the Medical College back in Richmond were deeply involved in the epidemic, of which more hereafter.

The armistice on November 11 brought intense relief, especially to the French, who had been bled white during more than four years of carnage. Joy was unrestrained in the streets of Toul, as American and French soldiers joined in celebrating, and the *vin rouge* flowed freely. Such songs as "Madelon" and "Tipperary" rent the air, and a black band chimed in with a rousing rendition of "Dixie."

With the war over, Base Hospital 45 began dismantling its operation. Colonel McGuire returned to the United States slightly ahead of the rest, and the greatly admired Lieutenant Colonel J. Garnett Nelson commanded the unit until it was disbanded at Camp Lee on April 29, 1919.

The nurses returned on another ship. Chief Nurse Ruth Robertson praised them in the highest terms, saying that they had served far beyond the call of duty in cold, rain, and mud, with wholly inadequate equipment at first, and impossible quarters. Working long hours, they managed to get things into reasonable shape, despite the difficult circumstances.

Army Surgeon General Ireland commended the entire unit, calling attention to its readiness for service and patriotic devotion to duty, and the professional excellence of its personnel. A bronze tablet commemorating the unit's contribution was unveiled in McGuire Hall in 1941 during the twenty-first reunion of the Base Hospital 45 Veterans' Association.

An MCV graduate who made a significant contribution to the war effort in World War I was Colonel William L. Keller. He served as director of professional services for the American Expeditionary Force, and was decorated by this country and France. At the end of the war he was named chief of surgical services at Walter Reed Hospital and professor of military surgery at the Army Medical School.

Back at MCV, all medical students had been inducted into the Student Army Training Corps in September 1918. They bivouacked in the Blues' Armory and marched to the college for classes. When the deadly influenza epidemic broke out that fall, the students were pressed into action as orderlies at John Marshall High School, which had been converted into an emergency hospital with 1,000 beds. Students also served at other points in Richmond and elsewhere. All schools, churches, and theaters in Richmond were closed, and over 800 persons died. So much time was lost by the students and faculty in helping with the epidemic that commencement was postponed from June 3 to June 15, to make up for the canceled classes.

All kinds of absurd rumors concerning the Germans had been flying about while the war was in progress. They were said to have spread the flu germs that killed from 300,000 to 350,000 Americans during the fall of 1918. They were also alleged to have put ground glass in flour manufactured in this country. Professors Charles C. Haskell and E. C. L. Miller, of the MCV faculty, embarked on a novel experiment. They ate ground glass to prove that it was not harmful, and survived in good style.

The year 1918 brought the death of Dr. Christopher Tompkins, one of the major figures in Medical College of Virginia history. "Dr. Tompkins gave himself so unsparingly and unselfishly to his college duties, and the demands of an enormous general practice, that his health was seriously impaired," the *Virginia Medical Monthly* declared. He had been connected with the college in one way or another since his graduation in 1870, most especially as dean from 1893 until 1913. He was professor of anatomy from 1880 to 1884 and of obstetrics from 1884 to 1889. His high standing in the profession was evidenced by his election six consecutive times to the presidency of the Southern Medical College Association.

Dr. Tompkins pointed out in his farewell address as dean in 1913 that a compilation in 1911 by the American Medical Association showed "that of all the medical colleges in the United States, and taking them in the order in which their graduates passed the various medical examining boards, the Medical College of Virginia stood fourth." Those ranking above MCV were (1) Rush, in Chicago; (2) Johns Hopkins, and (3) Cornell, "and about one hundred and forty behind them." Dean Tompkins said he had long been in favor of a union of the Medical College and the University College of Medicine, but that his health was not of the best, and he had made it clear sometime previously that he "neither desired nor expected to be a member of this consolidation." He was given a loving cup by the faculty as a tribute of affection and esteem.

The entry of the United States into World War I caused a reversal of the policy of maintaining an all-male student body at MCV, except in the School of Nursing. With so many men in the service there was need for women graduates in the schools of medicine, dentistry, and pharmacy. Students in all three schools voted unanimously in November 1917 for admitting the ladies, and the Board of Visitors and faculty followed suit. The first women were enrolled in the fall of 1918. The results were excellent, Dean A. L. Gray reported the following year. He said the situation was "eminently satisfactory," insofar as the medical school was concerned. These matriculates' work was "well up with the best, and in some classes they head the list," he said.

The first woman graduates in the three departments were: Medicine—Innis Steinmetz, Hamilton, Canada, 1920; Dentistry—Esther Margaret Cummins of Petersburg, Constance O. Haller of Wytheville, and Tillie Lyons of Roanoke, 1922; Pharmacy—Margaret Ella Savage of Norfolk and Ruth Vincent of Richmond, 1921. The 1922 class in medicine included Margaret Nolting and Mary Baughman, who became well-known practitioners in Richmond.

Another development at this period was the organization of Crippled Children's Hospital in 1920 as "the Orthopedic Department of the Medical College of Virginia for White Children." The beloved Dr. William Tate Graham was surgeon-in-chief and chief of clinical service.

The Dooley Hospital, the gift of Major James H. Dooley, was opened in 1920 at MCV. Major Dooley made an initial donation of $40,000, and when this wasn't enough, he added $11,000. The hospital was built for patients with contagious diseases, but was first used for white orthopedic and then white pediatric cases. When the great new MCV hospital opened in 1940, the children were moved there, and the Dooley was used thereafter for clinical laboratories.

The rating of MCV by the American Medical Association as a Class A school was stressed in several college *Bulletins,* beginning in 1914. For the session of 1915–16, two years of college work was the new requirement for premed students, including physics, chemistry, biology, and a modern language. The dental course for 1917–18 was increased from three to four years, and the school was rated Class A, one of only fourteen in the country. It fell to Class B in 1922 but promptly extended the course to five years, and got back its A rating in 1925. Requirements for entry into the School of Pharmacy were raised to two years of high school work in 1917–18, and to four years in 1921–22. The school held membership in the American Conference of Pharmaceutical Faculties.

Standards at the college were being tightened, but it appeared that not enough was being done. The school's Class A rating was placed in serious jeopardy by the report of Dr. N. P. Colwell, secretary of the Council on Medical Education of the American Medical Association, and Dr. William Papper, representing the Association of American Medical Colleges. Their devastating findings appear in the minutes of the Board of Visitors executive committee for October 20, 1919. The report's staggering conclusion follows:

> Because of its inadequate supervision of preliminary credentials; because of its almost total lack of qualified, full-time salaried teachers; because of the confusion resulting from crowding together classes of medical, dentistry and pharmacy students; because of the poorly arranged laboratories; because of its total lack of constructive research; because of its failure to obtain adequate post-mortems; because of its poorly developed library and museum; because of its lack of adequate supervision; because of the lack of adequate organization of its faculty and because of failure to use to even a moderate degree the clinical facilities available, this college does not belong and should not be retained among acceptable medical schools.

The foregoing was kept within the bosom of the Board of Visitors. The report appeared only in the minutes of the board's executive committee, and was not carried in the minutes of the full board. The report all but recommended that the MCV's Class A rating be withdrawn, but it stopped just short of taking that final step. Dr. Colwell warned that unless the college furnished evidence of "a thorough reformation before the classification of medical schools . . . in the spring of 1921, the Medical College will not be placed in Class A."

President McGuire, not surprisingly, was shocked by the findings, and said to the board: "Dr. Colwell's hostility to our school is obvious in every paragraph. . . . his prejudice and unfairness will be apparent to any disinterested person. Some of the criticisms are constructive and beneficial. Others are ungenerous and unkind, and many show either lack of knowledge of facts or willful perversion of the truth."

Dr. McGuire conceded that "we are far below the standard required with respect to full-time paid teachers." He believed that "if we can correct this criticism, the other faults complained of can easily be remedied or satisfactorily explained." Class A schools were required to have "at least twelve paid teachers who devote their entire time to medical teaching." It was decided to move at once to meet this requirement. By June 1920 six of the twelve full-time teachers had been obtained. These, however, were not department heads.

The MCV faculty adopted resolutions declaring that President McGuire should have the authority to determine the policy and personnel, and expressed "entire confidence in his fairness and ability." Two months later the executive committee of the board wrote Dr. McGuire that "if there had been better discipline in the faculty, much of this criticism would have been avoided." It went on to say: "A comprehensive schedule has been prepared setting forth the subject to be taught, the number of teachers for each subject, the part of the subject assigned to each teacher, and the number of hours to be given by him during the session. The curriculum set out in this schedule must be strictly complied with." A daily register would have to be signed by each teacher, and the dean would make a monthly summary and report it to the president. A full professor in each subject was to be responsible for the conduct of the course in that subject.

A bright ray of light shone in the gloom in 1921 when President McGuire reported to the board that "the graduates of last year passed the examinations of their respective medical, dental and pharmaceutical boards without a single failure." There were twenty-four M.D.'s in the group. Four years later, another fine record was made, the president announced. Of ninety-one medical graduates taking nine state boards, ninety passed. All thirty-four dentistry graduates, and all twenty-one pharmacy graduates passed their boards.

The Medical College was not deprived of its Class A rating in 1921, but its position was still precarious, and it was apparently placed on conditional probation.

Aid for the struggling institution came from the 1920 General Assembly, which raised the appropriation to the college from $20,000 a year to $40,000, and that for Memorial Hospital from $20,000 to $25,000 partly as a result of recommendations from Governor Westmoreland Davis.

The Richmond Chapter of MCV alumni sent a communication to the college in 1922 that was highly critical of conditions there. Among the signers were such prominent faculty members as Drs. C. C. Coleman, A.

G. Brown, Jr., A. Murat Willis, Clifton M. Miller, Beverley R. Tucker, J. Garnett Nelson, and Harry Bear.

"We realize the chaotic teaching conditions in the college and its hospital," this scathing communiqué declared, "and the consequent disaffection which exists among the students to a humiliating degree. We have viewed with alarm the apathy which exists among the teaching force, and the steady retrogression of the morale of both faculty and student bodies." The alumni expressed "a heartfelt desire to cooperate in every possible way in a concerted, constructive effort to the rehabilitation of the college and all that it represents."

The following week, Dr. E. C. L. Miller of the faculty conceded that while the Colwell report of the AMA "was so worded that it gave serious offense to most of us . . . as time has cooled our indignation we have seen more clearly that his criticisms were in many respects justified, and that his suggestions should be carried out." Dr. Miller went on to say that various changes were being made, and that if these can be properly implemented, "we shall have a school next year that we may be proud of, and the Damoclean fear of being put in Class B . . . will have vanished."

Drs. Colwell and Papper returned for a six-hour inspection in 1924, and their findings were much less caustic than those of 1919. They spoke of "a sincere desire on the part of the officers and faculty . . . to bring about the best possible clinical teaching," and expressed confidence that "many of the improvements referred to can and will be met."

Consolidation of the Medical College with the University of Virginia had been agitated at the very time in 1919 when the American Medical Association handed down its damaging conclusions as to conditions at MCV. The university authorities were probably not aware of the contents of that document, since it had been kept carefully under wraps, but they knew that the college was beset with problems, financial and otherwise.

Whereas in 1913 the president and board of the University of Virginia had favored a merger, and the plan failed because funds expected from the Rockefeller Foundation did not materialize, those same authorities were now strongly opposed to the plan.

A commission appointed by Governor Westmoreland Davis concluded, by a five to four vote, that a merger in Richmond was desirable. Alumni of the two institutions promptly ranged themselves on opposite sides of the question, as the legislature convened in 1922.

Statistics from the MCV catalogue for 1921–22 showed 2,532 doctors practicing in Virginia, of whom 266 were University of Virginia graduates, and 1,035 Medical College and University College of Medicine graduates. Graduating classes of M.D.'s at MCV were usually larger than those at UVA, and graduates of the latter school have tended to practice in other states in greater numbers. The university also has enrolled more students from out of state. As for the records made before the State Board of Medical Examiners, from 1904 to 1919, when MCV and UCM were separate institutions, the percentage of successful applicants was UCM 94 percent, UVA 93 percent and MCV 88 percent.

Such facts as these and various others were presented to the General Assembly of 1922 at hotly contested hearings. A referendum on sentiment among practitioners in Virginia, conducted by the *Virginia Medical Monthly* and published in its issue for July 1921, showed all three groups favoring a merger in Richmond by large margins, as follows:

	For Richmond	For Charlottesville
Physicians	1,461	322
Dentists	559	19
Pharmacists	984	90

Since the university had no schools of dentistry or pharmacy, the overwhelming sentiment of these two groups for Richmond is readily explained. Reasons for the preponderant preference among physicians for Richmond are less obvious although the larger number of MCV graduates participating in the poll would tend to give that group a distinct preference for their alma mater.

The Medical Society of Virginia and its organ, the *Virginia Medical Monthly,* favored the move to Richmond, as did the State Dental Association and State Pharmaceutical Association, the two latter organizations without a dissenting voice.

The brief on behalf of the MCV board, urging consolidation at Richmond, was prepared by William R. Miller, while that for the University of Virginia Alumni Association, in opposition, was the work of Milton C. Elliott. Noted experts were marshaled on each side of the issue. The principal argument in favor of Richmond was that clinical opportunities would be much greater there, whereas the strongest argument against moving the school from Charlottesville was that proximity to a university was more important than location in a large city. Most of the experts who appeared at the hearings said that a university affiliation should be the paramount consideration.

After the hearings were completed, the commission that had recommended merger by a five to four vote, took another ballot, and all nine voted for merger, five at Richmond and four at the university.

But the University of Virginia was not in favor of merger anywhere, and it put together a formidable group of Virginians in opposition. Included were U.S. Senator Carter Glass, eight congressmen, twelve judges and other influential alumni. When the showdown came, the Senate defeated the merger, 24 to 16. This ended all efforts to bring the two schools together.

With this plan down the drain, President McGuire approached President Frederic W. Boatwright of the University of Richmond on the subject of a possible union of that institution with the Medical College, under the auspices of the university. Dr. Boatwright visited the Rockefeller Foundation and the Carnegie Corporation in New York, in the hope of getting funds to finance the bringing together of MCV and U. of R. He got little or no encouragement. The executive committee of the university accordingly adopted resolutions saying that "the attitude of the New York boards . . . renders it impracticable at this time for the University of Richmond to take over the work of medical education in Richmond."

President McGuire was fully conscious of the need for a full-time executive head for MCV. His other responsibilities made it impossible for him to function with maximum effectiveness, and he urged repeatedly that a president be found who could devote all his time and energy to the problems of the college. These exhortations bore fruit, as will be seen in the next chapter.

A Reserve Officers Training Corps was established in the medical department at MCV in 1922. It was the twenty-fourth ROTC unit established in medical schools throughout the country. The object was to qualify selected students for appointment as reserve officers in the U.S. military forces. Physical training would be given mainly at summer camps.

Dr. John N. Upshur, who served with the VMI cadets at New Market in the Civil War, and was wounded, died in 1925 after a distinguished career as an MCV teacher from 1884 to 1899, and as a private practitioner. An editorial almost two pages long led the *Virginia Medical Monthly* as it saluted the passing of this eminent and much-admired man. Dr. Upshur was a charter member of the Medical Society of Virginia in 1870 and later its president. He also was president of the Richmond Academy of Medicine and the Tri-State Medical Association.

Dr. George Ross, another veteran of the New Market battle, surgeon for the VMI cadets in that engagement, and chief surgeon for A. P. Hill's Third Army Corps, died in 1926. A founder of the University College of Medicine, he occupied the chair of obstetrics. Dr. Ross was chief surgeon for the Southern Railway, and in private practice in Richmond for over sixty years. Extremely complimentary resolutions were adopted on his passing by both the Medical Society of Virginia and the Richmond Academy. "One can hardly overstate the winning effect of the princely personality of our lamented friend," said the Academy.

Dr. John W. Brodnax also died in 1926, mourned especially by the students. *Skull and Bones* had a huge headline, "MCV Mourns His Loss," and described him as "remembered and loved by many former and present students." He was professor of anatomy and an accomplished artist; the fine bust of Dr. Hunter McGuire in McGuire Hall is his work. His own portrait hangs in the college library, his name thereon misspelled "Broadnax."

17. Last meeting of the Medical College faculty before its merger with the University College of Medicine in 1913. *Bottom row, left to right:* Dr. George Ben Johnston, Dr. Henry H. Levy, Dr. William H. Taylor, Dean Christopher Tompkins, Dr. Charles A. Blanton, Dr. J. Fulmer Bright. *Middle row, left to right:* Dr. Lewis C. Bosher, Dr. J. McCaw Tompkins, Dr. C. C. Coleman, Dr. Clifton M. Miller, Dr. William P. Mathews, Dr. Frank M. Reade, Dr. J. Shelton Horsley, Dr. Ennion G. Williams, Dr. William G. Christian. *Top row:* Dr. Charles Robins, Dr. Greer Baughman, Dr. R. H. Wright, Dr. E. P. McGavock, Dr. A. Murat Willis, Dr. Beverley R. Tucker, Dr. Manfred Call, Dr. Charles M. Hazen.

FIVE

The Sanger Era Begins

THE TIME HAD COME for the appointment of a round-the-clock head of the Medical College of Virginia, if that institution was to survive. Amalgamation with the University of Virginia was no longer conceivable, and the college was in serious straits, both academically and financially.

The Board of Visitors offered the position to several eminent educators, but were turned down. The presidency of a tottering and almost bankrupt institution was hardly an inviting prospect. The visitors then invited Dr. William T. Sanger, the thirty-nine-year-old secretary of the State Board of Education for the preceding three years, to assume the responsibility. He accepted.

Dr. Sanger was not dismayed by the problems that confronted him when he took office on July 1, 1925, but his qualifications did not appear to be impressive. Born near Bridgewater College in the Shenandoah Valley, of German ancestry, his father was a minister in the Church of the Brethren and a licensed pharmacist. Sanger took his B.A. at Bridgewater and his M.A. at Indiana University. He taught psychology, philosophy, and education at Bridgewater, and then was a fellow in psychology at Clark University, Worcester, Mass., which institution awarded him a Ph.D. in psychology in 1915.

Sanger had wanted a Ph.D., in the basic medical sciences, in order to prepare for a career in clinical medicine, and he applied for admission to the Medical College of Virginia. But he had to abandon the idea because of serious eye trouble. He had inflammation in both eyes as a child, and became almost blind in one eye. The other eye suffered from progressive myopia, so that throughout his life he read with considerable difficulty.

Since he was without a degree in medicine, dentistry, or pharmacy, he came to the Medical College under an apparent handicap. Furthermore, for all his abilities, he was not impressive in appearance, nor was he possessed of what today we call charisma. It was jokingly remarked that he would never win a beauty contest. On top of all else, his administrative experience was limited to a brief deanship at Bridgewater College, one year as executive secretary of the Virginia State Teachers Association, and three years as secretary of the State Board of Education.

William T. Sanger was not fully aware of what he was getting into when he took over the presidency at MCV. Many years later he said: "When I accepted the post, I had no knowledge of the fact that there was a floating debt to two of our local banks, the notes of which had been endorsed by members of the board. I had no knowledge of a mortgage debt on Memorial Hospital, held by the Life Insurance Company of Virginia. I did not know there was a damage suit against the college by a dental student who was not awarded his diploma."

The new president was aware that in 1919 the Council on Medical Education of the AMA had found serious scholastic delinquencies that had not been corrected. He may or may not have been told before his acceptance of the full purport of those findings, namely, that the school was in danger of losing its accreditation. He said he had never heard of the famous Flexner Report of 1910, which pinpointed many earlier deficiencies.

In the face of these obstacles, Sanger took hold and moved forward. He would need time to demonstrate his effectiveness, but it soon became evident that this was no ordinary man. As Dr. W. Taliaferro Thompson, chairman many years later of the department of medicine, wrote, "He combined the best features of statesman, politician, beggar, scholar and administrator, and he had the optimism, energy and courage to solve the problems facing him."

He took office at a salary of $7,000, and things began happening at once. The Council on Medical Education had strongly insisted on the appointment of full-time, salaried heads of the departments of medicine, surgery, pediatrics, and obstetrics. By the following year Dr. William Branch Porter had been obtained for medicine, despite loud cries from the local medical establishment that full-time heads were not necessary. These objections will be examined more fully later.

Dr. Sidney S. Negus was invited to head the chemistry department, but was told by the head of a Virginia college that he would be foolish to accept, as "that institution will cease to function within five years." He disregarded the advice and became a much-admired member of the faculty.

The college had no endowment when Sanger took over, and a campaign for a million dollars was launched early in 1926, with Thomas L. Moore, chairman of the executive committee of the Board of Visitors, in charge of the effort. The goal of the students and faculty was $100,000, and it was oversubscribed in six days. Other results came more slowly, but at the end of Sanger's first ten months as president he was able to point to the following:

> $300,000 raised of a million dollar goal; $20,000 increase in the annual state appropriation; assurance of a new laboratory and outpatient clinic building; a new dormitory for nurses; organization of the school of nursing as an integral part of the college with its own dean; appointment of the first full-time professor of medicine, Dr. William Branch Porter; better supervision and improvement of teaching extension of the pharmacy curriculum under Dean [Wortley F.] Rudd from two to three years; Class A rating for the School of Dentistry; and reorganization of the central administration of the institution through creation of the administrative council.

The Medical College was barely "on the map" at this time for most Richmonders. President Sanger requested two students to stand at Seventh and Broad streets and ask everybody who passed during the rush hour, "Where is the Medical College of Virginia, please?" They found that "very few could give directions to these lost students," said Sanger.

The faculty was not meeting classes with anything like regularity, the president found. This was "the most persistent pressure from the students." The senior staff were appealing urgently for a teaching building, and there was great need for more hospital beds. The small size of the medical establishment at that time may be partially grasped from the fact that there were only sixteen residents.

In order to familiarize himself with medical schools of many varieties, Sanger visited thirty-two of them in the United States and Canada in the first few years following his taking over the presidency.

Questions had arisen from time to time as to whether the Medical College was a state institution. The matter came to a head when Governor Harry F. Byrd told President Sanger that, according to his information, the college was state-aided, but not a state institution in the fullest sense. Sanger presented convincing evidence that MCV was, indeed, a state institution. He showed that the Virginia Supreme Court of Appeals had held it to be such in its opinion handed down when Governor Cameron tried to fire the Board of Visitors in 1882. This made it possible for the college administration to argue successfully for larger state appropriations.

Dr. William Branch Porter, a 1911 MCV graduate, was brought from Roanoke as the college's first full-time salaried department head. He was required to devote from one-half to three-fourths of his time to the position, but was allowed private practice under certain restrictions, with a ceiling on his income. His appointment "created obvious unhappiness in the city, both within and without the faculty. . . . Some of the medical groups in Richmond were fearful that the new policy would . . . reduce the need for them as volunteers," Dr. Sanger said. "The critics were incensed not so much by Dr. Porter's appointment, but about the principle of whole-time professors in general." There was an outburst of criticism and adverse publicity in the press. President Sanger concluded that "the target of the opposition was not directed solely at whole-time medical teaching, but at the general program of development of the college, which was regarded as too competitive in several areas." He was disturbed by the criticism but not deterred from his plans.

Dr. Manfred Call, the dean of medicine, backed the president wholeheartedly in his determination to obtain full-time department heads. He pointed out in 1928 that "the majority of teachers in the clinical years of the medical course are on a voluntary basis, with a very small teaching load limited to one particular subject and without administrative responsibilities, unless the head of a teaching department." He added that "such teaching opportunities, no matter how interesting to the instructor or how faithfully the duties are performed, are but an incident in his professional life"; and that "his major interest is in the development of a clientele and the practice of his profession . . . oftimes in private institutions divorced from and in active competition with the college and its teaching hospitals."

Dr. Douglas VanderHoof, a John Hopkins graduate who had studied there under Sir William Osler, was the part-time chairman of medicine when Dr. Porter replaced him. He accepted the situation graciously, and was named to the Board of Visitors and its executive committee. Dr. VanderHoof not only rendered a conspicuous service to the Medical College but was active in Richmond church and civic circles for many years.

The most vocal objector to Porter's appointment, and to the whole idea of bringing in full-time department heads, was Dr. Murat Willis, part-time head of the department of surgery. Dr. Willis, co-founder of Johnston-Willis Hospital, and a highly regarded surgeon, took his case to the Board of Visitors. At heated hearings before the executive committee of the board in 1928, Willis charged Sanger with "ignorance as regards the problems of medical education and with incompetence in the management of the Medical College." Willis said further that "there is nothing in his past training that would in any way fit him for directing an institution for the education of medical men."

He presented a letter from Dr. Beverley R. Tucker of the faculty in which Dr. Tucker spoke of Sanger's "thoroughly inadequate qualifications," and expressed the "earnest belief that his continuance as president would lead to nothing short of disaster." (Later Tucker reversed this opinion completely, and became one of Sanger's greatest admirers.)

After extensive hearings, the full board and the executive committee voted unanimously that Willis had not proved his case against Sanger, and expressed confidence in the latter's "efficiency, ability and high character." Dr. Willis thereupon resigned from the faculty. He became increasingly distraught, to the extent that, tragically, on January 3, 1929, after performing an operation, he went into his office and shot himself. The Richmond Academy of Medicine, of which he had been president, held a special meeting to express its grief.

William Branch Porter turned out to be a brilliant choice for full-time chairman of medicine. Somewhat aloof in manner, and hardly an extrovert, he nevertheless made a tremendous contribution. Decades later, long after Porter had died, Sanger said: "I don't believe this college will ever adequately define the contribution he made here. His devotion and his competence were perfectly wonderful. He didn't always agree with his colleagues, but he was certainly levelheaded in most instances." Dr. Porter served as professor and chairman of the department of medicine from 1927 until his retirement in 1956. He was president of the American Clinical and Climatological Association. The *Virginia Medical Monthly* described him as "a superb diagnostician and a wonderful teacher." The William Branch Porter Professorship of Medicine was named in his honor, and in 1952 his former residents formed the William Branch Porter Society, which annually awarded an outstanding senior medical student a silver replica of the stethoscope given Porter by Sir William Osler. A memorial after his death in 1960, signed by H. St. G. Tucker, Jr., G. Watson James III, and Nathan Bloom, chairman, said, "Although he had no children, all of us whom he taught loved him as a father."

The next full-time department head brought in by President Sanger was Dr. Isaac Alexander Bigger, who joined the faculty in 1930, as chairman of surgery and surgeon-in-chief. A graduate of the University of Virginia medical school, he was at thirty, when he came to MCV, the youngest professor of surgery in the United States, according to the *Virginia Medical Monthly.* Dr. Bigger was a pioneer in thoracic surgery and was chosen president of the American Association for Thoracic Surgery.

On the twentieth anniversary of his coming to the college, forty of his former surgical residents gave him a dinner at which he was feted and presented with a portrait of himself and silver julep cups. *Skull and Bones,* the student newspaper, dedicated its current issue to him, and described him as "a man who holds the admiration and respect of everyone who knows him." And no wonder. It was said that he befriended innumerable people anonymously, and helped many students and nurses, both financially and spiritually with difficult personal problems.

"Ike" Bigger became so emotionally involved in his operations that he sometimes shouted imprecations at tense moments when a surgical assistant or a nurse failed to perform expertly. He is said to have frightened a young resident almost out of his wits when he burst out at him with an oath. Such near-tantrums were attributed to his deep concern for the patient, rather than to any lack of consideration for his associates. Many other surgeons are said to behave similarly under the stress of operations. Dr. Bigger's workday began well before 8 A.M. and ended at 10 or 11 P.M., a regimen that was believed to have hastened his death at age sixty-one.

He joined with Dr. J. Shelton Horsley in editing the fourth and fifth printings of Horsley's well-known work *Operative Surgery,* which appeared first in 1921, and went through two more printings. The Horsley-Bigger version appeared in 1937, and there was another edition in 1940. These two editions contained contributions by a number of MCV faculty, especially Bigger. They were internationally recognized, and were perhaps the most popular surgical texts of that time. The sixth and final printing was edited by Guy Horsley and "Ike" Bigger.

On Dr. Bigger's passing, resolutions were drafted for the Medical Society of Virginia by John Truslow, Carrington Williams, and Herbert C. Lee, and adopted by that organization. They said, in part: "He was the epitome of all the factors which compose the true image representing the dignity of man. No greater teacher ever lived. Countless operations in this country of ours are today being done because this is the way Dr. Bigger says to do them," the resolutions declared. And they went on: "His countless friends, patients, house officers, and students were immediately cast into profound sorrow at his untimely passing. Few men are indispensable. . . . Doctor Bigger was such a man. Brilliant, honest, humble, inspiring, friendly, fatherly, charitable, judicious, careful, earnest, faithful—are some of the adjectives that fit this man among men."

The Medical College was officially placed on "confidential probation" in 1935, following a survey by the AMA and would remain so for eighteen years. It had been so rated de facto since the extremely unfavorable 1919 survey, but the phrase "confidential probation" was not used at that time by the survey team. The fact that the college was thus rated from 1919 to 1953 was not known to the general public.

The third full-time department head to be added to the college staff was Dr. Lee E. Sutton, Jr., who was named chairman of the department of pediatrics in 1938. A graduate of Harvard Medical School, Dr. Sutton came to MCV in 1928 as associate in pediatrics. Four years later he was named dean of the medical school, and served in that post for a decade. He then was appointed professor and full-time chairman of pediatrics, and continued in that capacity until his retirement in 1958.

In 1953, at the close of his first twenty-five years as a teacher of pediatrics, his former residents gave him a testimonial dinner, and presented his portrait. He was pediatrician-in-chief at the Crippled Children's Hospital, and also served a term as president of the Children's Memorial Clinic. Virginia Polytechnic Institute gave him its highest award in 1962. The Sutton Memorial Lecture is delivered annually at the college on Pediatrics Day.

Student life at the college in the 1920s and 1930s had its ups and downs. With the onset of the Great Depression, the young men and women were often strapped for funds, but they made the best of it. Prohibition was in force until 1933, but like college students throughout the land, those at MCV presumably were not unduly hampered by these legal inhibitions. Surprisingly, there is little or nothing in *Skull and Bones* during this era concerning liquor or the lack of it. The Skull and Bones restaurant, operated almost continuously for over sixty years by the Shaiah family, was open for business in the 1920s. After repeal of the dry laws, students could relax there with a few beers.

Another divertissement at the time was campus politics—some of it unsavory, if a *Skull and Bones* editorial is to be believed. "Politics has become most disgusting at MCV," the student newspaper said in 1931. "It is no secret that cliques meet and first decide on the fraternities to be awarded the respective offices, the decision being based entirely on the fraternities' past history of office holding. . . . Such a system is demoralizing, diabolical, humiliating, and does not envelop even the faintest shadow of democracy. . . . What is the remedy? . . . Do away entirely with cliques, nominate the best man." In 1942 similar complaints arose. There was still a lack of democracy in college elections, since the dominant political group had nominated only one slate, *Skull and Bones* declared. It went on to say that the single slate was unconstitutional, because the constitution required two slates. The nominations were accordingly withdrawn, and two complete slates were named. A letter in the same issue of the newspaper from a student said: "Evidently crooked politics does not only take place in Germany and Hitler-dominated countries. . . . Hitler has 'blitzed' good old MCV."

Construction of the Medical College library was begun in 1931. It was a joint operation with the Richmond Academy of Medicine, which erected its handsome building adjoining it. This enabled the college and the academy to function in close collaboration. Medical students, interns and residents could use the academy's facilities, and members of the academy those of the MCV library.

Among the academy's treasures was the marvelous Joseph Lyon Miller Library of 3,000 medical books, many extremely rare and going back to the sixteenth century; valuable manuscripts; the largest collection of silhouettes of medical personalities in the United States; and thousands of rare old portrait prints and other engravings. (A detailed description of this remarkable collection can be found in Dr. Charles M. Caravati's book, *Medicine in Richmond—1900–1975*, pp. 99–104.) Dr. Miller willed the collection to the Richmond Academy on condition that it provide a fireproof home for these irreplaceable items. This led to the cooperative arrangement under which the college and the academy built simultaneously, and with buildings connecting. The collection is housed in an attractive room, with bookshelves on three sides, and silhouettes of famous doctors in cases. A brass plaque tells of the gift by Miller, and there are other plaques to noted members of the academy—Wyndham B. Blanton, Marvin Pierce Rucker, and Harry J. Warthen, Jr.

Dr. Miller was a 1900 graduate of the University College of Medicine, and his active professional life was spent in the small coalmining village of Thomas, W. Va. In this unlikely spot he assembled his astonishing collection from various parts of the world, and stored it in his dust-covered home. Requests for information from the Miller archive in Richmond come from all parts of the United States.

In view of the criticisms of the Medical College by AMA survey teams, it was gratifying that in 1932, for example, all seventy-four MCV graduates passed the Virginia State Board examination.

A graduate of the college at this time who later made a huge business success and became one of the major philanthropists in Virginia history was E. Claiborne Robins, who took his degree in pharmacy in 1933. Robins's munificent gifts of many millions were made to the University of Richmond, the Medical College and various other institutions. He served as president of the MCV Alumni Association, and in 1958 was awarded the honorary degree of Doctor of Pharmaceutical Science.

Reminiscing in 1968 concerning the means by which the college acquired property over the years, Sanger said:

> We have over thirty acres in Richmond now, but we had precious little when we started here. One thing we did was to get a good real estate man who would live with the job. He made drawings of every block in the area with the nature of the owner, the assessed valuation, frontage, etc. Each was to scale or relative scale, and the collection was bound into a number of books. When an owner or salesman would come in and say, "Well, I understand you want to buy property, and I've got so and so," I would say "What do you want for your parcel?" He'd name the price, and I would look at my little book and see whether it was in line. Sometimes we bought land when we didn't know how we were going to pay for it, but we always did ultimately. In time I bought over one hundred pieces of property, and others bought some, too.

In 1931 the maximum salary for professors was $5,000, and the depression made it necessary for the state to cut salaries twice. The cuts were later restored. In 1935 Sanger's salary was raised to $9,000 and in 1939 $10,000.

A notable temporary addition to the college faculty in 1935 was Dr. Albert C. Broders, a 1910 graduate, and head of one of the divisions of surgical pathology at the Mayo Clinic. Dr. Broders, who was internationally famous, remained at the college for a year as professor of surgical pathology and director of cancer research. He was with the Mayo Clinic from 1912 to 1950, except for the year he spent at MCV. The college conferred on him the honorary degree of Doctor of Science.

An idea of the progress in physical facilities that had been made since Sanger's arrival may be grasped from the fact that by 1936 the following six projects were under way: A central heating plant; a modern laundry; a $600,000 clinic and laboratory building on the site of the old Retreat Hospital; a dormitory on the northeast corner of Twelfth and Marshall streets; a complete hothouse for the school of pharmacy; and a tunnel system, for pipes and pedestrians, which by then had reached from McGuire Hall almost to Memorial Hospital.

The tunnel system was extended in succeeding years, until it became possible to go from the college to the Capitol underground, and to Monumental Church and the Richmond Eye Hospital, before the new Eye Hospital was built. Later another tunnel was constructed to Randolph-Minor Hall. The entire tunnel system by then covered about three-quarters of a mile.

Hunton Hall, named for Eppa Hunton, Jr., for many years a member of the Board of Visitors and its chairman for a time, was completed in 1938. It was a dormitory for hospital house staff and students, and in addition to bedrooms and baths contained lounges, reading rooms, a cafeteria, auditorium, and barber shop.

The ROTC medical unit was reinstated at the 1937–38 session, after a lapse of some years, with a resident officer, Lieutenant Colonel Edwin B. Maynard, professor of military science and tactics, in charge. Enrollment for the session was forty-seven freshmen and twenty-one sophomores. Dentistry and pharmacy students were admitted to the program in 1945.

The college celebrated its centennial in 1938, and combined it with Richmond's bicentennial observance of 1937. Fifty-seven panels and booths were set up in the college library and the adjacent Academy of Medicine building, under the direction of Dr. Wyndham B. Blanton. The exhibits showed medical progress in the preceding century. The schools of medicine, dentistry, pharmacy, and nursing each held a symposium, with the usual postgraduate clinics. The final program June 7 featured an address by Dr. Henry R. Christian of the Harvard Medical School. Dean J. C. Flippin of the University of Virginia Medical School was given the honorary degree of Doctor of Science. Three years later a committee was appointed by MCV to confer with a similar committee from UVA with respect to matters of mutual concern, specifically postgraduate education and possible joint faculty appointments.

A tribute to the Medical College Alumni Association was paid by President Sanger in 1938, when he said: "I do not recall a single year in my connection with the college in which the Alumni Association has been so constructive. Dr. Roshier W. Miller, president of the association, and members of his executive committee have been untiring in their plans and their field work."

The old First Baptist Church, adjoining the college on Broad Street, was acquired as a social center for college activities, and remodeled extensively. It housed the college post office, ROTC office, the College Dental Clinic, and the employees' health service. A dining room seating 200 was planned.

The A. D. Williams Memorial Clinic, replacing the outpatient clinic in the dilapidated Virginia Hospital, built in the early nineteenth century, opened in 1938. Adolph D. Williams gave $300,000 anonymously for the purpose, thus matching a Federal grant, and making it possible to construct the $600,000 facility. He provided $50,000 additional for equipment. When Mrs. Williams died she left $400,000 as endowment. These Williams benefactions were brought about principally through the persuasive powers of Dr. Stuart McGuire; a condition insisted upon by the Williamses was that a certain carpenter, a friend of theirs, be given steady employment until the building was completed. When Adolph Williams died he left $2 million additional to the Medical College.

One of the astounding episodes of the decade occurred when members of the Medical College and University of Virginia faculties were invited by the General Assembly to write a textbook for use in the public schools on the effects of alcohol on the human system. Prohibition had been repealed several years before, and school officials felt that a more objective study than the one concocted at the turn of the century, under the beneficent ministrations of the Anti-Saloon League, would be desirable.

Dr. Harvey B. Haag, professor of pharmacology and later dean of the medical school at MCV, and Dr. James A. Waddell, professor of pharmacology, materia medica, and toxicology in the UVA medical school, were chosen to do the work. They produced a book, 184 pages in length, late in 1937, and the State Board of Education pronounced it "a most valuable contribution . . . scientifically sound and very scholarly." The board ordered 10,000 copies.

But before the legislators could convene in early 1938, portions of the work leaked to the press. It appeared that Messrs. Haag and Waddell, while warning sternly of the effects of overindulgence, had actually said that small quantities of alcohol "may favor digestive activities" and "small quantities

. . . do not directly affect the heart or the blood vessels." Also, the statement was made that "it has been proved that we cannot abolish drinking by legislation nor frighten a person into sobriety."

Prohibition was no more, but the political potency of the professional drys was far from defunct. These subversive assertions aroused the Anti-Saloon League and the Women's Christian Temperance Union to furious activity. Only two weeks remained before the legislators met, but when they arrived in Richmond they found their desks piled high with outraged demands that the Haag-Waddell report be destroyed forthwith. Alcohol, they cried, must be pronounced a poison under every conceivable circumstance. The statesmen on Capitol Hill grabbed their hats and scrambled for the nearest bomb shelter. Only one or two out of 140 had read the book, but both branches voted to burn it immediately. One thousand copies, all that had been printed, were accordingly shoveled into the Capitol furnace, to a thunderous obligato of Bronx cheers. The text of the study was even banned from the official journals of the two houses, lest future generations be contaminated.

The harried authors succeed in retaining the copyright, and the book was published by the William Byrd Press of Richmond. The State of Vermont, with a gratifying show of intestinal fortitude, ordered 3,000 copies for use in its public schools. But the oldest legislative body in the New World had made an unholy spectacle of itself.

Harvey Haag, one of the authors of the book that had been given precisely the treatment being meted out at that time to books that Adolf Hitler did not regard as suitable reading for his *Kultur*-conscious Nazis, was one of the most popular members of the MCV faculty. "Harvey Haag Day" was staged annually by the sophomore class in pharmacy. Horseplay, some of it in questionable taste, was indulged in. (The senior class in medicine also held an annual jamboree, "taking off" the faculty. This one got so raw that it was ordered discontinued.) Following his retirement Haag was described in the *Scarab,* organ of the Alumni Association, as probably MCV's "most beloved alumnus." Famous for his wit, he was in great demand as a speaker at alumni meetings, and served as treasurer of the association for decades. Harvey Haag was president of the American Society for Pharmacology and Experimental Therapeutics and also of the American Therapeutic Society.

Pharmacy, as distinguished from pharmacology, was one of the prescribed courses when Hampden-Sydney's medical department opened at Richmond in 1838. A school of pharmacy was not formally established by MCV, however, until 1870. There was no separate program of instruction, and the course was offered in the medical school.

The University College of Medicine established a department of pharmacy, with a two-year course, when it opened in 1893. T. Ashby Miller was dean. The Medical College followed suit in 1897, and established a separate department, also with a two-year course, with Frank Reade in charge. After the institutions amalgamated in 1913, requirements were raised. Albert Bolenbaugh was the first dean after the consolidation. The degree of Ph.G. was continued and that of Bachelor of Science in Pharmacy was added. The course was expanded to three years in 1925 and to four years in 1932. This last included "a selected number of cultural subjects so essential to a well-balanced education." Several pharmacy fraternities were established in the school, beginning with Rho Chi, national honorary fraternity, in 1929.

The history of pharmacy at MCV would never be complete without reference to the major contribution made by Dean Wortley F. Rudd, who presided over the department from 1920 to 1947. At the unveiling of his portrait in 1956, Edward E. Willey, long prominent in Virginia's public life, and a former student of Rudd's said: "As a member of college boards, as a consultant of industrial corporations, and as an active member of various organizations interested in chemistry and science, he influenced young men to engage in many programs of scientific research." Dean Rudd taught in all four schools at the Medical College, and was president of several scientific associations. He received the coveted Herty Medal for his contributions to chemistry in the Southeast, as well as a number of honorary degrees.

The primitive origins of dentistry in Richmond are amusingly described by Mordecai in his *Richmond in By-Gone Days.* "In the days of my youth [late eighteenth century], only one *tooth-drawer,* who probably never heard the word dentist, did all the work and all the mischief in the dental line," Mordecai wrote.

> Peter Hawkins was a tall, raw-boned, very black Negro, who rode a raw-boned, black horse, for his practice was too extensive to be managed on foot, and he carried all his instruments, consisting of two or three Pullikins, in his pocket. His dexterity was such that he has been known to be stopped in the street by one of his distressed brethren (for he was of the church), and to relieve him of the offending tooth, gratuitously, without dismounting from his horse. His strength of wrist was such that he would almost infallibly extract, or break, a tooth, whether the right or the wrong one. I speak from sad experience, for he extracted two for me a sound and an aching one, with one wrench of the instrument.

Similarly, Hermie Wait Powell writes in her *Hundred-Year History of Dentistry in Virginia* that in the early days, "the calling of dentist seems to be considered open ground, into which any fellow who has impudence, some steadiness of hand, and a case of instruments, thinks himself free to take up a position."

The State Dental Association was organized in 1870 at Richmond. There was no course in dentistry at that time at the Medical College, and it remained for the University College of Medicine to institute one when it opened in 1893. Dr. Lewis M. Cowardin was the first dean. Three years later the Medical College organized a department of dentistry under the deanship of Dr. Henry C. Jones. The bitter rivalry between the two institutions flared up again when the MCV department sought membership in 1904 in the National Association of Dental Faculties. The application was approved, "in spite of violent opposition of those who ought naturally to have given our application favorable consideration," Dean Christopher Tompkins of MCV told his Board of Visitors.

The Virginia legislature passed a law in 1912 requiring all practitioners of dentistry to have an M.D. degree. This was found to be impractical, and the law was repealed two years later.

A four-year course, with graduation from high school as a prerequisite, was put into effect in 1917. One year of predental education was made a requirement in 1921, and this was raised to two years in 1937. After 1951 the course called for three years of college study.

Nursing was coming into its own as Sanger took over. The first dean of nursing at MCV was Elizabeth C. Reitz, appointed in 1925; she remained in the post until 1929. The profession was entering upon "a period of epochal changes not unlike those which came to medical education years ago," the MCV *Bulletin* declared in 1926. "Anticipating the present movement to put nursing education on a university basis in leading centers of the country, the Medical College has organized its school of nursing with its own dean and faculty, and given it rank coordinate with the schools of medicine, dentistry and pharmacy. . . . While nursing education is but a half century old in America, more women are pursuing it than all other types of higher education combined." Two years later the *Bulletin* said the MCV school was "one of the few Class A schools of nursing."

The new dormitory for nurses was constructed in 1928. It was named Cabaniss Hall after Sadie Heath Cabaniss, a pioneer nurse.

The nurses at the college let it be known in 1926 that they wanted to be "on an equal footing with the male population in matters of student activity." Their wish was granted, and they were allowed to vote in student elections and take part in dramatics, journalism, and what not.

The first hospital exclusively for black patients, St. Philip, was opened in 1920. The patients had previously been cared for in the basement of Memorial Hospital. Richmond citizens contributed $250,000 toward the cost of the new building. A school of nursing was established there at the same time. St. Philip received a bequest of about $130,000 in 1928 under the will of Mrs. Martha Allen Wise, and a tablet in her memory was placed in the lobby. Funds for a much-needed dormitory and education unit for the school of nursing were acquired in 1930—$80,000 from the General Education Board and $40,000 from the Rosenwald Fund. It was dedicated the following year.

A postgraduate summer clinic for black practitioners at St. Philip was begun in 1931, with funds from the Rockefeller Foundation. It was pointed out that there were approximately one hundred black doctors in Virginia, "many of whom . . . have not had the opportunity of an internship, and most of whom have no hospital connection." The executive committee of the Board of Visitors was enthusiastically in favor of the program, and hoped that it would become a model for the whole South. President Sanger stated in 1943 that the clinic was operated for nine years "as a pioneer endeavor of its kind in the nation, from outside funds, before the state supported the clinic."

Dr. Sanger reported to the board that a doctor on the MCV staff had "caused some disturbance at the St. Philip Hospital by objecting to the colored nurses using 'Mr.' and 'Mrs.' on charts." He said that the matter had been referred to the administrative committee of the hospital, and "no doubt could be adjusted without much difficulty."

After the passage by Congress of the Social Security Act, the U.S. Public Health Service established a course at MCV in public health nursing for blacks. Representatives of twelve states and the District of Columbia were enrolled when the classes began in 1936. The course was on the college level, and was designed to meet the need for additional nursing personnel in the southern states. It was offered to white students at the college in 1940.

The college honor system had its ups and downs, as was the case at other institutions. It had been revised in 1916 because of "dissatisfaction" and a system similar to that at the University of Virginia was adopted, except that students were not required to report violations by other students.

Ten years later this aspect of the system had been reversed, and reporting of violations by students was mandatory. *Skull and Bones* recognized that "every student dislikes and detests a gumshoeing, pussyfooting, tell-tale student," but it went on to say that "if this idea prevails . . . our honor system must fail." There was another alteration in 1927—a faculty member sat in on all trials but did not vote. Penalities were indeterminate, depending on circumstances.

The MCV faculty issued a statement in 1932 declaring that "the past inactivity of the honor system is not due to the students, but much of the responsibility rests with the failure of the faculty to report known violators, and to aid in impressing the principles of the honor code upon the members of the student body." The statement added that "the faculty is obligated to report any infractions of the honor code to the honor council."

Adoption of a college flag was a feature of the year 1938. It was presented to the college by the student body, and President Sanger thanked the donors, saying that the institution "has long needed a suitable flag." *Skull and Bones* described it as "a replica of the Red Cross flag, substituting green for red, with the seal used by the college in the center." Dr. Greer Baughman, professor of obstetrics, presented it on behalf of the students, and said: "White depicts the purity of purpose of the founders, and of those who have carried on without pay in most instances, in order that the green, which stands for the medical sciences, might fructify."

The death of Dr. J. Garnett Nelson in 1930 brought grief to many. A graduate of the University College of Medicine in 1900, he had served on the faculties of that institution and the Medical College. He had been president of the Richmond Academy, and the resolutions passed by it at the time of his death covered more than a page in the *Virginia Medical Monthly*. As a leader in Base Hospital 45 in World War I, Dr. Nelson held the rank of major and was chief of medical service until near the end of the conflict, when he was promoted to lieutenant colonel and placed in command of the unit. He was "greatly loved . . . by the entire command." Dr. Nelson was active as a leader in the Richmond Tuberculosis Association.

Dr. G. Paul LaRoque's death occurred in 1934, and was the occasion for remarkably affectionate and admiring resolutions passed by the Richmond Academy. "In the past forty years no teacher of medicine in this part of the country could fairly be called his peer," said the academy. "Should one doubt this statement, let him ask one of the thousands of students who have passed under his tutelage." Dr. LaRoque taught surgery on the faculties of both UCM and MCV for a total of nearly thirty years.

Another of the prominent faculty members to die during this period was Dr. Manfred Call, for seven years the highly respected dean of the school of medicine at MCV. Dr. Call died in 1936. A member of the faculty for thirty-four years, he was described by Dr. Harry J. Warthen, Jr., in the *Bulletin* of the Richmond Academy as "a truly great medical teacher," possessing "to a high degree the two most important attributes of a successful teacher: the ability to stimulate scientific curiosity, and the cultivation of professional honesty." His field was internal medicine, "but much of his time was given to affairs not directly connected with medical practice, for his judgment was so perfect that his advice was in constant demand by organized medicine as well as by laymen and troubled physicians."

The death of Dr. Joseph F. Geisinger in 1940 at age fifty-six brought many expressions of sorrow from his medical associates, his patients and his friends in all walks of life. The *Bulletin* of the Richmond Academy spoke of him as "one of our foremost urological surgeons" and "a teacher in the Medical College of marked distinction." An early volunteer in World War I, he edited the history of Base Hospital 45, taking the work of "some thirty or forty writers" and weaving it into "a smooth, even narrative of intense interest and charm." The *Virginia Medical Monthly* published resolutions saying that the Richmond Hospital Service Association [forerunner of Blue Cross] owed primarily to Dr. Geisinger "its conception, its origin, its final organization, its broad basis of fullest public service combined with sound financial conduct." The Manchester Medical Society passed resolutions saying, "Words completely fail when an attempt is made to pay proper tribute to a life such as his."

Another great loss was sustained in the sudden passing in 1940 of Dr. William G. Crockett, a member of the pharmacy faculty since 1920, described in *Skull and Bones* as a "beloved professor." A former president of the American Association of Colleges of Pharmacy, Dr. Crockett was a member of many professional and scientific organizations. Hampden-Sydney College conferred on him the honorary degree of Doctor of Science. The Crockett Memorial Laboratory was dedicated to him in the school of pharmacy in 1941.

Dr. Ernest C. Levy, who died in 1938, graduated from the Medical College in 1890, served on its faculty twice, and became one of the noted public health officials in the United States. As chief health officer of Richmond from 1906 to 1917, his work in eliminating typhoid fever and assuring the city of a sanitary milk supply gave him an international reputation. He was elected president of the American Public Health Association in 1922. The *Richmond News Leader,* in an obituary editorial at the time of his death, placed him "among the dozen men who have done most for Richmond in two centuries."

18. Dr. William T. Sanger, president of the Medical College, 1925–56, who became head of the institution when it was in serious trouble and in danger of closing down, and built it up to a position of eminence.

19. Dr. Ennion G. Williams, longtime MCV faculty member, whose administration of the State Department of Health was extremely distinguished.

20. Dr. William Branch Porter, first full-time department head brought in by President Sanger. As chairman of medicine he made a greatly valued contribution.

21. Dr. Isaac A. Bigger, obtained by President Sanger as full-time head of surgery, in which position he made a brilliant record.

22. Dr. Wortley F. Rudd, dean of the school of pharmacy for twenty-seven years, and nationally recognized in his field.

SIX

The New Hospital and the War

THE NEED FOR A MODERN, UP-TO-DATE HOSPITAL for the Medical College had been obvious for many years. It was realized that the college could not get rid of "conditional probation" and became a truly first-class institution until such a structure was acquired.

The public works program of the Roosevelt administration, initiated during the depression to create jobs, made it possible, at last, for an adequate hospital to be built. This was not achieved, however, without unexpected difficulty. Some of the members of the college Board of Visitors were opposed to accepting largesse from Uncle Sam; they saw it as an opening wedge to more centralization of power in Washington. Fortunately, in the end a majority of the board approved a resolution accepting the government's offer of a grant-in-aid for a new hospital and for remodeling the Egyptian building. Some board members stayed away from the meeting, rather than vote for the plan.

The PWA grant was for $1,444,800, but this was only a part of the total needed, since the federal authorities paid for only about 45 percent of the cost of any project. It remained for the Board of Visitors and other agencies and individuals to produce the rest of the $2 million required. Three Richmond banks had to be persuaded to lend the college nearly $1 million, and thanks to the efforts of William H. Schwarzschild and Eppa Hunton IV, who had succeeded his father on the board, the money was obtained. The General Assembly had to be persuaded to appropriate $250,000, which it did. The rest of the funds came from friends of the institution.

The cornerstone of the great new edifice was laid September 18, 1939. It contained "a white elephant with trunk upraised (a symbol of good luck);

a Jefferson nickel (to insure the hospital will never 'go broke'), and a roll book of the senior class in medicine (1940), with a photo of each student."

The eighteen-story, 600-bed hospital was opened on December 5, 1940, Founder's Day for the college's 103d session. Governor James H. Price and Dean Harvey E. Jordan of the University of Virginia medical school were among the speakers. Dean Jordan said the hospital "answers superbly the challenging cry of the noble medical tradition of this city." The sixteenth to eighteenth floors were not fully completed until 1949, when this was accomplished with the aid of a Hill-Burton grant.

Dr. Lewis E. Jarrett, director of the Hospital Division, stated that the imposing structure was "the most modern of its kind in America," according to "authorities throughout the country." The public swarmed to the building on the opening day, despite the cold, and formed two lines sometimes four, all the way from the City Hall. Some felt that the hospital would never be filled, and called it "Sanger's folly."

Rates were necessarily higher than in Memorial Hospital. Private single rooms would now cost from $5.75 to $8 per day, while ward patients would pay $3.35. Occupants of a private room for two would pay $5 each.

The three bears that stand in the courtyard in front of the building were the gift of the noted sculptress Anna Hyatt Huntington. She lived at Brookgreen Gardens, S.C., with her husband, Archer M. Huntington. The MCV *Bulletin* explained the animals' significance: "This highly prized group symbolizes those faraway days when Indian medicine men looked upon the bear, the strongest animal on this continent, as a demigod to whom he appealed for strength and power in the administration of primitive medicine."

World War II had exploded in Europe with Adolf Hitler's invasion of Poland in September 1939. It appeared increasingly probable that the United States would be drawn in, and Medical College officials were preparing for this contingency.

Twenty-nine seniors in the medical class would complete the four-year ROTC training course in June 1941, and be commissioned as first lieutenants in the Medical Reserve Corps, U.S. Army. Sixty freshmen, forty-five sophomores, and twenty-three juniors were taking the same course. Those enrolled were exempted from registration under the draft.

Organization of a class of Naval Reserve ensigns, "the first ever to be commissioned in a rank below lieutenant junior grade in the history of the Medical and Dental Corps of the Navy, is another first for the Medical

College," the MCV *Bulletin* declared in April 1941. "It is the first such unit in the U.S." Junior and senior medical and dental students were eligible for these commissions. Applications were on a purely voluntary basis, and the volunteers were commissioned at once as ensigns, on probation until after graduation. When the ensigns had had special training and had graduated from the college, they could apply for commissions as lieutenants junior grade, and if recommended by the college authorities, the commissions would be issued. The lieutenants would then be assigned to active duty with the Medical Corps, U.S. Naval Reserve.

Organization of a hospital unit for service overseas was the immediate objective of the college when this country entered the war in December 1941, following the Japanese attack on Pearl Harbor. Base Hospital 45 of World War I fame was reconstituted as General Hospital 45. While their titles were slightly different, the functions of the two MCV units during the respective conflicts were often the same.

Colonel Carrington Williams, professor of surgery, who had been with the surgical service of Base Hospital 45 in World War I, was chosen unit director. He did admirable work in organizing the unit. In contrast to the requirements in the previous conflict, when hospital units had to provide their own equipment, in World War II equipment was furnished by the federal government.

Dr. Williams was anxious to go overseas with the unit, but was found to be not altogether physically fit. Lieutenant Colonel John Powell Williams, chief of medical services, was accordingly named to succeed him as director. Major A. Stephens Graham was promoted to lieutenant colonel and named chief of surgical services. Dr. Alton D. Brashear was appointed chief of dental services, and Miss Anne F. Persons "principal chief nurse."

Confusion at the War Department in Washington was horrendous, and caused similar confusion with the unit in Richmond. There were seemingly endless waits. Finally the unit arrived at Camp Lee on May 15, 1942. Twenty-five percent of the members remained at camp, while the others commuted daily, usually from Richmond, a distance of forty-five miles. This went on for ten months, despite the fact that "units such as the 45th were intended for immediate overseas service, according to the surgeon general of the army."

The foregoing quotation is from Colonel Alton D. Brashear's lively account of the unit's more or less excruciating ups and downs, entitled *From*

Lee to Bari. Brashear was professor of anatomy at MCV and also held a degree in dentistry.

The unit was put on alert in September and all hands assumed that they were about to embark for the war zone. Fifteen other hospitals had left for overseas, and wild rumors proliferated at Camp Lee. Nobody knew whether General Hospital 45 was headed for Europe, the Pacific, or the Middle East. It wasn't headed anywhere. Not until March 10, 1943, did it receive orders to move.

The unit sailed, at last, from New York on March 21 aboard the *Andes,* a new British transatlantic liner converted to a troopship. Five thousand were on board, with lifeboats and rafts for only half of them. Furthermore, there was no escort until the ship neared its destination, Casablanca. Safe arrival there was a relief to all concerned. Dr. Brashear writes, with characteristic humor, that "like an ancient Arab, Major Kinloch Nelson came wobbling down the gangplank followed by six comely nurses." Dr. Nelson would serve as the unit's executive officer for a time.

Accommodations were allotted to the unit at Rabat, and the pleasant sojourn there was in dire contrast to the hardships the unit encountered later in Italy. Only bedbugs marred the stay in Rabat.

General Hospital 45 departed in the direction of Naples, November 30, 1943, but somehow got waylaid at a rain-soaked, windswept mudhole dubbed Goat Hill, the idea being that only a goat could survive there. "We had no chairs, lights, or tables," Dr. Brashear wrote. "There were no newspapers, radio, beds, sheets, heat, beer, ice cream, or water. We existed, either standing up half-awake or lying down half-asleep." These grievous tribulations finally ended, and most of the unit embarked for Naples on board the *Cameronia,* which had been attacked twice by submarines and bombers, but arrived at Naples December 19 without being sunk or attacked.

A tragic loss occurred when Captain Lewis T. Stoneburner III disappeared on a flight from Algiers to Bizerte. The plane on which this able young man was traveling was never heard from again. He had graduated first in his class at the Medical College, and had taken postgraduate training with the Harvard Medical Services. An annual lecture in his honor was established at MCV, and highly distinguished medical men are brought to the college from all over America.

The hospital unit was located near Naples in a great medical center at Bagnoli. It soon became an evacuation hospital, and the newly wounded poured in by the hundreds. The cold, foul weather at the front caused enormous numbers of noncombatant casualties also. Acute hepatitis and malaria were widespread. About half of all medical admissions were for neuropsychiatric problems, "acute battle reactions," Dr. Brashear wrote. The Anzio landings brought another avalanche of casualties. During the first two months in Italy there were as many patients as for the entire stay in Africa.

The Naples area was bombed from time to time, and some of the bombs fell close to the hospital, but none hit. Several other hospitals in the region were struck. Nearby Vesuvius got into the act, furnishing a flaming and thunderous obbligato to the explosions by staging its most tremendous eruption in forty years. This occurred in March 1944 and lasted for about a week.

Even more casualties flooded in during the spring and summer, as battles raged around Cassino and other points to the north, after which the Allied invasion of southern France swelled the total further. Surgeons worked around the clock, and no fewer than 1,285 operations were performed in June alone. Colonel Guy W. Horsley became surgeon-in-chief, succeeding Colonel A. Stephens Graham, who had been invalided to the U.S. as a casualty, and later was sent to the Southeast Asia command under Lord Mountbatten, where he had a significant role.

There were occasional interludes for relaxation in the hectic life of the 45th. These opportunities were seized upon for trips to nearby historic spots. Card games, baseball, and touch football also were indulged in, where possible.

The ordeal of long hours and overwork was compounded by irritating and contradictory orders from the high brass. Some of the comments and criticisms from these Olympian sources were baffling and infuriating, as the 45th felt that they made no sense. Amid tremendous bewilderment, caused by conflicting orders, the unit was directed in June 1945 to Bari on the Adriatic. The Germans had surrendered the previous month, and the unit was directed to take over the 26th General Hospital at Bari.

"We existed in an unhappy state of confusion as long as we were in Bari," the account declares. The heat was terrific, and there was a water shortage. "Expeditions to Cairo, Switzerland, and Northern Italy became a standard procedure for many." Several top officers were assigned to other units, along with all the nurses, and the enlisted men were widely dispersed.

When the 45th was officially declared inactive on September 30, 1945, following Japan's surrender, it had been operating for slightly more than thirty months since sailing from New York, and had cared for 36,000 patients, nearly one-fourth of whom were battle casualties. Only 65 died. The members of the unit returned to the United States by various routes.

The surgeon general praised the 45th in the most complimentary terms; "By its valor, it won the admiration and respect of all who were entrusted to its care. The service, cooperation, and loyalty of this unit, under circumstances never before encountered in the long history of conflicts, is worthy of the highest praise, and its achievements are an inspiration to all."

General Mark Clark, under whose command the unit served, was equally lavish in his commendation. He stated that the 45th "served with the greatest diligence, distinction, and bravery," and he added that there was "no way of estimating the number of lives saved by the valor and loyalty of the doctors and nurses in the 45th. . . . It was called upon during the bloodiest phases of battle to handle upwards of 2,000 casualties daily."

While the 45th was winning these accolades, things were happening back at the college. MCV's first full-time dean of medicine, Dr. Jacques P. Gray, arrived in 1942 to remain for four years. He was a graduate of John Hopkins and Harvard, and came to the college from the University of North Carolina, after serving on the faculties of the University of California and Stanford. Dr. Gray left in 1946 to accept the deanship of Oklahoma medical school.

Describing the impact of World War II on the Medical College, Dr. Gray said that "medical education has suffered and will continue to suffer for the duration of the present war . . . one-third of the members of the faculty are on military leave. . . . For the duration . . . the minimum requirement of three years of college work has been lowered to two years, by mutual agreement of the members of the Association of American Medical Colleges. . . . 'Round the calendar teaching and learning, as carried out under the accelerated program, offer the saving of one full year. The plan had advocates even before it was adopted generally."

The first interstate compact for higher education in this country was signed in 1943 between the Medical College and the West Virginia University school of medicine. The latter institution had only a two-year course at that time, and the third and fourth years would be completed at MCV. This trail-blazing agreement, the prototype for others arranged subsequently under the Southern Regional Education Board, resulted in the matriculation at MCV, over a seventeen-year period, of 342 students. About 20 were enrolled annually, and, overall, 335 were graduated. At the end of the period, West Virginia University established a four-year medical course, and the arrangement was terminated. Before the pact was signed in 1943, there were already more graduates of MCV in West Virginia than from any other medical school; this interstate compact increased the predominance of Medical College graduates there.

In addition to the war, MCV students had other tribulations, or thought they had. Governor Colgate W. Darden, Jr., had recommended, successfully, that students at William and Mary who were members of fraternities or sororities be forbidden to live in the houses maintained by those organization on the ground that they were "undemocratic" and placed a financial burden on parents. Students at the Medical College, and also at the University of Virginia, immediately jumped to the erroneous conclusion that the governor was intent on abolishing fraternities throughout the state. *Skull and Bones* commented: "When he steps on the 'two by four' campus at the Medical College, he will face new obstacles. . . . The dorms at MCV are incapable of housing all students who come from out of town." Nothing else was heard of this.

The "Don't Stick Your Neck Out" syndrome seems to have taken brief root in MCV at this time. "A Faculty Member" wrote *Skull and Bones* saying: "Of all the damnable weapons ever invented by man to tyrannize over his fellows, the advice 'Don't Stick Your Neck Out' is surely the most damnable. It kills initiative and makes cowards of us all. In our schools and colleges it reigns almost supreme and kills scholarship. Even the most inspiring teacher . . . can find his efforts reduced to naught by one sneering soul holding a class in thrall by the lash of his whip, 'Don't Stick Your Neck Out.' "

There was an uproar in May 1943 when George W. Bakeman, formerly with the Rockefeller Foundation, who became President Sanger's assistant in 1941, reported that rats had invaded McGuire Hall. They came from a dump behind the building, and began spreading out to nearby areas when a fire started in the dump. Bakeman reported that the rodents had "created a situation which is most unpleasant and actually alarming." He added that the animals "attacked anatomical material and undoubtedly have created other situations which should be corrected." Bakeman's statement was in a letter to Dr. Millard C. Hanson, city health commissioner, who replied, "We will make a renewed attack to improve conditions."

The attack was not entirely successful. On the night of October 17 two babies were bitten by a rat in St. Philip Hospital. One of them died, but an autopsy showed that the bite was not the cause. The other baby was worse bitten. Dr. Douglas VanderHoof, chairman of the executive committee of the Board of Visitors, stated that MCV officials were "profoundly distressed," and would take steps to prevent a recurrence, "sparing no efforts or expense." Black organizations in the community were badly upset, and demanded improved conditions at the hospital.

President Sanger conferred with Governor Darden concerning the ravages of the rats, whose operations were not too far removed from Capitol Square. There was a great stir in the press, with stories and photos. Preventive measures were apparently largely successful, as the excitement died down.

There was, however, a further series of protests over another aspect of the situation at St. Philip Hospital. Josephus Simpson, editor of the *Richmond Afro-American,* wrote Sanger in 1946 requesting that black physicians be admitted to practice at the hospital, and saying that if conferences failed "legal action is contemplated." The president replied that "ours is an educational institution with hospital privileges limited to members of the faculty. There are inevitably members of the profession, both white and Negro, who would welcome hospital staff privileges. That is generally true in other communities where institutions like ours are located." At a meeting of the Board of Visitors, that body reiterated that MCV hospitals have "a closed staff," and they did not "deem it advisable" to change the policy. No suit was filed by the complainants.

Ceremonies honoring J. R. McCauley, an official of MCV since 1904, and secretary of the Board of Visitors since 1905, were held in the spring of 1944. Known to the faculty and to thousands of students as "Mac," and sufficiently well acquainted with the residents to call practically all of them by their first names, McCauley was praised in the highest terms. He had missed only three meetings of the visitors since 1905; one such miss was because of illness, and the other two occurred when he attended alumni meetings. "Mac" had a unique collection of documents concerning the college from the earliest times which was well-nigh indispensable to historians writings about the institution. His daughter, Helen, presented his portrait to the college at the ceremonies.

The Medical College was going down hill in various directions in the middle 1940s, if the testimony of several deans and administrators is to be believed. Robert Hudgens, the respected director of the hospital division, told a committee headed by Dr. Frank Apperly, who invited his opinion, that "we are slowly gaining the reputation of treating patients as intruders . . . rather than as guests." He went on to say that "we mar our good appearance by little indiscretions, committed by both physicians and nurses . . . or by the attitude held toward patients in the clinics, gruff and commanding rather than gentle and solicitous." Hudgens said "a nice old-fashioned Negro woman" told him she would "rather die unattended than go to St. Philip Hospital, for she had heard so much about the 'meanness' of the nurses."

It was in the immediate aftermath of the war that these criticisms were heard, and it was understandable that problems had developed, in view of staff shortages, long hours, and inadequate pay. Hudgens pointed out also that the state "exercises 100 percent control over the policies of MCV, yet supplies only 12 percent of its funds, while the UVA receives 33⅓ percent." Over against the criticisms of the college it was emphasized that there were many pluses.

The foregoing derogatory observations were made in the fall of 1945. In the following year the executive committee of the Board of Visitors asked Hudgens and the various departmental deans to report on the situation.

Hospital Director Hudgens came up with a longer and more detailed series of criticisms:

> The Medical College is not well. What are the significant complaints? They are found in the criticisms and animosities recurrently directed at the Medical College. . . .
>
> (1) The Medical College has no declared policy in certain major orbits of activity and program.
>
> (2) The Medical College has graduated too many men who do not measure up to the level expected of a really good school.
>
> (3) Alumni . . . especially doctors, do not have enough pride, loyalty, and interest in it. Far too many are actually antagonistic and embittered toward their alma mater.
>
> (4) The Medical College is held in a sort of contempt by an astonishingly large segment of the medical fraternity of the state, which charges, among other things, unfair competition through subsidy, the pirating of patients, and discrimination in the allotment of hospital facilities.
>
> (5) Consultative or group study of patients and genuine teaching interest are neither actual nor likely when so many of the faculty must divide their time between teaching and private practice and, in order to have incomes commensurate with their training and ability, must devote themselves more and more to an ever-expanding private practice.

How was the institution to cope with so formidable a list of alleged shortcomings? Hudgens suggested "one corrective which offers possibilites . . . the adoption, implementation, and announcement by the board of adherence to the principle of a closed staff with fixed income provisions, and with uniform contracts in the matter of compensation and perquisites." He felt that "such a policy obviously meets the charge of no policy," and furthermore, "it assures the dedication to teaching which alone can raise the level of preparation of students"; and when this is achieved, "pride, loyalty, and support of alumni" would follow. In addition to these benefits, he argued that such a program would eliminate at once "the conditions upon which the medical profession of the state bases its charges of unfair competition, pirating of patients, and discrimination in facilities." On top of all else, Hudgens contended, such a program "removes the barrier to consultative or group study of the patient by removing for the teacher-physician both the necessity of holding and the incentive to hold the patient, in order to collect a fee for service."

Dean Jacques P. Gray of the medical school urged "clarification and definition of lines of responsibility and channels of authority, and of methods and procedure. . . . Further delay in facing these problems simply cannot be justified." He cited "salary, income limitation, and perquisites" as needing attention, plus "increases in salary levels, development of research . . . the perennial laboratory problem . . . relations between MCV and the medical profession and other groups." Dean Gray also spoke of problems with "morale within the Medical College, including faculty members, other professional and nonprofessional groups, students and others." He said that President Sanger had made some beginnings toward solutions.

Dean Wortley F. Rudd of the school of pharmacy mentioned the need for "clearly defined lines of authority extending from the president through the appropriate deans and administrative assistants to the lowest members of the institutional family, with responsibilities and authority of each officer plainly stated." He regretted that general faculty meetings, "when vital college problems should be discussed, are rarely held." Also, "the policy or lack of policy followed with respect to salary adjustments has resulted in a dangerous lowering of staff morale." Dean Rudd was of the opinion that "the chief weakness of the institution is the fact that our administrative policies are completely out of step with our physical development."

Dean Harry Bear of the school of dentistry made observations of a general character without substantive criticism, while Dean E. Louise Grant of the school of nursing was more specific and critical: "A low bottom existed when war 'hit' us, and conditions have not climbed upward, but have steadily gone lower and lower," she said. "The present [nursing] faculty is tired, discouraged, and lacking in faith at what at this point can be done. . . . many . . . are seeking out more satisfying experiences. . . . some are so fatigued and worn that they are actually ill. . . . Credit should be given to the constant efforts of our president, Dr. Sanger, and the two directors of the hospital division, Dr. Jarrett and Mr. Hudgens, for their cooperation and efforts." Dean Grant closed by recommending better terms of "employment, sufficient staff, good food, comfortable housing, and salaries comparable with those paid elsewhere."

The executive committee of the board, which had requested frank statements from the foregoing individuals, said it would study these findings, item by item, and deal with them at future meetings.

The MCV Alumni Association had taken on new life in the mid-forties, and it, too, had concerned itself with conditions at the college. It had become an incorporated organization, an alumni fund was launched, and a director of the fund appointed. There was to be an annual roll call conducted through class managers, and all other systems of solicitation were to be abolished, including annual dues and life memberships. Better service to alumni, students, and the college through the alumni office was the objective. Publication of the *Alumnus,* with news of the alumni, was begun. One bit of news was that the Gilmer family had produced no fewer than twelve medical graduates of the college. The latest was Walter Scott Gilmer, 1945, and the first Winfield Scott Gilmer, 1869.

A committee of alumni, headed by Dr. R. J. Wilkinson, studied affairs at the college and "much to the surprise of some members, we found a depressed feeling prevailing throughout . . . even the students admitted that their morale had been shaken." The committee stated that the primary cause for these conditions was "a lack of authority delegated to the dean of the medical school and the director of the hospital division." It believed that "the various departments of the college, particularly in the school of medicine, are not properly organized and coordinated," much of this situation said to be due to "inadequate salaries and a lack of delegating authority." But if the foregoing seemed to be, in effect, criticism of Sanger, it was not, for the committee praised him highly and urged that his salary be raised to $12,500.

In response to such criticisms as the foregoing, the Board of Visitors decreed in 1947 that the deans and department heads collaborate with Sanger in delineating their various duties. Sanger appointed an Administrative Council, composed of these officials, which met periodically for a couple of decades thereafter.

The Alumni Association purchased the antebellum Maury House at 1105 East Clay Street in 1947 as headquarters, and as a memorial to all the MCV alumni who had died in this country's wars. Total cost of the purchase and renovation was $63,000. The principal contributors were A. H. Robins Company and the E. Claiborne Robins family. The basement was leased to the Virginia Pharmaceutical Association for offices and the second and third floors to the Kappa Psi pharmaceutical fraternity. Lounges and office space for the MCV Alumni Association were located on the first floor. Dr. W. R. Payne, former president of the association, reporting for President R. J. Wilkinson, stated in 1949 that relations between the college and the alumni had improved greatly. He felt that this was due, in part, to the privilege extended to the association's president to attend board meetings; to frequent informal conferences with Dr. Sanger; to improved relations between the college and physicians referring patients to the college hospitals; to refresher and postgraduate courses offered alumni; and to the college's cooperation with the alumni in the development of their headquarters, and lending them money therefor. The *Alumnus,* organ of the alumni association, changed its name to the *Scarab* in 1952, and continued to publish news of the alumni. The association pledged $100,000 over a ten-year period to provide a large alumni lounge in one of the new dormitories, and the pledge was carried out.

Several MCV alumni were noted at this period as having made their marks brilliantly in various parts of the world.

Dr. George Green, who graduated in medicine from the Medical College in 1905, had a distinguished thirty-eight-year career in Nigeria as the first medical missionary sent to Africa by the Southern Baptist Convention.

In addition to MCV, he studied at the Southern Baptist Seminary in Louisville and also at the Royal College of Physicians and Surgeons in Edinburgh. He and Mrs. Green were sent out to Nigeria in 1906, and they traveled by ship, train, cart, and hammock to reach their destination at Ogbomosho. They established a hospital and dispensary in the basement of their home. Dr. Green performed surgery on the kitchen table, while his wife served as an amateur anesthetist. More than 2,000 patients were treated during their first year in Africa. It was sixteen years before hospital buildings were erected.

Dr. Green was a native of England, and when the British Empire celebrated the twenty-fifth year of the reign of King George V in 1935, Dr. Green and his wife were given Jubilee Medals in recognition of their service to British subjects (Nigeria was then a British colony). Shortly before Dr. Green retired, the king and chief of Ogbomosho presented to him the robe and insignia of the chieftainship of Ba'nisegun, recognizing him as "chief of the medicine men."

English-born Alice L. Randall, who graduated in medicine from MCV in 1928, was back in the United States after sixteen years in Assam province, India—decorated several times for her heroic work as a medical missionary. George V of Great Britain conferred on her the Jubilee Decoration in 1935, and George VI gave her the Coronation Medal upon his accession to the throne. The Indian government accorded her one of its highest decorations in 1944. Dr. Randall developed and expanded the American Baptist Hospital at Gauhati, India, from virtually nothing in the way of facilities or equipment, and only one American registered nurse, until it became famous throughout India and Burma. The hospital cared for refugees in World War II, as well as British and American soldiers. Dr. Gordon Seagrave, the celebrated author of *Burma Surgeon,* spent six weeks there in 1942 setting up a military hospital. Dr. Randall carried on without another doctor's assistance throughout this entire period until 1944.

Dr. William N. Hodgkin of Warrenton was another alumnus who made a great impact in his profession. A 1912 graduate in dentistry of the University College of Medicine, he was elected president of the Virginia State Dental Association, was a delegate to the American Dental Association for many years; was named to the State Board of Dental Examiners in 1930 and served for seventeen years, the last four as its president. Hodgkin was representative of that board to the National Association of Dental Examiners and the national board's president in 1940. He also served as president of the American College of Dentistry, and as a member of the Council on Dental Education, of which he served a term as chairman. Dean Harry Bear of the MCV dental school described his writings in dental literature as "models for future authors." Hodgkin was awarded the honorary degree of Doctor of Science by MCV in 1941.

Dr. William A. Morgan, a medical graduate in 1917 from MCV, rendered conspicuous humanitarian service to the Dominican Republic, performing seven hundred operations there for indigent patients. As related in *Reader's Digest,* a hospital in Ciudad Trujillo was named for him, and he received high honors from the government. On his return from the Dominican Republic he was placed in charge of otolaryngology at Doctors' and Sibley hospitals in Washington, D.C.

Dr. Randolph Lee Clark, MCV 1932, director and surgeon-in-chief of the University of Texas M. D. Anderson Hospital for Cancer Research, "not only directs its triple functions, teaching, research, and patient care, but was also responsible for the new hospital's existence," according to the *Scarab.* The hospital had only fifteen beds when he became director in 1946, "and its research was carried on in what had been a stable." Dr. Clark raised over $8 million, and the great modern facility was the result. He was also professor of surgery at the University of Texas Postgraduate School of Medicine, consultant to the surgeon general of the U.S. Air Force and to the medical division of the Oak Ridge Institute of Nuclear Studies. In addition to all this, Clark headed the Medical Arts Publishing Foundation, which he started, in partnership with R. W. Crumley, a former Chicago editor, and which published several medical journals. He was awarded the honorary degree of Doctor of Science by MCV in 1954, and in 1964 was one of thirty-five alumni of the Mayo Graduate School of Medicine to receive the Outstanding Achievement Award of the University of Minnesota at the Mayo Centennial Convocation. Dr. Clark married Dr. Bertha Davis, a 1932 medical graduate of MCV, and later a practicing anesthesiologist at the Texas Medical Center.

There were deaths of prominent faculty members during these years. Dr. Karl S. Blackwell, on the teaching staff of the Medical College for several decades, with a large practice and devoted patients, died suddenly of a heart attack in 1941. The number of doctors succumbing to heart attacks has often been noted, and coronaries have been termed "the doctors' disease." Dr. Blackwell was president of the Richmond Academy and the YMCA.

One of the most picturesque members of the medical fraternity in the city, Dr. Joseph A. White, died in his ninety-third year, after a long career as a pioneer ophthalmologist. As a postgraduate student in Germany during the Franco-Prussian War, he made a special study of war casualties. Dr. White founded the Richmond Eye, Ear, and Throat Infirmary in Richmond in 1879 and was the contributor of more than 200 articles to medical literature. He was a member of the first faculty of the University College of Medicine and later served on that of the Medical College. He retired as emeritus professor at age eighty-two. Dr. White was chosen chairman of the ophthalmological section of the American Medical Association and president of the American Laryngological, Rhinological and Otological Society. He was given a dinner in Richmond on his eightieth birthday, to which eminent medical men came from other parts of the country. "A.G.B.," evidently Dr. Alexander G. Brown, wrote in the *Virginia Medical Monthly*: "He golfs, he dances, he rides. He fox-hunts; he gives exhibitions of horsemanship (only last year) over the jumps at public horse shows. He works, he plays, he never tires." At age seventy-five Dr. White won a silver cup for horsemanship at the Deep Run Hunt Club.

He was succeeded as professor of ophthalmology at MCV in 1930 by Dr. Emory Hill, another eminent man in the field. Hill died prematurely in 1941, the year of White's passing. Resolutions of the Richmond Academy said he "had a brilliant mind" and was "an exceptional teacher, a wise counselor, an outstanding physician, and a cultured and courageous gentleman."

In the following year, Drs. Greer Baughman and Robert C. Bryan died. Dr. Baughman graduated from the Medical College in 1897, and was professor of obstetrics there from 1915 until his death. He served as a captain with Base Hospital 45, was president of the Richmond Academy and a founder of Stuart Circle Hospital. Baughman was also president of the Community Recreational Association and active in its affairs.

Dr. Bryan was on the faculties of both the University College of Medicine and the Medical College. He served abroad in World War I as a major in the medical corps. He was president of the American Association of Genito-Urinary Surgeons and a member of the American Medical Association's House of Delegates. Bryan was a founder of Grace Hospital.

Dr. Beverley R. Tucker's death occurred in 1945. He was described as "the pioneer neuro-psychiatrist of the South," and was also the author of several books and plays. After graduating from MCV in 1905, he established the outpatient clinic in nervous diseases there three years later. Appointed professor of neurology and psychiatry at the college in 1912, Dr. Tucker opened a small private sanatorium which in time became Tucker Hospital. He was active in many civic agencies and president of various medical organizations, as well as of the Westmoreland Club and the Society of the

Cincinnati in the State of Virginia. A founder of the Children's Memorial Clinic, he was chairman of the governor's first Mental Advisory Board at the State Penitentiary, chairman of the City Library Board, and a member of the State Board of Health. Few medical men of his time touched the life of the city and state at so many points or made so varied a contribution to its well-being.

23. West Hospital, opened in 1940, and one of the most up-to-date hospitals in the country at that time. Now slated for demolition.

24. J. R. McCauley, *middle of front row*, shown in 1938, his 34th year as a member of the MCV administrative staff. With him are twenty students whose fathers were matriculated by him. *Front row, left to right*: R. M. Ferrell, J. P. Jones, McCauley, J. M. Habel, C. F. James. *Second row:* J. W. Reed, W. P. Terry, P. J. Nutter. *Third row:* W. E. Vest, R. K. Clements, David M. Bear, R. L. Mason, T. S. Ely, E. L. Caudill, Jr., *Back row:* C. P. Parker, Jr., W. R. Jones, Jr., J. S. Rhodes, Jr., J. C. Hulcher, D. D. Gray, Jr., J. H. Moorman, Jr.

25. Dr. Baruj Benacerraf of the Harvard faculty, an M.D. of MCV, 1945, winner of the Nobel Prize.

26. Dr. Harry Bear, dean of the School of Dentistry, who built it up tremendously, and was president of two national dental organizations.

SEVEN

The Sanger Presidency Ends

COOPERATION BETWEEN THE MEDICAL COLLEGE and the University of Virginia medical school, and between the college and Richmond Professional Institute, was furthered in 1945.

The Medical College and the University of Virginia offered a two-week refresher course in general medicine, primarily to returning veterans. Lieutenant Colonel James P. Baker of the MCV faculty, who had served with General Hospital 45, and as its executive officer for a time, and Colonel Staige D. Blackford of the UVA faculty, chief of medicine in the university's Eighth Evacuation Hospital, were in charge. The course was to be held every three months for the next year, beginning at Charlottesville in December, and included lectures, clinics, ward rounds, and discussions. Civilian physicians were permitted to enroll, and some did.

President Sanger also indicated that his school and RPI were cooperating in several areas. He recommended, in order to make medical social work available to the college, that an annual scholarship of $250 be offered to a student in Medical Social Science for a two-year trial period at RPI, the student to give fifteen hours per week to apprenticeship training in social work. Dean Henry H. Hibbs of RPI said he would supplement this by $75. The plan was approved by the MCV Board of Visitors.

Further collaboration was made possible by a gift of $250,000 to MCV by financier Bernard M. Baruch with which to establish a center for teaching and research in physical medicine, with special reference to hydrology, climatology, and spa therapy. The MCV School of Therapy thus established would be named for Dr. Simon Baruch, father of Bernard Baruch, an 1862 graduate of MCV, Confederate surgeon, and founder of hydrotherapy in this country. RPI had been giving a four-year course in physical therapy, leading to the B.S. degree, and it was arranged for the fourth year to be taken at MCV. All degree candidates were to be admitted through RPI, while those desiring certification in a twelve-month course would register at MCV. The physical therapy departments of the MCV and St. Philip hospitals were redesigned for more efficient service, and equipped for the practice of all branches of modern physical medicine. Bernard Baruch attributed his own good health to hydrotherapy.

Until 1945 members of the MCV Board of Visitors had been serving for life. It was decided in that year to rotate the members, as was being done at the other state institutions of higher learning. Terms were to be four years, with not more than two terms for any member. The Alumni Association was instructed to submit three or more names to the governor as possible appointees.

Major General William F. Tompkins, ret., son of Dean Christopher Tompkins, who had had a highly successful career as a member of the War Department's general staff and in other important army posts, came to MCV as comptroller in 1947. Finances of the college "were in a lamentable condition," according to the Board of Visitors. General Tompkins "instituted controls and procedures and employed an adequate staff," and was made coordinator of financial operations. He was so successful that he later was named vice president for financial affairs, and was given the honorary degree of Doctor of Science in 1963.

General Tompkins was a classmate of Dwight D. Eisenhower at West Point, both graduating in the class of 1915. When President Eisenhower died in 1969, General and Mrs. Tompkins drove to Washington for the funeral. A series of calamities ensued. Mrs. Tompkins injured her thumb in the car. They stopped for lunch at Anderson House, headquarters of the Society of the Cincinnati on Massachusetts Avenue, before proceeding to the obsequies. While they were lunching, somebody broke into their car and stole their suitcases. They went on, nonetheless, to St. Alban's Cathedral, but on entering the grounds, Mrs. Tompkins fell and broke her arm. They never got to the funeral.

One of the most successful of all the departments at MCV is the Visual Education Department, now termed University Library Services. It began in 1947 under Melvin C. Shaffer, with a staff of two people. A third of a century later it was still under "Mel" Shaffer, and it had become internationally known. With a greatly enlarged staff it operated in the fields of art, photography, television, printing, and classroom services. Among its resources, as described by Dr. Sanger, are "an ultramodern color TV communications system in dentistry, a learning resource center incorporating a media library, and 250 study carrels for medical students. . . . it has played a key role in the graduate instructional activities of the college." The department expanded its operation after the amalgamation with RPI, and functions of the two institutions were consolidated, with the result that all audio, library, and media services are under a single direction. Technical aspects of the engineering program being operated over television in collaboration with Virginia Polytechnic Institute and the University of Virginia are handled through this expanded department. Shaffer retired in July 1984 as its head, and was succeeded by Dr. William J. Judd III, a Syracuse University Ph.D. and specialist in media, audio, and computers.

The well-nigh forgotten plan to merge the Medical College and the University of Virginia medical school was resurrected briefly in 1947, when Governor William M. Tuck became disturbed by the size of the financial deficits of the two institutions. He proposed that a "partial merger" of some sort might be desirable. Dr. Alan Gregg of the Rockefeller Foundation was asked for an opinion. He recommended strongly against any such plan, saying that "the long future of medical education in Virginia lies in the development of the medical school at Charlottesville." Dr. Sanger felt that the press had not given adequate publicity to the favorable references to MCV in the Gregg report. However, Sanger was not in favor of uniting the two medical schools, and said years later that he thought it would have been a mistake. He was not in agreement with the Flexner report's emphasis on the importance of a medical school's having a university affiliation.

A bequest of $1,000,000 came from Isaac Davenport of Richmond in 1947 to Memorial and St. Philip hospitals for the care of adults and children in their charity wards. Since indigent white patients were at that time in the new hospital, rather than in Memorial, the money would be applied there for those patients.

Another important development of the late 1940s was the establishment of the MCV Foundation, which was incorporated during the 1947–48 session. It undertakes to raise funds for the institution, and provides services and equipment that the General Assembly is unwilling to pay for. Holdings of the foundation in 1987 totaled approximately $32,000,000.

A program of continuing education, whereby the Medical College brought medical knowledge and techniques to the crossroads, was launched at about this time. Drs. James P. Baker and Charles M. Caravati were in charge for MCV. The college was allotted Southwest Virginia and the Southside as its principal areas of responsibility, and the first four communities where hospitals were brought into the program were Fredericksburg, Farmville, Suffolk, and Nassawadox.

Dr. Kinloch Nelson was given direction of this program in 1948, and he managed it effectively until 1963, developing it as a comprehensive postgraduate effort. In the latter year he was appointed dean of medicine, and another head of continuing education had to be chosen. Dr. Caravati, professor of medicine, was appointed assistant dean of medicine in charge of continuing education, and he remained in the post until 1972, when he retired as emeritus professor of medicine.

Continuing education was one phase of the Virginia Regional Education Program which grew out of President Lyndon B. Johnson's Public Health Service Act, passed in 1964 and concerned primarily with cancer, heart disease, and stroke. Dr. Eugene Perez was appointed director-coordinator of the regional program. A score of Virginia communities are now involved in continuing education, and medicine, dentistry, pharmacy, nursing, and other areas are covered. Clinics, conferences, and lectures are provided, plus TV courses, teaching exercises, and short residency training programs on campus.

President Sanger's reputation as an able administrator was spreading, as seen in the offer he received in 1948 to become director of the University of Maryland's medical center at a salary of $16,500. He was getting only $10,000 at MCV, but he turned the offer down. Soon thereafter his pay at the college was raised to $12,500, plus certain perquisites.

The death of Dr. Stuart McGuire on October 17, 1948, following a long illness, was a blow not only to the Medical College but to the medical profession. Confined to his bed since 1941, he nevertheless discharged many of his responsibilities, and his unconquerable will was manifest until the end. During World War I, when he was in charge of Base Hospital 45, he carried on with the best of them, never letting the fact that he had to wear a steel wire-mesh corset slow him down. He wrote in January 1919 that he had not a single day off since he went to Camp Lee the preceding April.

The famous Dr. William J. Mayo of the Mayo Clinic said that Stuart McGuire, in his younger days, exhibited "in his operations the finest technique of any surgeon of his age in America." During his career he was chosen president of the Richmond Academy of Medicine, the Medical Society of Virginia, the Tri-State Medical Association, and the Southern Surgical and Gynecological Association. And, of course, he was president of both the University College of Medicine and the Medical College of Virginia. Dean Wortley F. Rudd of the Medical College said that his "influence on medical education and medical practice, in all that these terms connote, will be counted far greater than that of any other man that Virginia has ever produced."

When the University College of Medicine burned in 1910, Dr. McGuire contributed $10,000 to the fund for rebuilding, and when the Richmond Academy of Medicine erected its new headquarters in 1931, he gave $15,000. It should be noted that these sums were the equivalent of at least $50,000 and $75,000 today. In his will, McGuire bequeathed more than $1,500,000 to the Medical College.

A lectureship in Stuart McGuire's honor was established at the college in 1929, with Dr. William J. Mayo as the first lecturer. World figures in medicine have been brought in annually for this lecture. Dinners in tribute to Dr. McGuire were given in 1934 and 1938, the former by the faculty and visitors of MCV, and the latter by members of the Richmond Academy. A handsome silver tray was presented to him on the earlier occasion. A disturbing event occurred when Dr. J. Allison Hodges fainted in the middle of his speech. He revived, and insisted on remaining for the rest of the program on a cot. At the dinner in 1938, Dr. J. Shelton Horsley, one of the great surgeons of his time, who served on the MCV faculty from 1903 to 1912, and in whose honor a lectureship was established there in 1947 by Dr. Guy W. Horsley, presided. He lauded Dr. McGuire on various grounds, saying that "he can carry his liquor as well as ever, he still plays a strong hand of cards, and his profanity is as impressive as in the days of his youth." Dr. J. M. T. Finney of Johns Hopkins was the principal speaker. When Dr. McGuire died after being confined to his bed for seven years there were countless encomiums.

Establishment of the school of hospital administration in 1949 was an important milestone. Dr. John Bell Williams, for a quarter of a century a valuable member of the MCV Board of Visitors, and for some forty years administrator of St. Luke's Hospital, introduced the resolution creating the school. Charles P. Cardwell, who had come to the college in 1940 as director of buildings and grounds, and six years later became director of hospitals, was co-founder of the school of hospital administration, which he headed. In that position he made a national reputation, and was awarded the gold medal of the American College of Hospital Administrators for his remarkable achievements. MCV conferred on him the honorary degree of Doctor of Hospital Administration.

In the late forties MCV's school of dentistry began accepting students from several southern universities that did not have dental schools. Students from the University of North Carolina came first, under MCV Dean Harry Bear, and others matriculated soon thereafter from the Universities of Florida and South Carolina, under Dean Harry Lyons. The arrangement continued until the late 1950s, sponsored by the Southern Regional Education Board.

President Sanger told the Board of Visitors in 1948: "We have the prospect of two Negro applicants for admission to dentistry, two for admission to medicine, and one to pharmacy." He was authorized to proceed with plans to send the applicants to predominantly black Meharry Medical College in Nashville. The General Assembly granted permission to MCV and UVA to establish annually twenty medical scholarships each at Meharry, and at Virginia State College ten. Recipients had to agree to engage in the general practice of medicine in a rural community of Virginia for a number of years equal to that for which scholarship aid was received.

The Bureau of Alcohol Studies and Rehabilitation opened in 1948 as an agency of the State Health Department, but was directed by Dr. Ebbe C. Hoff, a member of the MCV faculty. Dr. Hoff, a native of Kansas, won no fewer than six degrees from Oxford University (B.A., D.Phil., M.A., B.M., B.Ch. and M.D.). He came to MCV in 1946 as chairman of the department of neurological science, served as professor of psychiatry and physiology, and was appointed dean of the school of graduate studies in 1957. Hoff retained his post as director of the Division of Alcohol Studies until 1977. The General Assembly appropriated $1,000,000 in 1966 to establish under the division a center for research into the causes and treatment of alcoholism, with an adequate staff. Hoff was awarded the medal of the American Medical Society on Alcoholism.

Dr. R. Finley Gayle, Jr., chairman of the department of neurology and psychiatry at MCV for twenty years, and president of the American Psychiatric Association, described the alcohol program in 1949 as one of the earliest such programs anywhere. He said that it was run "as a combined in-patient and out-patient service," selection for admission being "in accordance with their [the patients] desire to receive help." The usual stay was about two weeks, but patients were followed as out-patients for a period of one year.

The twenty-fifth anniversary of Dr. Sanger's election to the presidency of the college was celebrated on April 27, 1950, with ceremonies in the old First Baptist Church, acquired by the college in 1939. Governor John S. Battle was among the speakers who praised Sanger for his remarkable achievements. A new automobile and a handsome engraved silver bowl were presented. Responding, the guest of honor spoke mostly of the institution's future needs. Commenting on the laudatory statements made by the various speakers, he said he was perhaps most touched by those of Wyndham B. Blanton, Jr., president of the Student Body Association, "because to me students come first, and their positive reaction to my sentiments was deeply rewarding."

Various aspects of the race problem were to the fore at the period. Overcrowding of patients in St. Philip Hospital caused what Charles Cardwell called "a critical situation." No adult beds for blacks had been added in Richmond since St. Philip was built in 1920, "except for a small, thirty-bed Negro hospital." Cardwell told the Board of Visitors that at St. Philip "all wards are badly overcrowded, and the emergency rooms are required to care for fifteen to twenty-five patients at a time . . . many patients spend their entire stay in the hospital on stretchers . . . some with known carcinoma, have been denied hospitalization because no beds were available." The place was also a fire hazard.

No substantial relief was afforded until two years later, in 1953, when Cardwell reported to the board that additional beds in Memorial Hospital had greatly lessened the overcrowding in both St. Philip and Dooley hospitals, and "increased the quality of patient care for Negro patients."

Still further relief came with the opening in 1956 of the Ennion G. Williams Hospital, which Charles Cardwell described as providing "200 additional hospital beds for Negro patients assigned to medicine, pediatrics, and psychiatry; 50 surgical and diagnostic beds for chest diseases, and 200 TB sanatorium beds to be operated for the State Department of Health." The entire hospital was exclusively for blacks. It represented the first substantial increase in hospital beds for blacks since 1920.

Dr. Ennion G. Williams, for whom the hospital was named, was a member of the MCV faculty from 1901 to 1923, and one of the most beloved and dedicated men in the history of Virginia medicine. The state's first commissioner of health, he was appointed by six successive governors to that position, in which he performed prodigies in drastically reducing such scourges as malaria, typhoid fever, and tuberculosis. When he died prematurely, in part because of overwork, the Richmond Academy's resolutions described him as having "the gallantry of Sir Philip Sidney, the sacrificial modesty of Walter Reed, the determination to conquer disease of Edward Jenner, and when aroused, the battle inspiration of Stonewall Jackson."

When Dr. Williams was beginning his medical career just after the turn of the century, he was left $468 in the will of Frances Richardson, who had been born in slavery, and was a domestic in the home of John L. Williams, Ennion's father. This sum was all the money that Ms. Richardson had when she died in 1902. It was a remarkable example of the affection that Ennion Williams inspired. He had attended her devotedly in her declining years and her last illness. With the money she bequeathed to him he bought some equipment for his first X-ray machine in Memorial Hospital. The X-ray department in the Ennion G. Williams Hospital was named for Frances Richardson.

It was becoming increasingly probable in the late forties that blacks would be applying for admission to the Medical College's various professional departments. In 1950 Miss Jean L. Harris sought to enter the medical school. The executive committee of the Board of Visitors voted unanimously to admit her, taking the view that "race shall not be a consideration in the admission of students." This was four years before the United States Supreme Court ordered such admissions.

Miss Harris, who was excellently qualified, entered the medical school in 1951 and made an exceptional record. Dean Truslow reported soon after her matriculation that she was making "extremely satisfactory" progress, and that "the students are accepting her without serious difficulties."

Following her graduation in 1955, she applied for an internship at the college and it was granted. Officials reported that she had no problems as an intern. She was appointed at MCV to direct the Center of Community Health. Later she was chief of the Bureau of Resources Development in Washington, and she held other important posts. Her success at MCV led to the enrollment of other blacks in all schools.

Dr. Wyndham B. Blanton, a member of a family with a long history of distinguished contributions to medicine, the son of Dr. Charles A. Blanton, for many years professor of children's diseases at MCV, retired in 1951 as director of the college's immunology clinic. He had held the post for eighteen years, and his associates in the clinic gave a dinner in his honor, and presented him with a silver bowl "in token of their friendship and admiration." He continued as a member of the faculty, that is, as clinical professor of medicine, until his retirement in 1958. Simultaneously, his son, Dr. Wyndham B. Blanton, Jr., was named assistant dean of medicine.

The senior Blanton's contribution as a member of the MCV faculty was important, but it was only one facet of an amazingly varied and productive life. He was the author of a most scholarly and authoritative three-volume history of medicine in Virginia from the earliest times, and then served as editor of the *Virginia Medical Monthly* from 1932 to 1942. Not content with that, he wrote a history of Second Presbyterian Church, was chairman of the board of Union Theological Seminary in Richmond, principal founder and first president of the Historic Richmond Foundation, and president of the Virginia Historical Society and the Society of the Cincinnati in the state of Virginia. All this along with a large medical practice. Dr. Blanton died in 1960.

The untimely death in 1950 of Dr. Harry Bear, dean of the school of dentistry, terminated a career of dedication to the advancement of the school and the college as a whole. A new building for clinical dentistry, the Wood Memorial, was under way at the time of his death, the faculty had been greatly expanded by the addition of a number of full-time teachers, and a department of dental research had been established. Dr. Bear had served as president of the American Association of Dental Schools and the American Society of Oral Surgeons and Exodontists. When his portrait was presented in 1951, Dr. John Bell Williams pointed out that under his leadership the dental school's enrollment had grown from 20 to 190. The executive committee of the Board of Visitors passed resolutions declaring that he "was never too busy to do kindly things for everyone about him. . . . Many will long remember his quiet humor, his tolerant attitude, his high sense of honor, his simplicity of manner, his earnestness in bettering his school, and his unfailing courage in his last illness." The Harry Bear Museum was established in the Wood Memorial Building. That structure was completed in 1954 with more than $1 million left for the purpose by Dr. Jud B. Wood and his wife.

Harry Bear was succeeded as dean of the dental school by Harry Lyons, who would become the leading figure produced by Virginia in the field of dentistry since Jamestown, a man who would achieve an international reputation. Before accepting the deanship, Lyons won from President Sanger an agreement to support his proposal to take the basic sciences out of the school of medicine and set them up in a separate "division" under their own dean. It was hoped and believed that they would ultimately become a "school," and that is what happened. Separate budgets for these departments, entirely divorced from the school of medicine, were established. This arrangement served greatly to promote the basic sciences and to bring a substantial increase in the number of graduate degrees achieved in those disciplines. Later, when Dean Lyons was a member of the Council on Dental Education, he persuaded the council to require, as a prerequisite for dental school accreditation, that dental school administrators be given full authority on matters pertaining to course offerings in basic sciences. This resulted in the adoption of such plans by many universities.

The year 1950 also saw the deaths of two other key figures in the life of the college, in addition to that of Harry Bear. These were Dr. Wortley F. Rudd, dean of the school of pharmacy for twenty-seven years and associated with the school for forty-six, and James R. McCauley, an official of the institution for forty-six years.

When the University of Maryland conferred an honorary degree on Dean Rudd, the citation said: "He has done as much if not more than any one person to advance the standards of pharmaceutical education and to elevate the practice of pharmacy." The W. F. Rudd memorial lecture was established in his honor following his death, and the first lecturer was J. Harold Burns, M.D., professor of pharmacy at Oxford University, who said Rudd was "one of those who played a dominant part in the development of pharmaceutical education." In 1956 the new organic chemistry laboratory for the school of pharmacy in McGuire Hall was named for Dean Rudd. His friends in the profession of pharmacy contributed the funds for the installation, which accommodated eighty students.

James R. McCauley came to MCV as business manager in 1904, and was made secretary to the Board of Visitors the following year. With the union of the two medical schools in 1913, he became secretary of the Board of Visitors executive committee and treasurer of the consolidated college. Stuart McGuire termed him the "unofficial historian of the institution" because of his remarkable collection of records and documents relating to the college's past. Two years before his death a no longer existent sunken garden and outdoor sitting area between Hunton Hall and the Ruffner School was named McCauley Court in his honor.

Work leading to the degree of Master of Science was being offered in 1948 at MCV in bacteriology, biochemistry, and pathology, and in the Baruch Center of Physical Medicine. Plans had been formulated for offering work leading to the Ph.D. for the first time in certain disciplines at the session of 1948–49. By the session of 1959–60 there had been a "striking increase in the proportion of graduate students working for the Ph.D.," according to the MCV *Bulletin.* At the 1963 commencement six doctorates were awarded and four masters. During the academic year 1965–66 there were seventy-five full-time graduate students, of whom twenty-six were working for the M.S. and forty-nine for the Ph.D. At the 1968 commencement, seven M.S. and six Ph.D. degrees were conferred, the largest number in MCV history down to that time—immediately preceding the coming together of MCV and RPI.

Two students were expelled in 1951 under the honor system, and there was a flurry of letters to *Skull and Bones* protesting their expulsion. Jennifer Ganakis, editor of the paper, said there had been so many of these communiqués that "an answer is compulsory." It was apparent, she declared, that "many of the students are not familiar with the school constitution"; and she added that "the action taken was entirely according to the stipulations of the honor code." Several letters complained that these students were expelled "while so many others go scot-free." She replied that the code provides that "if a student should see another committing a violation and does not report it, he is just as guilty as the infractor." The nature of the offense of the two expelled students was not made known. Since the code provided two penalties, and the first was "cheating—immediate expulsion," the presumption is that those who were "shipped" had cheated. The second category of penalties was for "indiscretion—lying, stealing, violation of athletic rules etc."

Skull and Bones, which had been functioning since 1915, was increasingly under fire. A committee on public relations recommended in 1953 that it either improve or go out of existence. They conferred with student leaders, and the paper was voted out as of September 1954. Students thereafter would provide news items for the *Medicovan.*

Dr. R. Blackwell Smith was named dean of pharmacy in 1947, as the youngest pharmacy dean in the country, succeeding Dean Rudd. He reported in 1951 that the school "has now been classified as a Class A school, as a result of the recent inspection by the accrediting group of the American Council on Pharmaceutical Education, this being the first definitive classification of this kind." The school was accredited in 1939, but certain specific recommendations were made for improvement, and these had now been carried out.

The school of medicine was removed from "confidential probation" in

1953, following an inspection by the American Medical Association, as noted in a previous chapter. The inspection team said it was impressed by the progress made, but called attention to "a number of persisting problems." One was "a tendency to inbreeding, with too few teachers who had received training outside the state." Faculty salaries were felt to be too low, and the physical separation of the basic medical sciences from the clinical departments was regarded as undesirable.

A hospital as a memorial to those who died in World War II was being planned in Richmond at this time, and President Sanger, ever on the lookout for ways to enhance the service and prestige of MCV, was anxious to have it placed in the Medical College area. Efforts toward that end were made, but the final decision was to locate the hospital on the Laburnum tract just west of Ginter Park.

The retirement from the faculty of Professor H. L. Osterud, Ph.D., in 1953 was the occasion for a remarkable outpouring of admiration and affection for both Dr. Osterud and his wife. The Alumni Association's meeting at Commencement was featured by extraordinary tributes and gifts to both of them. As *Skull and Bones* expressed it, "His day's work is never done, as long as there is a student who needs his assistance." The paper added that "he is a familiar sight on the last bus to Ashland at night . . . accompanied by some of his freshmen. Dr. Osterud knows which ones are lonely, desperate, in need of home cooking, and many graduates remember gratefully how Mrs. Osterud welcomed them into her home. . . . Some have given his Norwegian name to their sons." An annual Osterud Prize in anatomy was established.

More than 250 former residents and staff members in obstetrics and gynecology attended a ceremony in 1953, celebrating the twenty-fifth anniversary of Dr. H. Hudnall Ware, Jr.'s service to MCV. The occasion was planned by the Ware Residents Society, composed of his former residents, and many tributes were paid to him. The society established the Hudnall Ware Loan Fund in his honor with which to assist young residents in OB-GYN, and later presented his portrait to the college. The pavilion in the labor and delivery suite of the MCV hospital was named the H. Hudnall Ware, Jr., Caesarian Section Room. In 1969 Dr. Ware received the Obici Award for "outstanding contributions to the medical profession." He was president at various times of the MCV Alumni Association, the Richmond Academy, the Virginia League for Planned Parenthood, the Virginia Council on Family Relations, and the South Atlantic Obstetric and Gynecological Society.

Dissension reared its head in the department of ophthalmology in 1953 when Dr. DuPont Guerry III was appointed acting chairman of the department, pending the selection of a full-time chairman. Although Dr. Guerry was, and is, one of the most distinguished ophthalmologists in the United States, and he would later be elected president of the American Ophthalmological Society, the most prestigious organization in the world in this field, ten of the twelve members of the MCV department signed an indignant communiqué to President Sanger, protesting his selection as department head.

"The apparent methods employed in appointing Guerry remind one of the methods used by Hitler . . . in the 1930's" they wrote. "The ophthalmological faculty was indeed given a vote—but the vote had to be 'Ja' in order that it be counted. Our vote of no confidence is directed to a totalitarian system which has been allowed to develop in the state-supported institution, which should be in the first line of democracy."

Dr. Guerry had been appointed by Dean of Medicine John B. Truslow on the unanimous recommendation of a committee headed by Dr. I. A. Bigger. The executive committee of the Board of Visitors had confirmed the appointment unanimously.

Replying to the ten objectors, Dean Truslow said that Guerry "has made every conceivable effort to establish the harmony which he feels is so vital in the department, and he has contacted personally, and in most cases at length, nine or ten of the twelve members of the department. He has been under the distinct impression that he would receive their cooperation, and that they would accept his leadership in good faith."

The objectors dispatched another letter saying that "the designated chairman is the one individual who has not participated in the teaching and clinical functions of the eye department," and they feared "a loss of harmony."

The executive committee of the board held two more meetings, and heard arguments from everybody concerned, and again unanimously approved Guerry's appointment. The objectors were not appeased, so the committee held two more hearings, for an overall total of five. It did not change its position, and the Board of Visitors then approved the Guerry selection.

The appointment proved so successful that whereas Guerry had planned to hold the position temporarily, until a full-time head could be named, he was retained in the job for twenty years. During that period he strengthened the department in various ways, obtaining new equipment and employing prominent specialists. One would suppose that having created such an uproar, all the signers of the original protest would remember the controversy. But when one of them was asked for comment in 1984, he could not recall that the confrontation had ever occurred. An annual lecture in Guerry's honor was established in 1981.

The college was sponsoring intramural and intercollegiate baseball, basketball, and tennis in the early 1950s under the auspices of the Athletic Association. There was, however, little or nothing about the games in any college publication. The women students also had their sports. Known as the "Medicettes," they played basketball with an extra member on the team, making six on each side. Their games seemed to be entirely with "sextets" from local business organizations, such as the Chesapeake and Potomac Telephone Company.

The administration authorized the expenditure of $800 for color film showing activities at MCV, and the Alumni Association added $1,000. It was ready in 1956 and was shown to various groups, among the first being the Warsaw Rotary Club and the Men's Club of St. Stephen's Episcopal Church, Richmond.

Almost simultaneously, the college acquired an official song, "Hail Our Gracious Alma Mater." Dr. George Arrington, a 1952 medical graduate, wrote it to the tune of "Stenka Razin," and when first sung at an alumni dinner by the MCV chorus, it received a standing ovation. Sheet music for the song was available on the campus. A headline in the *Medicovan* read, "We now have an official song."

New trends in nursing education were discussed by President Sanger. "Nurse education is going through a rather abrupt transition, much the same as came to medical education a generation ago, paralleled later by dental education, pharmacy education, and other types," Dr. Sanger said in 1945. "During all such transitions, critics are numerous and vocal. Many of us remember the rather bitter protest against lengthening the medical course and, even more particularly, against lengthening the prerequisite preparation for the study of medicine. As recently as fifteen or twenty years ago printed comments on this subject were still appearing in the literature, and even more in medical or lay gatherings. . . . The development of new trends in nurse education is a typical social movement like those which preceded in kindred fields."

Sanger predicted two major developments "well-launched in the next half decade: widespread establishment of courses in education of hospital attendants, practical or vocational nurses . . . and the further development and extension of courses for the education of the professional nurse."

At about this time the nursing committee of the MCV board, of which Samuel M. Bemiss was chairman, expressed opposition to reducing nursing standards "below the minimum approved by accredited schools of nursing," and stated that "present standards of MCV cannot be reduced without injuring the school." It added, however, that "the imperative demand for nursing services should be met, in part, by training practical nurses," and the committee recommended "the establishment forthwith of a school for training practical nurses eligible for state registration." The view was expressed that "this school should ultimately provide for a two-year course."

This two-year course would not be established for some years, and then with results deemed unsatisfactory. The four-year basic baccalaureate degree program in nursing was adopted in 1952. The diploma and five-year degree programs were terminated.

In that same year the first unit of Randolph-Minor Hall, a residence hall and teaching center for the school of nursing, was erected. It cost nearly $600,000, plus $50,000 for equipment, all provided by the commonwealth. Four floors were added in 1956, and four more a few years later.

The building was named for Miss Agnes Randolph and Miss Nannie Jacqueline Minor. Miss Randolph was a great-granddaughter of Thomas Jefferson, and Miss Minor was the daughter of John B. Minor, famous professor of law at the University of Virginia. With Miss Sadie Heath Cabaniss, for whom Cabaniss Hall at MCV was named, they entered the nursing profession, at a time when ladies of gentle birth were not supposed to do anything but look after their families and possibly teach school. "The intrepid three," as described in *The First 125 Years,* a history of the Medical College, "began a new era of social work in Richmond." They founded the Nurses' Settlement for work among the poor, and out of this grew the Instructive Visiting Nurses' Association. Miss Minor was director of the IVNA for twenty years, and then for ten years was director of Public Health Nursing for the State Board of Health. Miss Cabaniss was the founder of nursing education under the Nightingale Plan at the Medical College in 1895. She was later director of the IVNA, and then the first rural public health nurse in Virginia. Miss Randolph graduated from MCV in 1914 in the first group of nurses to receive their diplomas from the college. Soon thereafter she was chosen executive secretary of the Virginia Tuberculosis Association, and subsequently was transferred to the staff of the State Board of Health, where she organized the tuberculosis bureau. Miss Randolph is credited with having done more to reduce the death rate from tuberculosis in Virginia than any other person.

Dr. Sanger's retirement as president in 1956 at age seventy was scheduled in 1954, and Dean R. Blackwell Smith of the school of pharmacy was slated by the board to succeed him. Dr. Smith was accordingly given a new post, assistant to the president, so that he might be groomed for the succession. Sanger was to become president emeritus in charge of development.

Dean John B. Truslow was leaving in 1956, after about five years as dean of medicine to become director of the medical branch of the University of Texas at Galveston. On the eve of his departure he issued a statement in which he praised several activities of MCV in the highest terms.

In the area of biophysics, MCV "has developed facilities unequaled in more than two or three of the great medical centers of the United States," he said. He was apparently attempting to say that only two or three such centers had facilities superior to those in Richmond. And "far more important than the facilities," he went on, "we have in the personnel under the leadership of Dr. William Ham a group of individuals of creative interests and productive possibilities outstanding in their own fields, and in the stimulus of other disciplines."

"In legal medicine," Dr. Truslow added, "we have developed a course widely copied all over the country." Under the leadership of Dr. Geoffrey Mann "we have an impact of legal medicine and medical ethics and medical economics upon our student body worthy of your attention . . . and we also have one of the two graduate schools in legal medicine in the U.S.—the larger of the two, in fact, for we have had two more graduates enrolled than at Harvard Medical School."

His final tribute was in the field of community medicine: "The identity of the professorship of community medicine with the directorship of public health of the city of Richmond has proven a valuable asset to our education program. The fact is that more people outside of this state identify the Medical College of Virginia with the Home Care Program of the city of Richmond than with any other single contribution our institution has made. Visitors from every continent on the globe have come to Richmond to see the Home Care Program, and its success, professionally, sociologically, and pedagogically has been extraordinary indeed."

The time had come for William T. Sanger's retirement at age seventy, as previously arranged. He and Mrs. Sanger were honored at a dinner on June 29, 1956, at the Commonwealth Club. They were lauded for their remarkable contributions, and given a chest of flat silver, and a handsome antique pitcher and tray. On a lighter note, Eppa Hunton IV, chairman of the executive committee of the board, presented Dr. Sanger with a silver teething ring, adorned with a blue ribbon, for "our baby chancellor, the first ever born at the Medical College of Virginia." This caused much hilarity. Dr. Sanger kept the teething ring thereafter in the top drawer of his desk, and chuckled every time he picked it up.

The Sanger presidency had begun in 1925, none too auspiciously, it appeared at the time. The Medical College was in serious straits, and Sanger did not appear to be too well equipped to solve its many problems. Indeed, it was predicted in some quarters that they were beyond solving. But these predictions turned out to be totally wrong. It was a long, hard struggle, and many obstacles and antagonisms had to be overcome, but Dr. Sanger not only put the institution firmly on its feet; he made a national reputation in the process. It took him nearly a third of a century, but by the time of his retirement he could view what he had achieved with much satisfaction. In the process of doing so, he had stepped on a goodly number of toes and aroused some little hostility; yet the results spoke for themselves.

President Sanger's accomplishments were of such magnitude that he was sought after by many medical institutions who wanted his advice and retained his services as an expert. He made no fewer than fifteen surveys for ten medical schools between 1945 and 1960 most of them in the South, but one in Michigan. For three years he made an average of eleven trips a year to the Vanderbilt medical school. He was awarded eight honorary degrees.

One would suppose that such manifold responsibilities would have occupied his attention to the exclusion of just about everything else, but this remarkable man found time for a great deal of activity on behalf of crippled children. He was on the board of the National Society for Crippled Children for seventeen years, for sixteen of which he was on the executive committee. He was president of the organization for a year, and was the first person to be awarded its gold medal.

Could a man with such a multitude of interests and concerns find time for any hobbies? It would seem not, but Sanger did. An expert horticulturalist, he cultivated 75 varieties of lilacs and 175 varieties of peonies. Not only so but he engaged in farming and stock raising on 136 acres in Bath County.

With him in a great many of his activities was Mrs. Sanger. She was widely felt to have been a major factor in his success, and her husband agreed. "My wife's judgment often startled me," he wrote in his memoir, *As I Remember*. "How was it arrived at so quickly and unerringly? If I did not follow it, I was sure to get my fingers burned." Dr. Robert V. Terrell, editor-in-chief of the *Scarab*, praised Dr. and Mrs. Sanger in the highest terms. Of Mrs. Sanger, the former Sylvia Burns, a freshman student with Sanger at Bridgewater College, Dr. Terrell wrote: "Not so well-known to the alumni is the gentle and unobtrusive yet accomplished Sylvia, to whom we owe far more than we can reckon." Thelma Vaine Hoke, secretary to Sanger for two decades and editor of the *Medicovan* and the excellent book on the college, *The First 125 Years*, termed Mrs. Sanger "the quiet loveliness behind his [her husband's] success." Mrs. Sanger quoted approvingly the words of a college president's wife in Illinois who said that the wives of college presidents were "janitors without portfolio," and that such a wife "must keep her home open for the sake of public relations and her mouth shut for the same reason." Mrs. Sanger also agreed with this lady's statement that "she wouldn't change places with anyone because of the opportunities the president's wife has for aiding the students who need someone in an unofficial position with whom they can talk over their problems."

Dr. Sanger did not accomplish so much without arousing antagonism in various quarters. There were those who felt that he was so singleminded in his determination to advance the interests of the Medical College that he sometimes forgot that other interests were involved. His critics said, too, that he devoted so much attention to getting new buildings that he failed to give sufficient thought to the college's other needs. In his defense he could argue that since the college had only four buildings when he arrived in 1925—the antebellum Egyptian building, McGuire Hall, and Memorial and St. Philip hospitals—it was essential that better facilities be procured. A first-class medical school could not possibly operate in such totally inadequate quarters.

It must be said that Dr. Sanger's personality was not his greatest asset, for he was not possessed of personal charm. This was simply another handicap that he successfully surmounted. As Dr. E. Randolph Trice said in reviewing the MCV president's memoir, "Those who knew Dr. Sanger best admired him most."

The Medical College and the University of Virginia medical school were in competition for appropriations, for professors, and for students. Yet Dr. Sanger made friendly gestures toward the rival institution on several occasions, most notably when he went before the General Assembly's finance committee in 1953 to urge upon the legislators, as the first medical need of the state, approval of the university's application for an appropriation toward its new hospital. He appeared at the request of the university's president, Colgate W. Darden, Jr.

Sanger was one of the founders of the Virginia Council on Health and Medical Care, and active in its affairs. This agency had as its principal objective the placing of doctors and dentists in areas of Virginia that were not being adequately served by these professionals. Many hundreds were placed in rural areas and small towns, as a result of the Council's efforts.

Dr. Sanger outlined his plans, following retirement, as follows:

> I shall endeavor to work closely with the administration and our board as an adviser, where practicable, shall continue as chairman of our building committee and work toward general institutional development; this will include funds for endowment and general support. I shall also tackle special projects from time to time, one of the first being concern for a superior informal education program for the students living in our new dormitories when completed. We want these students to meet many outstanding practitioners and scientists in small groups for questions and discussions.

Sanger retired as chancellor in 1959, and was elected chancellor emeritus and educational consultant, with compensation. He was also the first executive director of the MCV Foundation.

A number of highly distinguished faculty members at MCV were lost by death in the years from 1948 to 1954.

Dr. W. Lowndes Peple, professor emeritus of surgery, died in 1948. A graduate of the University College of Medicine in 1897, he taught at that institution as well as at MCV. Dr. Peple "devised many useful surgical implements which were widely adopted," the *Virginia Medical Monthly* declared. Major Peple was chief of surgical service for Base Hospital 45 in World War I. Witty and companionable, he made friends easily. He was on the staff of St. Luke's Hospital for many years.

The highly useful career of Dr. Roshier W. Miller was ended in 1950 when he was killed in a traffic accident. A graduate of UCM in both medicine and pharmacy, he served on that institution's faculty from 1897 to 1913, and then on the MCV faculty until 1947. Dr. Miller's great practical ability was put to good use when he supervised the construction of McGuire Hall after the 1910 fire destroyed the UCM building, and when he served as building committee chairman for the erection of the Richmond Academy's handsome headquarters in 1932. He was three times president of the MCV

Alumni Association, chairman of the city school board for many years, president of the Medical Society of Virginia and the Richmond Academy.

Dr. M. Pierce Rucker, noted obstetrician, editor of the *Virginia Medical Monthly* for a decade, and author of books and many articles, died in 1953. He taught at MCV for twenty-seven years, and was a special lecturer at Duke University on the history of obstetrics. Dr. Rucker wrote for medical journals in both this country and Europe, and conducted extensive research. He was the author of *Pen Profiles and Floral Eponyms,* edited by Dr. E. M. Holmes, Jr. The book contained sketches of thirty medical leaders from the eighteenth century to date, plus information concerning about 125 flowers that are named for medical men from many lands. Dr. Rucker was president of numerous medical organizations, including the American Association of Obstetricians, Gynecologists, and Abdominal Surgeons, the Medical Society of Virginia, and the South Atlantic Association of Obstetricians and Gynecologists. He was chairman of the city Board of Health for several years. "To his colleagues he was the scholar whose interests were unbounded and whose store of information was truly astonishing," said the *Virginia Medical Monthly.* "To his patients he was always the wise physician, counselor, and friend."

Dr. Claude C. Coleman, founder of the MCV's department of neurological surgery, died in 1953. A resolution of the Medical College board's executive committee termed him "one of the last surviving pioneers who had carried American medicine into undisputed world leadership in the field of neurological surgery." Dr. Coleman graduated from the college in 1903, and was on the staff from 1910 until 1951. He received many national honors. Thirteen prominent neurosurgeons who had trained under him came from all parts of the United States in 1949, on the thirtieth anniversary of his founding of the department, and give him a dinner and a silver platter engraved with their names. Dr. Coleman's portrait was presented to the college in 1951.

The year 1953 also ended the career of Dr. Alexander G. Brown, a graduate of the University College of Medicine in 1898. He was on the faculty there until 1913 when the two medical schools joined, and then taught for many years at the Medical College as professor of clinical medicine. Dr. Brown was editor of the *Virginia Medical Monthly* for fifteen years, beginning in 1919 when the Medical Society of Virginia bought the publication. Brown possessed marked literary ability, and his articles in the monthly were notable. He was president of Stuart Circle Hospital. Brown was also a member of the executive committee of the Virginia Historical Society, president of the Sons of the Revolution in Virginia, and a member of the Society of the Cincinnati and the Society of Colonial Wars.

The death of Dr. William Tate Graham, one of the great pioneers in orthopedic surgery, and founder of the Crippled Children's Hospital in Richmond, now the Children's Hospital, was another tragedy of the year 1953. He launched the hospital in 1919 in his basement office on Franklin Street, following a serious polio epidemic, with Miss Nannie J. Minor as his collaborator. Children with twisted and paralyzed limbs felt toward Dr. Graham as toward a father whom they could love and trust. Many a child who seemed certain never to walk again was able to do so, thanks to his compassionate and wise treatment. He was surgeon-in-chief at the hospital as long as he lived. Dr. Graham joined the Medical College faculty in 1913 and remained there as professor of orthopedic surgery until his retirement in 1948. He was appointed to the State Board of Health in 1923, became its chairman three years later, and served in that capacity until his death. When that occurred, the bellboys and other employees of the hotel where Dr. Graham lived were as distraught as anyone, so great was his capacity for friendship. Commenting on his life and achievements, the *Virginia Medical Monthly* described Dr. Graham as "a man with a warm personality, a gifted and beloved teacher, a conservative and devoted surgeon, with a keen sense of humor . . . a deep love of people with whom he always made friends."

The brilliant career of Dr. Everett Idris Evans came to an abrupt end in 1954 when this forty-four-year-old international authority on the care and treatment of burns died of a heart attack. Two years previously he had been a visiting lecturer at the University of Edinburgh and the Royal College of Surgeons in London. Dr. Evans was surgical consultant to the Atomic Bomb Casualty Commission, Far East Command (Japan), and chairman of the National Research Council's committee on burns. He was awarded a certificate of appreciation by both the U.S. Army and Navy for his contributions to scientific research. Dr. Evans joined the MCV staff in 1947. Tributes came from all parts of the world at his passing, and the *Virginia Medical Monthly* remarked that "admiration for his scientific abilities is often expressed in terms of personal warmth and genuine fellowship." A lectureship in his honor was established at the Medical College.

Dr. J. Fulmer Bright, who also died in 1954, was chiefly known for his service as mayor of Richmond for sixteen years, longer than any other occupant of that office, but he was a highly regarded member of the MCV faculty for a dozen years before his entry into politics. He was a graduate of the college in 1898, and his ability as a teacher there was praised by a committee headed by Dr. J. Morrison Hutcheson.

Finally, it was in the year 1954 that Dr. John Powell Williams died, at age 60. He gave up a large practice to devote his life to teaching. As chief of medical services at the McGuire Veterans Administration Hospital, and professor of clinical medicine at the Medical College, he made a superlative record in the training of internists. McGuire's was the first veteran's hospital in the United States whose program of teaching internal medicine was approved by the American Medical Association, and this was largely due to the ability and devotion of Dr. Williams. His leadership as chief of the medical service for General Hospital 45 in World War II was "acknowledged by all former members of that organization to be the guiding factor in the success of the outfit," the Medical Society of Virginia's resolutions declared. And it went on to say concerning Dr. Williams: "As an intense patriot, as a courageous soldier, as an outstanding medical officer, as a beloved civilian physician, and as an honored teacher there has seldom been an equal in this society. Finally, as an esteemed and wise counselor, a delightful companion and a loyal friend there is no replacement for this man."

27. Three presidents of the Medical College: Dr. William T. Sanger, Dr. Stuart McGuire, and Dr. Samuel C. Mitchell.

28. Dr. Charles M. Caravati, greatly distinguished member of the MCV faculty and winner of numerous highly prized awards.

29. Dr. Beverley R. Tucker, pioneer neuropsychiatrist, longtime MCV faculty member, public-spirited citizen and author.

30. Dr. Thomas W. Murrell, distinguished member of the dermatological faculties of both the University College of Medicine and the Medical College.

EIGHT

The College Under President Smith

Robert Blackwell Smith was elected president of the Medical College of Virginia in 1956, and was inaugurated on December 17 of that year. Dr. Joseph C. Robert, President of Hampden-Sydney College, parent institution of MCV, was the speaker.

Dr. Smith, a Ph.D. in medical sciences from the University of Chicago, had taken a B.S. in pharmacy at MCV in 1937, and an M.S. from the University of Florida in 1938. He was an able student. Dr. Smith succeeded Dean Rudd as dean of pharmacy in 1947, and for the two years preceding his election as president served as assistant to President Sanger, as previously noted. He had been a pharmacologist in the U.S. Food and Drug Administration, following his graduation from the University of Chicago in 1941, and was acting chief of the agency in 1945. For four years in the fifties he served on the committee on food protection of the National Research Council, and was a recognized consultant in several fields, including bread additives. Because of his competence in the latter specialty, he was named to head a commission on the subject in Geneva, Switzerland.

"Bob" Smith was born in Petersburg in 1915, over his father's drug store at the corner of Washington and South streets. His brother, W. Roy Smith, also a prominent alumnus of MCV, and its rector, relates that young Bob arrived just as Barnum & Bailey's circus parade was passing. Dr. Julian Beckwith, the physician in attendance at the birth, remarked to the family, "Barnum & Bailey just passed by and left you a little monkey."

When President Smith took over in 1956, he may have felt somewhat inhibited by the presence of Dr. Sanger as chancellor. He seems to have moved forward forcefully in his new position, despite the fact that he could have felt that Sanger was "looking over his shoulder."

The opening of the new student dormitories, situated between Ninth and Tenth, and North and Leigh streets, was an early event in the Smith administration, although they had been begun under Sanger. They housed more than 350 students, and since the boarding and fraternity houses near the college had disappeared, the need for the dorms was obvious. Dr. Sanger explained at the dedication that the program "means much more than a place to sleep and rest; it means an opportunity for students to enrich experiences by associating together outside of classes; it means developing college spirit; above all it means giving 'informal education' a chance to supplement routine class and clinic work." He said distinguished guests and selected members of the MCV staff would be invited to meet with the students late in the day or in the early evening for informal discussions "on broad cultural fields."

The four buildings were named for Florence McRae, MCV librarian for thirty-three years; Augustus L. Warner, one of the founders and first dean of the college when it opened in Richmond in 1838; Wortley F. Rudd, dean of pharmacy for twenty-seven years; and Harry Bear, dean of dentistry for thirty-seven years.

The Virginia Federation of Women's Clubs launched a drive in 1959 for funds toward the cost of a $95,000, two-million-volt X-ray machine known as a Maxitron. It would be useful for treatment of cancer. Members of one junior women's club washed automobiles, manned gas pumps, and wiped windshields at a Richmond service station. Several clubs sponsored window displays in department stores, or gave teas and benefit dances. The federation raised approximately $50,000. The Maxitron was placed in an addition to the Ennion G. Williams Hospital. The American Cancer Society contributed $43,350 toward the overall cost of $165,000.

Other building projects completed at about this time were the annex to McGuire Hall, relieving congestion of the basic sciences teaching area; a 565-car parking garage at the eastern end of Clay Street; and renovation of St. Philip Hospital.

A shocking event was the murder in Monroe Park by a robber of Dr. Austin Dodson, who was en route to a performance at the Mosque. Dr. Dodson was an internationally known urologist, the author of two texts that were "standard student and post-graduate texts throughout the country," and an admired member of the MCV faculty since 1931. He was credited with building the urology department at the college. He was also active in the establishment of Richmond Memorial Hospital.

Creation of the Hunton Memorial Eye Bank, with a donation from Eppa Hunton, Jr., was an interesting and important innovation. The Lions Clubs lent their financial support. It was soon seen that the Eye Bank could operate more effectively if it had control of its own budget, and the Old Dominion Eye Bank was accordingly incorporated as an autonomous, nonprofit corporation. The Hunton organization continued to operate as a research foundation. By 1959 about a thousand persons had signed pledge cards saying they wished to donate their eyes. The Eye Bank has furnished corneas for transplants around the world.

A curriculum planning committee, headed by Dr. Wyndham B. Blanton, Jr., assistant dean, produced "Objectives in Medical Education" after some fifteen months of "arduous discussion and consideration." It was adopted by the faculty in 1960, and a curriculum evaluation committee staffed by Dr. Edwin F. Rosinski then assumed the task of appraising the effectiveness of the medical school's curriculum, a task that led ultimately to its complete revision.

Dr. W. Taliaferro Thompson was named in 1959 to succeed Dr. William Branch Porter, who had retired, as professor and chairman of the department of medicine. He was at that time chief of the medical service at McGuire Veteran's Administration Hospital. Dr. Thompson had been on the teaching staff of the college since 1945, and associate professor of medicine since 1954.

Dr. Robert Q. Marston, a 1947 graduate of MCV and both a Markle and a Rhodes scholar, was appointed in 1959 assistant dean of medicine and associate professor, with responsibility for student affairs and admissions. Dr. Marston left two years later to become director of the medical center and dean of medicine at the University of Mississippi, and then vice chancellor. In 1968 he was appointed director of the National Institutes of Health, and after several years in that post became president of the University of Florida.

An important milestone was reached in 1960 when the General Assembly appropriated $4.4 million for the much-needed Medical Education building. A federal grant of $1,378,000, already made, brought the sum in hand to the desired amount. The structure's completion in 1963 made possible the expansion of the entering class from 84 to 128 members. For the first time there would be appropriate teaching and research quarters for the clinical departments. In addition, the departments of pathology, physiology, biophysics, and biochemistry would be housed there with additional space for biochemistry. Convenient study facilities for students also were included. Visual education, a computer center, a laboratory for human genetics, graduate studies in the medical sciences, and headquarters for continuing education also were in the twelve-story structure, two of which were below ground.

An idea of the statewide service being rendered by the college could be grasped from statistics published in the *Medicovan.* Almost two-thirds of the dentists practicing in Virginia and more than three-fourths of the pharmacists were MCV graduates. Of the two thousand trained physicians in the state, almost two-thirds were educated at the college. Of some five hundred students enrolled in the state-supported schools of professional nursing, MCV was educating over 60 percent. The various schools at MCV enrolled in 1958 students from ninety of the ninety-eight counties in Virginia. The college hospitals served 32,000 in-patients representing ninety-six counties, while the clinics recorded 93,000 patient visits, representing service to eighty-eight counties.

It was gratifying that Betty Anne Jones of Cleveland, Virginia, scored the highest grade in the United States in 1961 on the national certifying examinations of the Registry of Medical Technologists in the American Society of Clinical Pathology. She scored 179 out of a possible 200. Three other MCV students scored 176, 177, and 178, while the lowest score among the MCV contingent was six points above the national mean. Dr. Henry G. Kupfer, director of the school of medical technology, and other faculty members were being congratulated.

The following year two members of the faculty won significant awards. Dr. John L. Patterson, Jr., won the Research Career Award, and Dr. Sami I. Said the Research Career Development Award, both of which were made by the National Heart Institute of the National Institutes of Health.

On the centennial of the Civil War in 1961, Dr. Harry J. Warthen, Jr., of the Medical College faculty, created a remarkable medical exhibit of that conflict in the headquarters of the Richmond Academy, with Dr. E. Randolph Trice as chairman from the Academy. Warthen also created an American Revolution Bicentennial Exhibit in 1976. Both received much favorable attention, especially the Civil War exhibit, which attracted visitors from all over the world.

The United Daughters of the Confederacy presented a chapel in memory of Confederate president Jefferson Davis to the college in late 1960. It is on the seventeenth floor of the hospital. Mrs. Murray Forbes Wittichen, president general of the UDC, made the presentation and Hudson Strode, Jefferson Davis's biographer, was the speaker. A few months after the dedication the MCV *Bulletin* reported that the chapel "overflows each Sunday morning with patients in wheelchairs and on stretchers with their families and friends, and with employees." Between Sundays "it is used by individuals and small groups for prayer and simple communion," said the publication. The MCV hospitals had had a hospital chaplain for the preceding twenty years, provided by the Interdenominational Religious Work Foundation, but no suitable chapel. In 1966 Dr. Glenn Pratt was appointed associate professor of ethics and director of religious activities, a new position. He was a former military chaplain and a paratrooper in the Korean war.

President Smith was understood to feel that President Sanger had been too much concerned with "bricks and mortar." He was aware also that the American Medical Association was critical of the lack of advanced research at the college, and of the fact that so many of the faculty had been trained in Virginia. So, in accordance with plans initiated by Sanger, he proceeded to bring in a number of department heads from out of state, and to emphasize the need for research.

One of those brought in was brilliant Dr. David Hume of Harvard. When the search committee from the Medical College visited the Harvard Medical School to look into young Dr. Hume's record and interview him, they were told, in effect, that Hume would either give MCV the best surgical department it ever had or he would wreck it. He succeeded in the former objective and almost in the latter.

Controversy surrounded him from the time of his arrival in 1956 as successor to Dr. I. A. Bigger as full-time head of the surgical department. Dr. Carrington Williams had been serving without pay as acting head of the department, pending the choice of a permanent chairman, and he was extremely critical of Hume's modus operandi. He told the Board of Visitors that Hume's "ability is beyond question, but his ruthless management has led practically to a dictatorial power which apparently he extends so far as possible to other departments."

Dr. John M. Meredith, a leading surgeon in Hume's department, wrote President Smith that he had been "puzzled by a barrage of criticism and harassment from the chief of surgery," and he went on to say: "Never in my thirty-two years' experience in three medical schools have I ever encountered nor heard of such petty carping on such thin, flimsy matters." Meredith said Hume was trying to get rid of him and Dr. Charles F. Troland.

Dr. Lewis H. Bosher, Jr., was another surgeon in the department who was treated in a similar manner by Hume. Bosher's specialty was thoracic and cardiovascular surgery, and he said Dr. I. A. Bigger had told him that he would be in charge of this branch of surgery. When Dr. Carrington Williams went to Harvard with the committee that was checking out Hume before he was called to MCV, he reported that Hume said he was not interested in thoracic and cardiovascular surgery, and therefore would not be in conflict with Bosher's section. Yet when Hume came to Richmond, he took over and operated on a number of such cases at McGuire and the Medical College hospitals.

The Hume-Bosher controversy came to a head in 1962 at a meeting of the Board of Visitors. It had been sizzling for months, and a great many of the faculty were sympathetic to Bosher. He was an able surgeon, although some of its associates considered him to be temperamentally difficult. He was outspoken in his criticism of Hume, his superior. Hume's methods grated on the nerves of numerous persons who came into contact with him, but he was determined to have his way, and he was so valuable to the college that the board hesitated to thwart him. The board reprimanded Bosher for "defiance of properly constituted authority," but agreed that Bosher's "responsibility and authority in the area of thoracic and cardiovascular surgery within the division of general surgery be restored." This appeared to be a victory for Bosher, but two years later Hume wrote the board that the arrangement was unfortunate and impossible. He recommended the creation of a division of thoracic and cardiac surgery within the department, choice of its head to be left to him. His request was granted, and Dr. Hume got Dr. Richard R. Lower from Stanford University. Lower would become internationally famous. Bosher remained in the department until 1979, and then joined the staff of Chippenham Hospital, where he established the cardiac surgical program. He was also instrumental in setting up a similar program at Henrico Doctors' Hospital.

It should be obvious from the foregoing that whereas Hume aroused widespread antagonism, he got spectacular results. Dean of Medicine Maloney became so exasperated with him at one point that he fired him. The board promptly fired Maloney. Both firings were soon retracted.

Despite the controversies that swirled about the head of David Hume, even his worst detractors had to concede his great ability and his stupendous drive. He had performed the world's first kidney transplant at Harvard medical school in 1951, when in his early thirties. After he came to MCV five years later, and achieved additional fame, surgeons came from various areas of the globe to visit his department and learn of his innovative techniques in kidney transplantation, in immunology, endocrinology, and other basic clinical sciences. Hume was a strong advocate of a university affiliation for MCV.

He received numerous national awards while at MCV, including the Francis Amory Prize of the American Academy of Arts and Sciences, the Valentine Award of the New York Academy of Medicine, the Distinguished Service Medal of the University of Chicago, and the Distinguished Achievement Award of *Modern Medicine.* All this brought great prestige and many grants to the Medical College, and the department of surgery was greatly improved.

Expanded facilities for Dr. Hume's department had been made available in 1962 with construction of the Lewis L. Strauss Research Laboratory, named in honor of the Richmonder who had served as chairman of the Atomic Energy Commission. At a cost of $342,000, provided by foundation grants, a state appropriation, gifts from admirers of Admiral Strauss, and other sources, the building provided operating facilities, animal quarters, and laboratories.

Dr. Hume had been on the college faculty for sixteen years in 1973 when he piloted his private plane on a trip to California. After landing at Van Nuys Airport and transacting his business, he told Paul S. Hungerford, Jr., chief pilot of the Great Atlantic and Pacific Aeroplane Company, that he planned to return to the East that night. Hungerford informed him that fog was approaching and advised him to postpone his departure until next day. Hume, who was reluctant to take advice from anybody, went up, hit a mountain, and was killed. He was fifty-five years old.

At his memorial service from St. Stephen's Episcopal Church, Richmond, Dr. Francis C. Moore, chairman of the surgical department at Peter Bent Brigham Hospital in Boston, termed him "a restless genius," and said "he carried out the first of a long series of organ transplants that truly changed the face of surgery and medicine throughout the world."

A memorial signed by Drs. Walter Lawrence, Jr., Carrington Williams, Jr., and Hunter H. McGuire, Jr., of the MCV faculty said that "the adoration of his patients is indescribable," and that "he transformed the lives of hundreds of people who knew and worshipped him . . . students idolized him." It was largely due to him that MCV "came to be recognized as one of the most exciting medical schools in the nation. . . . talent poured into the faculty, money poured into his research projects." David Hume's death was indeed a tragic loss.

President Smith had brought to MCV a number of department heads and others from outside the state in the late fifties and early sixties, in the hope of meeting the criticism of the AMA that the college had too many Virginians on its faculty and not enough researchers. Some of these newcomers, like Dr. Hume, were none too considerate of the veteran members of the teaching staff over whom they were given control.

Dr. Carrington Williams expressed the opinion to the Board of Visitors that "President Smith does not have a proper view of the medical school, and is permitting research to replace clinical teaching as the prime function of the school." This view would be echoed the following year by John P. Lynch in his much-discussed and debated address accepting the presidency of the Richmond Academy.

The Medical College came under fire in late 1961 and 1962. A Richmond physician, name unknown, got hold of a letter from a "faculty evaluation committee" at the college, and gave it to the *Richmond News Leader*. He told the paper that the committee's report reinforced his opinion that the college was drifting away from its primary responsibility of turning out practitioners who could heal the sick, and was becoming involved instead in paperwork, bureaucracy, and excessive concentration on research.

The *News Leader* thereupon published an editorial (November 4, 1961) entitled "Foggy Days at MCV." It not only castigated the college for what it saw as the institution's drift away from its primary mission, but was scathing in its references to the committee report as "a work of classic illiteracy." The language of the evaluation group, said to have been composed largely of recently appointed members of the college faculty, was indeed couched in horrendous and nearly incomprehensible prose. The newspaper's comments stirred up something of a storm.

A still greater uproar occurred when Dr. John P. Lynch, of the McGuire Clinic, a prominent part-time member of the clinical MCV faculty, assailed the institution in his inaugural address as president of the Richmond Academy of Medicine (January 9, 1962). He expressed the view that the college was excessively concerned with research, at the expense of teaching students how to treat the sick. He also found "little real empathy on the part of the faculty . . . with the state of Virginia and her sick." Dr. Lynch charged, furthermore, that "areas of cooperation between our medical school and other health facilities and situations in the state have become progressively narrower and narrower."

Medical Dean Maloney said he considered Dr. Lynch "disloyal, unethical, insulting, and his behavior despicable." The Board of Visitors requested the General Assembly, which was in session, "to review the policies and programs of the college and report its findings." Dr. William C. Gill Jr., president of the Richmond Academy of General Practice supported Dr. Lynch with a statement alleging overemphasis on research at the college, adding that "there is a philosophy of 'ivory tower' medicine instilled in the students completely foreign to the clinical practice of medicine."

Germane to this whole discussion was the fact that the federal government had begun handing out millions of dollars for research. In earlier times, little money for this purpose had been available at MCV, and when funds began flowing out of Washington in the 1950s, there was a natural eagerness on the part of medical schools to beef up their research facilities. Many of the incoming faculty members at MCV seized eagerly upon these grants; they were especially anxious to stress research, since some of them believed the Medical College was an inferior institution, and greater research was, in their view, essential. As a matter of fact, such an objective was a worthy one, provided its pursuit was not carried to extremes.

Following his address, Dr. Lynch appointed a committee from the Richmond Academy of Medicine with the request that it appraise the charges against MCV. It was composed of three former presidents of the Academy, and was headed by Dr. Guy W. Horsley, immediate past president of the Medical Society of Virginia. The other members were Dr. Thomas W. Murrell Jr., counselor from the Richmond district for the Medical Society, and Dr. W. Linwood Ball, past vice president of the American Medical Association, and current delegate to the AMA. Horsley was on record as saying that "the medical schools should spend more time preparing young doctors to be clinicians rather than teaching all of them to be purely research fellows and professors."

The committee received eighty letters from members of the Academy, in response to a request for their views, and conferred with two hundred Richmond physicians. It also met with the educational committee of the Medical Society of Virginia, and with a national survey team from the

American Medical Association and the American Association of Medical Colleges which had recently visited MCV at the request of that institution's administration, following Lynch's address.

This survey team was in Richmond on February 19–22, and it completed its preliminary report before the Horsley committee did so. In its conclusions, which were repeated in its final report, the team stated that there had been no overemphasis on research at the college. On the contrary, it urged that there be greater emphasis. It also gave enthusiastic support to the college's curriculum, and to the "truly remarkable progress" that it found the institution was making. Dean Maloney was credited in the report with a large share in this progress.

The survey team strongly criticized what it took to be lack of communication between MCV and the medical community. It said this lack of communication was evidenced, for example, in numerous instances where local practitioners sent patients to the college for treatment and never received any information from the institution concerning the disposition of their cases.

Whereas the national survey team reached preponderantly favorable conclusions, the Horsley committee from the Richmond Academy, which made a much more thorough and prolonged inquiry, presented what it considered to be constructive criticism in several directions. Its able report, written by Dr. Murrell, found that many full-time and part-time faculty members at MCV were frustrated and dismayed by conditions, brought about in large measure, the report declared, by the combined attitudes of a fairly recently appointed group of administrators and department heads who were said to have undertaken their responsibilities with the "dedicated belief that the Medical College prior to their arrival was a fourth-rate institution in a desperate condition." And whereas the Horsley committee found multiple examples of friction, unhappiness, and even fear, the national team said it was impressed by what it termed cooperative faculty attitudes. It did concede that there was "a vigorous group of dissenters . . . [who] eloquently expressed their misgivings."

The Horsley committee, in what was no mere "town and gown" appraisal, declared that "qualities of leadership, humility, maturity, absolute integrity, judgment, sympathy, and diplomacy have been lacking in some of the recent appointees." A number of specific instances, demonstrating a lack of the foregoing qualities, were mentioned. The committee referred, furthermore, to a surgical procedure at the college which it pronounced flagrantly unethical. As for the research program, it said it had "no authority" to evaluate it, "nor does it profess to be qualified to judge the quality of this work."

The committee also stated that "a party was sponsored by a department head for college personnel at the Valentine Museum during the past Christmas season at which behavior was tolerated which was a disgrace to the Medical College and the state of Virginia."

This same department head, Dr. David Hume, had staged a similar soiree the preceding Christmas on college property. His entire staff, including nurses, orderlies, and others of both races were invited, and an extremely insidious "fish-house punch" was served. Unaware that the punch packed a gargantuan wallop, many of those who partook succumbed in short order. A leading MCV faculty member who was invited reports that when he arrived, he found the revelers "laid out in rows." Members of the administration showed up and were horror-struck. They decreed that no such party be held at any time in the future on college property. Consequently the event was moved the following year to the Valentine Museum, which granted permission, little realizing what was coming. An executive of the institution arrived at the height of the orgy, and ordered everyone off the premises.

Some positive good resulted from the focusing of attention on the college by the *News Leader* and Dr. Lynch. Highly regarded Charles P. Cardwell, Jr., director of hospitals, was named vice president of MCV, "with general responsibility in the area of community relations." Dr. W. J. Hagood, Jr., of Clover, retiring president of the Virginia Academy of General Practice, was appointed consultant to the college on general practice, that is, in the neglected area of the "family doctor."

A couple of faculty members who were centers of controversy departed shortly thereafter for other posts, and others followed suit subsequently. The able and admired Dr. Kinloch Nelson was elevated to the deanship of medicine when Dr. William F. Maloney left to accept the associate directorship of the American Association of Medical Colleges. Members of the Medical College faculty began attending meetings of the Richmond Academy in larger numbers than before, thus promoting better understanding between the faculty and the "uptown doctors." There were at that time, 309 doctors who had uptown offices and who lectured at MCV. Only seven received part-time monetary pay; the rest were limited to patient privileges.

Dr. Harry J. Warthen, Jr., editor of the *Virginia Medical Monthly,* himself a longtime member of the MCV clinical faculty, summed up the controversy in a well-balanced editorial. He concluded that "unquestionably, good has come from all this, for the air has been clarified." And he went on to say: "No differences exist that a little humility on the part of the newcomers, plus good will on the part of the natives and a mutual forbearance will not resolve."

Carter O. Lowance, confidential brain truster to four governors, had joined the staff of MCV in 1958 to become assistant to President "Bob" Smith. "Few have come to MCV who in such a short time won the friendship, admiration, and respect of administration, staff, and personnel," the *Medicovan* declared. Governor Albertis Harrison wooed Lowance back to the Capitol in 1962, to the distress of President Smith. "I don't know what we shall do without him," he said. And the elevator operator also was distraught. "Why y'all let that nice man go 'way from here?" he asked.

Colonel John H. Heil, retired former commanding officer of the Richmond Quartermaster Depot, who had been appointed assistant comptroller in 1960 and comptroller the following year, was named assistant to the president two years later, succeeding Carter Lowance.

The Medical College was one of twenty-two institutions of higher learning affiliated with the University Center of Virginia, a cooperative organization designed to make available to each member certain educational resources of the other members. President Sanger hoped that the University Center would be located in the immediate vicinity of MCV, but this did not come to pass. The Medical College participated in the visiting lecturers' program, the library program, the research program, the Eastern studies program, and the cooperative professors program of the center.

MCV's first full-time head of the department of neurology, succeeding Dr. Weir Tucker, was appointed in 1963. He was Dr. Cary G. Suter, a physician who was trained at the University of Virginia and who was for two years at the Mayo Clinic on a traineeship of the National Institutes of Health. He came to MCV in 1951 as assistant professor of neurology, and ten years later was made associate professor.

Dr. Tucker's record as part-time head of the department was highly praised by Dean William F. Maloney, who said that "great progress was made in developing an excellent educational program." Tucker said divisional growth made necessary a full-time head.

In the same year Dr. Ralph Ownby, Jr., was appointed full-time professor of pediatrics, and the first full-time director of the consultation and evaluation clinic. Dr. Ownby discontinued his private practice to accept the position. In 1970 he was named medical director of the Crippled Children's Hospital and an occupant of the Jesse Ball DuPont professorship for the handicapped child at MCV.

Dr. John Wyatt Davis of Lynchburg, who graduated from the Medical College in 1930, was the first winner of the Medical Society of Virginia's annual Robins Award "for outstanding community service." The award recognized "his work with the graduating classes of UVA and MCV . . . and in the field of public relations, and his role as a member of the medical advisory board of the United States Junior Chamber of Commerce." Davis was president of the American Geriatrics Board and the Tri-State Medical Association. A heart attack in 1969 did not slow him down. He died five years later.

A bequest of more than $1 million to the college for research in arthritis came from Dr. Charles Walter Thomas of Floyd, who died in 1964. An MCV graduate in 1903, Thomas practiced in Floyd, Patrick, and Henry counties.

The appointment of Dr. Kinloch Nelson in 1963 as dean of medicine as successor to Dean Maloney, brought to that position one of the unique personalities in the college's history. A University of Virginia graduate, he came to MCV in 1929, and from that time forward made a secure place for himself in the esteem of his associates. Before assuming the deanship he had held the positions of professor of medicine, head of the out-patient department, director of continuing education, director of the home care program, chairman of the interim committee of deans, and consultant in internal medicine at McGuire Veterans Hospital. The *Scarab* termed him "major-domo extraordinary, one of the most popular members of the faculty, who has much to do with the molding of the student in the clinical years, and who, by virtue of his constructive thinking, tact, sympathetic understanding, and genius for inspiring friendship and loyalties is assigned tasks and called on for advice and assistance by the highest and the lowest at the school, regarding problems ranging from the most personal to the most scientific."

As evidence of the foregoing the university named the elaborate, newly completed clinical facility the Nelson Clinic in 1972. Kinloch Nelson Student Honors Day was instituted, with presentation of student research, recognition of exceptional students, and a guest speaker.

After retiring from the deanship in 1971, Dr. Nelson joined the staff of the Medical Society of Virginia as coordinator for continuing medical education. "I tried retirement and it damn near killed me," he exclaimed on taking the new post. He retired from that in 1984. He was awarded the Presidential Medallion at the 1985 commencement in recognition of his outstanding contributions to VCU.

Possessed of a puckish sense of humor, Nelson decided to snicker publicly at physicians whose signatures are totally illegible. He arranged for a selection of these inscrutable scrawls to be published in the *Virginia Medical Monthly*, but made it plain that physicians were not the only offenders. "Hell," he said, "I have a lawyer friend whose signature is absolutely the worst I've ever seen. I've known some knotheads," he went on, "who seem to think it is some kind of status symbol to sign their names so you can't possibly read 'em. I don't get that at all!"

Dr. Nelson wondered how the poor pharmacists ever deciphered these hieroglyphics. The *Virginia Medical Monthly* published a letter the following year from Kenneth W. Schafermeyer, executive director of the Virginia Pharmaceutical Association, protesting the "illegible prescriptions written on hospital blanks," despite the fact that "regulations require that prescriptions for controlled drugs bear the *printed* name, address, and telephone number of the practitioner." This regulation is violated "in a large number of instances," he said, with the result that the pharmacist is prevented from calling the physician because his name is illegible."

President R. Blackwell Smith said in 1959 that the General Assembly at its 1958 session had "provided funds to begin implementation of the full-time clinical facility idea, and took the requisite step toward providing the essential physical facilities, that is, the medical education building." It is reliably reported that some alumni lobbied the General Assembly in opposition to appropriations for full-time faculty.

A dissent from the prevailing view of medical educators that the college should be completely staffed by full-time teachers and department heads, came later from the highly respected pen of Dr. Thomas W. Murrell, a pioneer skin specialist and member of the MCV faculty for half a century, for twenty-five of those years professor of dermatology and syphilology. Dr. Murrell had been given the honorary degree of Litt.D. by the college in 1955. At age eighty he lectured at the University of Beirut, and he was also visiting lecturer at several American medical schools. He wrote papers on the history of medicine and the Civil War. In the *Virginia Medical Monthly* for January 1962, Dr. Murrell, then emeritus professor, wrote, in part:

New minds have been brought here because of the necessity of full-time teachers, and there has come into being, not too positively expressed, the view that this is a trend to the time when the college will be fully staffed by full-time men, and the "closed staff" will be realized as something that is good and to be desired. It is entirely debatable, even if possible, that a closed staff is desirable. There is too much to be said on the other side. . . .

When an idealistic youth decides to enter the almost holy gates of medicine, he nearly always picks out a man he wishes to emulate. Many students are convinced they have a "call" or a certain fitness for a special department. They do not know that what they think of as a "call" is the interest aroused in them by contact with a dynamic personality. The dynamic is much more likely to be met in the part-time man who has achieved success in the outer world. Example: when Dr. Stuart McGuire was teaching, a majority of the boys thought they were especially fitted to do surgery.

Dr. Murrell died in 1964, aged eighty-four. A newly designed dermatology clinic was named for him in 1973. The first Thomas W. Murrell lecture was delivered at the dedication.

His son, Dr. Thomas W. Murrell, Jr., has been a member of the Medical College staff for forty-five years and clinical professor of dermatology for fifteen years. In addition to caring for his large private practice, Dr. Murrell has found time for an amazing number of professional and civic services. He has been president not only of the Medical Society of Virginia and the Richmond Academy, but also of the American Dermatological Association, and was given the Obici Award for outstanding contributions to medicine. He served as president and chairman of Blue Shield of Virginia, president of the Christian Children's Fund, of the William H., John G., and Emma Scott Foundation, and the Country Club of Virginia, as well as a member of the RPI Board of Visitors and the vestry of St. Stephen's Episcopal Church.

The fact that fewer MCV graduates in medicine choose a specialty as a career than graduates of medical schools in the country as a whole was made known by Edwin F. Rosinski, Ed.D., associate professor of medical education and director of research in that subject at the college. He found that for the period 1951–60 approximately 70 percent of medical graduates throughout the United States chose specialties, whereas only 56 percent of Medical College graduates made that choice. Those going into research and teaching were 4 to 5 percent for both groups. Hence some 40 percent of MCV graduates were general practitioners, compared with 25 percent for the rest of the country. This result was achieved through the emphasis and encouragement given to the training of the "general practitioner," and later the "family physician," through two decades by both Drs. Sanger and Smith, effectively assisted by Dr. Kinloch Nelson.

Dr. Harry Lyons became dean of dentistry in 1951, and remained in the post until 1970. A native of Lexington, Virginia, he was a leader in the state and national dental associations, and won numerous awards and honorary degrees. He stated that throughout his deanship not a single graduate of the school failed a state board.

From three to five continuing education, or refresher, courses for active practitioners were held each year during Lyons's deanship. There was also an annual homecoming, at which graduates of the dental school and their spouses came back to the college. As many as five hundred of them were on hand for some of these affairs.

The impressive Lyons dental building was opened in 1968, and named for Harry Lyons in 1971, one year after he retired. It cost $4 million, half of which was provided by the state and half by the federal government.

The Virginia Dental Association launched a campaign in 1981 for a $2 million endowment for the school of dentistry, designed to give it a new potential in the market for academic talent. Dr. James E. Kennedy was then dean. The MCV Foundation assisted in the drive, and former Dean Lyons was extremely active. Dr. Charles Fletcher of Alexandria, president of the Virginia Dental Association, was chairman of the effort. Cocktail parties were held over a wide area and the $2 million goal was reached. Dr. Lyons gave $200,000 of the amount, and Dr. Edward Myers, a retired Norfolk dentist, a member of the MCV Foundation Board of Trustees and of the MCV Board of Visitors, gave $100,000.

Awards conferred on Harry Lyons are almost too numerous to enumerate. Among them were the Alpha Omega Alpha Achievement Award; William J. Gies Award, American Academy of Periodontology; William J. Gies Award, American College of Dentists; Maimonides Award of the State of Israel; Virginia Association of Professions Distinguished Service Award; and the Distinguished Service Award of the American Dental Association, its highest award.

Dr. Lyons received honorary degrees from Temple University, New York University, Manitoba University, and Washington and Lee University. He served as president of the Virginia Dental Association, the American Dental Association, the American Association of Dental Schools, the American Academy of Periodontology, and the American College of Dentists, the only Virginian to have served in all these various capacities and one of only five persons in history who have done so. He served four terms as speaker of the House of Delegates of the American Dental Association, and was named MCV's outstanding alumnus of 1985.

Dr. Warren Weaver, chairman of the department of chemistry and pharmaceutical chemistry at MCV, was named dean of pharmacy when Blackwell Smith was elected president of the college in 1956. He had joined the faculty six years before, and held a B.S. degree in pharmacy and a Ph.D. in pharmaceutical chemistry from the University of Maryland.

Dean Weaver explained that in the years before World War II "you went to a physician only when acutely ill; you went to a pharmacist for health information." There was a revolution after the war, he said. The new antibiotics and sulfa drugs, and preparation of drugs by industrial manufacturers, made the pharmacist an interpreter of physicians' orders to the patient. He was doing more prescriptions and doing less compounding."

"One out of five patient days in some general hospitals are related to misuse of or reaction to drugs," Dean Weaver pointed out, "so pharmacists can do much to avoid this." The school of pharmacy at MCV seeks to focus on the idea that pharmacy is a personal health service, the chief goal being better health care through rational drug therapy, he said.

A training grant by the National Institutes of Health in 1960 for graduate studies in the department of chemistry and pharmaceutical chemistry made the school at MCV "the first school of pharmacy in the country to have a program of this sort."

A seminar for pharmacists was sponsored annually by the school in conjunction with the Virginia Pharmaceutical Association, and considerable enthusiasm was expressed by the participants. These refresher courses for druggists were regarded as extremely helpful, and at times applicants had to be turned away for lack of space. There were also extracurricular activities.

The school's first advanced degree, an M.S. in pharmaceutical chemistry, had been awarded in 1954. Other M.S. degrees would be offered later, as well as Ph.D.'s, and in 1976 the Ph.D. in Pharmacy was added.

Dean Weaver served as president of the American Association of Colleges of Pharmacy, was a member of the board of directors of the American Foundation for Pharmaceutical Education, and secretary of the Virginia Council on Health and Medical Care. The Virginia Pharmaceutical Association named him its "pharmacist of the year" in 1963. The University of Maryland school of pharmacy conferred on him its Honorary Alumnus Award in 1969.

A lecture hall in the great new Blackwell Smith pharmacy-pharmacology building was named for him. Dr. Weaver retired from the deanship in 1981, but continues to teach at MCV from time to time.

The nursing situation at the college was highly disturbing in the 1940s and 1950s, owing to a shortage of nurses, related in part to World War II. Drs. Carrington Williams and Harry J. Warthen, Jr., argued in 1946 in the *Virginia Medical Monthly* that it was unnecessary to compel nurses to take such elaborate training, "since a nurse graduating in two years is adequately trained for bedside nursing," whereas "for those with superior preliminary training, or desire and ability to specialize, the postgraduate year or years would offer unlimited possibilities."

The foregoing argument did not get immediate results, but a committee was finally appointed to visit several schools where two-year courses for nurses were offered. It reported that such a course should be instituted at MCV. President Smith approved, and so did the board. The course was offered in the fall of 1958. Graduates received the degree of "Associate in Science in Nursing," and were deemed qualified to "write the examinations for registered nurse licensure in Virginia." The course was fully accredited by the National League of Nursing, and was approved by the Virginia State Board of Nurse Examiners. It included such courses in general education as English, history, and sociology.

The two-year course lasted for only six years. A committee headed by Dr. Richard A. Michaux, longtime member of the MCV surgical faculty and then a member of the Board of Visitors, recommended unanimously "that the course be abolished," effective with the opening of the 1964 session, and the board agreed. Dean Doris Yingling of the nursing school had suggested this action, her contention being that in a teaching hospital, the nursing course should be four years. Other teaching hospitals, it was pointed out, including that at the University of Virginia, did not offer two-year courses. It was contended, too, that enrollment in the two-year course at MCV was declining, and that there was pressure for admission to the four-year program.

Wards in the MCV hospitals were closing in 1969 for lack of nurses, and Dr. Warthen returned to the attack in the *Virginia Medical Monthly.* "The educators are primarily interested in training the Chiefs, but there was relatively little concern as to how many Indians were provided to staff the hospitals," he argued. He was supported by Sadie Barton Snellings, R.N., of Mary Washington Hospital, Fredericksburg, who wrote in the same publication: "The nurse from the baccalaureate program can tell you numerous types of carcinoma of the colon, but can she care for a patient with a colostomy? Not likely."

The St. Philip School of Nursing was closed in 1962, after operating since 1920. Blacks had been admitted since 1954 to the Medical College school of nursing, thanks to the efforts of Dr. Sanger, and separate schools were no longer needed.

Mrs. Mayme Wilson Lacy, historian of the St. Philip Alumnae Association, was honored by having an annual award sponsored by the association named for her. She was the first black nurse to receive professional rank at MCV, and in 1953 was the first black appointed assistant director of nursing service at the college.

After MCV's consolidation with RPI to form VCU, Dean Yingling pointed to the advantages of university affiliation. It was now unnecessary, she said, to employ persons from other institutions to teach such subjects as English, history, psychology, and sociology to the nurses.

A master's program in nursing was approved in 1967. A new high-rise, air-conditioned women's dormitory with quarters for 432 students was opened and named Cabaniss Hall, as was the previous nurses' dormitory. The latter structure was renovated for teaching purposes and renamed the Nursing Education Building.

Dean Yingling came to MCV as dean of nursing in 1958, and by the time of her retirement in 1981 she was the dean of nursing with the longest tenure in the United States. A native of Baltimore, she received her B.S. in nursing education from the University of Oregon. She later earned a master's in guidance and Ph.D. in higher education from the University of Maryland. Miss Yingling organized the University of Nevada's first nursing school, and then was called to MCV as dean. Under her leadership, the school in Richmond was the first to offer a Master of Science degree in nursing; the first to staff a full-time continuing education department for nurses; and the first to employ a full-time director of nursing research. She was accorded the high honor of being made a University Professor.

Graduates of the MCV nursing school ranked first in the mean score of the Registered Nurse Licensure Examination in 1966, 1967, 1968, and 1971, in competition with the other Virginia nursing schools.

In 1974 the school sponsored the first Eastern Conference on Nursing Research in Williamsburg. Such a conference is now sponsored by the colleges and universities in the East on a biennial basis.

Dr. Gloria Francis was elected to the American Academy of Nursing in 1975, the first person from MCV thus chosen. She was associate professor and director of nursing research. Her book, *Promoting Psychological Comfort,* was named book of the year by the *American Journal of Nursing.*

The shortage of nurses in so many hospitals was seriously affecting MCV in the seventies, and an increase in salaries for nurses was obtained in 1978, thus helping to relieve the pressure.

Dean Yingling aided in developing a cooperative master's program with the University of Virginia school of nursing, whereby representatives of the two schools teach and work together for the benefit of nurses throughout the state. The plan is said to have become a model for the nation.

Miss Yingling is credited with getting rescue squad services from the West End of Richmond to serve largely black Church Hill, and she initiated faculty and student work in the city jail. The Virginia Federation of Women's Clubs awarded her a Certificate of Merit in 1967 for "outstanding achievement in developing a creative approach to health education." The Doris B. Yingling Scholars Programs and the Doris B. Yingling Nursing Research Award were established at MCV in her honor.

Monumental Church, erected in 1813–14 on the site of the terrible theater fire in 1811 in which seventy-two persons lost their lives, was found by its vanishing membership to be no longer operable as an Episcopal congregation. After various vicissitudes, it was given to the Medical College Foundation in 1965 "as a chapel or religious center for persons of all creeds, denominations, and faiths, and for other purposes of the college." The Sunday-school building adjoining was remodeled and renovated in 1959, and named Teusler Hall in honor of Dr. Rudolph Bolling Teusler, who graduated from the college in 1894, and became a medical missionary to Japan in 1899. He founded St. Luke's Hospital there and the country's first school of nursing and remained in Japan until his death in 1934. Teusler Hall was demolished when Monumental Church was restored some years ago. In 1983 the church was given to the Historic Richmond Foundation, since the MCV Foundation did not feel that it was equipped to make the best use of the storied edifice. A drive for $200,000 to complete the restoration of the church was begun by the foundation. The Beers-Newton house, adjoining the church and owned by it, is the property of the MCV Foundation, and is used for patient counseling and other purposes.

The Civil War Centennial Center, built to commemorate the one hundredth anniversary of that conflict, had served its purpose in 1965, and became the property of the college. It was renamed the Jonah L. Larrick Student Center, in honor of the man who was YMCA secretary for a third of a century until his retirement in 1959. Larrick was popular and admired, and was called the "unofficial dean of the students."

The building, when converted, contained a cafeteria, private dining rooms, music rooms, rooms for art exhibits and film showings, lounges, and game rooms. Speaking of games, the college has had only intramural sports since that time, including basketball, softball, tennis, and volley ball.

The Nelson Clinical and Self-Care Unit opened in 1967—seven stories, including physicians' offices, laboratories, radiology facilities, plus a restaurant and a bank. The center includes rooms for sixty ambulatory patients on the fifth and sixth floors. They must be able to go unassisted to doctors' offices in the MCV complex. They keep medication in their rooms and take it themselves. A nursing station is available on one floor. Patients occupying the facility wear street clothes and may have meals in the restaurant on the ground level or light refreshment in lounges. Members of patients' families who wish to remain overnight may do so.

The effects of hypertension on bridge and golf players were studied by Dr. Milton Ende of Petersburg (MCV, 1943), and the results reported in the *Virginia Medical Monthly*. Dr. Ende found that both pastimes occasionally caused hypertension to rise to disturbing levels, especially between marital partners at the bridge table! Thirty bridge players were scrutinized, and "a majority had trouble sleeping the night they played," while one-third recorded pulses of 100 or better while engaged in the game. Of the sixty-seven golf players studied, all but one of whom walked rather than use a cart, Dr. Ende found that one out of ten showed "a dangerous rise in diastolic pressure." More than half reported that they were depressed for one or more days after they had mutilated the fairway with their inept approaches to the green. "Professionals reacted the same as the duffers," he said, "and a small wager tends to create much more tension." However, Dr. Ende's conclusion was that "the stimulation of the game in the majority of cases was harmless."

One of the most distinguished pharmacists ever to graduate from the Medical College is J. Curtis Nottingham, who was given the honorary degree of Doctor of Pharmaceutical Science in 1966. He was the first full-time secretary of the Virginia Pharmaceutical Association, and the first Virginian since 1871 to be president of the American Pharmaceutical Association and then chairman of the association's Council. Mr. Nottingham was named "pharmacist of the year" by the Virginia Pharmaceutical Association in 1964, and at other times was president of the Medical College Alumni Association and of the National Conference of State Pharmaceutical Association Secretaries. He was named MCV's distinguished pharmacy alumnus of 1985.

A number of eminent faculty members died during these years. Dr. William H. Higgins, a member of the teaching staff of the medical school for over four decades, was emeritus professor of clinical medicine at the time of his death in 1957. In his honor, his many patients, friends and faculty colleagues raised a fund for an annual award to a member of the house staff perpetuating Dr. Higgins's "high standards of medical practice." He was chairman of the City Board of Health, and president of the Richmond Academy and the Richmond Heart Association.

His son, Dr. William H. Higgins, Jr., has carried on in the same tradition of public service. Like his father a graduate of the Johns Hopkins medical school and a president of the Richmond Academy, he was a member of the MCV faculty for several decades. Furthermore, he has found time for serving longer than anyone on the board of the Virginia Museum of Fine Arts (twenty-five years), during which he occupied the presidency and also the acting directorship of that organization, and more recently the chairmanship of the building committee for the huge new West Wing. Not only so, but in 1984, when he was carrying the heavy load of the last-named committee chairmanship, he was also chairman of the Greater Richmond Community Foundation, which raised $1.4 million for the restoration of the carillon war memorial in Richmond.

Dr. R. Finley Gayle, Jr., who died in 1957 at the age of sixty-five, had been chief of the department of psychiatry and of the psychiatric and neurological division of the hospital since 1939. He served as president of the American Psychiatric Association, the Southern Psychiatric Association, and the Virginia Neuro-Psychiatric Society. The R. Finley Gayle Observation and Treatment Center at Southwestern State Hospital was named in his honor a few months after his death. His son, Dr. R. Finley Gayle III, also an MCV graduate and associate professor there, who had entered private practice with his father, died prematurely of a coronary in 1979, aged fifty-six. He too had been president of the Virginia Neuro-Psychiatric Society.

Another eminent professor emeritus was lost in 1958 when Dr. Emmett H. Terrell died. A former president of the American Proctological Society and fellow of the American Medical Association, Dr. Terrell was chairman of its section on gastroenterology and proctology. He was a member of the MCV faculty from 1901 to 1947 and president of the Richmond Academy. Terrell was awarded the William and Mary Alumni Medallion for eminence in his profession.

Dr. Howard Masters, a graduate of the medical college in 1919, a member of its staff for thirty-eight years, and since 1939 associate professor of neuropsychiatry, died in 1959. He was president of the Memorial Guidance Clinic, of the Virginia Neuro-Psychiatric Society, the Mental Hygiene Association of Virginia, and the Tri-State Medical Association. Dr. Masters was president of the board of directors of the Tucker hospital for a decade and a half, and president of the National Association of Private Psychiatric Hospitals. He was also a member of the college of electors of the Hall of Fame in New York.

Dr. Porter P. Vinson, head of bronchoscopy at MCV since 1936, a specialty in which he was internationally known, died in 1959 when on a trip to Rochester, Minnesota, where he had gone for a checkup. He had been one of the first fellows in medicine at the Mayo Clinic, following his graduation from the University of Maryland in 1914. Dr. Vinson was appointed later to the staff of the clinic as a consultant in medicine, with a special interest in diseases of the chest. He was regarded as an authority on diseases of the esophagus, and when he came to Richmond, he had written more than 125 papers on chest diseases. At MCV he was professor of bronchoscopy and gastroscopy and was training students in the newer field of endoscopy. Vinson was president of the Mayo Foundation Alumni Association in 1941.

Dr. Frank L. Apperly, who joined the MCV faculty in 1933 as professor of pathology, died in 1961. A Rhodes Scholar from his native Australia, at Oxford he received the degrees of B.A., M.A., Doctor of Medicine, and Doctor of Science. He was a member of England's Royal College of Surgeons. Dr. Apperly returned to the University of Melbourne and again received the Doctor of Science degree, and was named head of the department of pathology. He was the author of many scientific articles, and was a former student of Dr. William Osler. He served in the British Army in World War I as a member of the medical corps. Mrs. Apperly was a graduate of the University of Dublin and active in Richmond as an actress in theatrical organizations.

Dr. Fred M. Hodges, for many years a clinical professor in the MCV department of radiology, and chosen emeritus professor in 1958, died in 1961. He was president at various times of the American College of Radiology, the American Roentgen Ray Society, the Southern Medical Association, and the Richmond Academy. He and Dr. William T. Graham started the Gamble's Hill Community Center and counseled it in its useful work. Hodges frequently examined patients who suspected that they had cancer, but he told the author of this volume that when he found no evidence of the disease, he made no charge—although under such gratifying circumstances most patients would have been more than ordinarily receptive to a bill, even a larger one than normal.

One of the most admired teachers at MCV, Dr. Sidney S. Negus, died from a stroke in 1963 while visiting friends in Port Washington, New York. He had been chairman of the department of biochemistry for thirty-five years, and had retired in 1962. Dr. Negus calculated that in a teaching career extending over half a century he had taught about ten thousand young people in their prep school, camping, college, and medical school days. At the time of his retirement his portrait was presented to the college, and an auditorium in Sanger Hall was named for him. Some years later an annual lecture was established in his memory.

The years 1962 and 1964 were devastating, in that during those years four greatly admired members of the faculty were taken prematurely by death, each in his fifties, three of them presidents-elect of the Richmond Academy, and the fourth serving his presidential term at the time.

Dr. John M. Meredith, chairman of the division of neurological surgery, having succeeded Dr. C. C. Coleman in that position, died in late 1962. He would have taken office as Academy president the following month. Dr. Meredith had graduated from the University of Pennsylvania, and came to MCV in 1941. He was the author of more than 130 articles in his field.

The community had hardly recovered from the shock of Dr. Meredith's passing when Dr. Charles M. Nelson died suddenly. He, too, was president-elect of the Academy. A memorial committee headed by Dr. John Robert Massie, Jr., who himself would die suddenly less than two years later, said that Dr. Nelson's passing "leaves an unbelievable gap in the ranks of the Richmond medical community. . . . it is hard to accept the fact that he has left us." The resolution went on to say that Dr. Nelson's "wide range of talents enabled him to excel in such divergent fields as medicine, golf, fishing, painting, sculpture, and bridge." "Monk" Nelson was a graduate of the University of Virginia medical school, served a residency at MCV under Dr. I. A. Bigger, and then was associated with Dr. A. I. Dodson in the practice of urology. At the time of his death he was professor of clinical urology at MCV.

Another great loss was sustained in the untimely passing of Dr. Morton Morris Pinckney in mid-1964. "His death from an unusual type of hepatic cancer is particularly difficult for us to accept," the *Virginia Medical Monthly* declared. "Mike" Pinckney was a man of exceptional personal charm and possessed of great ability. He founded the endocrinology clinic at MCV. In World War II he rose to the rank of lieutenant colonel, was assistant chief of medicine for the 45th General Hospital, and was awarded the bronze star. Resolutions of the most complimentary nature, stressing his exceptional talents as a physician and the affection felt for him by his patients were adopted by a memorial committee.

Dr. Pinckney was prevented by death from taking over as president of the Richmond Academy, and a few months later the occupant of that post died of a coronary attack. This was Dr. John Robert Massie, Jr., whose end came on a fishing trip in Florida. He was an enthusiastic fisherman, huntsman and golfer. He graduated from the Medical College in 1934, and was president of his class in both his junior and senior years. "No man was more widely loved by his patients," said the resolutions adopted by a memorial committee from the Academy. "His very presence seemed to lend hope to those hopelessly ill." A "brilliant surgeon," he served with the 45th General Hospital in World War II, and was discharged with the rank of major. At the time of his death "Bob" Massie was not only president of the Academy but also of the Medical College Alumni Association, and vice president of the Southern Surgical Association. At MCV he was assistant clinical professor of surgery. His funeral in his native Goochland County was attended by a huge throng of mourners from Richmond and the surrounding area.

A man who lost most of his family to the Nazi murder squads in World War II died in 1964, after seventeen years on the Medical College faculty, where he "gained national and international recognition through his research and publication," the *Virginia Medical Monthly* declared. He was Dr. Henry C. Kupfer, who was chosen chairman of the division of clinical pathology at the college in 1956. Three years later he was appointed to the National Committee for Teaching Clinical Pathology, "and served with distinction as chairman of a subcommittee of this group." Dr. Kupfer was born in Poland and was a graduate in medicine from the Charles University in Prague.

One of the most notable and talented MCV alumni was lost in 1962, when Dr. Walter Edward Vest of Huntington, West Virginia, died, aged eighty. A native of Floyd County, Virginia, and a graduate of the Medical College in 1909, Dr. Vest was "a towering figure . . . leader and president of many organizations, as editor and author, as a Shakespearean scholar, as wise counselor to many far and near, and as a skillful and knowledgeable physician," said the *Medicovan.* President of the Alumni Association, he "was alert to spot worthy students, to recommend them for admission and often advise them." Dr. Vest visited the college often and contributed generously to it. He was awarded the honorary degree of Doctor of Science in 1939. In a truly exceptional tribute, President Sanger was asked to represent the college at Vest's funeral.

Dr. Russell Cecil, a Medical College graduate famous throughout the world, died in 1966. The son of the Rev. Dr. Russell Cecil, pastor of Second Presbyterian Church, Richmond, Dr. Cecil graduated from MCV in 1906, and, after study in Europe and at Johns Hopkins University, joined the faculty of Cornell University Medical College in New York, where he remained. Dr. Elam Toone of the MCV faculty wrote that as early as 1925 Dr. Cecil became "undoubtedly the best-known American physician in the world" by virtue of his novel idea that old-style medical textbooks by single authors were outmoded, "since the scope of medical knowledge was far surpassing the capacity of any single individual to encompass." He accordingly "proposed a book in which each . . . field would be covered by an acknowledged authority. The result was that in a few years Cecil's *Textbook of Medicine* had become a standard in the medical schools of the English-speaking nations," and by 1966 had sold over twelve million copies in English alone, not counting translations into many foreign languages. Dr. Cecil was also nationally known for his work in arthritis, and was the first president of the American Rheumatism Association, and medical director of the Arthritis Foundation. He was given the American Medical Association's highest accolade, the Distinguished Service Award, in 1962. The citation mentioned especially his original and unselfish work in arthritis.

31. Dr. R. Blackwell Smith, president of the Medical College, 1956–68.

32. Dr. David Hume, internationally famous surgeon and storm center during his years at MCV.

33. Dr. Harry Lyons, dean of the school of dentistry, 1951–70, president of five national dental organizations, and winner of numerous awards and several honorary degrees.

34. Dr. Doris Yingling, dean of the school of nursing, 1958–81, longest tenure in the United States. Named a University Professor.

NINE

A Magician at Work in Education

A MORE UNPROMISING BEGINNING than that of Richmond Professional Institute, the other component of Virginia Commonwealth University, would be hard to imagine. Launched in 1917 in three unfurnished bedrooms on the third floor of a former residence on the site of the present Virginia State Library, with no students and a one-man faculty, it seemed destined to fade promptly from the scene. Then, too, this was the eve of our entry into World War I, which appeared to make the founding of an educational institution especially difficult. (I wish to acknowledge my great indebtedness to Dr. Henry H. Hibbs's book, *The History of RPI*, for many of these facts concerning the institution's beginnings.)

The amazing individual who embarked at thirty years of age upon this quixotic quest was Henry H. Hibbs, one of eight children of a Baptist minister in western Kentucky, and, as few nowadays seem to realize, an amateur magician in his youth. When in high school, Henry Hibbs and his friend Henry Manning toured Kentucky mountain villages in a horse and buggy, impressing the yokels and picking up some spending money. Hibbs did the magic and Manning the primitive movies. It would take all of Hibbs's prestidigitation to make a success of the school that he would launch years later in Richmond.

His impecunious father made some wise investments in coal mines, and hence was able to send young Henry to Brown University. At that prestigious Ivy League institution the youth not only took his B.A. degree, majoring in sociology, but he became deeply interested in the problems of urban communities. He made it a point to get into contact with civic and social agencies in Providence, and to learn something of their modus operandi. It was a strong motivating force in his lifelong concern with urban affairs.

Following his graduation in 1910, and a bicycle tour of Europe, Hibbs enrolled in the School for Social Workers in Boston. Along with his work there he matriculated at Brown University for an M.A. After completing that course successfully, Hibbs enrolled in Columbia University, New York, in quest of a Ph.D. He got it in 1916. His dissertation dealt with "Infant Mortality: Its Relation to Social and Industrial Conditions."

Young Hibbs had visited Richmond years before, and he spoke later of his "veritable worship of the city and its memories." It was natural, therefore, for him to find Richmond a place where he would like to make his career.

A group of private citizens invited him to come to the city in 1917 to head the newly organized Richmond School of Social Work and Public Health. The chairman of the committee was the Rev. Dr. J. J. Scherer, the beloved pastor of First English Lutheran Evangelical Church, on Stuart Circle. Dr. Scherer served as chairman of the school's board until 1925, when the institution was taken over by the College of William and Mary. The board then became advisory, and Scherer continued as chairman until his death in 1956. Virginia Commonwealth University's dormitory at the corner of Harrison and Franklin streets is named for him.

When Hibbs arrived to head the impecunious school, with not even a room to meet in and a grand total of $400 in the school's bank, he began scrounging around to find quarters. He was introduced to John Hirschberg, chairman of the City Administrative Board, and Hirschberg told him he could use, rent free, three former bedrooms on the third floor of a building occupied on the two lower floors by the Richmond Juvenile and Domestic Relations Court. As there was no furniture in the rooms, Hibbs began buying second-hand chairs, tables, and a desk. Several straight chairs were acquired for $1.00 each, an office chair for $4.75 and a typing desk for $8.00. It was six months before a used roll-top desk could be found, at a cost of $25.00.

The institution Hibbs was launching in these munificent surroundings was to be for the education of social workers and public health nurses. It would be called the Richmond School of Social Work and Public Health until 1939, when the name would be changed to Richmond Professional Institute.

When it opened in October 1917, Hibbs was the only full-time teacher, as well as school head, janitor, and jack-of-all-trades. His salary was $2,000 a year, if the money could be found. Another full-time teacher was added four months later when Mrs. Bessie A. Haases became the instructor in public health nursing. She functioned for the first half of the semester, and was succeeded by Miss Maude E. Morse in the second half. In addition, Miss Loomis Logan was a part-time teacher in social work.

Since the United States had entered the world war, Hibbs was subject to the draft. The secretary of war assigned him to service in Richmond, where he was to carry out the plans of the American Red Cross for training women to work with the families of soldiers and sailors.

The first student to enroll in the school was Miss Mary Dupuy of Prince Edward County. Thirty students, all women, had been registered when the institution opened on October 11—seven in social work, and twenty-three in public health nursing. There were also twenty-four students in special wartime Red Cross Home Service Institutes. The juvenile court adjourned on a day in June 1918 to permit the commencement exercises to be held in the courtroom. The graduates included four caseworkers, eighteen public health nurses and eighteen Red Cross Home Service workers.

Dr. Wortley F. Rudd of the Medical College of Virginia faculty, vice chairman of the Board of Directors (trustees), offered the use of rooms at the college for night classes, but this proved to be of no help, since the students refused to use them; nauseating odors from the nearby anatomical laboratory "made them sick."

Hibbs realized that if his school was to get off of the ground it would have to involve some leading businessmen who could raise money for its operation. F. B. Dunford, a businessman, was treasurer of the board, but he was the only person from the business community who was active in the school's affairs.

The war gave the young director an opening. He had just arrived in Richmond when he read in a newspaper that many doctors in rural communities were leaving for war service. He took the article to State Health Commissioner Ennion G. Williams and Dr. Roy K. Flannagan, the assistant commissioner, and asked them if four-month courses training graduate nurses for work in counties with few, if any, doctors would be considered "essential war service." They agreed at once that it would, and promised to help, if needed funds could be raised. "Training Nurses to Take Doctors' Places" would be the slogan.

Henry Hibbs became acquainted with Wyndham R. Meredith, a prominent Richmond attorney, and explained the plan to him. Meredith was much interested, and said he knew the very man to assist with the fund raising. This was John M. Miller, Jr., who was about to be elected president of the First National Bank. Meredith took Hibbs to Miller, and the latter was immediately impressed. He agreed to head the campaign for funds and named Tazewell M. Carrington and I. J. Marcuse, two other leaders in the business community, as vice chairmen.

These men called together other prominent citizens to hear young Hibbs tell his story. The latter prepared carefully for this crucially important occasion. He and Miss Lila Spivey, a registered nurse and student at the school, rehearsed their presentation so well in advance that when they gave it to the group, with photographs of Miss Spivey ministering to ailing children in rural Wythe County, from which most of the doctors had departed, those present promptly opened their wallets. Everyone contributed, two as much as $1,000 each, and two others $500.

Mr. Miller continued to hold meetings in the succeeding years, down to about 1925, and approximately $73,000 was raised overall. The American Red Cross gave $10,000 additional, and the War Work Council of the YWCA $3,000.

A department of recreation was added to the curriculum in 1919, with Miss Claire McCarthy, for many years active with the playgrounds in Richmond, as the first student.

The first catalogue described the School of Social Work and Public Health as a strictly urban institution, "the first of the kind in the South," and unlike a conventional college or university. This ambitious appraisal seemed a bit incongruous, in view of the primitive quarters occupied by the institution. It soon became apparent that a new home for the school would have be found. The vestry of historic Monumental Church rose to the occasion in 1919, and offered the adjoining three-story Beers-Newton house at 1228 East Broad Street rent free.

While the Beers-Newton house, built in 1839, provided more commodious quarters than had previously been available, there were definite problems. The bathroom was in a separate addition, reached by going out of doors. Then, too, the structure was located in what might almost have been termed the tenderloin, since it was near the just-abolished red light district, and almost next door to "jail alley." Night students were reluctant to enter the area. The "urban problems" with which the school concerned itself were a bit too close for comfort at the address.

So in 1923 there was another move—to an old residence at 17 North

Fifth Street, across the street from the YWCA. Rent was $75 a month. The gymnasium and cafeteria of the "Y" were available to the students.

Again, this was no final solution. There had to be a more suitable building in a better location. Conferences were held with President J. A. C. Chandler of William and Mary with regard to the possibility that that institution would take over the school. Chandler agreed that William and Mary would maintain the school in Richmond, provided it acquired a permanent building "in a good central neighborhood." It was recommended that this building be the Saunders-Willard house, 827 West Franklin Street, at the corner of Shafer Street. Erected in the 1880s by E. A. Saunders, and a typical example of late Victorian residential architecture, the commodious, three-story structure, with a large basement, and stable in the rear, offered many more possibilities for the school's headquarters than any of its previous homes. In recent times this residence had been occupied by Joseph E. Willard, U.S. Ambassador to Spain, and then by the University Club.

There remained the all-important question of how to acquire the building. Once more the business community was appealed to, and it came through handsomely. Tazewell M. Carrington was chairman of the drive for funds, and a total of $103,925 was raised. This was more than the $73,000 cost of the house, plus $23,000 for repairs and alterations.

Possession of Founders' Hall, as it was called, was obtained on June 1, 1925, and the remodeling began. This was one of many examples of the ingenuity of Henry Hibbs in adapting old houses, stables, and lofts to the needs of his institution. The kitchen in the main house became a classroom, and a new kitchen and dining room were put in the basement. To quote from Dr. Hibbs's history: "The director's [Hibbs's] office and the general office were located in the large sun parlor which then stood on the Shafer Street side of the building. A second classroom was arranged in the rear parlor on the west side, and a third classroom on the second floor rear, above the old kitchen. The other parlor was used for a library. The second and third floors were used as a dormitory for women."

The foregoing was an example of how, over and over again, residences that had seen better days would be rehabilitated and used for educational purposes. And the adjoining stable provided an even more striking example. To quote Dr. Hibbs: "The old stable in the rear . . . was an unusually fine brick structure of one and one-half stories with a gable roof and dormer windows. There were two rooms on the first floor, the front one for the carriages and buggies, and the rear one for the horse stalls. The upper floor contained coachman's quarters in the rear and the hayloft in front. In remodeling the stable all the partitions and the entire upper floor were removed, and the whole stable made into one large room, about 40 × 60 feet. A new maple floor was laid. This made a small gymnasium, with a high ceiling."

The acquisition of Founders' Hall and the stable behind it was merely the beginning of what would be a whole series of purchases, by one means or another, of properties throughout the immediate area, most of them somewhat down-at-heel, but all of them more or less susceptible to use for teaching purposes. Much of this was made possible by the Great Depression. Property values plummeted, and Hibbs was quick to pick up houses and subsidiary structures at bargain prices. Students who were unable to pay tuition at more expensive colleges became available for his low-cost school. The Works Progress Administration, another spin-off from the depression, was an additional godsend to the School of Social Work and Public Health. So was the National Youth Administration.

Another calamity, World War I, had made it possible, as we have seen, for Hibbs to persuade John M. Miller, Jr., to raise critically needed funds in order to train nurses to take the place of physicians absent in the services. Now it was the economic catastrophe of 1929–30 that gave the ingenious Hibbs another opening.

Whereas President Chandler of William and Mary seemed at first to take a keen interest in the little school, "the faculty [of W & M] was monumentally disinterested," according to Hibbs, "and Dr. Chandler increasingly adopted the faculty view," Rozanne G. Epps, director of VCU's evening, summer, and off-campus studies, has pointed out.

For the first year in the new building at 827 West Franklin, the total full-time enrollment was 52, with 393 part-time students, mainly at night. There were three full-time teachers, in addition to Director Hibbs—one each for social work, public health nursing, and recreational leadership. William and Mary contributed four part-time teachers, and there were five additional part-time teachers in night classes.

Mrs. Virgie A. Chalkley began her service as hostess at Founders' Hall in 1926, and impressed the students with her constant concern for their well-being. She also had charge of the dances.

Several full-time teachers who would be associated with the school for many years joined the faculty soon thereafter. These included Miss Theresa

Pollak, founder of the School of Art; Miss Aileen Shane, professor of social work; and Dr. Margaret L. Johnson, who would become dean of students.

Peeping Toms were a problem outside the women's dormitory until it was pointed out to the girls that they were not pulling down their shades. A further complaint came from citizens in the immediate vicinity who protested that the young women made too much noise telling their dates goodnight on the front steps of Founders' Hall. There was another stir when a workman caught a live possum in the matted ivy on the roof of a porch behind the hall. He took the animal home for his dinner.

The opening of the School of Art in 1928 was a significant milestone in the ongoing development of the institution. The School of Social Work and the School of Public Health Nursing were the two original schools, and Recreational Leadership had been added in 1919. A night college, or extension division, had been opened the following year.

Miss Theresa Pollak was the inspiration, from the outset, for the School of Art. She has given the facts in some detail in her engagingly written memoir, *An Art School: Some Reminiscences.* Miss Pollak described the initial events as follows: "In the spring of 1928 I participated in a group showing of paintings at the Woman's Club, after which Mr. Charles Smith, then a free-lance commercial artist, and Mr. William Young of Young's Art Shop, both having seen my work, told me that Dr. Hibbs was building a studio in a remodelled stable, and planning to start a real art department with classes in drawing, painting, and related subjects. They both suggested me for the drawing and painting job, and so I had my first interview with Dean Hibbs."

The interview was altogether satisfactory in one respect, since Hibbs told her that she was to teach "a day class in the school if I had as many as five students." The slight hitch was that she had to produce the students. This she proceeded to do. "I spent hours on the telephone," she wrote, "calling up everyone who to my knowledge had ever evinced an interest in art." When the class convened in September, there were about twenty students, well beyond her expectations. As a result of this success, Miss Pollak was permitted to offer a night class and also another for children on Saturday mornings. The School of Art, which would become nationally known, was in business.

The other early school that would achieve a national reputation was the School of Social Work. Hibbs said it was the first of its type in the South.

Founded in 1917, the original requirements for admission were maturity and the ability to work with people. It was not until some twenty years later that schools of social work throughout the country required college graduation for admission. This requirement was added in 1939–40. Several decades later this School of Social Work would become the largest, as well as the oldest, graduate school in the academic division of Virginia Commonwealth University.

An interesting phase of the school's activity began in 1928 when young Miss Alice Whiteside (now Alice Whiteside Jorg) came to Richmond, after studies at Harvard, Boston University, and Columbia. She gave afternoon and evening classes for adults in public speaking, the world's great plays, and play production. The following year Hibbs asked her to head a department of speech and drama, which she did for a dozen years. There was only a bare stage when she arrived, and absolutely no equipment with which to present dramatic productions. Within six months she had somehow managed to persuade Richmond firms and individuals to contribute the funds for what the *Richmond* magazine called "a beautifully equipped small theatre." Miss Whiteside also gave day classes designed to teach social workers how to produce simple plays and pageants, to provide entertainment for camps and playgrounds.

The institution founded by Henry H. Hibbs revolved to a large extent about him and Mrs. Hibbs in the early days. Mrs. Hibbs was scholarly, like her husband. She was the former Jessie Rowe Persinger, and they met when both were students at Columbia University. Miss Persinger, the daughter of a Methodist minister from Alabama, was getting her M.A. in mathematics at Columbia when he was getting his Ph.D. They were married in 1918, the year after he founded the School of Social Work and Public Health. She taught math for two years at Richmond's John Marshall High School.

The School of Social Work and Public Health remained small until after the close of World War II, and for most of that time was centered in Founders' Hall. Even after the Allison mansion at 910 West Franklin Street was acquired in 1938 as the Hibbs residence, and for other purposes, Dr. and Mrs. Hibbs had a close relationship with the girls. Anne Powell, later Mrs. Dave E. Satterfield III, who graduated from RPI in 1943, and was voted May Queen and "most beautiful" in her senior year, said the Hibbses were almost like a father and mother to the students.

They served nothing alcoholic to the undergraduates, either during or after prohibition. Mrs. Hibbs was a prohibitionist. Dr. Hibbs went along with her views on this, and may well have been in agreement. Although the punch at the Hibbses' receptions was never spiked, the girls seem to have taken this in stride. Mrs. Hibbs was especially popular with them, and taught them riding, making no charge. She is said to have had a fall from her horse on one occasion and to have broken both arms, but to have remounted and ridden home.

The school had been a branch of William and Mary since 1925, but no state funds were appropriated for its support until 1940. This seems to be the only example in Virginia history of a state institution that got no state appropriation over a period of fifteen years. The fact that Hibbs managed to keep it going under such circumstances is another evidence of his ingenuity.

Despite obvious handicaps, he succeeded in securing for $85,000 the huge Ginter mansion at Franklin and Shafer streets, built in 1888 by Major Lewis Ginter at a cost of $250,000—an enormous sum in that era. It had been serving as the Richmond Public Library, but the library was moving to its present location at First and Franklin. John M. Miller, Jr., was once more the financial genius who worked out a plan for purchasing it over a period of years with loans and student fees. William and Mary put up $10,000 toward the needed amount. The building was of crucial assistance in providing space for a variety of school purposes. It would later become the administration building for the academic campus of VCU. The large brick stable was turned into the A. A. Anderson Gallery of Art, thanks to the generosity of Colonel A. A. Anderson, a wealthy artist and patron of the arts. Hibbs learned that Colonel Anderson was in Richmond, told him of the availability of the Ginter hayloft for an art studio, and secured his financial assistance. The colonel was anxious to exhibit his own work, and did so in the stable, after its rehabilitation.

Another valuable acquisition is these years was the Ritter-Hickok house on West Franklin Street just east of Founders' Hall, built in 1855 and picked up in 1939 for the bargain price of $17,500, thanks to the depression. To the depression was also due the fact that the house was put in order with WPA funds. During the Civil War, when it was in a relatively rural area and had kitchens, outhouses, and smokehouses, one or more of these structures was used as a prison for spies, according to a wartime issue of the *New York Herald.* This last has not been verified, however.

From 1938 to 1942 the school acquired a dozen additional properties on West Franklin, Park Avenue, and Shafer Street. The total price for all of them was $115,000, although they were appraised at $288,600.

Three other fine residences were brought into the orbit of the school somewhat later—the A. D. Williams house at Franklin and Laurel streets, the Millhiser residence at 916 West Franklin, and the Frederic W. Scott mansion at 909 West Franklin. The last-named, the most imposing of the three, is used only in part by the school, as Mrs. Elisabeth Scott Bocock, daughter of Mr. Scott, occupied a portion of the building. After her death in 1984, members of her family continued to occupy it.

These and other handsome houses along Franklin were gradually purchased, and were restored and preserved—a great service to the city, and to the maintenance of its architectural heritage. The three blocks from Monroe Park to Ryland Street were placed on the Virginia Landmarks Register and the National Register of Historic Places in the 1970s. The great trees that line the thoroughfare almost form an archway above, like a cathedral nave.

The RPI Foundation, an outgrowth of the citizens' committee which aided the fledgling school in its early struggles, was of crucial importance in assisting in the purchase of numerous properties. As time went on, apartment houses were acquired and turned into dormitories.

The changing of the school's name to Richmond Professional Institute in 1939 was a factor in enabling it to obtain more funds. Also, the state made its first appropriation in 1940. It was for only $10,000, but was at least a beginning. This small sum was increased gradually during the decade until by the 1950–52 biennium the state appropriation was $99,540 per year.

The name Richmond Professional Institute was affixed to the school at the suggestion of John Stewart Bryan, president of the College of William and Mary, who felt that although the school was affiliated with the college, it was an entirely different type of institution, "of the occupational, technological or professional type," and hence should have a distinctive name. There seemed to be general agreement that the change was appropriate, and RPI was born.

What manner of man was this Henry H. Hibbs, who had performed such prodigies in getting Richmond Professional Institute under way?

His was not an ebullient or outgoing personality. "I don't think anyone was really close to Dr. Hibbs; he was an aloof person," said Maurice Bonds, head of the fine arts department. Yet "there were little warm contacts through the years." Bonds mentioned that "occasionally you would break through his authority figure, which he definitely was, and you would see a very human side—for instance, when he had his little red-haired grandchildren out in the street playing with them."

"It wasn't unusual," Bonds went on, "to see Dr. Hibbs walking or running around the campus with plumbing tools—or running behind someone who had plumbing tools." It is even recorded that a teacher looked out of her classroom window and saw the top of a man's hat coming up a ladder in her direction. As the moving figure came abreast of the window, it turned out to be Hibbs, who bowed, removed his hat, said "Good morning," and continued on to the roof, which he wished to examine.

Dr. Hibbs lost a joint from one of his fingers when he caught it in a door on a railroad train. He began losing his hearing at a fairly early age. One consequence was that he felt reluctant to drive a car, and Mrs. Hibbs did most of the driving. For years they used a Model-T Ford, or "tin lizzie," which was jokingly christened "Lizzie Borden" after the accused ax murderess from Massachusetts.

When Hibbs held a committee meeting, he was said to turn off his hearing aid quietly after he had said his say concerning some question before the group. The others would them express themselves, and after they had concluded, he would reputedly turn the hearing aid back on and say, "Now this is what we've decided to do."

He had a reproduction of a Renoir nude on his desk, under glass, but would raise the glass quickly and put it out of sight if someone was coming to his office who might raise a question.

As a student, Maurice Bonds went to class one day in shorts. A few hours later he was called to Hibbs's office. "Young man," said the prexy, "don't you ever let me catch you going to class in shorts." Looking back in 1976 on this episode, Bonds remarked wryly, "I believe girls come to class today with practically nothing on."

This interview with Maurice Bonds was one of some sixteen conducted by Professor Alden G. Bigelow, of the history and political science faculty, in the middle and late seventies with prominent figures in the school. In providing this oral history for students of the institution, Dr. Bigelow performed a genuine service.

Mrs. Mary S. King, secretary to Hibbs from 1956 to 1970, described him in another Bigelow interview as "one of the kindest, most thoughtful men I've ever known, and he is also a genius." Mrs. Jane Bell Gladding, former dean of women, for whom the new dormitories were named in 1984, agreed that Hibbs was a genius.

Mrs. King also noted that he was always tinkering around in the workshop after hours, and "this made noise and disturbed some of the students in class." One day he found a cardboard sign on the door, in red ink: "Cut out the damn noise!"

Hibbs was "a humorist," in the opinion of James L. Dunn, director of special projects for the office of university advancement, who worked under him for many years. "He had a story adaptable to every situation," said Dunn. "Invariably it would relate to his many experiences and encounters as the leader of RPI."

One of the ladies of the State Board of Motion Picture Censors told Hibbs she heard he had been sick, but did not know of it until he had recovered, and added that she would have sent him flowers, had she been aware of his indisposition. "Don't bother about the flowers," he joked, "I would have liked to have had some of those little bits that you snipped out of the movies."

He had an eagle eye for any sort of waste around the campus. "A light had been left on in a lecture room," Jane Bell Gladding said, "and Dr. Hibbs demanded to know 'What's that light doing on? There's no lecture going on here.' "

Like Mrs. Hibbs, he was fond of riding, and also of fishing. He caught an eight-and-a-half pound bass, twenty-two-and-a-half inches long, in a Chesterfield County pond. He was also a collector of old prints, and gave his collection of Richmond prints to the Valentine Museum.

The Hibbses had two daughters, Jessie and Mary Sue. Jessie married Nathaniel J. Hawke and Mary Sue married James V. Doss, Jr. Mary Sue was president of the RPI Student Government Association in her senior year. She died of leukemia in 1964—a terrible blow to her parents. Her father was so broken up that some doubted that he would be able to continue as head of the school. But he did.

After the School of Social Work and the School of Arts were established, courses in chemistry and biology were added in the early 1930s, with Dr. Doris Fales as head for the next two decades.

A major development in 1937 was the opening of the School of Distributive Education, originally known as the School of Store Service Education. Dr. B. H. vanOot, head of the bureau of trade and industrial education of the State Department of Education, was responsible for this addition to the curriculum. Hibbs admitted later that he had never heard of distributive education when vanOot told him that he (vanOot) could provide funds for two-thirds of the teachers' salaries for such a school. The offer was accepted, and the catalogue announced that the new school would be "for the training of men and women for executive positions in department stores, mercantile establishments, advertising and other distributive trades, and also for the training of teachers of retailing and salesmanship in schools, colleges and evening schools, staff training in stores, etc." Miss Louise Bernard was the organizer and first director of the school. She devoted full time to the task for several years and then functioned on a part-time basis until 1957. Here was an excellent example of the sort of schooling provided by Hibbs's institution which was not to be had anywhere else in Virginia. It fitted in with Hibbs's view that the primary object of his school was to furnish students with the means for earning a livelihood by the study of a profession. There was, however, provision in the curriculum for the liberal arts and the humanities—on a small scale, at first, but gradually expanded.

At the same time, it was contended that the student "should be permitted to devote the greater part of his or her time . . . usually about three fourths, to the study of the professional subject chosen." Also: "The decision as to what classes the student should take in each of his years of study should not be made by a general college faculty but by a professional faculty, with the help of professional associations or advisory committees made up of leaders in the profession or occupation concerned." These principles, it was argued, "were merely the basic principles and practices of the so-called land grant colleges or universities." The president of one of the largest such institutions was quoted as saying that "there are certain areas . . . which demand specialized training from the very start of the undergraduate's education."

Professional areas to which the Richmond Professional Institute extended its operations included art, design, music, music education, business, distribution, advertising, accounting, real estate, professional drama and speech, occupational therapy, commercial art, costume design, interior decoration, nursing, law enforcement, dramatic art, and other fields.

It is little short of incredible that the school found it possible to expand into these areas of study with such miserable financial support for several decades. Many wondered how the institution managed to function at all, but Hibbs was not dismayed. Long afterward he wrote: "These lean years were not a time of frustration or complaint. Rather they were a time of planning, research, and of developing new methods of doing things by ingenuity and persistent problem solving. In fact, the period . . . was a time of great progress along many lines." He pointed out that the campus was greatly extended; enrollment jumped from 51 full-time students in 1925 to 451 in 1940 and 1,107 in 1952; full accreditation by the Southern Association of Colleges came in 1953. By then the curriculum had been expanded from the two original schools to well over a dozen schools or divisions. "Moreover, none of these duplicated the work of other colleges in Virginia," Hibbs wrote. "All were different, and some were the first of the kind to be offered in the South."

The foregoing was accomplished despite the fact that faculty salaries were the lowest at any state institution in Virginia. It was not until the middle or late fifties that RPI's pay scale was brought into line with the lowest-paying state supported institutions.

Hibbs listed a number of lessons that he said he had learned during those "lean years": A mid-city location has real advantages in that it makes possible the employment of highly qualified teachers on a part-time basis, "just as schools of medicine have done for years." Also, "a reasonable number of old buildings can be economically and efficiently used by an urban school."

This type of plant can be utilized more efficiently, as shown by a survey of classroom use by the State Council of Higher Education in 1964. It showed that RPI had "far and away the highest average number of periods each week in which its classrooms were used . . . 33.4 periods per week as compared with an average of 18.9 periods per week" in all state-supported colleges, and 17.0 per week in the country as a whole. RPI was listed in the top ten percent in the nation in this regard. Furthermore, the need for scholarship aid in such an institution as RPI was less than that at many schools, since business establishments provided numerous work opportunities for students. In addition, housing for undergraduates could be made available in the neighborhood, and many students lived at home.

The school of art, founded in 1928 in a converted stable by Theresa Pollak, was a success from the first. Marion M. Junkin joined her in 1934, "and we were a good team," she wrote. "The two of us together planned and formed the character and objective of the school." Junkin taught at RPI for eight years, and then at Washington and Lee University for many more.

Miss Pollak had studied at the Art Students' League in New York, where nude models were routine, but they were by no means routine in conservative Richmond. Hibbs was afraid to allow such models, and was willing to go no further than two-piece bathing suits. But he attended a burlesque show in New York, where the girls wore only G-strings. With this example in mind, he relaxed a bit on his return to town, and decreed that G-strings would be permitted in art school, and the men would wear shorts.

"We finally got so we left off the G-straps, and the men wore just the athletic straps," Miss Pollak explained in later years. "An elderly woman went to the governor and complained because we had nude models." Nothing came of it.

There was a bit of a dustup on one occasion when a young woman was posing in the nude, and there was loud knock on the door. When the door was opened, her husband burst in. "He made quite a scene, he was furious," Miss Pollak said.

She was not against all modern art, by any means, but she had serious reservations concerning certain latter-day manifestations. "Music has become in large part noise; subjective, expressive painting has become hard, schematic, ugly, or minimal," Pollak wrote in 1968. "A shoe, any object, becomes ART because an artist deigns to sanctify it with his signature."

When the first exhibit of contemporary art was brought to the school, she took her children's class to see it. "A somewhat pompously dressed woman" delivered a blast against what she saw there. "I could dip my skirt in a bucket of paint and do something better than that," she snorted, Miss Pollak said, "designating a very lovely Kandinsky of the early free-flowing period." The irate lady pronounced it "an insult to God and humanity for you to bring those innocent children to see these monstrosities." With that, "she flounced out of the gallery."

The art school was "severely censured" by the central administration for presenting, as part of its Art Festival, the dance act of Robert Morris and Yvonne Rainer. "As I think back on the great beauty of this performance," Theresa Pollak wrote in 1968, "and the lasting effect it has had on me, I cannot but feel that it was well worth the reprimand. . . . The large gym was filled to capacity. . . . The dancers, completely nude and facing each other in close embrace, advance slowly and rhythmically across the narrow walkway, steps measured to loud speaker music and accompanied by readings from the notebooks of da Vinci. . . . The effect was pure and classic. One felt somehow the whole of life and its meaning had passed before one."

Miss Pollak's credentials for founding the art school were altogether obvious. An artist of marked talent, in later years she had group exhibits in galleries in New York, Richmond, at the University of Virginia, and elsewhere. She won awards for painting in New York, Richmond, and Norfolk, and is represented in permanent collections in various Virginia museums and institutions, and in private collections in New York, Washington and Richmond.

During the early years of the school that would later become RPI, the student body—almost 100 percent female—was highly respectful to members of the administration and faculty. There was nothing remotely comparable to the cantankerous, even insolent, behavior of many northern and western student bodies nearly half a century later, when deans were thrown down steps, and other faculty members were manhandled. *Atlas,* the student newspaper, was seldom, if ever, critical of the administration. There was a mild flurry of adverse comment when new rules were announced concerning the cutting of classes, but this subsided promptly.

Atlas, edited in 1932 by Harriet Montague, did assail some of the more preposterous carryings-on of the students in what was called "Duc Week"—later spelled "Duck Week." This was the week in the early fall when the freshmen (that was the term used then for incoming females), were subjected to somewhat ridiculous high jinks or mild hazing. *Atlas* pronounced this "undoubtedly the most painful experience one undergoes during his four years of college." The paper pointed out that "a majority of the time-honored institutions of advanced learning have long since abandoned this custom in order to raise their standards of culture and refinement."

The appeal was not heeded. Finally, in 1941 Hibbs directed that most of the monkeyshines be dropped, and that "the only dress requirement that freshmen have to follow is the wearing of 'Rat Caps' on campus." This rendered obsolete the directions appearing in the same issue of the student newspaper, directing freshmen to wear "odd socks and gloves, flat-heel shoes, sun glasses, white blouses and dark skirts, and minus make up, nail-polish and jewelry." It was further stated that "boys, like the girls, are subject to the same mad costume rules . . . rat caps, duck signs, sun-glasses, trousers three inches above the sock top, with no suspenders, green and gold bow tie."

But Prexy Hibbs apparently relented two years later, for the student paper said at that time: "Every day will bring the freshmen to school in different apparel . . . aprons, green and yellow, bows cocked at absurd angles atop even more absurd hair-dos . . . masculine members with delicately rouged cheeks and generous applications of lipstick."

These carryings-on were abandoned during World War II, but in 1948 "Rat Week," as it was then called, was back with a vengeance. Males were now enrolled in great numbers, and they were again required to doll themselves up in ridiculous ways.

All of which brought forth acid commentary from a minority of the masculine contingent. A junior signing himself "Howard Fitch" wrote a letter to the *Proscript* (*Atlas* had changed its name to *Proscript*), denouncing these "childish antics," and adding: "Ask anyone in the psychology department the reason a person would want to strut around with an arm-band of authority, a look of scorn, and a fat, loud mouth. The last guy to do these things . . . was shot and hung upside down in a filling station in Italy."

Another student, Harry Wyland, Jr., supported "Fitch," saying, "It would seem far more practical to devote the considerable energy which goes into harassing freshmen into some activity which would genuinely integrate these students into RPI life."

But the freshman class signed a communiqué saying "we have profited much from Rat Week," and the same issue of the *Proscript* took a similar stand. Lester Simpson, another student, asked a teacher in the psychology department for his view and the professor laid it down that Rat Week is "a good sign" and went on to say: "It shows that the student body has some spirit, and this sort of thing is a spirit builder. We certainly need it here." Rat Week was observed thereafter until RPI joined with MCV in 1968.

RPI had the same alma mater song as William and Mary, and this led to suggestions that RPI should have its own song. The two institutions were affiliated from 1925 to 1962, but it was contended that the William and Mary alma mater was to the same tune as several alma maters in other sections of the country, and this was felt to be unsatisfactory. The *Proscript* lamented in 1940 that the students didn't know the song, and that it had to be "printed at the end of the convocation program to assure the dean, faculty members and school speakers that we do have a school song." When RPI was separated from William and Mary in 1962, there were renewed calls for a different alma mater, especially since the William and Mary song contained the words "William and Mary, loved of old." A contest in 1963 for a new composition brought no satisfactory results.

While it was affiliated with William and Mary, RPI's colors were the same as those of the Williamsburg college, namely, green, gold, and white. In 1963 RPI adopted its own colors, blue and gray. With the establishment of VCU in 1968, both branches of the university adopted black and gold.

RPI's honor system had its ups and downs over the years. An editorial in *Atlas* in 1933 stated that "our honor system is not being supported by the student body as a whole. . . . There is something fundamentally wrong in a system when it permits the theft of books, gym clothes, money from pocketbooks and even information. . . . let us uphold our honor system."

The system wasn't really a system, "except informally," Dr. Hibbs said many years later, following his retirement. He was its staunch supporter throughout his tenure as head of the institution.

Atlas printed the honor code in 1936. The code called for expulsion for lying, cheating, stealing or violation of a written pledge. It urged students to report violators.

There were numerous editorials during the 1940s on the honor system, and several students were expelled for violating it. The *Proscript* denounced cheating and plagiarism in 1947, and spoke of students "condoning" these offenses. About three-fourths of students interviewed by the paper said they would not report violators. Later in that year some 400 undergraduates demonstrated in support of the system, despite what were termed "innumerable honor code violations." The *Proscript* upheld the code strongly throughout the 1940s and 1950s. There were quite a few expulsions.

Professor Alden Bigelow felt that the system worked well in the 1950s, and Jane Bell Gladding agreed. "But then it broke down and sort of disappeared," he went on. "We were changing from an elitist to an egalitarian society . . . honor systems are identified with a more elitist group." Bigelow said he used to walk out of his classroom during quizzes, "but now [1975] I stay." Professor E. Allan Brown, head of the English department, said: "I have given up trying to monitor in any way. I simply give them the material, give them the test. . . . I grew up under a rigid honor system at Chapel Hill; it worked." Dr. Brown added that he didn't know if the RPI honor system "was ever formally dropped . . . it simply withered."

The system continued functioning spasmodically in the early sixties, and several students were expelled for violations. The *Proscript* expressed outrage over checks being run at the library exit of books and briefcases, saying the library evidently was unaware that an honor system exists at RPI. But by 1965 half of 132 students interviewed pronounced the honor code "totally ineffective." Yet a few months later two students withdrew from college rather than stand trial. In 1966 the students voted 629 to 66 to abandon the policy of expulsion for failure to report another's violation, but the Student Congress refused by a close vote to make the change.

35. Dr. Henry H. Hibbs, founder and head of Richmond Professional Institute, and Mrs. Hibbs. She was much beloved by the students.

36. Richmond Professional Institute had its beginnings on the third floor, 1112 Capitol Street, site of the Virginia State Library. (From a painting by Belle Worsham).

37. Students in the Richmond School of Social Work and Public Health, afterwards RPI, in training for Red Cross service in World War I. Henry H. Hibbs, *back row, left.*

38. Founders' Hall, the former Saunders-Willard house at 827 West Franklin Street, to which the school moved in 1925.

39. Lewis Ginter mansion, Shafer and Franklin streets, which became the administration building.

40. Miss Theresa Pollak, founder of the RPI school of art in 1928, and its inspiration for years thereafter, contemplates one of her paintings.

TEN

Hibbs Is Succeeded by Oliver

WORLD WAR II CHANGED THE WHOLE COMPLEXION of the Richmond Professional Institute by bringing in hundreds of male students under the GI Bill, whereas until then the institute was almost solidly female. Enrollment jumped in 1946 to 1,168 full-time matriculates, of whom 458 were men, including 374 veterans. In 1940, on the eve of the war, there had been only 476 full-time students, of whom about a dozen were males. Before the war, furthermore, Hibbs was the only male administrative officer, and most of the teachers were women, but after the conflict ended men were increasingly employed in administrative and teaching positions.

Three alumni of RPI lost their lives in the war. Horace A. Bass, who joined the naval air force in 1941, almost immediately after the attack on Pearl Harbor, was killed in the South Pacific. James Henry Booth also gave his life in the war, and Lee G. Crutchfield, Jr., was killed at Fort Ord, California, early in the action.

Several faculty members were summoned for war work. The first of these was C. Hart Schaaf, associate professor of government and public administration. Beginning with the second semester of the 1941–42 session, RPI instituted various courses designed to prepare students for wartime activities, such as nursing, first aid, nutrition, recreation, and social work.

When the Korean War broke out in 1950, many RPI students were called up in the draft or the reserves. Permission was given by the administration to these men to complete their studies under special conditions. Eighty percent of the faculty and student body voted in favor of establishing an

ROTC. President Harry S. Truman announced deferments for college students who were maintaining adequate scholastic averages.

One of the men who joined the faculty at this period was Dr. E. Allan Brown, a Ph.D. in English from the University of North Carolina, who came in 1951. He said he found Hibbs "rather intimidating" in his first interview. As he left the room, Hibbs called out to him, "By the way, you are the only teacher in your department with a Ph.D.—that makes you chairman." During the conversation he noted that when the phone rang on Hibbs's desk, "a bright light came on, the signal that the phone was ringing." Since Hibbs was deaf, he had rigged up this arrangement so he would be sure to answer the phone.

An idea of the low salaries paid at that time to faculty may be gained from the fact that as head of the English department, Dr. Brown received $3,420 for nine months. Hibbs told him that he would have to teach only fifteen hours, since he was chairman, whereas the others would teach eighteen. There were six on the English faculty during the fifties, whereas in the seventies there were forty-nine full-time. The first B.A. in English was offered in 1965.

Brown said he taught for years in attics, basements, and parlors, not to mention a furnace room. The department finally got a room to teach in at 1128 Floyd Avenue in the old Cathedral elementary school. Brown stated that the policy of the institute was to admit "almost anybody" as a student, since the administration wanted to give everybody a chance, but "it was hard to get a degree." If the student proved himself, "fine, he would stay"; if he didn't, "out he went."

Brown was enthusiastic concerning Mrs. Hibbs, whom he described as "a very lovely person." She would have delightful receptions for all the faculty, who numbered fewer than one hundred at that time.

The first entirely new building constructed on the campus was erected in 1951, following the release of $249,000 for the purpose by Governor John S. Battle. This was the "multipurpose" gymnasium on the 800 block of West Franklin Street. It was only 77 by 108 feet, and would have to be enlarged, but it was a landmark. Twenty-two buildings had been acquired by RPI up to that time, none with state funds.

One of the most popular courses at RPI over a long period was the sociology class of Dr. Alice Davis. Her lectures were reliably reported to be in such demand that would-be listeners stood outside when the classroom would not accommodate them all. Gypsy Rose Lee, the famous stripper, a friend of Dr. Davis, was a guest lecturer more than once in the 1940s. She seems to have appeared in normal attire, and there was no publicity. A more bizarre attendant was a monkey, brought to class by a student, Speck Henderson, who said he wanted to find out "if monkeys behave like human beings." The simian emptied a girl's pocketbook and proceeded to eat a tube of lipstick, after which it consumed some chalk and a bag of potato chips. A decade later the class was regaled by Sally Rand, the famous fan dancer, who was appearing on the midway at the Virginia State Fair. Sally, admitting to age fifty-three, lectured to standing room only, and was greeted with loud clapping on her arrival twenty-nine minutes late. She thanked those present for "the nice applause for me with my clothes on." She had lectured previously at Harvard and Johns Hopkins. Her discourse at RPI covered such subjects as bottle babies, the Oedipus complex, evils of the Marxist manifesto, extrasensory perception, vaudeville pratfalls and custard pies, and the art of the dance. Sally said her fans symbolized the flapping of wings in the moonlight, but she conceded that she had been arrested numerous times for "indecent exposure." Presumably in the interest of scholarship she had presented a set of her fans to the Chicago Historical Society.

Goldfish gulping, a divertissement that prevailed on campuses a decade or two previously, was unaccountably revived briefly in 1950 at RPI by James Hubbard and James Ring, two undergraduates. Hubbard swallowed three of the piscatorial specimens and Ring two. The *Proscript* recorded the epoch-making event. No digestive catastrophes appear to have resulted.

Efforts to form an RPI Alumni Association culminated in 1950 in the establishment of such an organization at a two-day homecoming. It was pronounced an "overwhelming success," with more than 150 alumni or alumnae in attendance. Jack Creasy, '42, was elected president. Formation of the association was to some extent the outgrowth of the founding of a Richmond chapter of alumni the previous spring, with Frank Duffy as the student spark plug. Mrs. James B. (Kathleen) Bullard, '41, who would be active in RPI and MCV affairs for several decades, was elected president. A Washington chapter was formed late in 1950.

With William O. Edwards of the faculty as "alumni coordinator," over 150 alumni attended the homecoming dinner in 1963. Homecoming the following year was by far the most successful yet held, with 750 alumni and their families on hand. Some 260 attended the dance. G. William Norris, later a member of the VCU board, was reelected president.

Separation from William and Mary was being discussed as a desirable objective in 1951, and Kathleen Bullard, as president of the Richmond alumni, strongly supported the move. She said separation was a necessity, if the college was to grow strong and prominent in its own right. "It would mean some loss of prestige," she conceded, "but RPI must learn to walk alone." President John Pomfret of William and Mary agreed that gradual separation was desirable, as did representatives of the RPI Alumni Association. The actual breach would not come until 1962.

So long as the affiliation with William and Mary continued, no married woman could hold an administrative position with RPI. Rosamond McCanless, longtime librarian, said that when she took the position, she had to "give my word that I wouldn't get married." She was "engaged at the time, but I hadn't set any date." Miss McCanless also had a few problems with works deemed obscene by some. Joyce's *Ulysses* and Boccaccio's writings were available in the library, by virtue of her decision. Also, a certain novel which she and Hibbs felt was "plain pornography" was on file, with Hibbs's approval, since a faculty member had ordered it.

Thefts of books from the library were almost unknown in the early days, in sharp contrast to the situation today, when books disappear by the hundreds at VCU and many other libraries. And by the same token, articles of all kinds now are stolen on campuses in this very different era.

The RPI library had a difficult time at first. Located on the first floor of the converted Ginter stable and carriage house, known then as the A. A. Anderson Gallery of Art, it had about 7,000 volumes in the 1930s, and employed a part-time librarian. Miss McCanless, an M.A. in English and B.A. in library science from the University of North Carolina, became the first full-time librarian in 1938, and a program of expansion began. When another floor was added to the building in 1940, the library moved to the second floor. The number of books rose to 16,000 in a short while, and there was steady growth thereafter. The librarian took two salient steps—she raised the fine for overdue books to five cents, and she ordered the students to take their feet off of the tables. In 1968 Miss McCanless said the collection totaled 86,000 volumes, but that it ought to total at least 500,000. First construction of the James Branch Cabell Library was about to begin.

On a subject unrelated to the library, Miss McCanless told of a "night watchman who used to go around the dorms at closing time making notes, such as "Ritter-Hickok h & k (hugging and kissing). He would always be giving these reports. . . . Once we had a young lady up because she had been kissing somebody and hugging right out on Franklin Street at 5 in the afternoon." She was given "a talking to."

Race relations seem to have been better at RPI than at most educational institutions. From the very outset, Dean Hibbs showed no prejudice, and blacks were enrolled in the graduate school of social work, founded about 1930. When six blacks applied for admission to undergraduate evening classes, all Hibbs wanted to know was, "Have they got the money?" They had it, and they were enrolled. Professors William E. Blake, Jr., Alden G. Bigelow, and E. Allan Brown agreed that race relations were exceptionally good at RPI. When the U.S. Supreme Court handed down the epoch-making ruling against school segregation in 1954, a large majority of students queried by the *Proscript* favored it. Two years later the paper expressed "intense dislike" for the doctrine of "interposition," supported and acclaimed by the *Richmond News Leader* as supposedly conferring on the states the right to "interpose" their power against the federal authority.

World War II and the demands that grew out of it were responsible for several significant developments at RPI. The School of Occupational Therapy was instituted in 1942 to serve the needs of the GIs and other young people disabled by military wounds or industrial accidents, as well as disease. It was the first such school in the South, and for a dozen years was headed by Miss Elizabeth Messick.

An interrelated development of genuine importance was the founding in 1955 of the School of Rehabilitation and Counseling, the second purely graduate school at RPI, social work being the earliest. This School of Rehabilitation was one of the first of its kind in the United States, and over the years trained more graduates than any of the other such programs in this country. Its function was to enable college graduates to counsel and help injured, afflicted, or disabled persons to hold jobs and lead satisfying lives. The school had an extremely important role in enabling RPI to attain university status. From the outset it received substantial support from the federal government, and hence did not have to struggle for survival, as so many other RPI departments did. In the 1970s it received from the U.S. Department of Health, Education and Welfare the rating of "highest honor," and in 1985 the federal government made a grant of $212,500 for the work. Dr. Howard Garner of the School of Education was in charge.

The School of Business, which has become so important to Richmond, had its origins in the needs of returning veterans after World War II. There had been a few beginnings before the conflict, but it was not until the session of 1946–47 that the school was formally organized. By 1949 half of the hundreds of veterans enrolled at RPI wanted to take business courses. By 1957–58 the State Department of Education began to assist the school. It would become RPI's largest department, with thousands of students.

Engineering and architecture courses also had their inception in the years immediately following the war. RPI and Virginia Polytechnic Institute made an arrangement whereby engineering and architecture students could attend RPI for two years and VPI for the next two, at the end of which time the B.S. degree would be conferred by VPI. This arrangement would be more fully developed in later years. There was also the School of Engineering Technology, offering a two-year terminal program for technicians in drafting and design, construction, architecture, electronics, civil engineering, and chemical technology.

One of the most important of all the educational contributions of RPI, and its successor VCU, is made by the evening school and summer school. These are especially valuable and significant in their contribution to the urban thrust of the institution. For about a decade and a half there has been a registration of about five thousand persons, with some six thousand additional day students who take courses at night, for a total of eleven thousand overall. These schools are among the largest of their kind in the United States. Obviously so great an enrollment gives substantial numbers of Richmonders a direct interest in the institution and its well-being, especially since the majority of the registrants are mature citizens, many of whom have daytime jobs.

Dr. Hibbs showed great interest in the evening and summer schools. Rozanne Epps, long their director, wrote that "Dean Hibbs often went to the classrooms at the first meeting in order to register the students and to determine whether or not enough tuition would be available to permit the class to run." There were times when the total enrollment exceeded that of the rest of RPI. R. Hill Fleet became head of the operation in 1950. He was succeeded by Melvin E. Fuller, and in 1964 by John A. Mapp, whose notable contribution will be noticed hereafter.

Marked increases in appropriations by the state to RPI in the 1950s were highly significant in the forward advance of the institution. Strange as it must seem, it was not until 1951 that RPI was allowed to present its case for greater appropriations to the governor, although the other state institutions had enjoyed the privilege for many years. Dr. Hibbs took advantage of the opportunity to stress the enormous disparity between the salary scales at RPI and the other urban college at Norfolk, on the one hand, and the pay scales at the remaining state-supported schools, on the other. At the same time, he contrasted the overall appropriations to the two groups. He showed that whereas the appropriation per student at RPI was $148 and at the Norfolk college $197, it was $788 at Virginia State, $553 at Longwood, $434 at Madison, and $363 at Radford. "Do we really do this?" Governor John S. Battle exclaimed on seeing the foregoing figures.

The result was that the appropriation to RPI rose from $99,540 per year in 1950–52 to $171,110 each year of the following biennium, and to $414,413 by 1958–60. In addition, as noted earlier, the first phase of the gymnasium on Franklin Street was constructed, and in 1956 an additional $382,000 made possible the completion of the building, the first structure at RPI built with state money.

Soon thereafter what came to be known as the Hibbs Building was erected at the corner of Shafer Street and Park Avenue, with classrooms and a variety of facilities. The first phase was completed in 1958–59, and was quite properly named for Dr. Hibbs. The second phase was added in 1967. The large and impressive Hibbs Building was an essential addition to the growing institution.

Hungarian refugees were flooding into this country in 1956–57, fleeing from the Russians, who had brutally crushed the Hungarian revolt of 1956. Louis Teykaerts, a Hungarian student at RPI, was head of Richmond Hungarian Relief, and other RPI undergraduates cooperated generously in raising funds and contributing food and clothing. The *Proscript* participated enthusiastically in the campaign. Most of the paper's staff were present when a group of twenty refugees arrived at 3:30 A.M. on board a U.S. Air Force plane from Camp Kilmer, New Jersey. They helped to show the new arrivals to their Richmond homes.

Another Hungarian refugee enrolled in RPI's advertising course in 1958. He was Jack Csaky, who had a hair-raising escape from the Russians when they moved into Hungary in 1944. The Csaky family, parents and three children, left everything behind and lived mainly in caves or in the woods during the winter of 1944–45. They arrived at Dresden, only to run into the Russians. The Csakys somehow escaped by the narrowest of margins—swimming a river, although two of them couldn't swim and had to grasp a log. They found their way to Munich, where they worked on a farm. In 1950 they managed to get to the United States, and obtained employment on a farm in Hanover County, Virginia. Years later Jack Csaky opened an advertising agency in Richmond after his graduation from RPI, and his brother, A. Steve Csaky, became Richmond's deputy chief of police.

Two alumni of RPI became successful authors—Nedra Tyre and Tom Robbins.

Nedra Tyre was a graduate of the School of Social Work and had been an instructor in the sociology department. By 1954 she had published four books, the latest of which was *Journey to Nowhere.* The *New York Times* said that in this work Miss Tyre had upheld her reputation as one of the most talented additions to the ranks of mystery writers.

Tom Robbins, a gifted and original author who leaped to best-sellerdom as a novelist a few years ago, was editor of the *Proscript* in his student days, and also wrote a column, "Walks on the Wild Side." In an editorial published in 1958, Robbins defended RPI from its critics, as follows:

> RPI is different. Because it is different we have been subjected to a quantity of unjustified criticism. Many Richmonders chuckle when told "I go to RPI," "You mean that queer school?" they bray.
>
> If we could only find a way to fritter away time at football games and fraternity meetings we might become respectable. If we could duplicate the wardrobes owned by students at institutions where the women dress like those sterile, bony creatures in *Vogue,* and the men are so Ivy League even their souls have belts in the back, we might become socially acceptable.
>
> We are proud that we are different. Proud that our college years are not wholly occupied with petty, superficial things. Proud that we are a professional school, that we maintain professional standards and an adult curriculum. Proud of our hard work, creative ability, and freedom from convention.
>
> Cobblestone is a more firm foundation on which to build than the green grasses of academic snobbery.

A couple of months later Robbins again rushed to the defense of RPI when Bill Stern, the radio sportscaster, made the astonishing statement that colleges that don't take part in intercollegiate football are potential breeding grounds for communists. "Young people," Stern said, "are charged with emotional electricity, and if this energy is not directed into proper channels it will be released into improper ones."

Robbins ridiculed this thesis: "If the young Red continues to think and to read and to mature, and if he has turned to the left to compensate for some physical or psychological inadequacy, he soon recognizes Communism as bitter folly and directs his energy to causes more worthy of his time and talent." This cogent and logical riposte did contain the solecism "irregardless," but was otherwise couched in Robbins's lucid and forceful prose.

As a novelist, Robbins is wholly unconventional and unpredictable. His novels to date are *Another Roadhouse Attraction, Even Cowgirls Get the Blues, Still Life with Woodpecker* and *Jitterbug Perfume.* Such titles are sufficiently bizarre, but the books' contents are even more so. Consider the cast of characters in his latest work, *Jitterbug Perfume,* as described by Randy Sue Coburn in a hilarious recent interview with the author in the *Richmond Times-Dispatch,* for which newspaper he worked as a copy editor for a couple of years after his graduation from RPI: "This time, Robbins' cast includes a 1,000-year old janitor, a genius Seattle waitress, the shabbily genteel proprietress of a New Orleans perfumery, and a Timothy Leary-type character named Dr. Wiggs Dannyboy, who established the Last Laugh Foundation to explore immortality and brain science. The lusty goat god Pan, a minor presence in each of Robbins' previous novels, is a full-fledged character here, showing up at Descartes's funeral to declare, 'I stink, therefore I am.' "

For many years there were complaints of vast indifference in the ranks of the student body toward the affairs of the Student Government Association. There was difficulty in getting candidates to run for office in the association. Officers had responsibility for the Honor Council, and it was suggested that the council should be separately elected. In 1959 the president of the Student Government Association divided nonsupporters into three groups—those who "work and do not have time for that sort of thing"; those who claim "they never see announcements, no one ever tells them anything is going on"; and those who "see no sense in student government, when it is ruled by the administration, so they could not do anything anyway."

There were many exceptionally pretty girls at RPI during these years, to judge from photographs appearing in the *Proscript.* "Queens" of this and that were chosen, including an "oyster queen" who didn't like oysters, and "sweethearts" of various kinds. A particular star was Genie Spencer of Martinsville, a music major who won three titles in three weeks in 1959—she became Radio Queen of the South in Miami, tied with another girl next day for Miss Beautiful Legs, and then went on to walk off with the Miss Caribbean title in Havana.

Following the murder of Dr. Austin I. Dodson in Monroe Park in 1959 there was talk by city officials and others concerning the desirability of RPI's taking over the park. It was said to be a danger area and haven for nocturnal criminals. Dr. Hibbs welcomed the proposal, if it could be arranged, but it never was.

There was longtime agitation for closing Shafer Street to traffic between Franklin Street and Park Avenue, in order to provide students with a place to relax on the small "cobblestone campus." RPI asked the City Department of Public Works in 1959 to introduce an ordinance in Council to close the street. The ordinance, or one like it was finally adopted in 1967. This sorely needed step made it possible for the undergraduates to use the street and its immediate purlieus for various types of meetings and events, musical or otherwise. They had held what was said to be the first street dance in Richmond's history on Shafer in 1948, with orchestral music, but few such events had been possible.

The time had come for Henry H. Hibbs to retire. Dean or Provost Hibbs—he never assumed the title of president—was seventy-two, and had headed RPI and its predecessor institution for forty-two years. It had been more than four decades of coping with every sort of obstacle, and he had surmounted most of them in a manner that few other men could have equaled. Imagination, ingenuity, versatility, and dogged determination characterized his tenure, coupled with a willingness, even eagerness, to tackle any problem, from adding a new department with no funds in sight, to fixing a leaky pipe when no plumber was around.

"For the lifetime of the school he fought to make RPI a great urban center of learning," Robert Andrews wrote in the *Richmond Times-Dispatch*, "and today at 5 P.M. [at the close of the session in June 1959], he retired and his job was over. He put on his battered straw hat and strolled out of the quiet building for the last time."

The school would develop extraordinary momentum shortly thereafter, thanks to the separation from William and Mary, which gave it an identity of its own, the appointment of its own distinguished board, and vastly increased state appropriations—all of which could never have happened without the leadership and drive shown by Henry Hibbs over the decades.

There were many tributes to him as he relinquished the position, and began his retirement with Mrs. Hibbs. Andrews wrote that Hibbs seemed surprised by the numerous plaudits in the press, and in letters to him from various directions, as well as by the honorary LL.D. conferred on him by the University of Richmond.

The leadership shown by the new head of RPI was, of course, an important factor in the institute's forward surge during the 1960s. He was Dr. George J. Oliver, coordinator of branch activities, head of the Department of Education, and Director of Extension for the College of William and Mary.

Oliver was equipped with a more outgoing personality than Hibbs. He also possessed a keen sense of humor. One of his favorite stories concerned a conversation he had with a five-year-old boy who was enrolling in school on the Eastern Shore for the first time. "Well, young man," said Oliver, "do you know your ABC's?" "Hell no, I ain't been here but five minutes," was the reply.

Mrs. Oliver, a graduate of Hollins College, was a lady of unusual charm. She was extremely popular with the faculty and their spouses, as well as the students. She and Oliver made an exceptional team.

Oliver had the title of provost at first, as Hibbs did in his later years, but he was made president during the year following his formal installation in late 1959. At his inauguration he expressed the view that RPI would continue to provide "a type of educational opportunity not available in other state institutions," but he voiced the hope that "an even larger place" would be found for the liberal arts, without lessening the quality or breadth of professional education. A School of the Arts and Sciences was established by vote of the Board of Visitors in 1965, and a dean for the school was named.

President Oliver said he learned in his appearances before the General Assembly that they knew little about RPI, and when he asked for larger appropriations they were uninterested.

The State Board of Higher Education recommended a separate Board of Visitors for RPI. At the General Assembly's session of 1962 Governor Albertis S. Harrison endorsed a proposal for complete divorcement from William and Mary and a separate board, and the measure was passed. The governor appointed a Board of Visitors composed of exceptionally prominent citizens, probably the most distinguished board of any state institution. J. Rhodes Mitchell, executive vice president of the Chesapeake and Potomac Telephone Company, was the rector.

One of the board's first concerns was to improve the "image" of RPI in the public mind. A good deal remained to be done in this regard. The average Richmonder had the impression that the school was a bit weird, with an unprepossessing student body composed of unconventionally dressed young men and women rejoicing in grotesque coiffures and decidedly grievous attire.

Yet student interviewers for the *Proscript* found in 1963 that both students and others had favorable views of the institute. Members of the School of Social Work queried 507 persons for the paper. Of those attending RPI, three out of four rated the school and faculty as excellent or good, while two out of three of the nonattendants expressed themselves similarly. Those familiar with the school were favorably disposed on the whole, but the *Proscript* expressed the view that "there is a very real need for more and better public relations."

Enrollment in 1960–61 totaled 6,964, of whom 2,036 were full-time day, 348 part-time day, 2,372 attended the evening college, 1,125 were in adult classes, and 1,083 in summer school.

The department of distributive education conducted forty-eight institutes and clinics in the state during the session. The School of Music sponsored the Richmond Regional High School Band, and was host to the Central District All-State Choral Festival, and the School of Rehabilitation Counseling put on institutes and workshops, including twenty-two in the preceding five years. The School of Social Work was conducting twice-a-year institutes in cooperation with the National Institute of Mental Health. The School of Business and School of Distribution were offering adult programs to provide in-service training, retraining, and upgrading of employed persons.

Progress under the Oliver administration was slow at first, but the forward movement soon picked up speed. An appropriation of $563,000 made possible the erection in 1962 of the first phase of a science building on Park Avenue, and the second phase was acquired a few years later.

The Citizen's Foundation, which had played so vital a role in the development of the school over the years, changed its name in 1963 to the RPI Foundation, and the organization became increasingly useful to RPI.

President Oliver's proposed budget, as submitted to the General Assembly in 1964, was drastically slashed in the appropriations committee. By that time RPI had won such public support that there was a strong adverse reaction, and the school's backers were heard from. Webster S. Rhoads, Jr., and Robert Archer Wilson of the Board of Visitors appeared before the committee in vigorous protest. The impression they made was so favorable that the committee reconsidered, and RPI got nearly $1,500,000 additional for capital outlays. The legislators also made it possible for the institute to buy the Scottish Rite Temple, in order to convert it to a teaching facility.

By the time the General Assembly of 1966 convened, the lawmakers were in a more expansive mode, and RPI was treated handsomely. Among other things they appropriated $1.39 million for a physical education addition to the gymnasium on Franklin Street; $1.36 million for the first half of the new library building (the upper floors would be completed with a $4.5 million appropriation by the 1972 General Assembly); and $1.9 million for a new School of the Arts building on Harrison Street. As stated by Dr. Hibbs in his history, the General Assembly of 1966 did more to help RPI "than it had done in the entire period of about forty years before." Important in this connection was the fact that Governor Mills Godwin had praised RPI and Norfolk's Old Dominion College in his opening address to the legislators. He pointed out that "last fall, they ranked first and second, respectively, among Virginia's four-year institutions of higher learning in terms of total students enrolled." Both, he said, "are doing a job of which we are all proud." By the fall of 1967, RPI had a total head-count enrollment of over 10,000, and its facilities were enormously improved. The figure of 10,000 includes the number of students of all types who had matriculated, many of them taking only one course. The figure for "full-time equivalent" students was considerably less.

Instruction at RPI was being offered on three levels: The Junior College: the first two years of the four-year degree curriculum, the two-year terminal programs in technical fields, and the first two years of general education in arts and sciences. The Senior College: the last two years of the four-year professional curricula, with concentration on the major field leading to the bachelor's degree. The Graduate School: offering advanced work in professional areas leading to the masters's degree, and certificates in special fields for the college graduate. The master's degree was offered in several disciplines, in addition to those available in the two graduate schools of Social Work and Rehabilitation Counseling.

A highly important acquisition in 1964 was the twelve-story Monroe Terrace apartment building, to be used as a dormitory for women. It was sold to the RPI Foundation for the remarkably low price of $300,000. Bonds were offered by the state at low interest rates to make the purchase and remodeling possible. The dormitory was named for Margaret Leah Johnson, beloved dean of students, who had joined the faculty in 1930 as the first full-time professor. A Ph.D. of Columbia University, Margaret Johnson was universally popular. Her cairn terrier "Davey" was her constant companion, and was a familiar figure on the campus. Carl Shires, the first male editor of the *Proscript,* wrote: "Contrary to all known canine laws, Davey is excessively tender to cats. Next to a bone, he'd rather play with cats." Miss Johnson died of cancer in 1959.

Student dress and grooming was a lively subject of controversy during the 1960s. An editorial in the *Proscript* in 1959 by "C.S." was scathing in its criticism. "It seems impossible to persuade some to abandon greasy levis and sockless feet and to apply razors to bearded chins," said the writer. "The idea persists that in the search for truth . . . you must look like a down-and-out sharecropper without access to hot water or even five-day deodorant pads."

President Oliver was strongly in agreement with the above, and the following year he delivered an ultimatum as to student and faculty beards. A student and a professor were ordered to remove their whiskers, and they complied. It was laid down by the administration that men's shoes "should be polished," and "all men should be clean shaven, and with hair trimmed and cut in a conservative manner." These requirements were dropped in 1963–64, but the order went forth that "shorts, Bermuda shorts, and blue jeans are not acceptable attire for the campus." Bermuda shorts would be permitted in warm weather, "but not short shorts."

The Campus Improvement Committee was formed, in response to criticisms of the students' appearance, and urged better grooming, but at a meeting of more than a hundred undergraduates, a majority favored freedom of choice. The CIC opposed beards, extremely long hair and mustaches on males, and black leotards, excessive makeup and sloppy smocks on girls.

The issue of student dress and grooming got into court in the fall of 1965, when three students sought to register and were turned down because of their long hair and beards. One of them shaved and got a hair cut, but the other two sought a temporary injunction from the Virginia Supreme Court, ordering RPI to register them. They were turned down.

The American Civil Liberties Union entered the case, claiming that the college was "arbitrary, capricious, and unreasonable" and had violated the constitutional rights of free expression, due process of law, privacy, and protection from cruel and unusual punishment. The ACLU went all the way to the United States Supreme Court, after the Richmond City Court and the Virginia Supreme Court turned it down. The nations highest tribunal refused to hear the case.

With such encouragement from the courts, the administration announced that all beards and long hair were "out," except with permission of the dean of men, and that long sideburns also were "not in order." A student could be dismissed for failure to comply. The board of directors of the Alumni Association supported the administration unanimously.

With the completion of the addition to the Hibbs Building, the student lounge there, appropriately dubbed the Slop Shop, was rechristened the Rotunda. But the premises remained as slovenly as ever, and it was still called the Slop Shop by nearly everyone. "It would seem that any name other than the Slop Shop would be a misnomer," said the *Proscript*. "It's like putting a 'Keep Clean' poster in a pig pen." Fifteen years later it was still the Slop Shop.

Students rejoiced in 1964 over the acquisition of the first remotely adequate student center in nearly half a century—the former Millhiser residence at 916 West Franklin Street. Previously they had had no central meeting place of the kind, with Shafer Street, out-of-doors, almost the only space available. The Catholic Woman's Club had occupied the orientally designed Millhiser House in previous decades. Offices for campus organizations were installed, together with a snack bar, Ping-Pong table, card rooms, and lounge.

The problem of whether to have fraternities and sororities came to the fore in 1961–62, and a referendum was held. It was stipulated that at least two-thirds of 1,500 students voting was necessary to legalize the organizations, but only 688 students voted, 439 for and 249 against. This was supposed to close the issue. Some surreptitious groups—"clubs" for men off campus and sororities for women—had been meeting. Five clubs or fraternities remained active, while the sororities disbanded.

President Oliver announced in May 1963 that the administration had decided that fraternities and sororities could perform "no desirable function" for a downtown professional school where so few students lived on campus. These organizations were accordingly banned, effective January 1, 1964, and any student continuing as a member after that date would be subject to dismissal. The five fraternities were dissolved. They had Greek letter names, and they indicated that they might become clubs and operate off campus.

The administration also decreed that there could be no "unchaperoned parties where girls are present, and names of chaperons must be submitted in advance."

Rules covering the consumption of alcohol underwent many vicissitudes during these years. In 1958, just before the retirement of Henry Hibbs, the *RPI Bulletin* contained the following Draconian admonition: "The possession or consumption by RPI students or their guests of alcoholic beverages of any kind or alcoholic content anywhere on the campus, or in any college building, dormitory, residence hall, or boarding place is prohibited; nor may any alcoholic beverages of any kind or content be served or consumed at any dance, picnic, or other social function given in the name of the college or sponsored by any other organization or group."

Prohibition had been repealed a quarter of a century before, but the soul of blue-nosed Bishop James Cannon, Jr., who had presided over the Virginia Anti-Saloon League, hovered ominously over Richmond Professional Institute. It would be interesting to know how many hundred violations there were annually of these incredible regulations.

In 1959, when Oliver took over from Hibbs, the foregoing rule was omitted from the *RPI Handbook,* and it was not until 1963–64 that another regulation was promulgated. It was less drastic, and declared the "consumption of alcohol of any kind anywhere on the campus or in any college building is in direct violation of state statutes, and is strictly prohibited. . . . Alcoholic beverages are not permitted at any college-sponsored off-campus activity." This regulation was repeated almost annually for the rest of the decade.

Student sentiment with respect to this matter was in sharp contrast to that prevailing in later years, if the Student Government Associations's constitution affords an accurate index to undergraduate preferences. As announced in 1964, this document provided that "possession or consumption of alcoholic beverages is prohibited at any student function," and stiff penalties were prescribed. The rule had been in effect previously, but the penalties were new. Attendance at student dances in 1965 was distressingly low, a fact attributed by the *Proscript* to the foregoing anathema pronounced upon the possession or consumption of beer, wine, whiskey, vodka, brandy, or schnapps.

In 1969–70 the rules were extensively relaxed. There were certain restrictions as to who could attend functions where alcohol was served, and it was stipulated that there had to be supervision by a faculty member for groups of up to forty persons, and two faculty couples for larger assemblages. Then, as evidence of rapidly changing times, it was stated in the student newspaper in May 1970 that free beer was served at a meeting near Ashland, sponsored by the Interfraternity Council. Fraternities, by then, had been legalized.

By 1969 the drug menace reared its hideous head at VCU, as it did at many other colleges and universities. Three coeds were arrested on drug charges after a six weeks' investigation by police. The drug problem had been growing in Richmond, with the campus and the adjacent Fan district as areas of concentration. It would be a threat for many years thereafter, although less so than in many institutions.

Consumption of alcohol, particularly beer, was uninhibited on the nearby 800 and 900 blocks of West Grace Street, especially the latter. This area had been lived in by doctors and other prominent citizens, but it had become run down, and many of the homes had been bulldozed. Others had become virtual rats' nests, and would soon be replaced by retail establishments of various kinds, including beer emporiums of substantial magnitude.

Drug dealers would do business along the store fronts on the 900 block in the late 1960s, and there were prostitutes in the area. The *Proscript* reported regularly concerning the goings-on, noting the extracurricular lager consumption by undergraduates, especially at night, and the somewhat lurid behavior of other citizens. For example, a husband and wife had at one another with butcher knives, while another loving duo became so mutually hostile and irate that one of them heaved an alarm clock at the other, and it went through a plate glass window.

The 900 block contained a drugstore, music hall, several taverns and restaurants, and other establishments. There were topless dancers in one restaurant in 1969 and also later. A motion picture house that tried to make a go of it with movie classics and foreign films found patronage so inadequate that it closed in 1962. Three years later it opened as a sleazy, X-rated establishment that continues to operate. The 900 block was being invaded at night in the 1980s by a rough, even criminal, element from other parts of the city.

In an examination of the scope and mission of RPI, published in 1961, it was set forth that "the large majority of the educational services provided by RPI are not available in any other institution, public or private, in the state of Virginia." Furthermore:

> The department of commercial art . . . is the only one east of Chicago and south of the Rhode Island School of Design; the department of interior design is the only such program of collegiate rank south of the Pratt Institute and the Parsons school of design in New York City; the department of fine arts is the only institution in the East south of New York City providing professional education in the area; the school of distribution is the only such school in the South; the same thing is true of the school of occupational therapy. The graduate school of social work is the only such institution between Washington, D.C. and the University of Tennessee in Knoxville.

Subjects in general education offered at RPI included English, history, government, economics, modern languages, biology, physics, chemistry, mathematics, philosophy, psychology, and sociology. All applicants for admission were required to take the tests of the College Entrance Examination Board.

William O. Edwards, veteran member of the staff, stated that "the RPI faculty had one thing in common; we bragged about our institution at a time when we had very little." He added that "in 1964, 80 cents of every dollar spent here for maintenance and operations was generated through the enterprise of the institution itself." Virginia higher education "will never see that demonstration again," he went on. "In the same year the University of Virginia was receiving 80 cents from the taxpayer for every dollar spent, and generating only 20 cents."

Dean's list requirements at RPI in 1961 were among the highest in Virginia, the *Proscript* declared. Of twenty-six colleges and universities answering a questionnaire, only four had requirements as stiff, the paper said. In order to make the dean's list at RPI in early 1961, the student had to have 60 percent A's, 40 percent B's and no C's. Only twenty-two of 2,302 full-time students made the list. At least twenty-two Virginia colleges required a B or B-plus average, and only Emory and Henry, which required straight A's, was clearly tougher than RPI, the college paper asserted. A few months after the foregoing was published RPI lowered its dean's list requirement to an overall average of 2.5 and no grade below a C.

RPI was having headliners as speakers during these years. Such public figures as Buckminster Fuller, General Maxwell Taylor, Aaron Copland, Edgar Bergen (and Charlie McCarthy), Art Buchwald, and Drew Pearson presented a variety of programs.

President Oliver pointed out that "only since World War II has the urban university come to full flower as distinctly identifiable and characteristically different from the traditional American college." He went on to say that "the ability of these urban universities to respond quickly to the need for new programs and to handle great numbers of students has created a quiet but very real revolution in higher education in America. Many urban schools have grown from small professional units to great universities offering both professional programs and traditional liberal arts curricula."

A survey of attitudes toward RPI was prepared in 1963 for the RPI Foundation by Sidney Hollander and Associates. Returns were obtained from 154 alumni and 100 parents, as well as 60 community leaders in all parts of Virginia. Comparisons were drawn with the University of Virginia, VPI, William and Mary, Randolph-Macon, and the University of Richmond.

Community leaders said that RPI "is the institution they know least about and regard the least favorably" among the six under consideration. They ranked it last as to average scholastic ability of students and quality of instruction. Even among parents and alumni, RPI was placed next to last in the amount they see and hear about these schools in the press and on the air. Community leaders also rated it a "poor sixth in scholastic standing, wealth of students' families and general reputation." All this is hardly surprising, in view of the fact that the other five institutions are far older and more firmly established, with the standing that comes from a prestigious faculty, relatively adequate appropriations, large and influential bodies of alumni, and so on.

However, parents and alumni praised RPI on various grounds. "They consider the faculty competent and devoted, the level of instruction high, and the curriculum varied and practical, with many specialized courses. The art department is mentioned most often, by far. . . . They look upon RPI as a haven for the serious student whose principal concern is getting an education, especially a technical or specialized one. Among sixteen phrases, the four most frequently heard from parents and alumni were "an asset to the city," "an asset to the state," "an asset to the business and professional community" and "an asset to cultural life."

No school came close to the School of the Arts in the esteem of parents and alumni. Forty-two percent put it at the top; occupational therapy was next with eleven percent, and the others were still lower. "Art," as used at RPI, connoted not only the "field in general" but dramatics, fine arts, and commercial art.

Despite its obvious difficulties, RPI in 1965 had achieved the largest on-campus enrollment of any Virginia college or university, according to the State Council of Higher Education. RPI's total was 7,855, Old Dominion had 7,417, University of Virginia 7,429, and VPI 7,204. There were 4,410 day students at RPI and 3,445 evening college students, about 88 percent of them from Virginia. The school of business was largest, with 749, followed by art with 669, education with 603, social science with 296, and distribution with 251. The summer session in 1967 had the biggest enrollment in the state, with over 4,000 students in day and evening study. Situated in the urban corridor, with its rapidly expanding population, RPI was, and is, admirably located to develop as a truly great urban center of learning. The faculty was being worked harder than in most such institutions, with a faculty-student ratio of 20 to 1, whereas the ratio in most similar schools was 14 to 1. The RPI faculty was teaching an average of fifteen hours a week as compared with twelve for the average such college.

The school was providing instructional activity outside the regular curriculum, such as seminars, extension classes off campus, institutes, short courses, workshops, TV and radio courses, and special evening or summer programs. During the session of 1966–67 "more than 300 special or continuing education offerings were conducted, coordinated by the center for continuing education, with over 3,100 enrolled."

Religious activities on the campus were being conducted by clergymen and laymen from the various denominations, most of which had churches in the neighborhood. In addition to the established religious groups, about ten others also were functioning, albeit on a much smaller scale. These sects, mainly from the Far East, were as follows: Divine Light Mission, Transcendental Meditation, Maharaji Ji, Maharishi Mahesh Yogi, Baha'i, Nichiren Shosha of America, Krishna Yoga, Kundalini Yoga, COGS—Children of God, and Inter-Varsity.

Alumni activities were showing important progress. William O. Edwards was alumni coordinator, and although charged with other faculty duties, he had succeeded in putting together a list of some 3,000 alumni in the United States and overseas.

In that same year, 1964, Edwards was named director of development for RPI, and instructed to institute a badly needed enlarged program of public relations. He was also authorized to employ a staff member in his office, charged with responsibility for alumni activities. The alumni fund, the first annual giving program of the college, was launched, and the association made its first major financial contribution to RPI.

During President Oliver's term of office state appropriations were greatly increased and numerous important buildings were acquired or begun. Reference has been made to the purchase of Monroe Terrace. In addition, the Hibbs building was extended, the School of the Arts, School of Business and science buildings and the library were gotten under way.

When it was announced that the library would be named for James Branch Cabell, the Richmond author, Mrs. Cabell agreed to give the library some 3,500 books from her husband's personal library, and 5,000 letters from authors with whom he had corresponded. A handsome room was provided to house the collection.

Dr. Oliver announced in 1966 that he would retire from the presidency the following year, after eight years in office. He was sixty-eight, and said he wished "to have time to do more of what I want to do." A committee, headed by City Superintendent of Schools H. I. Willett, was named to seek his successor.

Dr. Oliver would be relinquishing the presidency in 1967, the year that marked the fiftieth anniversary of RPI's founding. Homecoming for alumni, various ground-breaking ceremonies, and the installation of a successor to Oliver would be important features.

41. Hibbs Building, named in honor of the founder.

42. A group of pulchritudinous RPI cheerleaders.

43. Shafer Court, where the students relaxed for many years before the building of the Student Commons.

44. John A. Mapp, chief architect and inspiration for the RPI Evening and Summer Schools, among the largest in the United States.

45. Tom Robbins, RPI graduate and nationally known author of such works as *Even Cowgirls Get the Blues* and *Jitterbug Perfume*.

46. Dr. Francis J. Brooke, member of the RPI faculty and later provost of the academic campus of VCU.

47. The gymnasium on Franklin Street.

48. Dr. George J. Oliver, president of RPI, 1959–1967, under whom the school obtained much larger state appropriations.

49. Rhoads Hall, dormitory named for the late Webster S. Rhoads, Jr., an influential member of the Board of Visitors.

50. Dr. Roland H. Nelson, Jr., president of RPI, 1967–1968.

ELEVEN

A University Is Born

SENTIMENT WAS MOUNTING in the early and middle sixties for the evolution of Richmond Professional Institute into a full-fledged university. Having broken away from William and Mary, which had inhibited it from offering degrees in the liberal arts and the humanities, the school was now in a position to provide such degrees, and to develop its curriculum and teaching staff on a more ambitious scale. Its able and forward-looking Board of Visitors was in tune with this concept, and anxious to promote it.

In September 1965 RPI had the largest enrollment increase in its history, and plans were being considered "for the development of an educational program directed toward achieving university status." B.A. degrees in English and history were being offered for the first time—a small thing, in itself, but symptomatic of the direction in which the school was moving. Then came the establishment of a School of Arts and Sciences, with a dean of its own, and a graduate school, also with a dean.

The movement for a newly created university in Richmond was given decided impetus in 1965, when the Higher Education Study Commission, of which State Senator Lloyd C. Bird was chairman, declared that the Richmond area needed a "bold new development, with the establishment of a major university under state control." It went on to say that this could best be accomplished through the union of RPI and MCV. Senator Bird was a graduate of MCV, and long interested in its affairs.

His report pointed out that affiliation with a university would be a significant step forward for the Medical College, since many authorities favored affiliation of every medical school with a university. Furthermore, "an announcement has been made that no additional institution of this [unaffiliated] type will be accredited by the national accrediting association in medical education."

"The great lack in the Richmond area," the Bird report declared, "is for a substantial graduate school, which would offer a fairly wide range of subjects leading to both the master's and the doctor's degrees. The Medical College does offer opportunity for doctors' degrees, but only in the sciences closely associated with health." Advanced chemistry was felt to be especially important to the industrial development of Richmond, but the courses in chemistry at MCV were heavily oriented toward medicine rather than industry. Hence the need for a different type of instruction in the projected university.

Cooperation between the Medical College and the Richmond Professional Institute was already fairly well advanced, as was pointed out in 1965 to the MCV board by Dr. Edwin F. Rosinski, of the Medical College faculty. President Smith was authorized to appoint a committee to discuss further cooperative arrangements with representatives from RPI. The boards of the two schools approved the joint offering of a doctorate in clinical psychology, if authorized by the State Council on Higher Education. And Rosinski went on to say: "There are many other areas of cooperation—students taking courses at RPI, faculty members from RPI teaching at MCV, visual education facilities at MCV being used by RPI on an as-available and cost basis." He expressed the belief that "a great deal more cooperation has been achieved between the two institutions than is found between schools of a university." Rosinski added that "the enthusiasm and spirit this committee has engendered has made it one of the most successful" such enterprises he had observed. Members of the board expressed pleasure, and commended him and his committee for their progress.

Further evidence of collaboration between the two schools was noted in another 1965 report. It stated that RPI was providing instruction in history to students in the nursing school at MCV; that MCV hospital administration students were studying data processing at RPI, and would begin their study of advanced statistics and economics there in 1966; and that MCV students were enrolled in the RPI summer school.

The 1966 General Assembly, on recommendation of Governor Mills Godwin, adopted a joint resolution creating a commission to plan for the implementation of the Bird Commission's proposal for a state university at Richmond, to be created by the amalgamation of RPI and MCV.

The result was the Wayne Commission, headed by Edward A. Wayne, president of the Richmond Federal Reserve Bank, and an exceptionally able citizen. The commission as a whole was composed of well-qualified persons.

Chairman Wayne appeared before the MCV board's executive committee in September to explain the plans for the new center of learning. President R. Blackwell Smith stated that he was not aware of any disagreement as to the need for an urban university in Richmond. He added that the Medical College faculty was particularly enthusiastic over the proposal. Wayne "emphasized that the plan was not to *merge* MCV and RPI, but to establish a new state university with the two schools as components." Despite this admonition, the terms *merge* and *merger* continued to be used for years thereafter, in the press and elsewhere.

Chairman Wayne appeared before the executive committee of the board again in April of the following year. "The deans, Dr. Sanger, and President Smith spoke of the importance of being affiliated with a university, and endorsed the establishment of a new university with the college as a component," the minutes declared. The full Board of Visitors then approved the concept unanimously "in principle," and awaited the report of the Wayne Commission.

That report was unanimous, and recommended the establishment, effective July 1, 1968, of "an urban-oriented state university in Richmond to embrace and build upon the Medical College of Virginia and the Richmond Professional Institute" and to be named Virginia Commonwealth University.

The report went on to say that "an urban-oriented university is unique in that its basic philosophy concentrates on meeting the needs of an urban population living and working in an urban environment. The city is truly its living laboratory." Discussing the particular requirements of the city and its environs, the report declared:

> The Richmond metropolitan area has a critical need for graduate programs, particularly in the physical and behavioral sciences, and in professional education. These and other advanced programs in the performing and applied arts, the communications media, and state and municipal government were identified by many individuals and groups as being sorely needed to upgrade the economic, physical, and social well-being of the area and its citizens. . . . The industrial plants, especially those with substantial research divisions now located in the area, plus large government installations within commuting distance, have all indicated a sense of urgent need for such offerings.

Three consultants from Temple University aided in the preparation of the report. Temple was considered especially significant for the commission's purposes, since it is "a multi-campus university in a university environment." Also, "its development represents a response to community needs for advanced education with programs scheduled to permit the combination of full-time employment and part-time education." Temple's inclusion within its complex of a health sciences division, with a large hospital, and a variety of out-patient clinics made the parallel even closer.

The Wayne Commission stressed the thought that "today, of ninety-nine medical colleges in operation or planning to open soon, only nine are not affiliated with a university." Furthermore, "in the three basic areas of responsibility of a medical college and medical center—education, research, and patient care—strong affiliation with a university is of paramount importance."

The report recommended that both the Medical College and RPI remain on their present sites. The Elko Tract of 2,400 acres in Henrico County, owned by the state, and already developed with streets, gutters, sewers, light, and water, with much room for expansion, was available. However, it was felt that the Medical College should stay where it was, and that it would take "at least five years" to make the Elko tract ready for the academic campus. In addition, the city as a "living laboratory" would be eliminated, and hence the "urban university" concept would be unrealizable.

Other sites were proposed and inspected, including the Swift Creek area of Chesterfield County, several in Hanover County, the Broad Street Station–Parker Field area of Richmond, and the Southside–River Front–Hull Street area. All were rejected.

The commission included an assertion with respect to Oregon Hill which, understandably, alarmed the residents of that area. The specific statement was as follows: "Transition in land use of the area south of the present RPI properties to the river appears inevitable. . . . The commission believes that the time factor involved will provide ample opportunity for gradual transition from current land use without working severe hardships on those who may be affected." While this projection may have seemed logical at the time, no such plan is now entertained, and its inclusion in the report has caused concern on the part of some Oregon Hill citizens.

Substantial financing was proposed by the commission to get the new center of learning "off the ground." It asked for $300,000 "for use during the 1968–70 biennium to finance the development and/or expansion of selected undergraduate and graduate programs, to provide for administrative staff for the university, to support a professional study of long-range library needs, resources, and facilities sufficient for an urban university, to develop a comprehensive and detailed university master plan." Also recommended was the appropriation of one million dollars "for the acquisition of properties, and the planning and construction of facilities as may be approved by the governor."

The ground had been so well-prepared that the Senate approved the foregoing 39 to 0 and the House 89 to 0. Virginia Commonwealth University was in business.

But there were hurdles to be surmounted, especially the strong resistance of various MCV faculty members, students, and alumni to the union of their college with a much younger and less prestigious institution.

Walter S. Griggs, Jr., wrote his Ph.D. dissertation at William and Mary in 1979 on "The Influence of Accreditation on the Development of the Medical College of Virginia into an Institution with University Affiliation," and argued that accreditation was the controlling factor in bringing about the amalgamation of the two institutions. It was undoubtedly an important element in causing the leadership at MCV to approve the joining together of the schools. Also, as Griggs points out, many of the faculty and alumni at MCV were unaware of the accreditation problem, and consequently were not convinced that the establishment of Virginia Commonwealth University was necessary. "But when those at MCV discovered the problems facing MCV, they decided to support the merger while trying to keep MCV independent," Griggs wrote.

It is interesting that some at RPI also were unenthusiastic concerning the proposal, and argued that they were not the weak party to the consolidation. The RPI administration felt that in all probability "MCV needed RPI more than RPI needed MCV," Griggs found. It was their view that whereas their institution "had some minor accreditation problems," it had "gained acceptability with, and increased funding from, the Virginia General Assembly." Furthermore, some RPI students and alumni objected to the plan, saying that MCV's reputation "is highly exaggerated in the minds of its own people," "it is quite mediocre," "good but not a topflight school."

While the RPI administration felt that their institution was not "the weak party," they nevertheless "in both their public and private comments viewed the merger as a positive good for both institutions." The Board of Visitors was "strongly committed to this view," the faculty agreed, and both schools felt that money could be saved through elimination of course duplication, and consolidation of budget, personnel, and purchasing departments.

President Smith of MCV appointed a committee in 1967 to consider the action of the General Assembly in providing for the establishment of Virginia Commonwealth University. Dr. Kinloch Nelson, dean of the medical school, was chairman.

In its findings, the committee cited several authoritative reports of medical agencies which had studied the problem of university affiliation with medical schools, all of which concluded that medical education "is best conducted in the cultural and investigative atmosphere of a university." The committee's conclusion was as follows: "The Medical College of Virginia would benefit greatly by becoming a part of a *university of the first rank.* The advantages outlined above, plus the tremendous clinical facilities it has always enjoyed, would increase strikingly its capacity to provide education in the health-related sciences in Virginia and the nation. . . . A *university of the first rank* should be developed in the Richmond area. Medical College of Virginia and Richmond Professional Institute should be the nuclei of such a university, which would be of incalculable value."

The stress placed by the committee on the necessity for developing a university to rank with the best caused speculation as to whether the committee had in mind a more comprehensive institution that the urban university envisaged in the Wayne report. At the same time, it was obvious that the report envisaged developing the desired center of learning from the union of MCV and RPI.

The strength of the opposition to the plan became apparent when the General Assembly convened in 1968. MCV alumni in the legislature and other friends of the institution obtained the passage of an amendment to the Wayne committee's recommendations providing that "the college, schools, and divisions heretofore existing as the Medical College of Virginia shall, as of July 1, 1968, be designated the Medical College of Virginia, the Health Sciences Division of the Virginia Commonwealth University." The purpose of this was to downgrade as far as possible MCV's connection with the newly established institution, and to subordinate VCU. Years later, Edward A. Wayne stated that "this amendment was intended to continue the independent status of the Medical College," and "in effect, it delayed the hope for creation of one university for a generation."

Not content with the foregoing, the General Assembly in 1970 passed a resolution stating that "the Board of Visitors of the Virginia Commonwealth University be requested to take the necessary action to maintain the identity of the Medical College of Virginia as an individual college, existing within the administrative framework of the university, and be it further resolved that the board be requested to confer diplomas that are in keeping with those heretofore conferred by the Medical College."

Response to the foregoing was kept to an absolute minimum by the Board of Visitors, which was completely out of sympathy with the resolution. The name of the Medical College was made somewhat larger on the diploma, and the college seal was added.

Scarab, the organ of the Alumni Association, took a poll of its readers, in an effort to ascertain prevailing sentiment concerning the union of the two institutions. A total of 186 replies were received, and only 18 were adversely critical. A few of the more scathing comments follow: "When I hear anything concerning VCU, what comes to mind is a group of long-hair hippies and pot users"; "it made me sick when MCV merged with RPI, and when I look at the seal of VCU, it makes me more ill"; "I may cut that stupid VCU symbol (the same as the panel on Playtex girdles) off my diploma"; "what sick old billy had this idea to merge these two to start with?"

Schechter and Luth, a New York firm, interviewed many members of the faculty and students at MCV, and most of them were favorably disposed. Yet, as with the *Scarab* poll, there were heated comments in opposition. Some of the printable ones follow: "I am nauseated by the appearance of students at RPI. I wouldn't give one of those slobs a job"; "RPI is a school for misfits and kooks"; "the community is not sure whether RPI is a baby or a monster"; "the merger will grossly degrade the MCV's prestige and standing"; "RPI is dirty, MCV is clean."

The Medical College Alumni Association was dominated at that time by opponents of the consolidation. As Walter S. Griggs, Jr., expressed it in his Ph.D. dissertation, the association "elected to retain its separate identity . . . which deprived the new university of the support of many MCV graduates." Also, "even the MCV Wives Club refused to join with the newly established VCU University Faculty Wives Club. The peacocks did not want to peck hors d'oeuvres with the chickens."

This was carrying matters entirely too far, but it was understandable that some Medical College alumni felt such loyalty to their alma mater that they reacted negatively to the establishment of a university in which MCV tended to be slightly submerged.

An example of this feeling, albeit in the reverse direction, is seen in the attitude of Dr. E. Latane Flanagan, who attended the University College of Medicine throughout most of his medical career, before it joined with its rival, the Medical College of Virginia, in 1913. Dr. Flanagan ended by spending his senior year at MCV and getting his diploma there in 1914. "As an old UCM man he found it difficult to admit that he graduated from the Medical College of Virginia," said the *Virginia Medical Monthly*.

Arguments in favor of the establishment of Virginia Commonwealth University are well-summarized by Dr. Wyndham B. Blanton, Jr., a graduate of MCV and later assistant dean of medicine there and rector of VCU. Dr. Blanton pointed out in the *Scarab* that affiliation with an institution offering courses in liberal arts and the sciences "will strengthen the medical sciences." Health science schools "profit from a close relationship with a university faculty concerned with sociology, anthropology, psychology, and related behavioral sciences," he declared, "as well as faculty in economics, engineering, and community planning." A broader base for continuing education programs will be available, he added. There will also be a new library available to the health sciences division, recruitment of faculty by MCV will be helped, and union of the two schools will eliminate "objections voiced by national foundations, granting and accrediting agencies." Dr. Blanton urged MCV alumni "to seize every opportunity to contribute to this newer, potentially greater source of Virginia health science education."

The union of the two schools took place on July 1, 1968, as scheduled, but a strong element inside and outside the Medical College was far from pleased. Despite the approval voiced by many in positions of authority at the institution, there was only a grudging acceptance by this group of objectors. However, opposition declined gradually as the years passed, and as the benefits of the consolidation became more and more obvious. Today, it seems only a question of time before such feelings disappear completely.

51. Edward A. Wayne, president of the Federal Reserve Bank of Richmond, and chairman of the commission which recommended that RPI and MCV be brought together as a single institution.

52. Dr. Wyndham B. Blanton, author of the definitive history of medicine in Virginia, editor of the *Virginia Medical Monthly* for a decade, and head of the immunology clinic at MCV for eighteen years.

53. School of Pharmacy faculty, 1967. *Front row, left to right:* Dr. Herbert J. Welshimer, Russell H. Fiske, Dean Warren E. Weaver, Dr. John Andrako, Dr. Werner Lowenthal, Dr. J. Doyle Smith. *Second row:* Dr. Charles Clayton, C. Eugene White, Dr. Edwin S. Higgins, Dr. Arthur Cammarata, Dr. Roscoe D. Hughes, Dr. Kenneth S. Rogers. *Third row:* Dr. Said Khalil, Dr. Lynn D. Abbott, Jr., Mrs. Annie S. Leeper, Dr. Carolyn T. Edwards, Dr. Frederick J. Grundbacher, Dr. Alfred J. Richard. *Fourth row:* Dr. Alfred N. Martin, Dr. William L. Banks, Jr., Dr. Milton L. Neuroth, Dr. Joseph J. McPhillips, Dr. Anthony M. Ambrose, Dr. Bartholomeus van't Riet, Mrs. Caroline G. Jackson, Norman L. Hilliard. *Fifth row:* Miss Lucy M. Harvie, Dr. Kenneth E. Guyer, Jr., Dr. James F. Stubbins, Dr. Marvin R. Boots, Kenneth E. Moore, Dr. Robert E. Thurber.

TWELVE

The Brandt and Temple Presidencies

DR. ROLAND H. NELSON, JR., head of the Duke University School of Education, and a graduate of the Harvard School of Education, succeeded Dr. Oliver in 1967 as president of Richmond Professional Institute. Young and personable, he quickly made a favorable impression on the Richmond community.

Nelson took over at a time when RPI was showing remarkable progress in various directions. Under the presidency of George Oliver, and with the great impetus provided by an exceptionally competent and dynamic Board of Visitors, the school showed the following for the period 1962–68, as recorded by Robert A. Wilson, rector.

Direct effects—

1. Financial support in operating funds from the state of Virginia quintupled, and capital funds from the state increased twelvefold.

2. Public opinion regarding the college, as evidenced by the press and civic leadership, progressed from sometimes "bad" to enthusiastic approval of the college as an important part of a new state university.

Collateral effects—

1. The campus area was more than doubled, and the value of the plant more than tripled.

2. Enrollment tripled and so did the number of graduates.

3. Curriculum was broadened with the addition of four new schools and nineteen new degrees.

4. Faculty numbers more than doubled, although on the basis of advanced degrees held, its competency remained relatively stable.

Faculty holders of the Ph.D. rose from 15 percent to only 19 percent during the six years. Numbers of degrees awarded to students increased spectacularly, however. Bachelors degrees awarded in 1962 totaled 277 and masters 44, whereas by 1968 the figures were 794 and 109.

The salary problem at RPI was a real one in the middle sixties, but by 1968 there was considerable improvement. In 1964 the governor had authorized a faculty pay scale based on the national average for similar institutions. This raised the incomes of the teaching staff, but not enough to reach the national level. Four years later the increased wage scale for the school was as follows: professors, $12,500 to $17,000; associate professors, $10,000 to $13,500; assistant professors, $8,000 to $11,000; and instructors, $6,000 to $8,500.

The General Assembly of 1968 provided appropriations that President Nelson pronounced "quite adequate"—something of a milestone in the pronouncements of college presidents, who are not wont to express such sentiments.

Citizens of Richmond's Fan had become more favorably disposed toward the school, John E. McDonald, Jr., president of the Fan District Association, said. He stated that the association had become better informed concerning the aims and functions of an urban institution, and was helping the school's neighbors to be more understanding. In the past, he declared, the "so-called hippies" were the most vocal element, but he felt that the neighborhood "is appreciating the other students at RPI," and "the more the neighborhood learns about the school, the better the relationships are going to be."

The war in Vietnam had been going on for some years. A poll in 1965 by the *Proscript,* which queried about 150 students and faculty, found 80 percent in favor of U.S. forces remaining in Vietnam. The following year, students gave 230 pints of blood to the war in one week. Again, 80 percent of 227 students questioned felt that this country should stand firm. But by March 1968 sentiment had changed, and the Committee to End the War in Vietnam met in Shafer Court, with about 150 others, for a peace vigil. Those in charge said the U.S. policy was a result of misinformation, noninformation, and propaganda. The group urged peace at once, regardless of the policies of other nations.

In October 1968 sentiment on the campus against the war had mounted. A nationwide uproar was created when a student, Jack Kelso, announced that he would "burn a puppy" in protest against the deaths of Americans in Vietnam. Kelso apparently had no intention of burning a puppy, but he got the public's attention. Members of the Society for the Prevention of

Cruelty to Animals joined with other outraged citizens from coast to coast in loud and vehement protest. There was a rally of some 500 persons in Monroe Park, at which it was surmised that the "puppy burning" would take place. Kelso, a member of Students for Liberal Government, was the first speaker and he was greeted with a goodly number of boos. A representative of the National Students Association also spoke, along with others. Virtually all the speakers were against the war. Puppies may have been present, but none was committed to the flames.

A brand new Board of Visitors had taken over at Virginia Commonwealth University. It included several members of the RPI and MCV boards, as well as additional appointees. The first order of business was to find a president for the university. Meanwhile the heads of the institution's two component parts, Drs. Smith and Nelson, were given the title of provost. Smith stated that he did not wish to be considered for the presidency, but preferred to remain as chief administrator and academic officer at the Medical College.

While the search for the new head was proceeding, Fred O. Wygal, who had been acting president of Longwood College some years previously, was named executive administrator of VCU. He was primarily a manager and caretaker, bridging the temporary gap, and he carried out those duties acceptably.

The *Proscript* endorsed Roland Nelson for the university presidency in the strongest terms, saying that he "possesses rare qualities of understanding, forthrightness and openmindedness," and "has captured the imagination of students, faculty, and administration alike." While this could well have been true of the students, and he stood high in the community, sentiment among RPI administrators and faculty was divided. As for the Medical College, leaders there were determined not to accept him as the overall university head. They did not want *anybody* from RPI in charge of MCV, since they regarded RPI as inferior. Furthermore, there was a real question whether a man of Nelson's limited administrative experience could handle the complex job of running a large medical school.

While the search was proceeding for a president, Webster S. Rhoads, Jr., of the prominent Richmond department store family, who had been indefatigable as a member of the RPI board, died suddenly. He had served as a member of the executive committee and as chairman of the property and finance committee. The new high-rise dormitory on Franklin Street opposite Monroe Park was named for him. Rhoads Hall was dedicated May 17, 1968 with Governor Mills Godwin as the principal speaker.

In the following month, Roland Nelson accepted the presidency of Marshall University, and Dr. Francis J. Brooke, vice president for academic affairs, was named acting provost of the academic division. He had come to RPI from Centre College, Danville, Kentucky. Dr. Brooke had a most painful experience soon after his new appointment. He was kicked in the face by a pony, and sustained a broken nose and several damaged teeth, necessitating stitches. He seemed, nevertheless, to carry on remarkably well, with scarcely any interruption.

Dr. Smith was having serious health problems, and in January 1969 he resigned as provost of the health sciences division, effective July 1. His appointment as professor of pharmacology was extended for six years.

Colonel John H. Heil, vice provost of the division, was named acting provost, and served effectively. Versatile Colonel Heil had an LL.B. from the Jefferson School of Law, and a master's from Columbia University in physical education, was a graduate of the U.S. Army Command and General Staff School, and had commanded the Richmond Quartermaster Depot. After the new president of VCU was selected, he was named assistant vice president for health sciences. And in 1981 he would receive a fellowship from the National Endowment for the Humanities for a year's study at the University of California at Berkeley.

There had been substantial achievements under President Smith. The number of full-time faculty had grown since he took office in 1956 from about 175 to 407, the *Medicovan* declared. Four residence halls were completed, the medical education building (renamed Sanger Hall and later enlarged), was built in 1965, and a new 432-bed women's dormitory, Cabaniss Hall, was erected. The Jonah L. Larrick Student Center was dedicated, and the clinic center for self-care patients was completed. Some of these projects were begun under Sanger. The MCV advisory board stated in resolutions that "dramatic progress" had been made under Smith—enrollment doubled, capacity of the institution increased, value of the property quadrupled, many full-time positions added, and the school's reputation enhanced.

"Bob" Smith had sought admission to the medical school in his college days, and had been rejected. He accordingly entered the school of pharmacy. Smith never got over his rejection, and when president, frequently taunted the medical faculty because of it. "I wasn't good enough to be admitted to your school, and now I'm president of the college," was the burden of his too-often-repeated song. It offended the medical men considerably.

Dr. Smith's health declined steadily and he died in 1971. More than a decade later the handsome, new $12 million pharmacy-pharmacology building was named for him in recognition of his accomplishments. E. Claiborne Robins contributed $1 million of this amount.

Nearly two hundred persons were screened, and several were interviewed, when the Board of Visitors conducted its intensive search for the best person to serve as the first president of Virginia Commonwealth University. Dr. Warren W. Brandt, executive vice president of Virginia Polytechnic Institute, was the final choice, and he accepted. Brandt was forty-five years old, a native of Michigan, and a Ph.D. of the University of Illinois in analytical chemistry. He had taken his B.S. at Michigan State, and was class valedictorian. As a Guggenheim Fellow he spent a year at Oxford, and then headed the department of chemistry at Kansas State and was associate dean of arts and sciences at that institution. He also served as secretary-treasurer of the American Chemical Society, and had written forty publications in technical journals and books in various areas of analytical chemistry. Warren Brandt was obviously a highly regarded scholar in his field, he had had valuable administrative experience, had been at VPI for five years and knew the state.

Mrs. Brandt, the former Esther Cass, was also a native of Michigan, and unusually attractive. She and Warren had met as students at Michigan State—in a chemical lab, of all places, for she, too, was a chemist. Esther Brandt became a laboratory technologist and worked in that capacity while her husband did graduate work. They had two children.

They arrived in Richmond to assume the presidency about June 1, 1969, and chose a house at 1201 Loch Lomond Court as their residence. Administrative offices would be at 910 West Franklin, which had served both Hibbs and Oliver as living quarters.

There was unrest on campuses throughout the United States in the summer of 1969, and VCU was no exception. It had begun the previous year, following the assassination of Martin Luther King, Jr., in Memphis. The Vietnam war also contributed importantly to the collegiate turbulence all over America. Things had been relatively quiet at VCU, although there was apprehension in April 1968 following the murder of King, and evening classes were canceled two nights. Women were directed to be in their dorms by 7 P.M., with no exceptions. There was, however, no serious disorder.

About a month before the Brandts arrived in Richmond, thirty students visited Acting Provost Francis J. Brooke in his office (May 2, 1969). They made the usual "demands"—more black faculty, more black students, more Afro-American studies. Added to this was another demand—that the first rector of VCU resign from the Board of Visitors because of his "segregationist tendencies and racist philosophy." The rector was Virginius Dabney, the author of this volume. The *Proscript* said this demand was "absurd," and suggested that the group "present proof of the slanderous statements against Mr. Dabney." The only black on the board, James E. Sheffield, said the charges were without foundation, and Governor Godwin came to the rector's defense, saying he had "rendered a great service to the state." Dabney said he had no intention of resigning. Five days later the militant blacks declared: "We want all our rights, we want them here and we want them now," but the demand for the rector's resignation had been withdrawn, since the committee concluded that "it lacked information to justify asking the administration to take any action." The group "occupied" Brooke's office the next morning for a few hours, but it was entirely peaceful.

There were demonstrations and marches in many cities during October 1969 in connection with the war in Vietnam and what was termed "moratorium day," October 14. Hundreds of VCU students and others heard speakers in Monroe Park demand an end to the war and withdrawal of U.S. forces. Some two thousand or more, in a line stretching from the Richmond Public Library to Capitol Square, marched peacefully to the capitol, after a folk mass and memorial service in the Cathedral of the Sacred Heart. En route the marchers sang "The Battle Hymn of the Republic," and carried American flags, placards with skulls, and a sign "Stop It!" In the square there was a moment of silence for the eight hundred Virginians killed in the war. The gathering was dismissed with the admonition, "Go in peace, to work for peace among all men and nations."

Agitation over Vietnam was escalating in the spring of 1970, especially after four students were shot and killed by national guardsmen at Kent State. President Brandt ordered the flag on the campus flown at half-staff as a sign of mourning, but refused to call off classes. Some students advocated a three-day strike to force President Nixon to bring the troops home. A rally of hundreds of undergraduates in Shafer Street voted not to strike, and both the Student Government Association and the faculty senate opposed a strike. A small group of students went ahead and struck anyway.

There were fire bombs, several fire alarms, and "a whole rash of bomb threats," but it appeared that some of those responsible were not students. It was a time of considerable tension and apprehension, but when it was over, VCU had come through with few scars. Eppa Hunton IV, the rector, said that in his opinion, no other institution in Virginia, especially the state-supported schools, had emerged from the recent upheaval as unscathed as VCU. He expressed thanks to Dr. Brandt and the entire administration, as well as the campus police.

When the war in Vietnam ended, Major Floyd H. Kushner of Danville, an MCV MD, class of 1966, returned from over five years in North Vietnamese prisons. He had arrived in Vietnam in 1967. Soon thereafter the helicopter in which he was riding hit a mountain, and he was the only survivor. Dr. Kushner was injured and was incarcerated in the prison camp at Quang Nam, where he lost sixty-five pounds, and was the only man captured before 1968 who survived in that camp. After three years of near-starvation there he had to march fifty-seven miles along the Ho Chi Minh Trail to Hanoi. This turned out to be a minor blessing in disguise. "I was damned glad to get to North Vietnam, to get to a jail," he said. "I thought it was splendid there." The food was much better, he declared, and he gained back forty of his lost pounds.

Disorder unrelated to Vietnam alarmed the VCU community in 1969. There were two rapes in December on the 1600 block of Monument Avenue during night class hours. A walking student police patrol was organized to check the campus at night, and the university police offered the coeds a course in basic self-defense. There were more assaults in the 1600 and 1700 blocks of Monument, and the 1100 block of Floyd. An attempted rape in Shafer Street was broken up when a dozen students chased and caught the attacker.

A rather incredible series of events occurred in 1971, according to the minutes of the Board of Visitors. President Brandt reported that a rape occurred at about 8 A.M. in the Pollak art building outside the dean's office. The secretary involved refused to give any assistance, would not work with the artist who wished to sketch the assailant, and said that if the man were caught, she would not help in the prosecution. No explanation of this person's amazing attitude seems ever to have been forthcoming. There had been an attempted rape three days earlier and several obscene phone calls.

By 1971 there was vigorous agitation by a black student leader, Jim Elam, again alleging "racism" in the university. Other members of Students for an African Philosophy joined in. Failure of the institution to renew the contract of Vincent Wright, assistant dean for student affairs and a militant black, was cited. Forty-two black teachers and administrators urged his reinstatement. The university said he had "failed to fulfill administrative duties."

The first full-time black professors had been employed by RPI in 1967—Dr. Regina Perry of the School of Arts, and Dr. Rizpah L. Welch in the School of Education. Many blacks held part-time teaching positions. President Brandt stated in 1970 that the employees at VCU were 36.8 percent black.

In a speech at VCU in 1972, Dr. Nathan Wright, of the New York State University faculty, said whites have "honkified minds." He did not make this charge against any particular institution or organization. In that same year the *Commonwealth Times,* successor to the *Proscript,* inaugurated a black section, in which members of the race were allowed to let off steam and air grievances, real or imagined. At times "revolution" was advocated, and hatred for "whitey" was expressed. Marcellus O. Howard, a black student, called such inflammable writing "blatant racism" that had caused "irreparable damage."

The U.S. Department of Health, Education, and Welfare (HEW), which was pushing hard in every direction to improve the status of minorities, sent a delegation to VCU in 1974 to see what made the desegregation policies there "work so well," as the *Commonwealth Times* expressed it. They were interested, among other things, in why blacks chose VCU in preference to their own predominantly black schools. Most of those interviewed said that the financial aid offered at VCU was the deciding factor.

Warren Brandt was inaugurated as president on November 11, 1970, with some 240 delegates from universities, colleges, and learned societies in attendance. The inauguration took place during what was called "university week," and a program was offered designed to "give students, faculty, and the community an opportunity to discuss vital urban problems . . . [and] be helpful in defining goals, identifying priorities in fulfilling its [VCU's] mission." An effort was made to publicize the university's role as an urban institution, and receptions, exhibits, seminars, lectures, and a drama production were features. Tom Wolfe, the nationally known Richmond-born writer, was a speaker. The elaborate program was arranged under the chairmanship of H. I. Willett, Richmond superintendent of schools for twenty-three years, who had joined the VCU faculty as a part-time professor of school administration and consultant on urban affairs. Dr. Willett would be a crucially important factor in the operation of the university as a consultant to three presidents, and as acting president himself for nearly a year.

There was the very real problem of the hostility of an influential faction at the Medical College and among the alumni, toward the west campus, formerly RPI. As president, Warren Brandt was determined to unify the institution and promote amicable relations, but diplomacy was not his forte, and in moving too quickly and abruptly to bring the medicos into line, he "got their backs up." A more gradual and more tactful approach would have achieved better results.

Brandt held luncheon meetings with community leaders, in order to explain the aims of VCU, and made himself known to these important Richmonders. They acquired a better understanding of the school as a result.

Dr. and Mrs. Brandt were teetotalers, and alcohol was seldom, if ever, served at their private functions. This was a minor matter, but it ran counter to prevailing custom. When the Board of Visitors was first entertained by them, Esther Brandt asked the arriving guests, "Will you have cranberry juice or tomato juice?" "I don't believe it!" muttered a more or less bibulous member of the board.

By 1971 there was a full-time faculty of 565 at VCU's academic division, and adjunct faculty of 250. Admissions of students had to be limited by the availability of facilities and staff, and only half of the 6,500 applications could be accepted for 1970–71, although many were "definitely college material." The number of new faculty with doctoral degrees was increasing steadily.

The departure of Dean of Students Charles M. Renneisen in 1970 to accept another position caused genuine distress, especially among the undergraduates. He had made an "instant hit" with the students in the academic division, said the *Proscript,* which had urged him as president, succeeding George Oliver. President Brandt also praised Renneisen in the highest terms, saying he had made many friends for VCU.

Ralph M. Ware, Jr., was named director of development for VCU, a position he had held with MCV. He would also assist with the General Assembly. He was a pharmacy graduate of 1942, lectured in the school of pharmacy for thirteen years, served as secretary to the State Board of Pharmacy from 1952 to 1962, and was chosen pharmacist of the year by the Virginia Pharmaceutical Association in 1958. In 1960 he was elected president of the National Boards of Pharmacy.

Ware retired in 1986, but it was announced that he would continue to work on part-time assignments. J. William Doswell was chosen to succeed him as assistant to the president for legislative relations. Doswell had formerly served as director of external affairs for the Central Intelligence Agency, and he also served as president of J. W. Doswell Public Relations in Richmond for twenty-one years.

William O. Edwards was named director of university relations, and given responsibility for interpreting VCU to the public and assisting the president on special assignments. Edwards would also represent the university on the federal government's programs, and coordinate all university publications and news services. He served on the Richmond City School Board from 1970 to 1980.

James L. Dunn, assistant director of development at VCU became director of alumni affairs. He had directed the placement service on the academic campus from 1964 to 1970, and was given the first distinguished service award of the Virginia College Placement Association. Dunn had been instrumental in founding the association, and had served as its president. It grew under his leadership into two hundred representatives of Virginia colleges, and of businesses that seek employees on campuses. The Virginia association became a model for other state placement organizations.

Dr. Warren H. Pearse, assistant dean of medicine at the University of Nebraska, became dean of medicine in 1971, succeeding Kinloch Nelson, who had retired from the position, after serving as dean for eight years. Pearse reported in 1975 that the health sciences division had been trying for some time to recruit more qualified students from disadvantaged areas, and that rural recruitment was proceeding well. He said the rapidly expanding family practice residency program was attracting "both our own and the other schools' rural graduates."

Dr. Paul D. Minton, of Southern Methodist University, was named dean of the School of Arts and Sciences in 1972, succeeding Dr. J. Edwin Whitesell, who relinquished the post to devote full time to the teaching of English. One of Paul Minton's claims to fame was his coining of the phrase "skins full of students," to denote student enrollment, that is, "VCU has 16,000 skins full of students."

The police forces of the two campuses merged following the joining together of RPI and MCV, with Major T. R. Benson in charge. Average age was in the late thirties, and the force had the same basic training as the Richmond and state police. There was plenty of need for the force, as evidenced by the fact that in November 1970—chosen at random—there were 163 offenses, including breaking and entering, carrying concealed weapons, drug violations, assaults, vandalism, obscene phone calls, and passing bad checks. Some years later, unfortunately, Major Benson was arrested on a charge of burglary of university property and possession of a stolen machine gun. He received a twelve-month sentence, after pleading guilty.

A Criminal Justice Institute opened at VCU "for law enforcement and administration to aid local governments improve administration of criminal justice." Courses were offered in police-community relations, narcotics and drug investigation, and jail operation.

With the retirement of Harry Lyons as dean of dentistry, the Medical College began a search for his successor. Dr. John A. DiBiaggio, dean for student affairs and advanced education at the University of Kentucky College of Dentistry, was selected. He was a D.D.S. of the University of Detroit. Dr. DiBiaggio served for about five years, and then accepted appointment as executive director of the University of Connecticut Health Center. He was later elected president of the university, and then president of Michigan State University.

The Virginia Academy of Science gave its Ivey F. Lewis distinguished service award to Dr. Roscoe D. Hughes, retired chairman of biology and genetics at MCV. It was the highest award of the academy, conferred "periodically" on an outstanding Virginia scientist for significant contributions toward the activities of the academy.

The first Edward A. Wayne Medal for distinguished service to VCU was presented in 1971 to Eppa Hunton IV, the university's second rector. (The cast had been presented to Mr. Wayne). Hunton had served on the MCV board from 1932 to 1951, for several years as chairman. He was reappointed in 1954 and was placed on the VCU board in 1968. His father, Eppa Hunton, Jr., was appointed to the MCV board in 1913, and Hunton Hall, a dormitory for housestaff, was named for him. He served as chairman of the board from 1925 to 1932.

Dr. Wyndham B. Blanton, Jr., began an illustrious eight-year service as rector of the VCU board in 1972, succeeding Robert A. Wilson in that position. Wilson had also served as rector of RPI, and both he and Blanton would be awarded the Wayne Medal.

It was made known that Dr. Lewis Diana, professor of sociology and anthropology, had spent the preceding fifteen years in a study of prostitution, and the psychology involved. He said he had begun the study by chance when he was an instructor at the University of Pittsburgh. In the course of his explorations, he said he had interviewed 479 prostitutes and over 500 clients. Diana emphasized in the interview with *VCU Today* that he was not "a dirty old man."

Dr. M. Thomas Inge, chairman of the English department, and a noted specialist in the field of the comic strip, was commissioned by the Smithsonian Institution to write an essay on the worldwide influence of American comic art.

Donald Shaner and Associates of Chicago urged Virginia to establish a powerful Board of Regents for the state, with authority to chop institutional budgets. The report alleged numerous instances of mismanagement, and poor use of space facilities. It even charged that VCU had 42,000 square feet of unused classroom space, which Warren Brandt promptly termed "baloney." The Virginia colleges and universities, as well as the General Assembly, rejected the findings of the Shaner agency. A super-board was deemed inappropriate for the Old Dominion, one reason being that the state legislature wanted to keep control over institutional spending. The General Assembly's Commission on Higher Education recommended instead that the State Council on Higher Education be given greater authority to review budget requests of the various schools, to approve or disapprove course offerings, and to seek coordination of the institutions of higher learning.

In the late sixties and early seventies student bodies throughout the United States seemed to vie with one another in seeing which could outdo the other in exhibiting the grossest forms of slatternly dress. VCU was no exception, of course, and there were numerous comments on the uncouth appearance of the students. Many seemed unaware that undergraduates everywhere in that era rivaled one another in attempting to be as odious-looking as possible. Ivy Leaguers, no less, went around shoeless, sockless and shirtless, with matted hair, straggly beards, holes in their pants, some sadly in need of soap, water and fumigation. The appearance of girl students was similarly revolting. The Vietnam war seemed to do something to a whole generation.

There was widespread disorder on campuses, including VCU. For example, a confrontation with the police took place on the 1100 block of Grove Avenue one October evening in 1970. The *Commonwealth Times* said the fracas was apparently stirred up deliberately by a small group of students who began taunting the cops when they answered a call from residents who objected to noise from a rock band. An officer chased and arrested an undergraduate who was jeering at him, whereupon beer cans, bottles, and bricks began raining down. The police were called "pigs"—a favorite epithet of that era—and the cry went up "Pigs today, bacon tomorrow!" A policeman was hit by a brick and injured, necessitating 100 stitches. Snapping dogs were brought in, several students were bitten, and seventeen arrests were made. The man who apparently threw the brick was not connected with VCU, however, but a welder. He got twenty years.

A more gratifying trend of the time was the willingness of college men and women to spend hours ministering to the disadvantaged and handicapped. In 1969–70, many undergraduates tutored in the public schools in order to assist pupils who were falling behind and in need of special attention. Others worked at Grace House "to help kids find life a little more liveable." Both operations fitted in with VCU's mission as an institution devoted to addressing urban problems.

About 800 students took part in a voluntary fast for the benefit of "the former state of Biafra" (the secessionist Eastern Region of Nigeria) in Africa. They gave up their accustomed evening meal in the campus cafeteria, costing approximately 50 cents, and contributed the money saved, about $400, to the relief fund. Someone stated next day that there was grave doubt that the funds would get past the Nigerians, who controlled shipments to Biafra.

Fraternities and sororities, which had been banned at RPI in the sixties—although welcomed at MCV—were authorized for the west campus in 1970. A petition with almost 3,000 signatures had been filed, asking permission for those organizations to function, and the Board of Visitors granted the request. Eleven were in the original group, and they constituted the charter membership of the Interfraternity Council. It was stipulated that there would be no discrimination on the basis of race, creed or national origin.

Dr. Francis J. Brooke, vice president for academic affairs, was high in praise of faculty-student relationships at VCU. "I think it is a closer, warmer relationship than I've ever seen in an institution of this size," he said in 1971, "particularly given the fact that we have a large percentage of commuter students." He cited the "fundamental seriousness of the student body. . . . Most of our students have decided what they want to do with their lives, and have set out to do it."

Homosexuals were accorded special attention in the *Commonwealth Times* early in 1971. "Out of the closets and into the streets" and "The Gay Revolution is here to stay" were given by the paper as their slogans. An apartment in the 1100 block of Grove Avenue was "the unofficial headquarters of the Gay Liberation Front in this area." Unnamed gays were quoted as to their gripes and objectives. They said that "in changing America, the Gay Liberation Front has aligned with women, black liberationists, particularly Black Panthers." The *Commonwealth Times* explained that it neither supported nor condemned homosexuals. Three years later, Jim Baynton, managing editor of the paper, wrote a series—the "straight's view," "the psychologist's view," "the legal view" and the "homosexual's view."

In that same year, 1974, the Gay Alliance petitioned the Board of Visitors for the right to be officially registered with the university for participation in university functions, and to have access to state funds. With only two dissenting votes, the petition was denied. The petitioners filed suit. Two years later, the Fourth Circuit Court of Appeals sided with the Alliance, and the board voted to allow it to register.

Rules for dorm visitation with the opposite sex were being relaxed gradually. In 1970 the following regulations were put into effect: Monday–Thursday, visitation from 6 P.M. to 10 P.M.; Friday, 6 P.M. to 1 A.M.; Saturday, 12 P.M. TO 1 A.M.; and Sunday, 12 P.M. to 10 P.M. Effective in 1973, the second and third floors of Johnson and Rhoads halls and the second floor wing of Rhoads were thrown open to males, making an overall total of 300 spaces available to males to 1,400 for females. In 1981 the headline on the campus newspaper proclaimed "Students Can Now Sleep Together," that is, twenty-four hour visitation was permitted in some dormitories. This last brought VCU into line with other universities in the state, the board was told.

Parking was the greatest need on the campus, in the opinion of 80 percent of the students, according to the Self-Study of 1972, of which Dr. Joel R. Butler of the psychology department was director, with Dr. M. Thomas Inge as editor. The faculty were probably in agreement. President Clark Kerr of the University of California once remarked that "the multiversity often seems to be a group of individual faculty entrepreneurs united only by a common grievance over parking." Construction of the huge parking deck at the Medical College in 1975, costing over $4,000,000, with five levels and 3,189 spaces, did much to relieve the situation. Transportation between the VCU east and west campuses had been facilitated by a system of buses.

The Self-Study found 70 percent of the students believing that "their instructors were performing in a highly satisfactory manner," and most "were satisfied with the curriculum in terms of preparing them for work." Nearly 70 percent wanted to expand the athletic program.

Dr. Richard I. Wilson, vice president for student affairs, and Dr. Alfred Matthews, dean of student life, were praised in the highest terms by Paul

Woody, editor of the *Commonwealth Times*. Woody quoted a former staff member of the paper as describing Wilson as "one of the most dynamic, exciting, and interesting administrators she had ever seen," and he added: "This is probably true, but she neglected to say he also plays shortstop pretty well for a left-hander. . . . he is also a pretty good man at the bat." Woody described Matthews as "the man whose name comes most often to mind when student activities are mentioned." He said both Matthews and Wilson were "accessible to students and interested in what they are thinking."

The small turnout of students in west campus elections was noted and deplored many times over the years. The school paper blasted the undergraduates repeatedly for their indifference, but with so large a proportion of the students living off campus, and a great many with jobs in town, there were reasonable explanations for much of it. There was a fairly comprehensive student government in the late sixties and early seventies, but during the 1971–72 session this organization voted itself out of existence. Lack of interest, heightened by concern over the Vietnam war, caused the demise of the system. A Student Union, which would have cost each student $70 a year, was voted down overwhelmingly in 1972 by those who took the trouble to cast a ballot. Other efforts were made to establish some kind of campus organization of the sort, but widespread indifference was always fatal. Finally in 1979 an Academic Campus Student Association was overwhelmingly approved in a referendum in which 20 percent of eligible undergraduates took part. It appeared to be doing well, considering the continued indifference of the great majority of students.

A mild sensation was caused in 1972 when the *Commonwealth Times* published three nude photos of Nancy Lewis, a married psychology student at VCU. She was modeling at Galaxy Galleries, "a recently operated Grace Street establishment (117 West Grace), with nude models and cameras available for amateur photographers." The management announced that there was "little pornographic satisfaction for anyone," and that "poses deemed lewd are forbidden."

Nudity became slightly prevalent on the west campus in the spring of 1974, when "streaking" was the rage at various colleges and universities. It began at VCU when six male students ran out of the Scottish Rite Temple at Park Avenue and Harrison Street, clad in their birthday suits, and rushed to the corner of the Cabell Library, at which point they jumped into a Volkswagen and disappeared.

Some twelve days later, on March 19, spring got into the bones of forty streakers of both sexes on the 800 block of West Franklin Street. They gamboled about from 11 P.M. to 2 A.M., with numerous male and female nudists running around or riding bicycles through the area. Hundreds watched and police showed up in force. Four persons were arrested for indecent exposure, and a dozen or so for disorderly conduct. Not all were students. A man who stood up stark naked in his convertible and was arrested, turned out to be a soldier from Fort Bragg. There were fines in police court for streaking and for disorderly conduct, some of the latter for calling the police "Pigs." This was the last of the streaking incidents.

The beer emporiums on the 900 block of Grace Street and nearby areas were lavishly patronized by students during the seventies. An incomprehensible poll of undergraduate sentiment found that ardent spirits were preferred to beer, but that one poll was the only evidence of any such predilection. In alluding to the reasons for patronizing certain taverns, the student newspaper made rhapsodical references to the quality and quantity of the "cold beer" served, and there were similar allusions to "beer blasts" and "keg parties" on and around the campus. It would be difficult, if not impossible, to find any real evidence that the boys and girls preferred drams of whiskey to steins of lager.

Fire, evidently set by an arsonist, did extensive damage in 1971 to the onetime president's residence on 910 West Franklin. Several irreplaceable things were destroyed, including valuable early nineteenth-century wallpaper which Mrs. John F. Kennedy had tried to acquire for the White House. Slight damage was done to several paintings. The person who set the blaze was never discovered.

The five-story $2,800,000 arts building on Harrison Street, named for Theresa Pollak, founder of the School of Art in 1928, was dedicated. It has an interior courtyard for exhibits, and enclosed areas under the second floor suitable for out-of-door work and exhibitions. The building includes over 113,000 square feet of floor space, with sixty offices, twenty-seven studio classrooms, a conference room, two reference rooms, the School of the Arts Library, and the Glaser Memorial Room, the gift of Milton Glaser.

Construction was under way for the addition to the McCaw-Tompkins Library on the Health Sciences Division campus. It would be equipped with modern lighting and central air conditioning. The first phase of the James Branch Cabell Library on the west campus had been completed, and the second phase would soon be ready. It would provide study facilities for 4,000 students, with a special study area and free lockers for applicants for graduate degrees. Both libraries installed electronic detection systems to prevent book thefts. Approximately 1,600 volumes were disappearing annually, about average for the United States.

The MCV hospitals were being seriously criticized in 1972, both by the Self-Study and also by a prominent delegation from the Health Sciences Division which called on Governor Linwood Holton. Those in the delegation were Drs. David Hume, Richard Lower, and W. Taliaferro Thompson, and John F. Imirie, Jr., vice president and chief executive officer for hospitals. They complained of conditions, and said there was a virtual crisis, with beds closing and lack of nurses and other personnel.

A committee headed by T. Edward Temple, secretary for administration under Governor Holton, made a careful study of these allegations, and reported to the governor. The board spent more than fifty hours in an effort to get to the bottom of the charges. The Temple Committee had said that the hospitals lacked a clearly defined mission, and the board responded by stating that the mission was threefold—to serve as a teaching laboratory for the Health Sciences Division, to support clinical research, and to participate in community affairs, especially in the care of indigent patients.

It was apparent to the board that major criticisms were to be made of the hospitals, and this was borne out by the Self-Study. It spoke of many inadequacies and shortcomings. At the same time, the study was high in praise of the facilities for intensive care.

As for what it considered flagrant deficiencies, it said: "A little soap and water all over the area would improve the image. . . . the parking situation for patients and their families is beyond belief. . . . we need an emergency ward ten times the size of the one we have. . . . dressing room facilities for students, house staff, faculty and nursing are totally inadequate," and so on.

On the favorable side, the several intensive care units were credited with doing "a beautiful job," and the report pronounced "the respiratory intensive care unit, the coronary intensive care unit, the general intensive care unit, and the cardiac intensive care unit all excellent."

Most of the criticisms cited above were no longer valid when the Self-Study of 1982–83 was announced. With construction of the magnificent new $60 million, 539-bed main hospital, replacing the sadly outmoded structure of 1940, and the subsequent $34 million renovation program, VCU was in a position to offer the most advanced and efficient health care to all.

Facilities for research were greatly enhanced in 1970 through the completion of an installation for animals in Hanover County costing nearly $400,000. Located on an eighty-nine-acre farm, it cared for horses, sheep, goats, pigs, and dogs. The building contained two surgical suites, two laboratories, supply room, office conference room, autopsy room, animal preparation and treatment rooms, veterinarian's office, and technicians' lunch room. A veterinarian is available at all times and makes regular visits. The smaller animals are not housed in Hanover but in Sanger Hall's animal quarters. These are cats, rabbits, rats, guinea pigs, hamsters, and mice. Each species of these smaller types is numbered in the hundreds, if not thousands, while the larger animals, in the county, are nothing like so numerous.

Sanger Hall had been opened in 1963, with an addition in 1970 and another a few years later. Dr. Daniel T. Watts, who had come to the Health Sciences Division in 1966 as dean of the School of Graduate Studies and professor of pharmacology, was "highly influential in planning the $9,600,000 addition to Sanger Hall," scheduled for completion in 1974, the *Medicovan* declared. Dr. Watts was a Ph.D. of Duke University, and came to VCU from West Virginia University. "This will be the first time in the history of the institution that basic science departments will have modern offices and laboratory facilities," he said. His title was changed later to dean of the School of Basic Sciences, and he was instrumental in greatly upgrading that school, with nationally recognized scholars.

The Virginia Federation of Women's Clubs donated over $45,000 toward purchase of the Clinac, a piece of the Health Sciences Division's radiation equipment. It was received by the division of radiation therapy and oncology.

A notable addition to the west campus took place when the fine, new School of Business building was occupied in 1972. Costing $3.8 million, with over 146,000 square feet of space, it contained 180 offices, 72 classrooms, and a large computer center. Across Main Street, the commodious science-education building was completed in 1976, and named for George J. Oliver, last president of RPI. The science building cost $3.9 million and the education building $2.749 million. They were connected with the School of Business building by a bridge across Main Street.

An important addition to the health sciences curriculum occurred in 1970 when Dr. Fitzhugh Mayo was added to the faculty as head of the newly established department of family practice. Dr. Mayo had been in private practice at Virginia Beach since his graduation in 1955. He would be "responsible for developing programs for the teaching of medical students and training of the house staff in providing primary, comprehensive, and continuing patient care furnished by one physician." The American Medical Association's Council on Medical Education had recognized the family physician as a specialist in 1969.

Dr. T. Winston Gouldin of Norfolk, president of the Virginia Academy of Family Physicians, wrote in 1974 that "family practice is the fastest-growing specialty." He called attention to the Millis Report, "the most influential document on medical education since the Flexner Report. . . . [which] pointed to the dire need for family physicians in this country." In 1938, 75 percent of all physicians were general and family practitioners, but by 1970 the figure had dropped to 19 percent. As Dr. Gouldin explained, this abrupt drop in the number of family physicians came about because "medical educators worked fervently to eliminate the general practitioner. They considered it an obsolete, antiquated relic of the horse and buggy era. . . . Students were openly coerced not to lower themselves to that level."

The Health Sciences Division of VCU established residency training programs in family practice at Blackstone, Fairfax, Newport News, and Virginia Beach. In 1974 its program was said to be "the second largest university department of family practice in the United States." Dr. Fitzhugh Mayo, its head, received two highly prestigious awards—the Thomas W. Johnson Award of the American Academy of Family Practice in 1974, and the Certificate of Excellence, highest award of the National Society of Teachers of Family Medicine, in 1983. Dr. Mayo was president of the Association of Departments of Family Medicine in 1980.

President Warren Brandt was a vigorous, athletic type, given to jogging and other forms of exercise. Suddenly, without warning, he came down with a neurological disease known as the Guillain-Barré syndrome, a sometimes fatal malady. He recovered, but the illness left him limping badly, and handicapped him in his remaining time as head of VCU.

In mid-August 1974 he announced that he planned to resign, effective October 1 "to seek new challenges." He said he had accomplished many of his objectives "over the past five years." Brandt would serve as special consultant to the Board of Visitors during the session of 1974–75. Some months later he accepted the presidency of Southern Illinois University.

Dr. Wyndham B. Blanton, Jr., rector, praised Dr. Brandt for "his numerous dynamic and innovative achievements." He went on to say that Brandt "has done much to meld the Medical College and the former Richmond Professional Institute into an urban university of standing in a united pursuit of goals." In addition, "faculty has been upgraded, standards raised; physical plant enlarged and improved; and enrollment increased to the extent that VCU is the largest institution of higher learning in Virginia, with more than 17,000 students."

The *Commonwealth Times* was high in praise of Dr. Brandt. Paul Woody, editor, spoke of his "upgrading of the student body at large, the faculty, and the physical facilities. . . . The governmental structure for the school had been set up during his tenure. There has been upgrading of budgets and vast physical development." Woody went on to say: "But as he always has, Brandt remained modest to the end. He gave much credit to Francis J. Brooke, provost of the academic campus, for the advances made in academic and faculty upgrading. He also gave credit to the deans, department chairmen, and faculty for much of the progress. . . . When it comes to fund raising, especially from the General Assembly, there are none better than Brandt. He always does his homework."

The foregoing appraisal by the *Commonwealth Times* was regarded by some as excessively complimentary. Dr. Brandt had indeed improved the academic standing of VCU and raised the level of scholarship on the faculty. During his tenure, thirty-two degree programs were added and two new schools were established—the School of Allied Health Professions and the School of Community Services. While more than $20 million worth of new construction had been completed or was under way, much of it was begun under RPI President Oliver. And if Paul Woody found Brandt always modest, others considered him to be able, but stubborn and opinionated. It should be emphasized, however, that Warren Brandt left Virginia Commonwealth University a distinctly better institution than it was when he became its first president.

The search for a successor was begun. In the interim, a committee ran the school, with T. Edward Temple, who joined the faculty the year before as vice president for development and university relations, as chairman. The other members were Francis J. Brooke, provost of the west campus, and Dr. Pinson M. Neal, Jr., provost of the east campus. All these men worked closely with Dr. H. I. Willett, consultant to three presidents, and Dr. Wyndham B. Blanton, Jr., rector.

Dr. Wayne C. Hall had been named vice president for academic affairs, succeeding Dr. Brooke in that position. He had come to VCU from the State University of New York, and had served previously at Texas A&M, and as director of fellowships and adviser for programs to the National Academy of Sciences. A pioneer in research in plant metabolism, Hall had published over one hundred articles in national and international journals.

With the conclusion of the search for a new president, T. Edward Temple was named to succeed Warren Brandt, effective June 1, 1975. A former city manager of Danville and Hopewell, he was a man of even disposition with considerable administrative experience. He had the ability to be firm without ruffling the feathers of persons with whom he disagreed. Soon after taking over, he said he was working on a plan for reorganization of the university's administrative structure. He also would seek to improve its image. The newly elected president declared that he would attempt to preserve the institution's liberal reputation, if by "liberal" was meant willingness "to try new things, to do things that other institutions fear doing."

Temple's "traveling road show," as he described it, an effort to interpret the school to the public, involved a great deal of travel throughout the state. He and members of his administration and teaching staffs had made their presentation by November 1976 to sixty members of the General Assembly and more than a hundred alumni in eleven cities and towns in all parts of Virginia. He felt that the results had been gratifying.

The Department of Rehabilitation Counseling established an alcohol education program in 1975. Graduates were regarded as qualified to be alcohol counselors. A graduate degree was offered, and it was said to be one of the largest programs on alcoholism in the United States.

The amount of beer consumed around the campus led to the imposition of stricter rules covering events where alcohol was served. No longer would it be possible to stage what the student newspaper referred to as "those nocturnal keg parties in the gym where you paid a dollar to get in, listened to loud music, and got so blasted drinking free beer that you had trouble walking out the door."

Under the new dispensation, all applications for large beer parties on university property would have to be approved by the student activities office. VCU police had to be on hand for such functions, an ABC banquet license obtained at $15 per day, and the police had to be paid $7.50 an hour. It was further decreed that at least 25 cents per glass be charged swillers of the suds, with "all you can drink" invitations banned. Furthermore, any gathering in residence halls potentially involving 200 or more persons had to be approved in advance, even if alcohol was not served. Police also were required to be on hand.

A few years later, in 1982, big "beer bashes" were being staged at frequent intervals, since there was "no problem getting licenses," Bill Schwartz, president of Theta Delta Chi fraternity, was quoted as saying in the *Richmond Times-Dispatch.* He added that the fraternity "threw a party every month, and made about $500 on each one to cover house expenses." But by 1983 this was no longer possible, since the Alcohol Beverage Control Board ruled the profits from such a carouse must go to civic, athletic, educational, charitable, political, or religious purposes.

On another front, the VCU music department was sadly strapped for adequate space and facilities. The former Grove Avenue Baptist Church was accordingly purchased for the department's use. Four other churches had been taken over by the university in past years: the former home of Grace Covenant Presbyterian, used by the drama department and for a cafeteria; Monumental Episcopal, being restored; and the old First Baptist and First African Baptist, historic structures, like Monumental, and saved from being bulldozed.

The Baptist Student Union on the west campus opened in two remodeled buildings on the 1000 block of Floyd Avenue. The $300,000 renovation was paid for by the Baptist General Association of Virginia. The Roman Catholic Diocese of Richmond provided temporary quarters for the Baptists while the building was being made ready.

The American Association of University Professors ranked VCU among the nation's 150 comprehensive universities. It was one of the three Virginia institutions placed in Category One. Almost simultaneously the National Science Foundation listed VCU among the top 100 universities on the basis of research effort.

The university's average score for entering students on the SAT examinations was 875, Jerrie J. Johnson, admissions director, said. He stated that this figure compared favorably with the national average. However, Johnson explained that "we put more emphasis on the high school transcript than we do on college board scores." Extracurricular activities also were taken into account.

Special distinction was achieved in 1975 by Colin M. Turnbull, professor of anthropology and sociology, when he was one of fourteen writers who won an Academy-Institute Award from the American Academy of Arts and Letters and the National Institute of Arts and Letters. A native of Scotland and graduate of Oxford, he said of VCU that "there is something exciting about a university that has problems, is still growing and not firmly entrenched in tradition." Dr. Turnbull had studied remote tribes in Africa for years, and was the author of two books telling of his experiences and observations, *The Forest People* and *The Mountain People.*

President Temple was formally inaugurated on December 4, 1975, at ceremonies in the Mosque. A couple of hundred colleges, universities, and learned societies sent representatives. Rector Blanton presided, and President Temple spoke.

Mrs. Temple, Polly Daniel Temple, was ailing and unable to attend the exercises. She would be ill much of the time thereafter, and would die in November 1976. Her illness and death were great trials to her husband, and caused a natural and unavoidable lessening in his efficiency.

The following March 6 he himself died suddenly of a heart attack, aged sixty-one. His passing was a grievous shock to the university and the community, in whose admiration and affection he had made a firm place for himself. Resolutions expressing sorrow, and paying extraordinary tributes to him for his character, ability, and dedication were adopted by both the Board of Visitors and the faculty senate.

Ed Temple had been in office for only twenty-one months, and consequently had not had time to carry out anything like all of his plans. But as the *VCU Magazine* expressed it, he "revamped the university's administrative structure, campaigned successfully for a new MCV hospital, and did much to improve relations between the two campuses."

Henry H. Hibbs, founder of RPI, died in Lexington, Virginia, about a month after Temple, on April 4, aged eighty-nine.

A scholarship in memory of Temple and his wife was established in 1983 by the university and the International City Management Association, since he had been a former city manager, and had taught a course in city management at VCU. The City Management Association also contributed to the scholarship, which would be awarded to students on the basis of financial need, previous academic achievement, and career potential.

H. I. Willett, consultant to both Brandt and Temple, was named acting president of the university, pending the selection of a permanent occupant of the position. He consented to accept the responsibility, despite the fact that his health was troubling him. As matters turned out, he served for almost a full year, and his contribution was of the first importance. Indeed, "Hi" Willett's marked administrative ability, combined with his knowledge of the institution, and his readiness to "talk turkey" when necessary, made him little short of indispensable.

He was given invaluable assistance and support by Dr. Wyndham B. Blanton, Jr., the rector. Blanton had served as rector for the preceding five years, would continue for three more, and was on top of every situation. As a graduate of the Medical College and former assistant dean of medicine there, he was especially well equipped to deal with problems on the east campus, but he was knowledgeable concerning the entire operation. Blanton retired from medical practice in 1973 to become vice president for medical affairs of Charter Medical Corporation, with his office in Richmond. He is a Holstein cattle fancier of wide reputation on his Cumberland County farm, was president of the Virginia Holstein Association, and was awarded certificates by VPI for his contributions to the dairy industry. He also served as president of the Virginia Council on Health and Medical Care, and in 1986 was elected president of the Virginia State Fair.

As the search for a successor to T. Edward Temple got under way, Virginia Commonwealth University had a total enrollment of over 19,000 students, with a full-time equivalent of 13,700.

54. Dr. Warren W. Brandt, first president of Virginia Commonwealth University, under whom the institution made significant progress.

55. The Jonah L. Larrick Student Center at MCV.

56. Dr. Kinloch Nelson, dean of medicine for eight years, winner of almost every conceivable award from the institution, and a legend in his time.

57. Dr. T. Edward Temple, second president of VCU, whose important accomplishments were cut short by his untimely death.

58. Henry I. Willett, who served as acting president of VCU, despite the risk to his health, and who made other valuable contributions to the progress of the university.

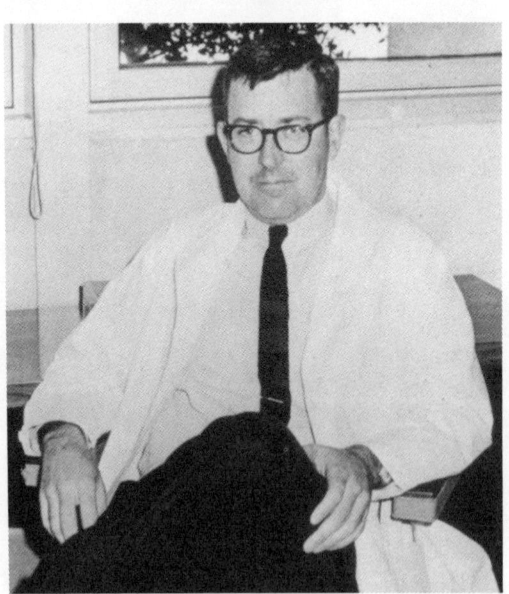

59. Dr. Hunter H. McGuire, Jr., member of the MCV faculty for decades, and chief of surgery at the McGuire Veterans Administration Hospital.

60. Dr. Carolyn McCue, at one time the only full professor of pediatrics at MCV, shown with one of her patients. She is the only woman elected president of the Richmond Academy of Medicine.

THIRTEEN

President Ackell Takes Over

THE FIRST VCU PRESIDENT to have broad experience in the field of health care as well as education and administration" was chosen by the Board of Visitors in November 1977 after a search begun the previous spring. He was Edmund F. Ackell, M.D., D.M.D., of the University of Southern California, selected from about two hundred persons whose records and careers were examined.

Edmund Ferris Ackell was born in Danbury, Connecticut, on November 29, 1925, the son of Ferris M. and Barbara (Elias) Ackell. He took his B.S. degree from Holy Cross College in 1949, after three years in the U.S. Naval Reserve, 1943–46. He then entered Tufts University, graduating with the D.M.D. degree in dentistry in 1953, and took postgraduate training at the University of Pennsylvania. Being desirous of acquiring an M.D. also, he matriculated at Case-Western Reserve, and the degree was duly forthcoming in 1962. An internship at Bellevue Hospital, New York, was followed by a residency at Meadowbrook Hospital. The academic world appealed to him, and he became professor of dentistry at the University of Florida. Soon he was made dean of the college of dentistry at the University of Florida, and then provost of the J. Hillis Miller Health Center and vice president for health affairs. From Florida he went to the University of Southern California, where he served as vice president for health affairs and special assistant for governmental affairs.

Aged fifty-two and vigorous, Dr. Ackell came to Virginia Commonwealth University at a time when a man of his executive ability and outgoing personality was needed. He soon made a place for himself in the Richmond community, became a director of the chamber of commerce and United Virginia Bank, and earned the respect of his peers throughout Virginia.

Ed Ackell is married to the former Carole M. Pryde, whose good looks and charm supplement his abilities admirably.

Before taking office, Ackell said in a Richmond interview that universities today are more oriented toward social concerns, the environment, and the community. He emphasized that he wanted to establish greater access to the community, and use the university's research and educational resources to meet social needs in an urban setting.

"Because VCU is growing up in a different time than other more established institutions, as a relatively new university, it will be different," he said.

VCU is one of three predominantly urban universities in Virginia, the others being Old Dominion and George Mason. Advanced degrees at such centers of learning are especially suited to addressing urban problems.

Ackell took office on February 1, 1978, and he lost no time in putting his ideas into effect. He found the university's academic disciplines organized in twelve schools—allied health, the arts, arts and sciences, basic sciences, business, community services, dentistry, education, medicine, nursing, pharmacy, and social work. This basic structure was to remain, but there would be modifications.

During the first seven years of his presidency, Ackell led a reorganization of the university's administrative structure and supported a major revamping of the university governance system. He instituted a totally new system for both short-range and long-range university planning, and began an annual process for setting and reviewing the university's institutional priorities. He also played an active role in faculty leadership, establishing not only the annual system of faculty awards and the annual faculty convocation, but also a new and revised set of faculty tenure and promotion guidelines, including the university's improved system for posttenure review of faculty performance. Ackell played a major role in several major personnel changes, including the recruitment of a number of new deans on both campuses and the hiring of new personnel to replace various vice presidents, as previous incumbents moved on to presidencies of their own or retired.

In 1978, the year Ackell took over, VCU ranked among the top one hundred institutions receiving federal grants for research and development. Virginia Polytechnic Institute was sixty-second, the University of Virginia sixty-seventh, and VCU ninety-sixth. In five years from 1974, VCU grants jumped from $12 million to $24 million, and by 1984 to over $30 million. In the latter year, VCU ranked among the top seventy institutions.

President Ackell told the Board of Visitors in 1979 that the School of Allied Health Professions—which was celebrating its tenth anniversary under Dean Thomas C. Barker, president of the American Society of Allied Health Professions—had some 500 students, of whom nearly 200 were seeking graduate degrees. The school had three "outstanding and nationally recognized programs," occupational therapy, physical therapy, and health administration. A year later he noted that the department of psychology was ranked by the American Psychological Association number eleven in the United States in production of publications in refereed journals. Also, the Virginia Treatment Center, "our principal off-campus practicum site, is ranked as one of the foremost research centers, based on the number of articles in refereed journals."

Fifty-eight Ph.D. candidates graduated at commencement in 1981, Ackell announced. This total "puts us well over the required fifty for our category 1-A status," he said.

Members of the Health Sciences Division were taking part in scientific gatherings all over the world—Moscow, Tel Aviv, Stockholm, Geneva, and Rome, for example—with expenses paid by the sponsoring agencies. In Moscow the VCU representative was chosen to preside over a group of six in his field.

One of the great triumphs in the university's history occurred when Dr. Baruj Benacerraf (MCV, 1942–45) was awarded the Nobel Prize in medicine and physiology. Chairman of the pathology department at Harvard, he shared the prize with two others. The award was made for "discoveries on how genetically determined cell structures determine whether a person successfully combats cancer and other diseases." It was explained that "the work [of the three scientists] has helped make transplant operations safer, and has contributed to explaining why some cancer cells are eliminated from the body while others remain." In 1985 Benacerraf was given the prestigious Rous-Whipple Award of the American Association of Pathologists.

Dr. Benacerraf was born in Venezuela of a Moroccan father and an Algerian mother. In the early 1940s he applied to twenty-five medical schools, and was turned down by all except the Medical College of Virginia. Because of World War II, the normal four-year course was crammed into three years. Benacerraf was "close to the top of his class academically," and his former classmates remembered him as "a brilliant and likable person." On his graduation from MCV in 1945, he joined the army and then embarked on a career of research. Before joining the Harvard faculty, he held various other faculty positions. Along with his chairmanship of Harvard's pathology department, he served as president of the Sidney Farber Cancer Institute in Boston.

Dr. Benacerraf stated that MCV "provided an excellent education" and permitted him "to compete on an equal basis with others educated elsewhere." He returned to class reunions at the college. "I will always feel affection for MCV and the people who helped me," he said.

Another award winner at VCU is professor James D. Pendleton of the English department. His plays have won many accolades, and have been produced by acting groups throughout America, as well as in other countries. Pendleton's *Rite of Passage* was chosen by the Eugene O'Neill Memorial Theater Center for inclusion in the 1979 drama-for-TV project at Waterford, Connecticut. He also received the North Carolina School of the Arts Playwriting Award for 1972.

Dr. B. W. Haynes, director of the burn unit at the Health Sciences Division since 1953, was announced as the winner of the Harvey Stuart Allen distinguished service award of the American Burn Association, the most prestigious award in the field of burn treatment.

President Ackell chose Dr. Wayne C. Hall, vice president for academic affairs, and later provost of the university, to act in his stead whenever he was temporarily absent from the campus.

Ralph M. Ware, Jr., former director of development, was appointed assistant to the president for legislative relations. He had been involved in long-range planning, legislative relations, and fund raising since 1966. Thomas A. Pyle succeeded him with the title of executive director of university advancement. Pyle, a management consultant with offices in Avon, Connecticut, had directed the regional alumni reorganization at Columbia University. He subsequently left VCU.

President Ackell was dissatisfied with various aspects of the Medical College Alumni Association, and early in his administration began taking steps toward revamping it. He told the association that its organ, the *Scarab*, "needs to be upgraded to be more in keeping with the medical center journals and information bulletins that are coming in from other medical centers around the country." The publication accordingly underwent a radical metamorphosis.

The MCV Association had adopted resolutions in 1975, 1977, and 1978 strongly reaffirming its intention to "remain an independent corporation," and in 1978 it voted "to oppose any effort to divide the MCV Alumni Association into associations for the six individual schools, and to stay independent." There were letters in the November 1978 *Scarab* from twelve alumni, all of whom said they wanted the association to remain unchanged.

But James L. Dunn, director of alumni activities, had been working on this impasse for years, and the alumni were beginning to realize that their reorganization wasn't getting anywhere with its obstructionist attitude. When Ed Ackell put his shoulder to the wheel, things began to happen. By September 1979 he and Dr. Robert O. Hudgens, president of the MCV Alumni Association, signed a far-reaching agreement, completely overhauling the association as follows:

> VCU Alumni Council will be organized for the purpose of communication and university-wide alumni relations programming; representatives of the Board of Trustees of the MCV Alumni Association will become members of the Council representing alumni of the Medical College. Each campus . . . shall be equally represented on the Council.
>
> Each of the six component schools represented in the MCV Alumni Association will organize a unit of alumni who studied in the particular school; the chairman shall serve as the school vice president of the MCV Alumni Association, beginning January 1, 1981; the dean shall serve as a non-voting member of the school unit leadership board.

The property at 1105 East Clay Street would continue as MCV Alumni Hall. "A study of utilization of the building will be undertaken."

The annual operating budget, previously funded by subscription, "upon adoption, will be submitted to VCU for funding." Furthermore, the annual giving program of the university, adopted by the Board of Visitors as the mechanism to obtain annual alumni support shall be the exclusive fund-raising appeal of those who studied at VCU. . . ." Staff may be employed by the association, the cost to be "included in the operating budget of the association."

The foregoing was approved by the Medical College Alumni Association executive committee and newly elected President Linwood S. Leavitt.

Truly there had been a drastic turnaround in the university's alumni affairs. It meant an enormous lot to the future of Virginia Commonwealth University to have its alumni well organized and soundly financed. By the fall of 1983, thanks to the new setup, the Alumni Activities office had put together a list of more than 52,000 alumni of VCU or its predecessor institutions, MCV and RPI. This was several times as large a list as had ever been compiled before, and it meant that this huge group of men and women could now be called on to aid VCU in achieving its many objectives.

The MCV Alumni Association and the VCU Alumni Association (Academic Division) would continue to represent their respective campuses, and alumni who studied in a particular school would, as before, sponsor activities appropriate to that school. Such events would be the Business School Alumni Symposium, the Dental School Homecoming, and the Social Work Institute.

Collections from the VCU annual fund were having a steady growth. They were $86,000 in 1975–76, $296,000 in 1980–81, $254,000 in 1984–85, $397,929 in 1985–86, and $494,407 to April 30, 1987.

James L. Dunn, who had been director of alumni activities since 1970, was named in 1984 to the newly created post of director of special projects for the office of university development. Stephen C. Harvey, assistant athletic director, was appointed to the alumni post, succeeding Dunn.

An important step in the development of alumni activities occurred in 1984 with the organization of the College of Humanities and Sciences Alumni Association. There are some 50,000 graduates of these schools, so that the significance of this organization is obvious. Dr. Patricia S. Geerdes, curate of Christ Ascension Episcopal Church, was elected first president, and the association gave its first association award to Anne Powell Satterfield (Mrs. David E. Satterfield III), '43, former rector of Virginia Commonwealth University and former president of the United Way for Greater Richmond.

Perhaps the notable advances made since 1968, when RPI and MCV came together to form VCU, and the new alumni organization instituted by Ackell, will help to create a more favorable attitude on the part of some alumni toward their alma mater. Dr. Rufus P. Ellett, Jr., of Roanoke, president of the MCV Alumni Association in 1974, said in a communication published in the *Scarab:* "Even though many of us have hated MCV on many occasions, and have stated 'if we ever get away from here we won't come back,' let me say to you that your basic education in your profession was obtained from MCV and allowed you to progress in your profession, and is partially responsible for your monetary worth today. . . . I feel it is only fair for us to support our alumni association."

It should be noted in this connection that at the time of Dr. John P. Lynch's caustic criticism of MCV, in his inaugural address as president of the Richmond Academy of Medicine in 1962, several alumni stated that they hated the college. It is a strange phenomenon. Perhaps such sentiments are no longer entertained.

In the spring of 1980, President Ackell suddenly found himself the victim of charges in the press that he was guilty of "conflict of interest." This "tempest in a teapot" was created by the *Richmond Times-Dispatch,* which trumpeted in large front-page headlines that Ackell was a director of the Whittaker Corporation of California, which had recently purchased General Medical Corporation, a concern doing substantial business with the Medical College of Virginia. The newspaper pointed out that Ackell was receiving a $15,000 annual fee for this directorship, whereas the law said that $5,000 was the limit, under such circumstances. It implied that there had been gross impropriety.

The VCU Board of Visitors made a thorough investigation, and the rector, Dr. Wyndham B. Blanton, Jr., announced the board's "firm and complete support of Dr. Ackell." He had served as a director of Whittaker since 1975, and had made it clear, on accepting the presidency of VCU, that he intended to continue. The board agreed to his doing so. Ackell explained that he had played no role in the acquisition less than two months before of General Medical by Whittaker, and that General Medical's relations with the MCV Health Sciences Division had not changed since that acquisition. He advised the board that he would continue to serve as a Whittaker director, but at a reduced yearly compensation of less than $5,000. That ended the matter until the General Assembly's session of 1984, at which time the law on conflict of interest was amended to remove the limit on compensation of any public official from any privately-operated corporation doing business with the commonwealth, provided the recipient stated that he or she had nothing to do with the letting of contracts between the government agency and the private corporation. The record showed that the amount of business being done in 1984 between General Medical and the Health Sciences Division was almost exactly what it had been before Whittaker bought General Medical four years previously.

Stuart Shumate, a member of the Board of Visitors, asked Dr. Ackell soon after he took over the presidency whether VCU would have to lower standards in order to increase black enrollment under pressure from the U.S.

Department of Health, Education and Welfare (HEW). The president indicated that he did not plan to lower standards but raise them. He went on to explain, however, that the university had a special services program on the west campus for a limited number of students who had academic difficulties.

This program had been instituted by President Warren Brandt. It was for the benefit of those who could not meet the entrance requirements, but gave evidence of being able to succeed in college.

The Self-Study of 1972 declared: "The needs of an urban society cannot be met through the admission of only those students who have demonstrated exceptional prior performance, as measured by standard criteria. Consideration must also be given to what are currently considered academically deficient students, as well as those who transfer with low grade point averages. This is particularly true in those instances where the potential exists for the graduate to return to an area of critical need." About two hundred undergraduates were, and are, enrolled in this program each year.

At the board meeting in September 1981 President Ackell described several varieties of "remedial and academic support activities." These included noncredit courses in elementary algebra, fundamentals of English composition, and so on. Courses also were offered as supplements to regular college-level classes. Some good students take these courses to hone their skills, Ackell said, as do a fair number of older students. This type of instruction also serves as a refresher course for persons away from college for a length of time.

While most of the special students are blacks, whites also are part of the program. Tutoring and counseling are offered, as well as summer courses in reading, writing, and arithmetic. A high school diploma or its equivalent is required for entrance, and the entrant must show academic potential.

The foregoing applies to the west campus only. At the Health Sciences Division admissions are handled by special selection committees composed of professionals in each field. There is no special services program and no quota system.

Blacks were getting increasing recognition on the west campus. As early as 1970, Jim Elam, a sophomore sociology major from Richmond, was elected president of the Student Government Association by a vote of 726 to 465. Elam limped and used a cane, the result of having been shot by a sniper in Richmond's West End in 1962, according to the *Commonwealth Times*. As evidence of further interracial progress, a black May Queen, Georgette

Twine, of Greenwich, Connecticut, was chosen in 1971. Blacks became still more influential on the west campus as time passed. In 1980 over 2,000 votes were cast in the Student Government Association election, and of the twenty-eight student senators chosen, eighteen were white and ten black. VCU had more black students during these years, and has more today, than any predominantly white college or university in Virginia.

The diversification of the VCU student body was commented on by Dr. Ackell in 1981. "It's more diversified than any campus I've ever been on," he said.

Diversification of a different sort seemed evident on February 19, 1979, when about 250 young men and women began throwing snowballs, chunks of ice, and mounds of slush at every motorist who passed the busy intersection at Laurel and Franklin streets. Police were called, and they ordered the crowd to disperse, only to be pelted themselves. "I almost got killed!" one of them exclaimed.

The fracas began at about 2 P.M., and caused virtual chaos at the intersection. It went on all afternoon, and brought hundreds of calls to police headquarters from irate motorists, according to Ray Lovenbury, who covered the event for the *Times-Dispatch.* Captain James W. Cheagle, acting inspector of the Richmond police bureau, came to the scene and commanded the youngsters to disperse. They responded with another volley of snowballs and ice chunks directed at his car. Some of the revelers were relatively well behaved and suggested to motorists that they close their windows on approaching the "danger zone," but others "seemed intent on breaking out windows," Lovenbury wrote. Snowplows were sent down Franklin Street toward Laurel, on the theory that this would intimidate the excited students. They were not intimidated. Finally, at around 5:30, they apparently had had enough, and the crowd dispersed.

President Ackell and vice president of Student Affairs Richard I. Wilson signed a letter criticizing the students for their "irresponsible behavior" which "went beyond good clean fun . . . caused harm to members of the larger community . . . and has, to a disproportionate extent, undone the positive effect of many services and many acts of kindness and decency performed by other members of our community."

The situation was compounded by the fact that a few days before, undergraduates had misbehaved at a basketball game with Old Dominion. As Bill Millsaps expressed it in his *Times-Dispatch* sports column: "Four bellicose patrons were vigorously escorted from the premises by the police. ODU

Coach Paul Webb made a nice, one-handed grab of a three-quarters-full beer can thrown from the upper deck. VCU starter Penny Elliott forgot for a moment that he was a basketball player and thought he was Muhammad Ali." An altercation between an ODU cheerleader and a VCU player caused spectators to heave cups of ice onto the floor, and there was a "shoving match." "A young fan came out of the stands and attacked the cheerleader," whereupon "four policemen subdued him and dragged him off." It was a stormy evening.

Dean Alfred T. Matthews said that these incidents caused VCU to get "bad press and TV coverage." Dean Wilson suggested that VCU students undertake a community program that "focuses positive attention on students and the institution."

The following year, however, President Ackell complimented the Ram rooters for behaving "in an exemplary manner" at the recent Sun Belt Conference game.

The students also demonstrated a commendable concern for the starving children of Cambodia by putting on a drive for funds that netted $3,500. Several local restaurants and night clubs contributed, along with entertainers who performed in Shafer Court.

The gays on campus got sympathetic treatment from the *Commonwealth Times.* It gave the cover and two more full pages to the gay movement, with special reference to a four-day gathering in Washington, attended by an estimated 75,000 persons. The college paper carried further sympathetic items from time to time.

Protection against rape was offered by the VCU Safety Escort Service, and an advertisement asked for more volunteers to aid in the work. Protection began in the fall of 1980, operating from 8 P.M. to midnight, Monday through Thursday. It was funded by student activity fees, and had the cooperation of the university administration and the police.

The neighborhood of the campus on Grace Street was much improved in the late 1970s when several blocks underwent a substantial facelifting. A large hospital, a huge supermarket, a multilevel parking deck, and a home for the elderly were in various stages of construction. The overall effect was greatly to enhance the area, so heavily frequented by VCU students, who were, in fact, its commercial lifeblood.

Ragged and tattered "street people" were hanging out along West Grace in the early 1980s. This did not comport with its improved image. These unfortunates entered the restaurants for a few minutes of warmth in the cold weather, only to be moved out by the police or the proprietors. Police officers referred the "street people" to shelters, but these filled early in the evening during the winter.

A feeling of unity was lacking in 1980 between many students of the east and west campuses, the *Commonwealth Times* concluded, after interviewing a number of them. Some felt that the joining of RPI and MCV was a fortunate thing, and would lead, in time, to an elimination of friction, but there was said to be a feeling on both campuses that unity was a fair distance from reality. Half-a-dozen students in the Health Sciences Division said they had little *rapport* with the academic end of the institution, while an equal number of the latter campus agreed. The local media were blamed for exacerbating the situation by referring to the medical campus as MCV rather than as MCV-VCU. One student, Martha Crawford of Clinton, South Carolina, felt that RPI was "too well known" for the name to be abandoned. "When someone asks me where I go to school, I'm going to say RPI," she declared. "I don't think the name Richmond Professional Institute will ever cease to exist."

City Council voted in 1980 to close the 900 block of Park Avenue, between Linden and Cherry streets, to traffic. This affected the overall traffic situation only slightly, but from thirty to forty parking spaces were eliminated.

Completion of the new parking deck on the block bounded by Main, Cherry, Laurel, and Cary streets, costing $3.3 million, served greatly to relieve the pressure for parking in the entire area. The deck contains four levels, with 1,018 spaces for cars. The city is allotted 320 for events at the Mosque, and there is free parking for parishioners of Sacred Heart Cathedral and Grace and Holy Trinity Church. Safety is stressed in the building, which contains thirty-two closed circuit cameras for constant surveillance, and the grounds are well lighted.

Would-be parkers are directed to the deck, by the elaborate system of signs erected in 1981. Those on the Health Sciences Division grounds were awarded first place by the National Health Science Communication Association.

Library resources of Virginia Commonwealth University were being steadily upgraded. Collections in the James Branch Cabell Library, when added to those in the Tompkins-McCaw Library, made available in 1983 a combined total of 900,000 volumes in all formats, of which 603,000 were books and bound journals, and 8,533 were current periodicals and serial subscriptions.

In addition to the valuable Cabell collection, and the papers of such Richmond authors as Frances Leigh Williams and Morris Markey (of the *New Yorker*), the Cabell Library houses materials assembled by New Virginia Review—a unique assemblage of little magazines and small publications. Such materials are available through interlibrary loans to readers in public and academic libraries throughout the Commonwealth.

A problem for more than one president of VCU was the fear of Oregon Hill residents that their homes were to be bulldozed for the benefit of the university. Residents of this area, extending from the expressway south to the river, met with President Warren Brandt, and presented petitions asking the university authorities to "declare publicly that no future expansion plans will destroy one house or remove one family from Oregon Hill." Brandt told them that a new master plan would be published in seven or eight months. The Wayne Report, as explained in an earlier chapter, said that VCU might have to expand to the river.

The master plan gave no such assurance as was requested, since the institution badly needed a couple of blocks on the northern end of Oregon Hill—bounded by the expressway, Cary Street, Harrison and Cherry streets—in order to construct an athletic complex centered around what was formerly the city auditorium. The university, which would soon have some 20,000 students, was without anything remotely resembling adequate athletic and recreational facilities, and the above-mentioned area was the only one available for such a purpose.

VCU got a good deal of unfavorable publicity in connection with this project. It was depicted in a TV program as "the big, impersonal university" ruthlessly planning to seize the property of defenseless homeowners, in order to build tennis courts for students. Earl Jenkins, a resident, headed the Save Our Homes Committee, which issued numerous statements, based, at least in part, on a serious lack of understanding of the university's plans. For example, VCU never had any intention of invoking the right of eminent domain, whereby homes could be confiscated for a public purpose. Dr. Ackell explained that of the nineteen property owners in the desired area, "quite a large number have already indicated an interest in selling because it *is* a declining thing, and more and more people are moving out." He added that "we are not going to force anybody to sell." Only five of the owner-occupants expressed an unwillingness to relocate, he declared.

A few of the five are still there, but the university acquired enough of the desired tract, without forcing anybody out, and the athletic complex that resulted was of extreme importance to the institution's students. Dedication of the 28,000-square-foot complex took place on November 1, 1983. The former city auditorium had been renovated as a gymnasium at a cost of $1.45 million, and the adjacent land was graded and put into condition for a great variety of athletic purposes at an additional expenditure of $500,000. The gym, which is available for student social events as well as athletics, contains locker rooms, bathrooms, shower facilities, and a vending area. There is a multipurpose court for basketball, team handball or racquetball, badminton, and volleyball. The upper level has four handball-racquetball courts and one multi-use court. The land across from the gym was graded for field sports and a running track. One large field is surrounded by a small jogging track. Two tennis courts were installed directly behind the complex at a cost of $100,000. Other activities offered or under way include aerobics, English horseback riding, martial arts, and running-stretching classes.

The former city auditorium, which is the central structure in the above-mentioned complex, was the scene of many significant public meetings and concerts in other days, before the building of the Mosque. President William H. Taft and would-be president William Jennings Bryan shook the rafters there with their oratory, the Rev. "Billy" Sunday held shouting revivals, and Ignace Paderewski, the world-renowned pianist, gave concerts in the grubby hall, despite its atrocious acoustics.

It is gratifying to report that this structure has been brought back to life, as it were, after it had served as a municipal garage and had been allowed to deteriorate badly. In making it the crux of its athletic and recreational facilities, VCU did so at a minimum of damage to the good citizens of Oregon Hill. Some of them are probably convinced, despite all assurances to the contrary, that the university has sinister designs on them for the future. Such fears seem entirely without foundation. There had been complaints that the students make too much noise in the gymnasium with their rock music, but otherwise the situation appears serene on Oregon Hill.

It was once the site of the handsome mansion "Belvidere," built by William Byrd III in the middle or late 1750s. "Belvidere," situated on a seventeen-acre tract bounded by today's Laurel, Holly, China, and Belvidere streets, has long since vanished, with all its dependencies and its serpentine wall, and the area is now covered with modest houses. The dwellers in those houses have no reason to fear that their peaceful sojourn near the banks of the James will be rudely disturbed hereafter in disregard of their well-being and happiness.

61. James Branch Cabell Library on the west campus.

62. School of Business, west campus.

63. Dean Warren Weaver, school of pharmacy.

FOURTEEN

Progress in the Eighties—East Campus

VIRGINIA COMMONWEALTH UNIVERSITY was making significant forward strides in the 1980s, and developing in many directions as an institution of the first rank. It had overcome most of the handicaps that beset it in earlier days, was more united in its outlook, and was now in a position to capitalize on its numerous assets.

Erection of the splendid new 539-bed hospital, costing $60 million, was a momentous milestone. This ultramodern structure at Twelfth and Marshall streets, which opened in 1982, gave a lift to the medical school, providing highly sophisticated facilities for patients and staff, as well as for research. The West Hospital, which dated from 1940, was exactly what MCV needed at that time, but had long since been outmoded.

The new fourteen-story hospital, with 600,000 square feet of floor space, made possible the consolidation of many services previously scattered throughout various buildings. The emergency rooms, some of the largest such facilities in this country, are among those consolidated. These rooms are divided into separate areas for medical-surgical, trauma, pediatric, labor and delivery, and obstetrics-gynecology patients. There are also consolidated and expanded operating and recovery rooms, radiology services, obstetrics-gynecology, neonatal and intensive care units.

All-weather walkways connect the new hospital with other hospital and clinical facilities. Closed circuit television is available at many locations in the building.

A $34 million renovation program for modernization of existing facilities is a vital part of the Health Science Division's plans. Minimal renovation is going forward for West Hospital pending determination of its further use.

This 437-bed, eighteen-story building, which has loomed above the surrounding area for nearly half a century, is to be used for classrooms, offices, and research until it is demolished, probably in the 1990s. North Hospital, formerly Ennion G. Williams, is being extensively renovated and enlarged for patient care. East Hospital, formerly St. Philip, erected in 1920, is to be demolished, while South Hospital, the onetime Memorial, built in 1903, is to be returned to the state.

In this massive medical complex, resident physicians' programs are offered in the following areas: anesthesiology, child neurology, dermatology, diagnostic radiology, family practice, general surgery, legal medicine, medicine-primary care, neurology, neurosurgery, nuclear medicine, obstetrics-gynecology, ophthalmology, oral surgery, orthopedic surgery, otolaryngology, audiology, speech pathology, pathology, pediatrics, primary care, plastic surgery, psychiatry, radiation therapy, rehabilitation medicine, thoracic surgery, transplant surgery, urology, and vascular surgery.

Families of patients from beyond a thirty-mile radius find comfortable accommodations free of charge at Zeigler House, 1006–8 East Marshall Street, only a block from the new hospital. This Hospitality House, in the former home of Frances Zeigler, dean of nursing in the 1920s, can accommodate twenty-eight guests in eight bedrooms with six baths. Cooking and laundry facilities are provided. Guests are referred to Hospitality House by the social services department or the chaplain service at the hospital.

Jacqueline Nichols, president of Hospitality House and special projects chairman of its auxiliary, was one of nine persons honored by the American Hospital Association in 1985. Mrs. Nichols was chosen as the outstanding volunteer for this region, comprising five states and the District of Columbia. She was in charge of the campaign which raised $250,000 for renovation of the Zeigler house.

Complementing the great new hospital on the VCU east campus almost perfectly, the federal government erected in 1983, across the James River from Richmond, the magnificent $120 million McGuire Veterans' Administration Medical Center. It replaced the long-outmoded VA medical center built during World War II.

This 814-bed hospital is intimately tied in with the VCU Health Sciences Division's faculty and student body, since both make constant use of its ultramodern facilities. Dr. John T. Farrar, of the VCU school of medicine, is chief of staff, with Dr. Hunter H. McGuire, Jr., of that school, as chief of surgery. James Holsinger, Jr., director of the McGuire VA Medical Center, wrote the *Richmond News Leader* concerning the importance of the center's relationship with VCU:

> The affiliation of McGuire Medical Center with Virginia Commonwealth University, particularly with the Medical College of Virginia, is important in developing outstanding clinical, educational, and research programs. . . . At the McGuire Medical Center staff physicians and other health-care professionals train residents and teach students. Residents rotate through the services of both institutions; in addition, MCV faculty members provide regular attending and consulting services to our veteran patients. The intellectual stimulation and excellence of an affiliated institution helps attract the very best physicians, nurses and other health-care professionals.

The Health Sciences Division of Virginia Commonwealth University is one of the few medical centers in the United States with an active combined program of heart, liver, cornea, and kidney transplantations. The cardiac transplant program is the second largest in the world, being second only to that at Stanford University.

Heart transplants began at MCV in 1968, and 131 such transplants had been done there as of May 1985. The feasibility of such a procedure had been demonstrated at Stanford in the late 1950s by Dr. Norman Shumway and his young assistant, Dr. Richard R. Lower. Dr. Lower came to MCV in 1965, and is professor and chairman of thoracic and cardiac surgery. He is internationally famous for his heart transplants and cardiac bypass operations at the Richmond institution.

Sixty-eight of these heart transplant patients were alive in May 1985. The longest survivor, as of that date, was Arthur F. Gay, a postal worker in Washington, D.C., who remained well and active thirteen years after his transplant. Current statistics show a 75 percent probability of survival for one year and 50 percent at five years. Without transplantation, these patients would have lived only a few days or months.

Only Stanford and the Health Sciences Division of VCU performed heart transplants in the 1970s, all others having become discouraged. One of the latter was Dr. Christiaan Barnard, who performed the world's first such operation in South Africa, after serving for a year as resident fellow under Dr. Lower. But the perseverance of Stanford and VCU paid off. There were no spectacular breakthroughs, but careful study of the problems and gradual improvement in coping with rejection brought better results. Insurance coverage for the extremely high costs also became available. When word got around that survival rates were rising steadily, many groups from this and other countries visited Richmond to bring themselves abreast of the latest developments. As a consequence, about twenty-five medical centers in the United States are now performing these transplants, and numerous others are planning to do so.

Legal problems arose in the early stages. A transplant by Dr. Lower and others in 1968 led to a suit for $1 million in damages, on the alleged ground that the man whose heart was removed was not dead at the time. Defendants in the suit were Drs. Lower, Hume, David H. Sewell, H. M. Lee, and Abdulah Fatteh, who were involved in the transplant. Various specialists testified that the man was dead, since his brain had ceased to function, whereas the plaintiffs contended that the death of the brain was not the proper criterion. The jury found for the doctors, and no damages were assessed. But the landmark case was not decided until 1972, and no transplants could be performed in the intervening four years.

The VCU Health Sciences Division was the first anywhere to devise the technique of flying in hearts and livers for transplants from distant points on a tight schedule of only a few hours. This program was launched in 1978. Herbert E. Teachey, Jr., transplant coordinator and administrator, who has served several terms on the board of the North American Transplant Coordinators Organization, is the key factor in this part of the procedure. The logistics are carefully worked out, and almost split-second timing is essential. Teachey is also involved with acquiring the materials for bone transplants by the orthopedic surgeons, for skin grafting by the burn specialists, and corneas for the ophthalmologists and the eye bank.

Dr. Lower, a modest man, is quick to point out that the heart transplants are the work of a team that includes Dr. S. Szentpetery and Dr. Timothy C. Wolfgang, "who have made major contributions." Dr. Wolfgang, who took his M.D. from Thomas Jefferson University in Philadelphia, is doing some of the transplant operations credited in the popular mind to Dr. Lower, while Dr. Szentpetery, a giant Hungarian, and summa cum laude graduate of the University of Budapest, is in charge of the transplants at the McGuire VA Hospital. These are carried out under the auspices of VCU, and are included in the total of VCU transplants.

Dr. Lower's other great contribution is in the area of coronary artery bypass operations. VCU was one of the earliest medical centers to begin this type of surgery when it launched the program in 1970. It was also one of the first, if not the first, to report an operation mortality of under 2 percent. About 90,000 such operations are now being done annually in this country, and about 700 of these are carried out at VCU. Latest statistics there show a mortality rate of below 1 percent, with 93 percent of patients remaining improved after five years, and 80 percent after ten years.

Unlike the more temperamental surgeons, "Dick" Lower remains calm during even the most difficult and tense operations. No oaths are hurled by him at bungling residents or clumsy nurses. If those around the operating table begin talking, a quiet raising of the eyes in their direction by Lower is sufficient to control the situation.

A native of Detroit, Michigan, he is an A.B. magna cum laude of Amherst College, which conferred on him the honorary degree of Doctor of Science in 1971. Dr. Lower also was accorded the *Ernst-Jung-Preis für Medizin* in Hamburg, the first American Surgeon to receive this prestigious award. He was chosen president of the Halsted Society in 1982. Lower is in demand as a lecturer in many countries.

Liver transplants were begun at the Medical College of Virginia in 1968 under Dr. David Hume, but the program was dropped because there was not an acceptable survival rate. A new drug and improved surgical techniques caused a revival of the program at VCU in 1984, the only such program in Virginia, and one of the few in this country.

Dr. Hyung Mo Lee, a Korean M.D. from the Seoul National University Medical School, is in charge of the liver transplant program. He came to MCV, trained under Dr. Hume, and is now president of the distinguished American Society of Transplant Surgeons. Dr. Lee has been professor of surgery at the Health Sciences Division since 1970, and is the author or co-author of hundreds of papers and abstracts. Coordinator for the liver transplants is Dr. Robert Carithers, department of medicine, with Drs. Wallace Berman, department of pediatrics, and Gerardo Mendez-Picon, department of surgery, as the other members of the "front four."

The first successful liver transplants were performed at VCU in 1984, and there was a survival rate of 50 percent from those four operations. Liver transplant operations sometimes take as much as sixteen hours, and the average cost is $80,000. Fortunately the insurance companies are paying a substantial part of this amount.

Kidney transplants also are being performed at VCU with considerable success. The first was done by Dr. Hume in 1962, and 627 have been carried out over the years, with 27 in 1984; there is a 70 percent survival rate after two years, and 95 percent for blood relations. The liver and kidney transplants are under the supervision of Dr. Lee, but the operations are being performed by Dr. Gerardo Mendez-Picon, a native of Spain and graduate of the University of Santiago de Compostela. Dr. Mendez-Picon trained under Dr. David Hume.

MCV's most ambitious operation of all took place in the spring of 1986, when the institution's first heart-lung transplant was performed successfully by Dr. Lower on Joey Holden, a seven-year-old Orlando, Florida, boy. After nearly four months in the hospital, Joey was released in August, ready to take part in sports and to return to school. Friends in Orlando had raised about $90,000 toward the cost of his operation and hospitalization. The future for Joey seems bright. MCV is one of only six medical centers in the United States that perform this operation.

Dr. Joan Brownie, of the State University of New York at Buffalo, a Ph.D. in management and policy analysis of that institution, took over as dean of nursing at MCV in 1982. The school was authorized in 1986 by the State Council on Higher Education to offer the Ph.D. in nursing.

Dr. Alastair M. Connell, a native of Scotland and dean of the college of medicine and the School of Allied Health Professions and professor of internal medicine and physiology at the University of Nebraska, was appointed in 1984 as vice president for health sciences, succeeding Dr. Lauren Woods, who had retired.

Dr. Woods, an M.D. and Ph.D., was a nationally recognized pharmacologist and researcher when he joined the MCV staff in 1970 as vice president for health sciences from the University of Iowa. His leadership, notable for a low-key yet strong management style, was a stabilizing influence on the MCV campus, according to Dr. John Andrako, associate vice president for health sciences. "He believed in hiring excellent leadership and then letting them do their jobs," Dr. Andrako said. Dr. S. Gaylen Bradley, dean of the school of basic sciences, spoke of Dr. Woods's "personal integrity in a job that is sometimes characterized by flamboyance; his concern for faculty, teaching, and patient care; and his quiet resoluteness during often stressful times."

Dr. Connell, on taking over as Woods's successor, lost no time in stressing the thought that "if there is one area that needs attention, it is teaching. . . . I don't think the medical center should be attempting to provide all the treatment in Richmond. Our primary mission is teaching." He also stated regretfully that "the doctor-patient relationship has become less personalized."

Dr. Connell said he was attracted to VCU because of its "fine, long tradition—it not only has a long history, but its recent history is one of major contributions on the national scene. Everyone in medical circles regards the medical center as first-rate, and that makes it a very attractive place to be, and a very challenging place to be."

A new dean of medicine was named in 1985, succeeding Dr. Jesse Steinfeld, who resigned in 1983, after more than seven years in the post, to accept the presidency of the Medical College of Georgia in Augusta. His successor is Dr. Stephen M. Ayres, an M.D. of Cornell University College of Medicine, chairman for a decade of the department of internal medicine at St. Louis, and medical director of St. Louis University hospitals.

When Dr. Steinfeld, a former surgeon general of the United States, took over as dean of medicine in 1975, soon after T. Edward Temple became president of VCU, there was quite an uproar. Word got around Richmond concerning his fervent and long-continued antagonism to the tobacco industry. He had been aggressive in urging the banning of all cigarette advertising, and had advocated an end to federal subsidies to tobacco farmers. Given Richmond's heavy involvement in cigarette manufacture, there was concern as to whether Steinfeld would continue his agitation. The concern turned out to be largely unwarranted; President Temple had a word with him, and he muted his militancy during his sojourn at VCU.

Steinfeld did well as dean at the local institution. Beverly Orndorff, the authoritative writer for the *Times-Dispatch* on medical and other scientific subjects, stated that he "has been generally highly regarded as MCV's dean by faculty members . . . a gentle, low-profile, but highly effective administrator who performs his duties with good humor."

During the two years following Steinfeld's resignation, before the appointment of Ayres, the interim deanship of medicine was filled by Dr. Leo J. Dunn, the much-admired professor and chairman of obstetrics and gynecology. He got his M.D. from Columbia University, working his way through. Dr. Dunn came to VCU in 1967 from the University of Iowa as the college's first full-time chairman of the department of obstetrics and gynecology, and built it up in important ways. He is a Markle Scholar, and the recipient of the Obici Award. Dunn holds or has held a number of significant national offices, including president of the American Board of Obstetrics and Gynecology, chairman of the Council on Resident Education in Obstetrics and Gynecology, and president of the Foundation of the American Association of Obstetricians and Gynecologists.

Dr. Stephen M. Ayres, the new dean of medicine, is the author of four books, has contributed chapters to numerous others, and has written more than two hundred articles and papers on medical subjects. He is a pulmonary physiologist, concerned primarily with the treatment of heart and lung disease. Dr. Ayres is a former chairman of the committee on smoking and health of the American Lung Association, president of the Society of Critical Care Medicine, chairman of the pulmonary disease advisory committee of the National Heart, Lung and Blood Institute, and holds many other prestigious positions in the profession. He is, or has been, on the editorial boards of nine medical journals.

Equal partnership between patient and physician is an objective that should be stressed in the training of doctors, Ayres believes. He has noted that many older patients are reluctant to ask their physicians questions, and he feels that this is a lingering effect of the "authoritarian stage" of medicine, "when the physician did all the talking and the patient obeyed his orders and was supposed to come back cured."

A patient ought to be able to have a personal physician, Ayres declared in an interview, agreeing with views expressed by Dr. Connell, and "if a patient becomes ill at night, he ought to be able to call that physician, and some house calls will have to be made." The new medical dean at MCV also stressed the thought that it would be instructive if physicians themselves became ill for about ten days; "it would help them understand what it's like to be sick."

The successor to Dr. David Hume as chairman of surgery is Dr. Lazar J. Greenfield, professor of cardiac, thoracic, and vascular surgery, who came to VCU in 1974, the year following Hume's death in an airplane crash. Dr. Greenfield is an M.D. of Baylor University, a former resident in the Johns Hopkins University Medical School, and a Markle Scholar, a coveted award to persons especially gifted in academic medicine. When appointed to the Richmond position, he was serving as chief of surgical services at the Veteran's Administration Hospital in Oklahoma City and professor of surgery in the medical center at the University of Oklahoma. His specialties are pulmonary embolism, shock, cardiac function, and vascular problems. He invented the Greenfield Sieve, used to prevent blood clots from getting to the heart. Dr. Greenfield edited *Complications of Surgery and Trauma,* with 67 chapters, 44 of which were contributed by the faculty and staff of the Health Sciences Division, or medical college. He is in demand as a lecturer in various parts of the world. In the fall of 1984, for example, he spoke at the International College of Angiology in Tours, France, and at the bicentenary meeting of the International College of Surgeons in Ireland. He is a student of medical problems in the American Civil War, and of the hospitals operated during that conflict.

Dr. Robert J. DeLorenzo, associate professor of neurology in the Yale University School of Medicine, took over the chairmanship of the department of neurology at VCU in 1985, succeeding Dr. Cary Suter, who continued as professor of neurology. Dr. DeLorenzo was awarded a $1.8 million Jacob Javits Neuroscience Investigative Award in 1986, the fifth VCU researcher to win such a grant.

Anthony Marmarou, Ph.D., professor of neurosurgery, also received a Javits Award, totaling nearly one million dollars.

Dr. Hermes A. Kontos, professor and vice chairman of internal medicine likewise was granted a one-million-dollar Javits Award in 1986. A few months later he was selected to receive the National Heart, Lung, and Blood Institute's new Method to Extend Research in Time (MERIT) Award.

A rare honor came to Dr. Andrew P. Ferry, chairman of the department of ophthalmology, when Queen Elizabeth II of Great Britain knighted him in 1981. Dr. Ferry had been appointed in 1968 an officer of the Most Venerable Order of the Hospital of St. John of Jerusalem for services performed in Jerusalem as director of the Eye Bank of Jordan, and was promoted to the rank of commander of the order in 1974. Sir Andrew was elected president of the Eastern Ophthalmic Pathology Society in 1984 and the American Association of Pathologists in 1985. Ferry was guest of honor at the meeting of the European Ophthalmic Society in 1978.

Dr. Henry St. George Tucker, Jr., one of the most respected and admired members of the medical faculty since the 1940s, who developed the endocrinology division, received a signal honor when he was voted the 1984 Upjohn Award as outstanding educator in the field of diabetes, a field in which he is internationally known. He is a former president of the American Clinical and Climatology Association, and of the Richmond and Virginia affiliates of the American Diabetes Association. Dr. Tucker received the Obici Award in 1982 and the distinguished service to medicine award of the VCU school of medicine in 1984.

Dr. Harold J. Fallon, chairman of the department of internal medicine, was chosen in 1985 chairman-elect of the American Board of Internal Medicine. He had served as president of the American Association for Study of Liver Disease, is a member of editorial boards of several medical journals, and serves as councillor to various medical commissions and associations.

A $200,000 award went to Dr. Philip S. Guzelian, Jr., when he was named the 1984 Burroughs Wellcome Toxicology Scholar. The award is made competitively by an especially appointed advisory committee. Dr. Guzelian, chairman of the division of clinical toxicology and environmental medicine at VCU, has been especially active in researching the harmful effects of the pesticides Kepone and Chlordane. Kepone has done untold damage to the fishing industry in the James River, and is also extremely damaging to humans. Guzelian developed a method for the detoxification of individuals exposed to it. In addition to the Wellcome Award he received a challenge grant in 1984 from the Virginia Environmental Endowment.

Dr. William J. Frable, professor of pathology, received the George Papanicolaou Award in 1983 for meritorious achievement in the field of cytology, from the American Society of Cytology, which he had served as president. His wife, Dr. Mary Ann Frable, professor of otolaryngology, was acting head of the department, 1976–78, and was named chief of staff of the Richmond Eye and Ear Hospital in 1985. Dr. and Mrs. Frable are noted rose cultivators in their Windsor Farms garden, and their roses have won many prizes. Dr. William Frable has won virtually every award in the Richmond Rose Show.

Dr. Dwain L. Eckberg, professor in the departments of medicine, physiology, and biophysics, will have an experiment on the first NASA space shuttle mission dedicated wholly to life science research. His project is one of twenty-three experiments, selected by NASA in an open competition between 350 scientists from the United States and abroad. The Eckberg experiment is expected to shed light on why people exposed to the weightlessness of space experience an abnormal reduction of standing blood pressure when they return to earth. The project involves measurements of heart rate changes provoked by changes of pressure in a neck collar to be worn by astronauts.

Dr. Nelson G. Richards, clinical professor of neurology in the VCU Health Sciences Division, was elected president in 1983 of the 8,500-member American Academy of Neurology, the first private practitioner to be chosen for that office. He is a leader in the fight to abolish professional pugilism.

A grant of over $900,000 from the National Institutes of Health was made in 1985 to Dr. Andrew J. Fantle, associate professor of obstetrics and gynecology. The sum was made available to finance a study of behavioral therapy for urinary continence in elderly women.

A grant of over $500,000 for the purpose of demonstrating the value of helping persons with head injuries adjust to their jobs, went to two MCV faculty members in 1986 from the National Institute of Handicapped Research. Dr. Jeffrey S. Kreutzer, director of rehabilitation psychology and neuropsychology, and Dr. Paul H. Wehman, director of the VCU rehabilitation research and training center, are the investigators under the grant, the largest the department of rehabilitation medicine has ever received.

A campaign for $1 million to establish an endowed chair in honor of Dr. Elam C. Toone, professor emeritus, has been launched by the division of immunology and connective tissue. Dr. Toone founded the arthritis clinic on the MCV campus in 1938 when there were no physicians specializing in what was then termed "rheumatism." Members of the immunology and connective tissue division are internationally known today for their contributions to arthritis research. Among those worthy of special mention are Dr. Shaun Ruddy, chief of the division, and Drs. Robert Irby and Duncan Owen. The proposed chair will be helpful in continuing and encouraging the work Toone began.

A bequest of $524,000 came to the Health Sciences Division in the will of George B. Bliley III, of Suitland, Maryland, formerly of Richmond. The will stipulated that the money was to be used for "research and development of long-range medical study."

The late Frank Loveall established a $600,000 student loan fund in memory of his wife, Dorothy Velma Clark Loveall, a 1936 graduate of MCV. The fund is managed by the MCV Foundation.

A notable addition to the university's Health Sciences Division took place in 1983, when the highly sophisticated Massey Cancer Center opened its doors. Costing more than $8 million, it includes fifteen separate types of cancer clinics to meet the needs of outpatients. There is nothing comparable to it in the rest of Virginia, and the center is recognized by the National Cancer Institute as part of a national network of cancer centers.

Its director, Dr. Walter Lawrence, Jr., chairman of the physical oncology division, is a former acting chairman of surgery at VCU and former chairman of the Commission on Cancer of the American College of Surgeons. He received the J. Shelton Horsley Award in 1973 for his work in cancer control, and the Distinguished Service Award of the University of Chicago School of Medicine in 1976.

The center is named for the Massey family of Richmond, which gave a total of more than $1.4 million toward the cost of the facility. Gifts came from William E. Massey; his wife, Margaret H. Massey; the family of the late Evan Massey; and the Massey Foundation. Richmond's Ethyl Corporation contributed $500,000.

More than 100 clinical specialists are involved in the work of the center. Over 25,000 outpatient visits are made annually to its facilities.

Organized treatment of cancer began at MCV in 1939, when an outpatient clinic for sufferers from the disease was opened, under the direction of Dr. George Z. Williams. A cancer center was officially established by the Board of Visitors in 1974, and the present widely ramified operation was gradually developed.

The main building houses radiation therapy, teaching and administrative areas, and research laboratories that were opened in 1984. An Oncology Clinic has been constructed in the new wing of the former Ennion G. Williams Hospital, now North Hospital, immediately adjacent to the Massey Cancer Center building, and was completed and opened in 1987. It contains outpatient examination and treatment areas, space for a special pharmacy for anticancer drugs, and for various rehabilitation activities, and an opportunity for specialists in the numerous areas to work closely together in caring for outpatients. Also included is an inpatient unit for cancer sufferers receiving either medical treatment or surgery.

Since its formation in 1974, the cancer center has been a prototype for interdisciplinary cooperation at the clinical, educational, and investigative levels. Research programs are supported by more than $4 million in grants from federal funds and private sources.

The executive committee of the center includes the following, in addition to Director Lawrence: William L. Banks, Jr., Ph.D., co-director, professor of biochemistry and surgery; S. Gaylen Bradley, Ph.D., associate director for research planning and development, dean of the School of Basic Sciences; J. Shelton Horsley III, M.D., associate director for clinical affairs and community services, professor of surgery; and I. David Goldman, M.D., associate director for pharmacology and hematology-oncology, chairman of the hematology-oncology division. Dr. Goldman was awarded a seven-year $2.5 million National Cancer Institute Outstanding Investigator grant in 1985 for the study of anticancer drugs.

A member of the staff whose gift of understanding and empathy is frequently praised is Dr. Susan J. Mellette, director of cancer rehabilitation and continuing care. She came to the Medical College in 1955 as a research fellow, and in 1962 was named director of the division of cancer studies.

Dr. Mellette won the J. Shelton Horsley Award in 1974 for the most outstanding contribution to cancer control in Virginia for the preceding year. She is now professor of hematology-oncology. Her remarkable ability to counsel and encourage patients has made her widely admired and beloved.

Bernard W. Woodahl, special projects officer for the center, works closely with Dr. J. Shelton Horsley III in the community affairs program area. He assists with program planning, and identifies lay and medical leaders in local communities who can be involved in the center's activities. Mr. Woodahl served for over a quarter of a century as executive vice president of the American Cancer Society's Virginia Division.

On another front in the fight against cancer, the National Cancer Institute made a grant of $693,000 in 1985 to enable up to 600 students of medicine, dentistry, and nursing to learn about the disease. The fund, which is to be expended in five years, also will be used to teach doctors and dentists already in practice concerning detection and treatment of cancer. Tobacco awareness seminars for students, with particular attention to the dangers of smoking, are a part of the program. Student health-care professionals also will go into rural areas, screening persons for cancer.

A bequest of $400,000 to the Massey Cancer Center was made in 1985 by Dr. Albert del Castillo, of Honaker, Virginia (MCV, D.D.S., 1912).

Overnight accommodations for families of pediatric patients receiving treatment at the college hospitals for cancer or other serious illnesses were established in 1980 by the Children's Oncology Services of Virginia, and the Richmond area McDonald restaurants. This Ronald McDonald House is located at 2330 Monument Avenue.

The above is one phase among many of the widely ramified and much-admired Children's Medical Center, the only comprehensive health-care facility for infants, children, and adolescents in the central Virginia area.

The CMC is actually a children's hospital within the larger hospital, consolidating all existing programs on the MCV campus having to do with pediatric research, education, and patient care. Internationally known Dr. Harold M. Maurer is professor and chairman of the department of pediatrics, a man of many distinctions, member of numerous boards and committees for state and national bodies concerned with his specialty, including the National Advisory Committee on Childhood Cancer. Dr. Maurer is editor of *Textbook of Pediatrics*, and on the editorial boards of the *American Journal of Hematology* and *Medical and Pediatric Oncology*.

The giant strides taken by the department of pediatrics in the past quarter of a century are noteworthy. As recently as 1960 there was only one full-time professor, Dr. Carolyn M. McCue. She is exceptionally able, the only woman ever chosen president of the Richmond Academy of Medicine, the recipient of several prestigious awards from the college and the alumni association. Obviously, however, the department under her chairmanship could not compare with today's operation, involving fifty full-time faculty members and a tremendous amount of advanced equipment.

Dr. William E. Laupus, who would be elected later to the presidency of the American Board of Pediatrics, became chairman in 1963, and the faculty had grown to six full-time members. Completion of the first stage of Sanger Hall in that year provided new space for research, and there were additions to the building in 1969 and 1974. By 1975 there were twenty-two full-time faculty, and new programs in neonatal intensive care had been added. This had been facilitated in 1972 by the consolidation and relocation of the pediatric service in newly renovated North Hospital.

Dr. Maurer succeeded Dr. Laupus in 1976, when the latter left to become dean of the Eastern Carolina Medical School. New programs in nephrology, infectious diseases, critical-care medicine, primary care, gastroenterology, and child psychiatry were developed. In 1978 a modern six-bed pediatric intensive care unit was added. In 1986 Dr. Maurer received the Distinguished Faculty Award for Excellence and the Dean's Award of the School of Medicine.

With the opening in 1982 of the new 539-bed hospital, pediatrics on the campus entered a new and more impressive phase. Using the high-quality facilities thus afforded, the VCU Board of Visitors created the Children's Medical Center.

The pediatric inpatient service is situated on the sixth, seventh, and eighth floors of the new hospital with 197 beds and bassinets. There are about 3,500 admissions annually, and an average daily census of 75 patients and 75 newborns. Some 3,500 deliveries a year take place in the hospital. Outpatient visits total approximately 50,000 annually.

There is an intensive care unit for critically ill medical and surgical patients, an adolescent unit to meet the special needs of those from thirteen to twenty-one years of age, and a child and adolescent emergency unit for emergency cases. This last also includes the Central Virginia Poison Center. Nonemergency outpatient services are provided in Randolph-Minor Hall, immediately adjacent to the Cancer Center. Pediatric group practice also is available there.

New technology such as is found in few other pediatric facilities is provided at the Children's Medical Center. Only about ten medical schools in this country have a high-speed jet ventilator, which breathes for premature infants, allowing their lungs to develop without being damaged by too much pressure. Only four centers have the apparatus that is brought into play at the CMC when the jet ventilator fails to keep the infant alive. This is a mechanism which actually does the lungs' work. So widespread is the fame of the Children's Medical Center that about one-third of the patients come from outside the central Virginia area, many from other states and foreign countries. More than one thousand applications for residencies are received each year.

Dr. Barry Wolf, professor of pediatrics and human genetics, was awarded the Science Museum of Virginia's Outstanding Scientist Award for his important discoveries with respect to biotin deficiency in babies.

A gift of $340,000 was received in 1985 from the Alfred I. duPont Living Trust for the endowment of the Jesse Ball duPont professorship in pediatrics. Mrs. duPont was born and grew up in the Northern Neck.

There is a close relationship between the CMC and the Children's Hospital (formerly Crippled Children's Hospital), located about four miles from the campus on Richmond's Northside. Dr. Ralph B. Ownby, Jr., of the MCV pediatric faculty is medical director of the Children's Hospital, and the teaching programs at the university are directly affiliated with the hospital. These programs include pediatrics, orthopedic surgery, ophthalmology, plastic surgery, and rehabilitation medicine. The director of pediatric orthopedic services is a full-time orthopedic surgeon who is a member of the MCV faculty.

The pediatric inpatient unit at St. Mary's Hospital in Richmond's West End also cooperates with the pediatric department at the Children's Medical Center. Dr. Edwin L. Kendig, Jr., of the CMC's faculty, is pediatric medical director at St. Mary's, and first- and second-year house officers from the center obtain part of their training there.

Dr. Kendig, who lectures on pediatrics all over the world, and is a former president of the American Academy of Pediatrics, with 19,000 members, joined the MCV faculty in 1958 as professor of pediatrics. A magna cum laude graduate of Hampden-Sydney, with Phi Beta Kappa, and holder of honorary degree of Doctor of Science from that college, Kendig took his M.D. from the University of Virginia, on whose board of visitors he served for eleven years. He was also chairman of the Richmond City Board of Health for eight years, and is currently editor of the *Virginia Medical Monthly* and president of the Virginia State Board of Medicine. The author or editor of several highly regarded works in the field of pediatrics, he edited *Disorders of the Respiratory Tract in Children* (1967), which was termed by Dr. Harry J. Warthen, Jr. "the definitive text on this subject" and "the first outstanding medical book in depth produced in Richmond during the past decade." The work contained contributions from twenty-nine collaborators, including seven from the MCV faculty. Dr. Kendig received the Louise Obici Award for exceptional contributions to medicine.

A three-day teaching conference is arranged each year in Williamsburg by Virginia Commonwealth University's pediatric department, with the Sutton Memorial Lectures, in honor of Dr. Lee E. Sutton, by nationally known authorities, on the program. Other similarly important speakers appear on the east campus each year at what is called the General Pediatrics Ambulatory Care Annual Conference.

Dr. Saul Krugman (MCV M.D., 1939) received the 1983 Albert Lasker Public Service Award for his studies in hepatitis, rubella, and measles, which culminated in the development of the hepatitis B vaccine, now licensed for use throughout the world. Dr. Krugman, a professor of pediatrics at New York University, discovered in 1960 that children could be protected against measles by means of a vaccine, and in 1969 confirmed that this was also effective in fighting rubella. Rubella has been practically wiped out in this country, and measles is "a medical rarity."

The school of dentistry acquired a distinguished new dean in 1985 when Dr. Lindsay McL. Hunt of Emory University came to the Health Sciences Division of VCU. Dean Hunt, a D.D.S. and Ph.D. of Baylor University in physiology, and winner of the Baylor gold medal for highest scholastic honors, was associate dean for academic affairs in the Emory school of dentistry and professor of oral biology. He has won important research grants and has delivered numerous papers and addresses all over the United States.

He succeeded Dr. James E. Kennedy, who had served as dean of dentistry at VCU since 1977. A D.D.S. of the University of Pennsylvania, Dr. Kennedy resigned to accept the deanship of the school of dentistry at the University of Connecticut.

Among the eminent faculty members at today's VCU school of dentistry are:

Richard P. Elzay, professor and chairman of the department of oral pathology, president of the American Academy of Oral Pathology and the American Board of Oral Pathology.

Richard Ranney, assistant dean for research, winner of the basic research in periodontal disease award, International Association for Dental Research, chairman of the oral science research awards committee of the association, and chairman of the American Academy of Periodontology research committee. Dr. Ranney received a five-year grant of $1.8 million in 1985 from the National Institute of Dental Research for inquiries into the nature of plaque and its prevention.

Dr. Daniel M. Laskin, professor and chairman of the department of oral and maxillofacial surgery, elected to a dental surgery fellowship in the Royal College of Surgeons in England. Dr. Laskin also was elected an honorary member of the Brazilian College of Oral and Maxillofacial Surgery and Traumatology and awarded the René Lefort Medal for contributions to his specialty.

F. B. Wiebusch, assistant dean for continuing education, man-of-the-year award and fellowship, Academy of General Dentistry.

An MCV alumnus in dentistry, class of 1947, John N. Pastore, a retired Richmond oral surgeon, is president of the Henricus Foundation, which is launching an exciting program to explore and, it is hoped, to restore, the original settlement of Henricus on Farrar's Island. The counties of Henrico and Chesterfield and Henrico Doctors' Hospital are cooperating in this overdue effort to excavate the foundations of, and perhaps rebuild the church, hospital, and school, which were virtually wiped out in the great Indian massacre of 1622.

Dr. W. Baxter Perkinson, Jr., a 1970 graduate of the dental school, where he made the highest grade point average achieved by any student in the school to date, is a talented watercolorist. He is donating the proceeds from sales of four of his paintings, depicting the four seasons, to the school of dentistry, and hopes to raise close to $250,000 in this way. Dr. Perkinson is a part-time clinical professor in the school, and is president of the Richmond Dental Society. He is a nationally known lecturer, and is the first winner of the Harry M. Lyons Outstanding Alumnus Award.

Another alumnus, class of 1947, is said to have revolutionized the practice of dentistry. He is Dr. Charles T. Barker of New Bern, North Carolina, who has designed functional equipment to make the patient more at ease. A lounge-type seat instead of a cast-iron chair, soft music, and an arrangement that puts the drills, hoses, and other tools out of sight are features. Dr. Barker's ideas are stressed in German textbooks, and his equipment has been installed in the prestigious Science Museum in London. He also devised a mobile dental health unit that travels from school to school, taking dental care to children from low-income families. Health officials from all over the world have come to New Bern to inspect the unit, says the *VCU Magazine.*

John S. Ruggiero, a Ph.D. in pharmacy from the University of Connecticut, and dean of pharmacy at Duquesne University, became dean at VCU in 1982, succeeding Warren E. Weaver. At the time of his appointment, Dean Ruggiero was serving with the Virginia Pharmaceutical Manufacturers' Association. He has received various awards for distinguished contributions, and has produced numerous publications. Dr. Ruggiero is a speaker on pharmaceutical subjects in all parts of the United States.

Among the notable members of the pharmacy school faculty are:

Paul Pierpaoli, president of the American Society of Hospital Pharmacists.

William R. Garnett, chairman at various times of sections of three national pharmaceutical organizations.

T. Reinders, recipient of many awards, including one for achievements in the professional practice of hospital pharmacy from the American Society of Hospital Pharmacists. He was also chairman of three different groups from two national pharmaceutical bodies, and recipient of three certificates of recognition for professional achievement. He received the VCU Distinguished Award for Teaching, 1982.

William H. Barr has been given the Federal Drug Administration Commissioner's special citation, and has been a consultant of the FDA for more than a decade. Professor and chairman of pharmacy and pharmaceuticals, Dr. Barr was called from California as a consultant when President Nixon had his attack of phlebitis.

Dr. John Rosecrans, professor of pharmacology and toxicology, received an international award in Belgium from the Society of Stimulus Research—a group he helped to found. The accolade was for his work with nicotine and other drugs that stimulate or depress the brain. Rosecrans was one of only three recipients of this, the society's "distinguished scientist" award.

The School of Basic Sciences has developed impressively, with nationally and internationally known scientists on its faculty. Dr. Daniel T. Watts, the first dean, to whom reference has previously been made, did much to build it up to its present eminence, as evidenced by the award to him in 1984 of one of the first two Presidential Medallions, signifying exceptional contributions to Virginia Commonwealth University. A scholarship in his honor was established on his retirement.

Dr. Watts was succeeded as dean by Dr. S. Gaylen Bradley, a Northwestern University Ph.D. in microbiology, who came to the Health Sciences Division from the University of Minnesota in 1968. Dr. Bradley was named professor of pharmacology and toxicology in 1979, after serving as visiting scholar the previous year in the department of pharmacology at Cambridge University, England. He also was an invited guest at various times with the Hungarian, Polish, and Cuban Academies of Science. Bradley has done hundreds of scientific papers and abstracts, prepared either by himself or jointly with others, as well as books and chapters in books. He was editor of the *Journal of Bacteriology*, 1970–77.

President Ackell has stated that the School of Basic Sciences ranks in the top ten in the nation in the number of degrees in biomedical disciplines. It offers advanced degrees in eight biomedical sciences, more than any other Virginia institution.

Four of VCU's programs in the basic sciences are nationally ranked—biochemistry, physiology, pharmacology, and microbiology. In a ranking of institutions on the basis of recent improvements in research, the National Research Council said in 1983 that all four of these programs were above the ninetieth percentile on the basis of recent improvement.

Dr. Louis S. Harris, chairman of pharmacology since 1972, was honored in 1983 by a $50,000 grant from Sterling Drug for the establishment of a visiting professorship. And in 1985 he received the Nathan B. Eddy Memorial Award, the highest international award to an individual for achievements in drug abuse research. He served for many years as a member of the United Nations committee on substance abuse, traveling to many countries of the world. Dr. Harris is the author or co-author of more than 200 scientific publications dealing with pharmacology, chemistry, and drugs. His department of pharmacology is one of the largest training programs in the United States, and is one of only two U.S. centers that evaluate new drugs for abuse potential. Harris received the VCU award for excellence in teaching, research, and service, 1984.

A number of other eminent scientists are on the faculty of the school. It is impossible to list all of their distinctions, but a partial list would be as follows:

Associate Dean William L. Dewey—outstanding lecturer, school of medicine, 1980–81; VCU award of excellence, for teaching, research, and service, 1983; President-elect, American Society for Pharmacology.

John Povlishock—first Javits neuroscience investigator award 1984; distinguished award for teaching, 1983; named "best professor" by four successive freshman classes.

Marino Martinez-Carrion—award of excellence, 1982; secretary-general, Pan-American Association of Biochemical Societies, 1981.

Judy Bond—executive editor, *Archives of Biochemistry and Biophysics;* associate editor, *American Journal of Physiology,* and *Cell Biology.*

Walter E. Nance—president, International Society for Twin Studies; board of directors and vice president, American Board of Medical Genetics; consultant in genetics, World Health Organization; Markle Scholar; university award of Excellence, VCU, 1985.

Robert L. Bolster—past president, International Study Group Investigating Drugs as Reinforcers, and of the Society for the Stimulus Properties of Drugs.

Steven Price—guest lecturer, USSR Academy of Sciences, and Tokyo Metropolitan Institute of Neurosciences.

George H. DeVries—Javits Award of $1.25 million for research on aspects of multiple sclerosis; distinguished scholar award, VCU, 1985.

Albert E. Munson—awarded $2.24 million by the National Toxicology Program to investigate how certain drugs and chemicals affect the body's immune system. He and his associates were also awarded $1.2 million by the national program in 1979 to develop possible procedures for the immunological study.

Charles Blem—curator of VCU's ornithological collection (largest in Virginia), and herpetological collection (64th largest in the world), given the VCU annual lecture award of the college of humanities and sciences for 1984.

Dr. Sidney Kaye, a 1956 graduate and former professor at MCV, was awarded the American Association of Forensic Sciences Alexander O. Gettler Award for outstanding analytical achievement in forensic toxicology. Dr. Kaye is professor emeritus at the University of Puerto Rico, to which he moved in 1962 from Richmond. His wife is also an M.D. of MCV (class of 1952).

The School of Allied Health Professions has an excellent standing among such schools. It has managed to achieve this despite the fact that it is spread over nine buildings. " 'Substandard' does not adequately describe some of the teaching spaces," says a school publication. "The university is courting a serious accident or even disaster by continuing to utilize some of these spaces."

The school was established in 1969 when Dr. Thomas C. Barker, who still heads it, was named dean. He had come to MCV two years before as director of the School of Hospital Administration, succeeding Robert S. Hudgens. Dr. Hudgens, president of the American Association of University Programs, had died the previous year. He had been at the college off and on for a decade and a half and was highly regarded. Barker, B.S., M.A., and Ph.D. of the University of Iowa, came to MCV from the Michigan Health and Security Institute, of which he was project director.

Owing to his ability as an administrator, he has managed to operate effectively, despite the lack of adequate space or facilities allotted the School of Allied Health Professions, and its grievously sprawling quarters. Included in the school are the departments of medical technology, radiation sciences, occupational therapy, patient counseling, physical therapy, health administration, nurse anesthesia, medical record administration, and gerontology.

Several of the foregoing are nationally recognized, and the department of physical therapy is internationally known. Susanne B. Hirt, now emeritus professor, headed the department for over thirty years. She received "every major accolade for her work as a clinician and educator," and was recently visiting professor at the University of Tel Aviv in Israel. Dr. Otto D. Payton, the current chairman, was visiting professor in 1984 at the University of Sydney, Australia. Dr. Walter Personius receives patients from all over the eastern United States.

Occupational therapy is a nationally ranked department, and the state's only department in that discipline. Scholarly endeavors as well as clinical practice are pursued by the teaching staff. Dr. Jeanne Madigan of the University of Chicago was recruited to head the department in competition with a number of other institutions. Originally established at RPI in 1942, it became a department in the School of Allied Health Professions in 1969.

Graduates of the department of health administration are sought after by hospitals and other health care institutions throughout the United States. Regarded as one of a handful of top departments in its field, it offers the Ph.D. degree as well as the traditional Master of Health Administration. This department grew out of the excellent school of hospital administration previously established at MCV. Recently, it was awarded two grants totaling $106,000 by Beverly Enterprises to implement management development programs and to provide stipends for students planning to enter long-term care administration. Larry Prybil, previously the talented head of this department, is now directing the administrative activities of the Sisters of Mary hospital chain.

The school of patient counseling also developed from a previous program at MCV, established in 1943 by the Rev. Dr. George D. Ossman. Today, under the Rev. Dr. A. Patrick L. Prest, Jr., it is turning out graduates who are in demand in many states. Dr. Prest is sought after in Europe, where he has several times addressed the International Congress on Patient Counseling. He also led a series of chaplaincy workshops in various parts of the British Isles.

Nurse anesthesia is another nationally ranked department, rated number one in the country by the American Association of Nurse Anesthetists. Professor Herbert T. Watson, the chairman, is considered "*the* outstanding nurse anesthesia educator nationally." The department originated the first graduate degree program in nurse anesthesia in the United States.

64. New 539-bed MCV Hospital, costing $60 million, with much sophisticated, up-to-the-minute equipment.

65. Dr. Richard R. Lower, internationally famous cardiac surgeon.

66. Dr. Walter Lawrence, Jr., director of the highly regarded Massey Cancer Center.

67. Dr. Leo J. Dunn, chairman of the department of obstetrics and gynecology, who has held several significant national offices in his field.

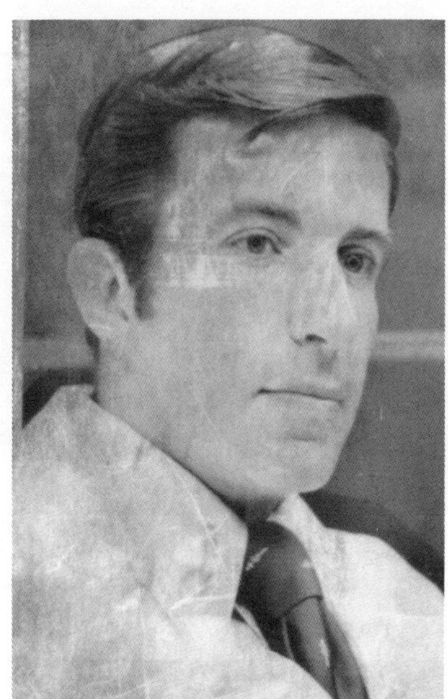

68. Dr. Lazar J. Greenfield, dean of the department of surgery, lecturer in various areas of the world and author.

69. Dr. John J. Salley, vice provost for research and dean of graduate studies.

FIFTEEN

Progress in the Eighties—West Campus

OF VAST IMPORTANCE TO THE WEST CAMPUS was the opening in 1984 of the new Student Commons, which had a universal impact and filled an urgent need. Thousands of students had been wandering around for years between classes, sitting on curbstones or lolling in Shafer Court or Monroe Park, weather permitting. Now, at last, they had a suitable place to meet their friends and relax.

Situated at 907 Floyd Avenue, and bounded on the other three sides by Main, Cherry, and Linden streets, the new Commons Building was dedicated January 17, 1984.

Even the *Commonwealth Times,* so often antagonistic to the administration, declared in an article by Rich Radford that the facility "opened to rave reviews from both students and faculty." Thousands came to the opening, many more than were expected.

This "student union" is similar to those in most U.S. colleges and universities. The first such union was organized in 1815 at Cambridge University, England, and the idea spread to the United States. MCV had been the only state-supported four-year college in Virginia without one.

The result of this lack was that west campus undergraduates had no proper place to meet and relax between classes or at other hours. In the 1950s and early 1960s they gathered in the snack bar in the Hibbs Building or sat on the wall on the west side of Shafer Street. When Shafer Street was closed, Shafer Court became available in good weather. Modest student facilities were opened in the Millhiser House at 916 West Franklin, and then in the Sitterding House at 901 Floyd.

All this was totally inadequate after the coming together of MCV and

RPI in 1968 to form Virginia Commonwealth University, with enrollment on the west campus of 15,000 or more. The Cabell Library was a place for study, but not for recreation and relaxation.

The new Student Commons solved the problem with three levels of facilities. On the lower level are the Deli-Pub, a 172-seat rathskeller with dance floor and wide TV screen, and the Stairwell Lounge. The main level includes the cafeteria, game rooms, lobby-lounge, and information desk. On the upper level are the multiuse ballroom, two small meeting rooms, administrative offices, and the student organization area. A theater adjoins the main building, and is connected by an upper-level bridge.

Completion of the commons was celebrated with a six-day program of special events, January 17–24, inclusive. The first one, immediately following the dedication, was "College Bowl Meets the Faculty," wherein VCU's College Bowl championship team encountered a team from the teaching staff.

Among the other events, extending over five days, were an afternoon of jazz, a comedy show, Black History Month preview, a chess tournament, billiards tournament and table tennis tournament, and an airband contest, with the climactic event the Super Bowl football game on the wide-screen TV in the Deli-Pub.

Exterior architectural design for the building was by VVKR of Alexandria. William Robinson and Terrill Dean, graduates in interior design from VCU, did the interior.

A second extremely important addition to the physical plant on the west campus was the completion of the $10.5 million Jane Bell Gladding residence center at 711 West Main Street, with accommodations for 864 students. Dedication of this commodious structure on April 24, 1984, only a few months after the opening of the Student Commons, provided much-needed lodgings for full-time undergraduates who had been occupying apartments in housing leased by the university some six miles from the campus near Henrico High School. Another 3,600 are housed in Rhoads and Johnson halls.

The residence center was completed in two phases, the first having opened in 1979. The official entrance is through the carefully preserved limestone facade of the Branch Public Baths, erected in 1911. There are four-, five-, and six-person flats and townhouse apartments, as well as suites. Also included are a game room with video games and vending machines, together with a laundry room offering coin-operated washers and dryers, plus a multipurpose meeting and recreation room opening onto a large outdoor patio.

Jane Bell Gladding, for whom the residence center is named, served both RPI and VCU, beginning in 1947 and ending with her retirement in 1974. A much-admired member of the teaching staff for more than a quarter of a century, she served as associate professor of chemistry, dean of women at RPI for a decade, and then associate dean of student life at VCU for four years. A Phi Beta Kappa graduate of Smith College, she studied under the renowned Dr. Alexis Carrel at the Rockefeller Institute for Medical Research. When she joined the RPI staff in 1947, it was as an assistant in the chemistry laboratory. Soon she was promoted to instructor and then to assistant professor. In those early days she taught eighteen or twenty hours a week, even twenty-three at one point. Mrs. Gladding was instrumental in the establishment of the Laurels Honor Society for women in 1970, later opened to men and women on both campuses. She was the Richmond Newspapers Christmas Mother in 1974, and two years later received the distinguished alumni award of the Collegiate Schools.

On the academic campus, the School of Social Work takes priority as the oldest of all the departments, and is also one of the best. When Henry Hibbs opened his little center of instruction on Capitol Street in 1917 it was called the School of Social Work and Public Health. From that modest beginning it became a graduate school in social work about 1930, and has come to be recognized as one of the superior graduate institutions of its type in the United States. When it entered the graduate field, the undergraduate courses were grouped in what was called the School of Applied Social Science.

Raleigh C. Hobson, who took his M.S. degree in social work in 1936, was one of the first small group of male graduates of the school. He became director of public welfare for the city of Richmond and then director of public welfare for the state of Maryland. Hobson also served on the RPI board. Dr. Hibbs had a hobby of collecting old prints and engravings, and as a token of esteem for Hobson he gave him an original woodcut by the famous Albrecht Dürer entitled *Christ Leaving His Mother.*

Dr. George T. Kalif was director of the Graduate School from 1945 to 1965, and he enjoyed a good reputation. But in 1965 a committee from the Southern Association of Colleges appraised the school, and found what it termed a lack of leadership and inadequacy of provision for development in four areas. The committee recommended that the school's accreditation be lifted by the council on Social Work Education. An appeal was taken from this finding, and a search for a new director began.

Dr. Richard Lodge of the University of Pennsylvania was chosen, and he took over as dean in 1966. By 1972 there had been a complete turnaround and the Council of Social Work Education said the school had a "program of distinction." It also found "an outstanding ratio of graduates placed with continued employment in the social work field." Dean Lodge was elected in that year to the post of executive director of the Council on Social Work Education and left VCU.

Elaine Z. Rothenberg, associate dean under Lodge, was chosen to succeed him. She had been with the school since 1960, and associate dean since 1967. Chosen social worker of the year for the Central Virginia area in 1965, she was a nationally known lecturer in the field. Mrs. Rothenberg retained the deanship for a decade, and then became acting assistant vice president for academic affairs, and the only faculty member now in the institution with the title of University Professor. A scholarship in her honor was established in the School of Social Work. She was director of the excellent University Self-Study for 1982–83. (Dr. John Andrako was named chairman of the steering committee, but found it impossible to continue, and Dr. Howard L. Sparks was appointed in his place. Dr. Ann Woodlief was editor of the study.) Dr. Rothenberg also took the lead in obtaining the renovation of the Franklin Street gymnasiums in 1984–85.

Grace Harris, a Ph.D. in sociology from the University of Virginia, and associate dean since 1978, was chosen dean of the School of Social Work to succeed Dean Rothenberg. Dr. Harris had been a teacher in the school since 1967, and the director of student affairs in 1975–76. She is one of two black deans on the academic campus; Dean Murry DePillars of the school of the arts is the other.

Dr. Edna F. Roth, professor in the School of Social Work since 1978, was elected in 1984 to the National Academies of Practice as a "distinguished practitioner of social work," the only member of that profession in Virginia to be so honored.

The School of Social Work Alumni Association was organized soon after Henry Hibbs founded the school, and has been active ever since, with regular meetings, large attendance, and a newsletter that goes to all members.

Of all the schools on the academic campus, the one most frequently mentioned as superior is probably the School of the Arts. It is nationally recognized, and the third largest art school in the United States. The two larger ones are the College of Fine and Applied Arts at the University of Illinois, and the School of Visual Arts in New York City, a private institution. The VCU school had over 2,000 full-time students in 1984 and 150 faculty members. It includes the departments of painting, sculpture, printmaking, crafts, music, dance, drama, fashion, interior design, and communication arts.

Theresa Pollak, who founded the school in 1928, was head until 1950, and remained on the faculty until her retirement in 1969. She relates in her reminiscences that the school fell into serious disarray some years after she relinquished the chairmanship.

It has "lost the last vestige of any sense of unity," she wrote, and she didn't see how "any one person could pull together, with any degree of harmony, the diverse interests and ambitions inherent in the various departments." But Herbert J. Burgart, who came as dean in 1966, did it, Miss Pollack says. "Young, vigorous, and enthusiastic, he has the ability to see things in the large and thus to organize, while at the same time he is aware of and sensitive to the individual," she wrote in 1969. Burgart held degrees of Ed.D. and M.Ed. from Pennsylvania State, and a B.A. from Long Beach State College.

Murry N. DePillars was an assistant dean under Burgart from 1971 to 1976. When Burgart resigned in the latter year to accept another position, DePillars became acting dean, and in 1977 was made dean. He is a Ph.D. of Pennsylvania State, an M.A. and B.A. of Roosevelt University, and an A.A. from Kennedy-King Community College. An artist in painting and also in pen and ink, Dr. DePillars' first love is jazz, a love which he acquired as he grew up in Chicago on intimate terms with some of the great jazz performers.

He is enthusiastic over prevailing attitudes in Richmond. "When I first came to Richmond," he said in 1985, "I was simply overwhelmed. I had never confronted an art environment like the one at VCU, one that was mutually supportive, where students seemed happy to be in school, and faculty seemed happy to be teaching. . . . People here take for granted what Richmond's got in terms of art. I hope the city and state recognize on a cultural level what they have in the arts community here."

In the early decades of the RPI school of art, its students were winning scholarships offered annually by the Art Students' League of New York. About ten such scholarships had been awarded by 1948. Others got fellowships from the Virginia Museum of Fine Arts, and had their work included in professional jury exhibits. Graduates of the school have obtained positions in some of the country's leading museums, and others have been employed as instructors in colleges and public schools.

Jewett Campbell, of the faculty, received the Governor's Award for the Arts in 1985, and the VCU President's Medallion in 1987.

The chairman of the drama department, Raymond Hodges, retired in 1969, after producing over 100 plays for the department. He joined the faculty in 1940, and served as chairman for thirty years. He was a one-man faculty at first, but the department expanded greatly by the time of his retirement. In 1985 the 257-seat theatre in the Performing Arts Center was dedicated in his honor as the Raymond Hodges Theatre.

Dr. Kenneth Campbell succeeded Hodges. Since coming to VCU from Auburn, where he headed the theatre department, he has done "sixteen things at once," as the *Commonwealth Times* expressed it. Between 1967 and 1973 Dr. Campbell founded "six theatre-oriented organizations and associations, which range from Children's Theatre to theatre programs in correctional institutions and penitentiaries."

The school of the arts became a member of the National Association of Schools of Design in 1969, and received accreditation in 1973. A great advance came in 1971 with the opening of its headquarters in the Theresa Pollak Building at 325 North Harrison Street. Seven of its departments are located there, together with a library, fashion costume museum, graduate studies, and development programs. Next came acquisition in 1976 by the RPI Foundation of the old Grove Avenue Baptist Church, which was converted into the VCU Music Center. Six years later, 1982, the great new $5.6 million Performing Arts Center at 922 Park Avenue was dedicated. It houses two of the school's departments, theatre and music. A 257-seat theatre and 502-seat concert hall are important features, together with administration and other offices; studios; dressing, practice, and rehearsal rooms; an organ suite; costume and scene shops; and set property storage space. An idea of the quality of programs offered in the center may be grasped from the fact that the first concert was given by the Vienna Symphony Orchestra, which hadn't played in the United States for ten years, and made one of its three stops at VCU.

When the Prague String Quartet gave a later concert there, the first violinist told President Ackell that he would rate the VCU concert hall as "one of the three best in the world."

The new dance facility at 10 North Brunswick Street is another important addition. With six multipurpose studios, a ballet studio, dressing areas, and a performance studio, it is presenting important dance programs, and brought the American College Dance Festival to Richmond.

VCU's department of fashion is the lengthened shadow of Hazel Mundy, who nurtured it from its early beginnings in 1936, and developed it into a topflight organization, highly regarded throughout the fashion industry, and frequently featured in *McCall's* magazine. Mrs. Mundy's sparkling personality and concern for her students caused her to be greatly beloved. When she retired in 1965, her portrait by Jeanne Begien Campbell was presented to the university.

She was succeeded as head of the department by Otti Windmueller, a member of the faculty since 1953, who continued as head until 1976, and made a great contribution. She introduced many innovations, including more emphasis on research, and student tours abroad. Despite her retirement she maintains contact with the department, and is in demand as a lecturer and juror.

The present head is New York couturier Theo Young, who has been placing graduates in the country's foremost design houses. Several students have been winners in the prestigious Drambuie Young Designers Competition—chosen over rivals from such nationally ranked fashion schools as the Chicago Art Institute and the Parsons School of Design. Enrollment in the VCU school is about 250 and growing steadily.

A particularly successful graduate is thirty-eight-year-old Roger Baugh, a native of Wise County, who was selected in 1986 Most Promising U.S. Designer—the coveted Cutty Sark Award, the Oscar for men's wear. Baugh has been on an international best-dressed list for the past two years.

Each year the school of the arts presents more than 300 concerts, exhibitions, workshops, lectures, recitals, and performances that are open to the entire metropolitan community. It publishes *Richmond Arts Magazine* and the *School of the Arts Journal.* The Anderson Gallery offers approximately fifty exhibitions each year, and has more than 20,000 art works in its permanent collection. The terminal degree in the school of the arts is the M.A., and 89 percent of the faculty have it. On the average, over 1,400 applications are received annually for the 500 openings.

Dr. Murry DePillars, dean of the school and a jazz aficionado, is given a substantial share of credit for the excellence of the VCU Jazz Orchestra. Under Doug Richards, director of Jazz studies, it has won three successive awards for the best scholastic jazz group in this country at Notre Dame's annual collegiate jazz festival. Its album, *The Tattooed Bride,* was judged the best collegiate jazz record of the year by *Downbeat Magazine.* Martin Williams, editor of special projects for the Smithsonian Institution, and son of the late Dr. John Bell Williams, longtime member of the MCV Board of Visitors, says that Doug Richards "trains musicians in the best possible way." Williams, a nationally recognized authority on jazz, has lectured frequently at VCU. Dr. Richard Koehler, VCU music department chairman, predicts that "in the not too distant future, the jazz department will be one of the leading schools of its kind in the country." Largely because of this orchestra's impressive accomplishments, John L. Clark, Richmond businessman, donated a 4,000-record collection of classic jazz to VCU in 1984. It is housed in a special room on the third floor of the James Branch Cabell Library.

An important breakthrough for the school of music came in 1984–85 when eight concerts, drawn from the twenty-seven concerts presented at the John F. Kennedy Center for the Performing Arts in Washington, were given at the VCU Performing Arts Center. These Terrace Concerts were under the direction of Marta Istomin, artistic director of the Kennedy Center. They were repeated in 1985–86.

Another significant development came in 1984, when the VCU Community Music School was absorbed into the VCU department of music. This school, founded in 1971, provides lifelong learning experiences for interested students, ranging from age four to senior citizens.

A listing of important graduates and other alumni of the school of the arts is extremely impressive. Some of them are eminent in more than one area of art, and a good many deserve much more than a mere recording of the name. A partial listing follows.

Painting—Nell Blaine, one of the foremost artists in the United States, given an honorary degree at the 1985 commencement; Judith Godwin, Ed Kerns, Marianne Stikas, David Wurtzel, Ward Jackson, Ulysse Desportes, Joe Haske, Daisy Youngblood, Richard Kivorkian. Most of the foregoing also do printmaking. Sculpture—Clifford Earl; Kimberly Spangler, also fashion modeling, and John Temple Witt, who did the statue of Bill ("Bojangles") Robinson in Richmond. Art history—Pearl Moeller. Illustration—Bill Nelson, who has done many covers for *Time* and *Newsweek,* and Mike Kaluta. Political cartooning—Hatley Mason. Design—Brett Lewis, Tim

Priddy, and Philip B. Meggs, author of the widely acclaimed *History of Graphic Design.* Theatre—Woody Eney, Barclay Lottimer, Stephen Furst, Michelle Harmon-Gulick. Interior Design—Roger Baugh. Fashion Illustration—Mel Odom. Communications Art—Bailey Dwiggins, who handles a large portion of NBC's TV sports. Photography—Emmet Gowin, Willie Anne Wright, and David A. Harvey, staff photographer for *National Geographic. VCU Magazine* said that Harvey's job as a photographer for the *Geographic* is "akin to batting cleanup for the Yankees, teaching engineering at M.I.T., whale hunting with Captain Ahab, or typing for Ernest Hemingway . . . the best working with the best."

The school of business at VCU is having a tremendous impact on Richmond's business and industrial community. Dean J. Curtis Hall, who has headed the school since 1962, and is nationally known, has seen the school grow from a small group to an enrollment of between 4,000 and 5,000 degree-seeking students. The school's commodious headquarters is equipped with a full range of computer facilities. Bachelor's degrees are offered in accounting, business administration and management, economics, information systems, marketing, and office administration. Master's degrees are available in accountancy, economics, business administration, science in business, and taxation. The Ph.D. is now being offered, also, and there is a large list of applicants, since the doctorate is prized in business and industrial management. Many of the school's classes are held in the evening so that executives and others can pursue their studies after hours.

The magnitude and quality of the operation are seen in the fact that there are 129 full-time faculty, 101 with doctorates. During the 1983–84 session members of the teaching staff published 191 books and articles. The school ranks among the top 16 percent of such schools nationwide accredited at the graduate and undergraduate levels.

Its Council on Economic Education encourages and promotes a better understanding of economics and the American economy among Virginia school administrators, teachers, community members, and the public. It is one of eight such centers in Virginia.

The school also includes the Virginia Real Estate Research Center, as well as the Alfred L. Blake chair of real estate. The latter was established by the late Alfred L. Blake, Jr., with a substantial contribution, supplemented by the Virginia Realtors Foundation, until it now has endowment of over $1 million, third largest endowment of its type in the United States.

Dr. James H. Boykin, director of the research center and occupant of the Alfred L. Blake chair, was chosen in 1985 as a fellow of the Homer Hoyt Institute of Post-Doctoral and Advanced Studies in Land Economics, one of only five economists in this country to be so chosen. He is also chairman of the Real Estate Center Directors and Chairholders Association.

Dr. Moustafa Abdelsamad, professor of finance and associate dean of graduate studies, has been named president and chief executive officer for the third straight year of the Society for Advancement of Management (SAM), an international association of management professionals and the oldest management society in the world. He is also editor-in-chief of SAM's *Advanced Management Journal.*

A chapter of Beta Alpha Psi accounting fraternity has been founded at the school, and community service is an important part of its agenda. Members have volunteered assistance to elderly and disadvantaged citizens with their tax problems, have provided free tutoring for beginners in accounting, and participated in United Way campaigns.

Students from the school of business have done extremely well in competition with undergraduates from other institutions. For example, those in advertising—a subject taught today in the School of Mass Communications—won for three straight years (1969–71) against students taking part in the district contest held annually in Charlotte, North Carolina, under the auspices of the American Advertising Federation. In 1976 a team of five undergraduates from the School of Business won a national championship from a field of twenty-five colleges and universities in the annual business games held at Emory University. Two years later, another team of five won in their division at the same business games, and piled up a score of ninety-three, as against an average of seventy-four for the other competing institutions.

Dr. J. Curtis Hall, dean of the school, received the John Robert Greer Award in 1983, the most prestigious accolade given to business educators. A native of Virginia, a magna cum laude graduate of Duke University, and an Ed.D. of Columbia, Curtis Hall is co-author of four textbooks, the most recent being in its fifth edition. He has served as head of innumerable agencies in the world of business education, including president of the National Business Education Association.

Like the School of Business, the Evening College and Summer School at VCU serve to bind the university to the community. More than 5,000 "after hours" students register each semester in the evening school for an offering of over 800 courses. Many of these students are mature men and women holding daytime jobs who wish to advance their careers or develop new interests, and more than half of them hold baccalaureate degrees. The variety of courses is remarkable. It ranges from computer hardware and software operations to Chinese philosophy, and from cell biology to real estate law. This is one of the largest evening colleges in the United States.

Like many schools at RPI and VCU, it had its struggles before becoming well established. Rozanne G. Epps, until recently the director, is authority for the statement that at one point, four classes were scheduled in a men's room! She outlined the means by which classes were arranged in the college's early days. "While it was not possible to hire a full-time teacher to teach a special-interest class to six students, it was possible to find five or six people in the community who were interested, and who would willingly pay tuition," she said. "The next step was to find someone who could teach the subject, pay him a stipend, and the class was off and running."

Mrs. Epps was chosen in 1985 by the Richmond YMCA as one of eleven "outstanding women" of Greater Richmond. Her work as director of evening and summer studies was mentioned especially, including her course "Focus on Choice," designed to help women clarify their educational and career goals, which "has become a model for others." She was appointed to the VCU Board of Visitors in 1986.

Degree-seeking students in the Evening College get the same degrees that are offered in the daytime classes, and regular faculty are available for about 60 percent of the courses. Degrees range from two-year associate degrees to doctorates. A Ph.D. in chemistry, for example, can be obtained by taking courses in evenings, on weekends, and in summers. No stigma is attached to Evening College sheepskins. There is even a holiday "intersession," a two-week miniterm between semesters for those desirous of "hitting the books" at that time.

Prominent business and professional men and women are on the faculty of the Evening School. For example, Samuel J. T. Moore, an attorney and authority on the Civil War, lectures there, and makes his presentation more vivid by appearing occasionally before his class dressed as Jefferson Davis.

The summer sessions are quite similar to those in the evening, with a comparable list of courses. Elaborate supplements are published periodically by the Richmond newspapers, giving a complete list of the hundreds of courses offered in both schools.

Members of the faculty and staff of VCU are permitted to sign up free of charge in each semester for one job-related course in the evening or summer school. Hundreds take advantage of this opportunity.

There is also the Off-Campus Credit Program, which delivers over 200 credit courses annually to a student body of more than 2,000 persons throughout the commonwealth. Anyone in the state wishing to take advantage of VCU's special resources may enroll, provided he or she is a high school graduate and meets other simple requirements.

A count was taken one morning about 1970, and it was seen that at least 300 people were commuting to the evening school from the Charlottesville area, and almost as many from the Peninsula area, especially from around Williamsburg. There were numerous other commuters from Petersburg, Hopewell, Prince George, Dinwiddie and Fredericksburg. The number of commuters is still large.

The evening and summer schools were in excellent hands with Mrs. Epps in charge, but it is generally conceded that the person who put these schools on the map, no pun intended, was John A. Mapp.

John Mapp joined the RPI staff in 1964 as director of the evening and summer school, and was in overall charge of adult programs. President Oliver was particularly interested in the summer school, and this was given special emphasis. The joining together of RPI and MCV in 1968 furnished a substantial fillip for the entire operation, and enrollment mounted rapidly.

Mapp's enthusiasm was contagious, and he communicated it to all with whom he came into contact. He introduced various innovations, including the holiday "intersession," as well as the arrangement for publishing the entire list of courses, together with other pertinent information, in advertising supplements to the Richmond newspapers. He served as dean of the Evening College and Summer School until his retirement in 1978.

Thousands of students from other colleges and universities matriculate in the VCU summer sessions. In recognition of his leadership in this field Mapp was elected president of the National Association of Summer Sessions. He was presented with a plaque by the Virginia Association of Summer School Deans for "outstanding services to State, Regional, and National Summer Associations, 1965–1978."

When John Mapp retired from the deanship, Jeff Comer wrote in the *Commonwealth Times* that he would "surely be missed," and that it was "his leadership that has made the evening college and summer school what they are today." Comer went on to state that he was "an administrator everyone speaks so highly of."

Former Dean Mapp was the first recipient in 1984, along with Dr. Daniel T. Watts, former dean of the School of Basic Sciences, of the newly created Presidential Medallion, in recognition of outstanding contributions to Virginia Commonwealth University by members of the university community.

One of the most unusual and innovative programs at Virginia Commonwealth University was produced for the School of Education by Ernest M. Gunzburg, who fled from his native Germany in the 1930s when Hitler took over, and came to the United States. He gave years of his time, with no compensation, to taping interviews with prison inmates, who describe in their own words their experiences in crime and their warnings to others. Then he raised the funds to put the plan into operation. President Ackell thanked Mr. Gunzburg for his "highly commendable" contribution to the university. This is only one of numerous patriotic and civic services rendered by Gunzburg since coming to this country.

Entitled "Your Life Today and Tomorrow," this program is designed to warn young people against a life of crime, and to get the message to as many of them as possible through the high schools. It is administered by Dr. John Oehler, dean of the School of Education, under the overall direction of Dr. Charles Ruch, former dean and now provost and vice president for academic affairs. Twenty teachers and counselors representing school districts from five Virginia counties and three cities, together with representatives of Oasis House, a Richmond youth service agency, met at Richmond in July 1984 for a two-day training session, under the direction of Gilbert Cumbia, co-editor with Dr. Richard Vacca of booklets issued as discussion guides. Several months later, thirty-two Henrico County teachers and counselors received similar training, and there were plans to continue these sessions with representatives of other schools throughout the state.

It is hoped that the plan will be adopted eventually all over the United States, and that this method of combatting the crime wave that has engulfed the country will prove effective by sending warnings to young people from those who are serving terms in prison for their misdeeds.

Also with headquarters in the School of Education is the Virginia Institute for Law and Citizenship Studies. Founded in 1978 by a group of young lawyers concerned by rising juvenile crime rates and young Virginians' disrespect for law, it has been strongly commended by the State Board of Education. The board was impressed by the institute's work in leading young people to be "more knowledgeable and responsible citizens." It has been instrumental in educating thousands of Virginia students concerning their legal rights and responsibilities. It provides speakers, printed and audiovisual materials, and teacher training in substantive law. The program is funded by grants from various foundations and legal organizations, and the VCU School of Education.

A program of Montessori teacher education, also is offered under the School of Education, providing accredited preprimary training for teachers of children from three to six. VCU is said to be the only state-supported American university that provides such a Montessori course.

A Ph.D. program in urban services, likewise under the School of Education, was one of the six doctoral programs offered on the west campus in 1985. Initiated in 1982, it is interdisciplinary in curriculum, design, and management, with a policy board drawn from several schools and Virginia State University. It furthers admirably VCU's urban mission.

The other disciplines in which the Ph.D. is awarded on the west campus are psychology, social work and social policy, business, public administration, and chemistry.

The chemistry department was notably strengthened by a $1.7 million bequest from the late Mary Eugenia Kapp, former head of the department and longtime member of the RPI and VCU science faculties. Dr. Gordon A. Melson, current department head, said Miss Kapp suggested in her will that the money be used for a professorial chair in her name, for fellowships, or for both, or for any other use the authorities desired. He estimated that the bequest would yield $100,000 annually, to be used for various purposes, including a lecture series. Dr. Kapp's friends knew that she was not short of funds, since, for example, she flew to Europe on the Concorde, but they were astonished at the size of her estate. She was highly regarded as a scientist and was the first woman chosen to head the Virginia section of the American Chemical Society. She also received the organization's Distinguished Service Award for 1969.

The department of psychology, which awards over 40 percent of all the doctoral degrees granted by the university, goes back to the earliest days of Henry H. Hibbs's School of Social Work and Public Health, when a part-time instructor taught a "course in psychology" in 1917. In 1925 Dr. Harvey deJ. Coghill, later a prominent psychiatrist in Richmond, taught a course in abnormal psychology. The department developed slowly until the 1940s when the B.S. and M.S. degrees were offered in what was then Richmond Professional Institute.

The department entered a new and much more significant phase when Dr. Edwin R. Thomas became head in 1957, a position he held until 1972. These were regarded as the department's most important years, and with the creation of Virginia Commonwealth University in 1968, Dr. Thomas was authorized to hire six new faculty, thus bringing the full-time staff to eighteen. The doctoral program was begun in 1971. When Thomas stepped down in the following year, he was succeeded by Dr. William Ray, under whom the department achieved further progress. Dr. John P. Hill, an internationally recognized scholar in adolescent development, later chosen president of the Society for Research in Adolescence, succeeded Dr. Ray in 1981. Hill resigned as department head in 1984, and Dr. Thomas V. McGovern served as acting head, pending the selection of Dr. Steven J. Danish in 1985 as his successor. Danish, a nationally recognized authority on counseling psychology, came to VCU from Penn State.

The department is granting an average of twenty doctorates a year, and has some thirty faculty members. It offers the B.A. and B.S. in psychology, and the M.S. and Ph.D. in clinical, counseling, and general psychology.

The degree of Doctor of Public Administration in the School of Community and Public Affairs goes only to persons who have had "an appropriate public management professional experience for a period of five years," and who have a master's degree or a postbaccalaureate degree in law or medicine. There is no full-time study requirement, and the applicants continue to be fully employed. Many courses are scheduled for intensive study on weekends. This doctoral degree is intended to provide advanced professional training for public executives with demonstrated administrative ability and a strong commitment to public service. Dr. Leigh E. Grosenick is program director.

In was not until 1962, when Richmond Professional Institute was separated from the College of William and Mary, that RPI was able to develop any degrees at all in such subjects as English and history. The Williamsburg institution did not wish to see duplication at Richmond, so that there was not even a B.A. in those two subjects until 1965. Today, twenty years later, there is still no Ph.D. at VCU in either discipline—only two special types of M.A. in English, and no M.A. of any kind in history. Reluctance of the State Council of Higher Education to authorize advanced degrees at the school also is an important factor, since M.A.'s in English and history are offered at several state institutions.

A comprehensive program designed to train students in writing publishable poetry, fiction, and drama has been authorized by the State Council, and is being offered by the English Department. Dr. Gregory Donovan is in charge. Applicants must submit a portfolio of work, and must also meet the general admission requirements of the School of Graduate Studies. The degree of Master of Fine Arts in creative writing is awarded. An M.A. in English/English education also is offered.

The head of the English department is Dr. Dorothy M. Scura, a Ph.D. of the University of North Carolina. Her dissertation dealt with James Branch Cabell and Ellen Glasgow, and she is widely respected as an authority on these writers. Dr. Scura is the author of *Henry James, 1960–1974, A Reference Guide,* and of several chapters in books, as well as papers and lectures dealing with various aspects of literature. She has also contributed to encyclopedias, and has served as president of the Women's Caucus of the Modern Language Association.

Dave Smith, a renowned poet, is professor of English. A Ph.D. of Ohio University, he is the author of eight books of poetry and several works of fiction and non-fiction. His verse appears frequently in the *New Yorker* and other periodicals, and he has received many honors, including the award for excellence in literature of the American Academy and Institute of Arts and Letters, and a Guggenheim Fellowship. He declined a lucrative offer from the University of Michigan to remain at VCU.

Maurice Duke, a University of Iowa Ph.D., is co-editor of *A Richmond Reader* and *Black American Writers,* senior editor of *American Women Writers,* and the compiler of *James Branch Cabell: A Reference Guide.* He has contributed many articles to scholarly journals, and has spoken to numerous groups. Dr. Duke was director of graduate studies in English at VCU, 1975–80, and director of creative writing, 1982–84.

Dr. A. Bryant Mangum, associate professor of English, received the distinguished teaching award at the 1984 convocation. Professor Arthur L. Engel's previously published *From Clergyman to Don: The Rise of the Academic Profession in Nineteenth Century Oxford* was issued in paperback in 1985. Dr. Ann Woodlief's *In River Time,* a book dealing effectively with the James River in many of its phases, appeared in the same year. Professor James D. Pendleton's successes as a playwright have been noted in a previous chapter. Dr. C. Williams Griffin, associate professor, who received VCU's distinguished teaching award in 1985, was unable to accept a Fulbright Fellowship because he was committed already to work underwritten by a grant from the National Endowment for the Humanities. Dr. Walter R. Coppedge is a Rhodes Scholar, a former president of the College of Charleston, and in 1985 was elected president of the Virginia Writers Club.

The chairman of the history and geography department is Professor Philip J. Schwarz. He is the author of *Jarring Interests: New York's Boundary Makers*, and of another book, soon to be published, *Twice Condemned: Slaves in the Criminal Laws of Virginia.* Schwarz has served on the editorial advisory board of the *Virginia Magazine of History and Biography.*

Professor James T. Moore, a University of Virginia Ph.D., was until recently chairman of the history department. He is the author of *Two Paths to the New South: The Virginia Debt Controversy, 1870–1883*, co-editor of *The Governors of Virginia*, and a member of the editorial board of the *Journal of Southern History*. Moore received the college of humanities and sciences lecture award for 1982.

Professor Melvin Urofsky, a Columbia University Ph.D., author of a dozen books and scores of articles, was named chairman of the history department in 1974, but after serving for several years he resigned the position to enter the University of Virginia law school. He won a J.D. degree there while continuing to teach at VCU. Urofsky is currently working on *Letters of Louis D. Brandeis* and a textbook on American legal history. He plans another book on the letters of William O. Douglas.

Dr. Susan Eastabrook Kennedy, also a Columbia University Ph.D., is the author of *America's White Working-Class Women: An Annotated Bibliography*, and of *If All We Did Was Weep at Home: A History of Working-Class Women in America.* She also wrote *The Banking Crisis of 1933*, and is in the process of writing two books on the career of Herbert Hoover. She has contributed articles to the *Dictionary of American Biography* and to scholarly journals. Dr. Kennedy has been a Perrine Fellow, Hoover Scholar, American Council of Learned Societies grantee and fellow, a Danforth Associate, and a Guggenheim Fellow.

Dr. William E. Blake, Jr., professor of medieval, renaissance, and reformation history, was the first president of the VCU faculty senate in 1960–61, and was chosen the outstanding faculty member on the west campus in 1969. Competing against eleven toastmaster's clubs in central Virginia in 1984, Dr. Blake won the toastmaster's championship. He drew an analogy between Britain's Loch Ness Monster and British humor, and expressed the strong suspicion that neither existed.

Dr. Joseph W. Bendersky is the author of the recent book *A History of Nazi Germany.* He previously published *Carl Schmidt: Theorist of the Reich,* which has been issued in Japanese and translated into Italian.

Dr. Harold E. Greer, Jr., with Harry M. Ward, wrote *Richmond during the Revolution, 1775–1783.*

The history department sustained a serious loss when Dr. Daniel P. Jordan resigned to accept the directorship of the Thomas Jefferson Memorial Foundation, and with it the management of Monticello. Dr. Jordan had been on the VCU faculty for fifteen years, and had made an enviable place for himself in the Richmond community. An excellent speaker, he addressed numerous gatherings on historical subjects, and won the College of Humanities and Sciences Lecture Award for 1983. He is the author of *Political Leadership in Jefferson's Virginia* and co-editor, with Maurice Duke, of *A Richmond Reader.*

VCU's physics department does not offer the doctorate, but it has been attracting attention. Dr. Cameron B. Satterthwaite, a pioneer in certain aspects of experimental physics, has been department head since 1979. The department has been gaining recognition in the general field of solid state physics and certain other fields such as theoretical astrophysics. A significant achievement was the department's sponsorship in 1982 of an international symposium at the university under the auspices of the American Physical Society and NATO.

Dr. Young Kim, associate professor of political science, was given the Distinguished Service Award of South Korea by that country's prime minister in 1984 for assisting South Koreans in legal matters. Professor Kim also made a report on attitudes toward unification of North and South Korea that forms "the basis of the South Korean government's unification policy."

A Free University for Senior Citizens, a novel concept that may be unique in this country, was launched by VCU in the fall of 1983.

A Free University for young people rather than senior citizens was tried in 1969 during the hippie era, when all kinds of novel experiments were in vogue. This Free University, which had no official standing, was opened at 735 West Broad Street. There were thirty classes on such subjects as "African Literature," "Democracy-Communism-Socialism," "Emotional Hang-ups," "Young Americans for Freedom," "Development of Pornography," and "Underground Publications." No credit was given, and classes were conducted "by anybody who feels himself competent," with students and faculty "operating on an equal basis."

"Diploma factories seldom produce anything but degenerate stereotypes who wish to maintain the status quo," the registration form declared, in words typical of that anti-everything era. A city councilman, a psychologist at the state penitentiary, representatives of the Southern Students' Organizing Committee, the president of the American Civil Liberties Union, and five VCU instructors constituted the teaching staff.

By April 1969 some 500 persons had enrolled, and ten more courses were added. Revenue from various functions was expected to support the operation. But one year later the whole thing collapsed. "Lack of interest and a standing debt of $2,000" were given as the reasons.

Persons sixty and older are eligible for the courses at the recently opened Free University, and professors emeriti from both VCU campuses are providing instruction. The program is housed in a variety of locations, including the Shepherd's Center of Richmond, an interfaith organization concerned with older citizens.

The idea for this university came from Dr. Howard L. Sparks, VCU's vice provost for continuing studies and public service. After polling professors emeriti and retired faculty, he suggested to the Rev. Robert Seiler, director of ministry to the elderly at St. James Episcopal Church, that he poll senior citizens as to whether they could be interested in such an operation. The response was highly favorable, and plans accordingly proceeded. Seiler, John A. Mapp, and others have been active in arranging the programs.

The interest has been so much greater than expected that whereas the classes were held originally at Grace-Covenant Presbyterian Church, they are now being given at various other sites as well. Subjects are much less "far-out" than those of a decade and a half ago. Sample courses are: "Traveling around the World," "Contract Bridge Strategy," "Exercise for Health," "Twentieth-Century America," "A Review of Practical English Grammar," "The Home Computer: Uses and Misuses," and "Gardening for Fun, Food, and Flowers."

The hundreds of senior citizens attending the classes express great enthusiasm for the quality of instruction and the significance that this opportunity has for them. Some come from as far away as Fredericksburg. They evidence their involvement by showing up in even the bitterest weather.

The Free University was awarded the silver medal for community service in 1985 by the Council for the Advancement and Support of Education. In the same year, John Mapp was elected to Richmond's Senior Citizen's Hall of Fame for his work with the university and other agencies for the benefit of the elderly.

In a different area of activity, VCU's archaeological research center, directed by Dr. Dan Mouer, has begun an intensive study of archaeological sites at Curles, the historic James River plantation on Curles Neck. Land here was owned originally by Richard Cocke and then by Nathaniel Bacon and others in the seventeenth century, and by the Randolphs in the eighteenth. The search has yielded dozens of important sites and thousands of artifacts.

70. Student Commons, with varied facilities for food, recreation, and student organizations, meeting a long-felt need.

71. Jane Bell Gladding and the new dormitories named in her honor.

72. Elaine Rothenberg, dean of the school of social work and then acting assistant vice president for academic affairs, the only VCU faculty member at this time with the title of University Professor.

73. Dean Grace Harris of the school of social work with two members of her faculty, Profs. Thomas Carlton and Beverly Koerin.

74. Dean Murry N. DePillars of the School of the Arts, an artist as well as a jazz aficionado.

75. Dean J. Curtis Hall of the school of business, a national figure in his field, winner of prestigious awards and co-author of several textbooks.

SIXTEEN

President Ackell and the Student Press

PRESIDENT ACKELL'S RELATIONS with the student press have often been strained, thanks primarily to the adversarial attitude and unreasonableness of some student editors. The situation during the session of 1984–85 was much improved, with a more objective point of view evidenced in the editorial sanctum of the *Commonwealth Times*, but a much different situation prevailed in several other years.

The *Proscript* was the student newspaper for decades on the west campus, until 1969, the year after RPI and MCV came together to form VCU. In that year the paper changed its name to *Commonwealth Times* and became a different type of journal. The *Proscript* was an excellent paper, and much fairer in its approach to the administration. It did not seem to be looking for reasons to attack the president, and it often reached a high journalistic standard. It also dealt exclusively with campus affairs, whereas the *Times* calls itself a newsmagazine and roams all over the map, dealing with city, state, and national issues. In fairness it should be stated that the *Times* has received a number of high journalistic awards. The paper was much less critical of Presidents Brandt and Temple than of Ackell.

Until 1970 the *Times* was the organ of the journalism department, but in that year it published some offensive remarks concerning the election of Jim Elam, a black, as president of student government. This episode, combined with the fact that the arrangement was causing a drain on the department's personnel and finances, led to the paper's separation. A media board was created to supervise the *Times,* and made answerable to the Council on Undergraduate Student Affairs.

Under Warren Brandt, the president was more accessible to the students than was the case under Ackell. Brandt came to VCU from a land-great institution, namely VPI & SU, and it is the tradition of land-grant colleges that their presidents are more readily available to students than the heads of many other centers of higher learning. Ed Ackell, in the latter tradition, holds to the view that in a university with some 20,000 students, it is difficult, if not impossible, to have an open-door policy that permits any undergraduate to drop in on the president at almost any time. There are too many demands on him, he feels, for that to be a feasible system. Instead, he meets regularly with representatives of leading student organizations.

His relations with the press got off to a favorable start when four members of the *Commonwealth Times* staff interviewed him early in his administration. In a wide-ranging discussion, Ackell impressed the journalists with his "great readiness to answer those questions and address those issues that surfaced during the interview," the paper said.

The president was not made happy, however, and neither were a lot of others connected with the university, when the *Times* published the salaries of all west campus employees making over $10,000 a year. This list appeared in both 1979 and 1980, to the great annoyance of department heads, and the embarrassment of many whose salaries were publicized. In a subsequent year the paper revealed the salaries on the east campus. All of which caused complications. It should be stated that the *Commonwealth Times* was by no means the only paper to carry these lists of academic salaries. A number of others, including several city dailies, did likewise, all of them invoking the so-called people's right to know.

But the stir caused by this publicity was equaled by the uproar occasioned when the *Times* carried an incredibly obscene interview containing virtually nothing but gutter language, and entitled "I'm Nasty and They Don't Like It." The foul-mouthed individual, who was given several columns of space, said he played in a punk rock band and had been in "mental hospitals, jails, and detention homes." It was easy to believe. The interview was not only offensive; it was utterly pointless, since it was hardly more than an avalanche of words, such words as had never appeared before in that or any other VCU publication.

President Ackell wrote a brief and quite mild letter in which he expressed "disappointment and displeasure." He added that "this kind of article does a great disservice to our institution, and raises a serious question in my mind about the appropriateness of the *Times* as it is presently identified with this university."

An almost frenzied retort from a score of students, most, if not all of them members of the *Times* staff, greeted Ackell's letter. It was termed "threat and intimidation," and the students went on to say: "It seems that Dr. Ackell, reacting feverishly, is speaking for a hearty bunch of big-money holders, who simply can't stand negative images . . . can't acknowledge filth. . . . VCU's tantamount attraction [described as "progressive attitudes and open-mindedness"] can never be dictated by muscle-headed image-makers."

The *Times* admitted subsequently that the punk rock interview was criticized by "many" students as well as by administrators, and that the paper and its staff were termed "Commonwealth Crimes," "Punk Rock Rag," "Neo-Bohemian Clique," and so on. One student wrote: "I have been reading with disgust about rats, punk rockers, and weirdos for four years. . . . The *Times* caters to a minority of ridiculous interests, mainly the staff." Another senior said the paper "does not accurately reflect the concerns of VCU" and "is damaging VCU's image, while the rest of us are apologizing for our campus paper."

The blast of criticism had a temporarily beneficial effect, for the president, in an interview in September 1982, said that there had been "a great improvement in the *Times*." However, he said he had made *VCU Today* the official university organ, and was using it for his communications. He was uncertain that the improvement in the *Times* could be counted on to continue. "Every place I've been we've always had a very active student newspaper that I've enjoyed." he said, "except this place. It's no secret."

Relations with the *Times* deteriorated again, as he anticipated. The account in the paper of a meeting between President Ackell and the faculty in February 1984 was termed highly inaccurate by the president. The *Times* reporter stated that a professor received "an ovation" when he charged that Ackell viewed the faculty as "the enemy." The account also said that when Ackell stated that department chairmen make most of the decisions at VCU, this was "received with spontaneous laughter." Dr. Ackell complained then and later that he and others were misquoted frequently in the *Times*.

The paper returned to the attack at the opening of the 1984–85 session with a front page display headlined "A President behind Closed Doors." Ronnie Greene, managing editor, wrote the story, saying that Ackell "has a history of being unattainable to faculty and students." He quoted several faculty members as claiming that they found it difficult, if not impossible, to see the president. The latter retorted that he meets regularly with both faculty and students.

Ackell spoke shortly thereafter to one of Professor Jack Haberstroh's classes in mass communications concerning his relations with the student press. He stressed integrity in reporting, and said he was unhappy with the *Commonwealth Times.* He had given interviews to the paper in the past, he said, "but when they started misquoting me" he began refusing to grant interviews.

Ronnie Greene spoke to Haberstroh's class some days later. He said he was unaware that anybody but Ackell had charged him with unfairness.

After both men had been heard, Virginia Church wrote in the *Times-Dispatch:* "Dr. Haberstroh said he thinks there was a feeling among the students . . . that 'Ronnie may have been unfair in not interviewing more students on their view of Ackell and his inaccessibility.' He added that both professors quoted in the story wrote Dr. Ackell personal letters disputing the accuracy of that story."

The president said consideration was being given to the establishment of another newspaper to displace the *Commonwealth Times.* It would be "up to the students" to decide whether money from student activity fees would continue to go to the *Times,* he declared. The paper was receiving $25,000 during the session from that source and about $2,500 a week from advertising revenue. George T. Crutchfield, director of the School of Mass Communications, said: "We are exploring the possibilities of establishing a more frequently produced laboratory newspaper which may serve the university community." The *Times* appears once a week, as does the laboratory paper now produced by mass communications, whereas a newspaper published several times a week is being considered.

President Ackell volunteered in the spring of 1984 to give the *Times* its first interview in three years. It went off well, on the whole, although Ronnie Greene, the interviewer, referred at the outset to what he termed Ackell's "nervous twitch," and to the allegations years before—grossly overplayed in the *Richmond Times-Dispatch*—of a supposed "conflict of interest" on the part of the president. Why Greene felt it appropriate to drag in this largely forgotten matter was not explained. The General Assembly at its 1984 session had made it abundantly clear that it took no stock in these charges, and passed legislation to insure that they would not be repeated.

Dr. Ackell answered Greene's questions in a friendly tone. He said his presidency "is the toughest in the state, because as a relatively new institution there were so many things that needed to be done," but "we're getting things organized."

"I keep getting offers to go to other institutions and other medical centers, but I turn them down," he said. He added that he wants to "get us through the fund drive program. . . . once that is over, in between three and four years. I will probably step down." The drive for funds was then in its preliminary stages.

Ackell said VCU is not trying to be "a Harvard or a Stanford." "We should compare ourselves with our peers . . . the very good urban-oriented institutions."

Black students at VCU have an organ of their own, *Reflections in Ink,* founded in 1978, and supported in part from student activity fees. Its staff at the outset were all members of the Black Student Alliance and the League of Black Journalists, and this probably is still true. The issue stressed most consistently in the paper is South Africa's apartheid. There are no references to the frightful atrocities perpetrated almost routinely by blacks against blacks in various African countries.

The tone of *Reflections in Ink* is less strident than might have been anticipated. In fact, its attitude toward the administration has been less obnoxious than that exhibited off and on by the *Commonwealth Times.* It protests what it regards as an inadequate number of black faculty, both tenured and untenured at VCU, and the small number of blacks in administrative positions. Such complaints are heard throughout this country at regular intervals, one reason for the shortage being that hundreds of institutions are competing for a limited number of qualified persons.

There have been two small, weak radio stations on the west campus—WJRB, operated since the early 1960s from various locations, such as a dormitory and a cafeteria; and since the middle 1970s WVCW which superseded WJRB and functions from 916 West Franklin Street.

VCU and RPI publications have won many awards over the years. It is impossible to list all of them, but some samples follow.

The *Proscript,* published by the RPI students for several decades was chosen the outstanding college paper in Virginia in 1961, and this was the third time in four years that it had been so chosen. Also, in 1961, it won first place among institutions in its enrollment class in the Associated Collegiate Press semiannual national contest.

For the third straight year the *Commonwealth Times* was named in 1979 the best college paper in Virginia, and in 1980 it received a national award at a New York City convention—first place among international college and university newsmagazines.

VCU Today was hailed in 1978 as one of the five top university newsletters in the United States by the Council for the Advancement and Support of

Education. In the same year it was selected as one of the top sixteen in the country by the National Scholastic Public Relations Association. In 1982 *VCU Today* won third place among internal newsletters in a contest sponsored by the International Association of Business Communications.

In the same year, *Research in Action* was named "the best external magazine" in this country. It also has received awards from the University College Designers Association, the Society of Illustrators, and the Council for the Advancement and Support of Education.

VCU Magazine, issued quarterly since 1971 by the alumni activities, was accorded high honors in both 1975 and 1976. In both years *Newsweek* rated it as one of the top eight such magazines in the United States, and the Council for the Advancement and Support of Education called it one of the ten best.

As previously noted, plans were being formulated in 1987 for a several-times-a-week laboratory newspaper to be produced by the School of Mass Communications, possibly in conjunction with *Commonwealth Times.*

The school offers the largest and most extensive program of its kind in Virginia. It includes public relations, advertising, broadcast news, and newspaper and magazine. Enrollment each year is around eight hundred.

The school's origins go back to 1948, when the first courses in journalism were offered at RPI. A degree program was instituted in 1950, with the first four degrees awarded in 1953. Jack R. Hunter, of the *Times-Dispatch* staff, was acting head of the operation for thirteen years, ending in 1970, and is still on the faculty. He was assisted by such part-time instructors from the local press as Omar Marden, Ed Grimsley, and Charles McDowell. With Virginia Commonwealth University established, and incorporating RPI, George T. Crutchfield was brought in as full-time head in 1970, and the program moved to the school of arts and sciences.

Crutchfield, a fortunate choice, came to VCU from the University of South Carolina, where he had taught for five years. He had taken his B.S. degree from Florida Southern College and his M.S. from Florida State, with additional graduate work at Syracuse University. This was followed by practical experience on several newspapers. Widely connected among newspaper agencies and organizations, Crutchfield has served as a consultant to the Dow Jones Newspaper fund, as a member of the advisory board of the American Press Institute, as an officer of the Association of Schools of Journalism and Mass Communications, and of Kappa Tau Alpha, national scholarship honorary society in journalism, with a chapter at VCU. All this has redounded to the advantage of the university.

The importance of the liberal arts is fully realized in the school which Crutchfield heads, and it is stipulated that the course shall be 75 percent liberal arts and 25 percent professional instruction. The school's news-editorial sequence—newspapers and magazines—was accredited in 1976 by the American Council on Education for Journalism.

The accrediting team said, however, that the quarters occupied by the school in the basement of the Franklin Street gymnasium had long since been outgrown, and the accreditation would be lost unless new and greatly expanded facilities could be obtained. Such quarters have been allotted the school in the projected new $13 million academic building on Main Street between Linden and Cherry streets. The structure, scheduled for completion in 1987 or 1988, will include a Virginia Communications Hall of Fame, and also will house chemistry, biology, mathematics, and physics. Facilities for the school of mass communications are to be among the most sophisticated and advanced in this country.

The school has had some extremely distinguished journalists on its faculty.

Dr. Edmund C. Arnold of the Syracuse University school of journalism joined the staff in 1975 as professor of mass communications, and retired only recently. He enjoys an international reputation in the field of typography and newspaper design, for he has redesigned such papers as the *Kansas City Star, Christian Science Monitor,* and the *Scotsman* of Edinburgh. Arnold is the author of twenty books and some 2,000 articles. The journalism fraternity, Sigma Delta Chi, named him the outstanding journalism educator in America for 1980. He received the VCU humanities and sciences lecturer award in 1981.

Dr. David Manning White, former chairman of the department of journalism at Boston University, came to VCU in 1975 as professor of mass communications. He has written a score of books, is an international authority on popular culture who has lectured in many parts of the world, and has been decorated by foreign governments. He is also a radio and TV commentator. White is a Ph.D. of the University of Iowa, and has been elected to the journalism and mass communications Hall of Fame at that institution. He retired from VCU in 1982.

Dr. Robert H. Bohle, assistant professor, won a National Teaching Award for Graphics and Design from the Poynter Institute in St. Petersburg, Florida—one of eight university professors to receive it. He was also one of thirty-five professional journalists and faculty members who took part in a recent seminar on newspaper design at the American Press Institute. He has since served as a lecturer at API.

Stephen Fleming, assistant professor in the school, is the author of a recently published book entitled *The Exile of Sargeant Nen.* It relates the experiences of a highly decorated South Vietnamese military officer who comes to Northern Virginia after the fall of South Vietnam.

For a dozen consecutive years the school has been awarded a grant by the Newspaper Fund for a summer editing internship program for the southeastern region. It is one of only five universities in this country to receive this grant. Dr. William H. Turpin, a much-admired member of the faculty, conducted this program for about a decade, but he resigned to take a position in Florida. The present conductors are George Crutchfield and Robert Bohle.

The school profits from the advice of a twelve-member advisory board of media professionals, headed by Alf Goodykoontz, executive editor of Richmond Newspapers. Graduates are highly successful in obtaining employment. Students and faculty have won a great number of national awards.

76. George T. Crutchfield, director of the school of mass communications, who is widely connected among newspaper agencies and organizations.

77. School of the Arts building, named for Theresa Pollak, who founded the school.

78. Dr. Thomas C. Barker, dean of the school of allied health professions, with several departments that are nationally if not internationally known.

SEVENTEEN

Athletics at VCU

ATHLETICS AT MCV AND RPI, AND AT VCU, has been a hit-or-miss proposition until recent years. Inadequate or nonexistent equipment and facilities made it impossible in the early days to have first-rate teams or, at times, any teams at all. Intramural sports have been significant at the three institutions, but intercollegiate competition has been spasmodic and difficult until recently.

The ups and downs of athletics at the Medical College of Virginia in the early part of this century were recited in chapter 4. With completion in 1970 of the new gymnasium east of the Larrick Center, students in the health sciences have been much better served. It contains an official basketball court and two smaller courts for intramural play, and space for volleyball, badminton, and indoor tennis courts. Billiards and table tennis, plus squash and handball courts, are on the second floor, as well as a weight and exercise room.

Students in medicine, dentistry, pharmacy, and nursing have a limited amount of time for athletics, but intramural sports thrive. In 1960, for example, on the eve of the opening of the new gym, 750 students were competing on twenty-one basketball teams, fourteen volleyball teams, eighteen softball teams, and fourteen golf teams, with tournaments in golf, tennis, table tennis, and billiards.

Richmond Professional Institute organized a basketball team in 1946, immediately following the end of World War II. Dick Wiltshire, who had starred in basketball and baseball at the University of Virginia before the war and had just been honorably discharged from the U.S. Marine Corps, was the first coach. He was paid $6 an hour for his services. The team practiced in a converted stable on Shafer Street and had no uniforms.

A further obstacle arose when the *Proscript* urged, just as the basketball season was getting under way, that intercollegiate competition for RPI would be "inconsistent with the best interests of the school and the student body." The paper, edited by Virginia ("Nikki") Calisch, said that a winning team would make it necessary for the members to spend too much time away from their studies. The *Proscript* advocated greater emphasis on intramurals.

Under such conditions, the basketball season was not a howling success, but the team won four games and lost eight—not too bad, under the circumstances.

The opposition to intercollegiate athletics expressed by the college paper seemed not to appeal to the majority as there were continuous efforts to compete with other institutions. Men's teams at RPI were known as the Green Devils and women's as the Devilettes. The Green Devils fielded teams in baseball and tennis in the spring of 1947. The Devilettes were competing in basketball and hockey.

By the fall of 1948 varsity letters were being awarded in men's sports—a green and yellow monogram. The soccer team was preparing to play Washington and Lee, University of Virginia, and Duke. The *Proscript,* which two years before had sought to prevent all participation in intercollegiate athletics, got out a special Sports Section. RPI was admitted in 1954 to the Little Six Conference, consisting of Randolph-Macon, Roanoke College, Bridgewater, Lynchburg, Hampden-Sydney, and Emory and Henry.

A key figure in VCU athletics for more than a third of a century was Ed Allen, who came to RPI from Rhode Island State College. He was head basketball coach from 1950 to 1968, head baseball coach from 1950 to 1975, and head soccer coach in 1950.

Under Coach Allen, VCU's basketball and baseball teams began offering real competition to rival institutions. The basketball team won six and lost six in 1957, finishing in third place among the Little Eight—the Norfolk Division of William and Mary having been added to make it eight. In the same year the baseball team had its best season up to that time. Yet attendance at athletic contests was extremely low—fewer than one hundred at most of them.

Other important personalities in the VCU athletic organization are Mrs. John ("Bet") Royster, director of women's athletics for twenty-years; Mrs.

Charlotte Birindelli, with the organization for fifteen years as tennis and women's basketball coach; and Earl McIntyre, ten years, assistant to the athletic director. Women's athletics became an integral part of the total athletic program in 1976–77, and women representing VCU began competing in the NCAA and the Sun Belt Conference.

The Devilettes had their best basketball season ever in 1960, winning nine and losing five. The following year the Green Devils won twelve and lost ten. By that time the Franklin Street gym was ready for use. Outdoor sports were usually in Byrd Park.

Following the school's separation from William and Mary, the Green Devils changed their name to the Rams. At the same time, the institute's colors were switched from green and gold to blue and gray.

In 1964 the women's tennis team won all seven of its matches, the first time that an RPI team had gone through an entire season undefeated. The stars were Tunie Dooley, Jean Cornwell, and Dot Neatrour.

A VCU crew was organized in the late sixties by Donald Bowles, who coached the oarsmen as they rowed on the James at Richmond. The crew operated for several years, and competed with teams from such institutions as East Carolina, University of North Carolina, and Alabama-Birmingham. Jim Storie was captain and later coach. Lack of interest caused the program to fold in the early seventies.

The men's basketball team won thirteen and lost nine in 1969, their best season to date. Lou Creech, who scored over 2,000 points for RPI during his career, and C. G. Winston were the team's luminaries. In the same year the baseball nine won twelve and lost eight. George Gay was the batting champ, while pitcher Don Clatterbough won six games and lost three. The following year the baseball team, with a 17-6 record, barely missed winning the small college title, which went to Hampden-Sydney. Gay was again the premier hitter.

Chuck Noe, who had coached at VMI, VPI, and South Carolina, signed a five-year contract with RPI in 1970 as athletic director and basketball coach. The Rams' basketball program underwent a rejuvenation under this leadership.

He began playing such teams as Minnesota, Syracuse, Missouri, and Memphis State. VCU, established only two years before, had great difficulty, at first, persuading these schools to play its teams, since they had never heard of the Richmond institution. However, Chuck Noe was persistent, and he not only played them, he defeated some of them, to their considerable consternation. For the years 1970–76 he compiled a remarkable 96-42 record, and put VCU on the basketball map.

In 1976 the athletic department had been in the red for several years because of budget problems. Internal strife on the men's basketball team prompted President Temple to investigate the situation. As a result of the foregoing circumstances he accepted Noe's resignation as director of athletics and men's basketball coach. At the same time he ordered that the two jobs be separated.

Dana Kirk succeeded Noe as basketball coach and Lewis Mills became athletic director. In 1978 the Rams compiled a 24-5 record. This was so spectacular that the General Assembly commended the team for having "brought honor to themselves, the University, and the commonwealth." Kirk was named Virginia college "coach of the year." He left in 1979 to accept the position of head coach at Memphis State and was succeeded by J. D. Barnett, who would compile the best record yet in wins and losses and make VCU a nationally ranked basketball power. Of which more later.

Meanwhile the VCU women athletes were compiling some impressive records. The women's swimming team, the Aquamarettes, placed fourth among 140 in the national meet at Arizona State in 1975. University of Miami, Florida, was No. 1, followed by Arizona State and UCLA. By early 1976 these VCU swimmers had piled up an amazing fifty-eight straight victories. They were finally defeated by the University of North Carolina.

Martha Quinlin, twenty-one-year-old junior phys-ed major, was named "grand champion all-around" at the national judo championships in Los Angeles in 1975. She was the holder of a first-degree black belt.

The women's volleyball team has made an astonishingly fine record in recent years. In 1975 it was 18-6 and won the state championship, which it proceeded to do for the next three years. It then had a streak of three more state championships in 1984, 1985, and 1986, with a record in 1986 of 43-3. The stars of the 1986 team were Kelly Baker, Idalis Otero, Candy Semerville and Karen Craweley.

Patty Dillon, co-captain of the women's swimming team, was named "student athlete of the year" at VCU's first all-sports banquet in 1978. She was undefeated in state competition for the previous three years and set six state records. She was selected for all-American honors for two straight years. Miss Dillon had a 2.9 grade average for her four years at VCU, and 3.0 in her major, physical education.

Another swimming sensation a few years later was Nancy Hall, a freshman, who "swam her way to an all-American title at the NCAA Division II championships in Orlando, Florida, in 1985." She was the "first VCU woman to make the national finals since Camille Wright swam the 200 freestyle in 1975," according to the *Commonwealth Times*. Nancy Hall finished sixth in the 200 freestyle with a school record of 1:54:58, and also set a school record time of 53.42 in a fourteenth-place finish in the 100 freestyle. The coach for these phenomenal swimmers at VCU was Ron Tsuchiga, who was in his twelth season.

In cross-country, Inge Schuurmans won the Sun Belt Conference championship.

In women's basketball, the best record was made in 1979 with 19 wins and 11 defeats. However, this good showing was achieved against relatively inferior teams, as VCU basketball was not yet competing in NCAA Division II. It did so in 1981–82 for the first time, and compiled a 13–11 record. In 1983 it moved up to Division I, and in 1985–86 had a 14-14 season. The leading star to date is Becky Crow, who played from 1979 to 1982, and made over 1,000 points.

The men's wrestling team had its best season ever in 1978, ending with 13 wins and 7 losses. Four of its members went to the regional competition.

President Ackell reported in 1978 that the Sun Belt Conference had invited VCU to join the seven other universities in the conference, and that the invitation was accepted. Each institution had to have six major sports in order to be eligible. VCU's were basketball, baseball, wrestling, golf, swimming, and soccer. The university also had tennis and cross-country teams in intercollegiate competition.

Dr. Ackell took a leadership position with respect to athletic scandals that were erupting in various parts of the country. He told the VCU Board of Visitors that "it is time for presidents to say 'We are going to do something about the problems athletics are having.' " He was one of twenty-three college and university presidents who met in Kansas City in 1983 at the invitation of the NCAA to consider these problems. Ackell represented the Sun Belt Conference at the gathering. It drafted a list of proposals designed to give the institutions better control over violations of NCAA rules. He was also an enthusiastic participant in the meeting of college presidents at New Orleans in 1985 which drew up much stricter regulations for the control of intercollegiate athletics.

The attitude of the university toward athletics is set forth in the Self-Study of 1982–83, as follows:

Intercollegiate athletics are a part of the extracurricular program at the university, with approximately 210 students participating. The public image of the university is enhanced by the sports program, in particular by the national recognition which has been given recently in basketball, swimming, tennis, women's volleyball, and women's field hockey. The basketball team was ranked in the top twenty of the nation in the 1982–83 season. The program has also helped gain the support of students, alumni, and the community for the university.

Academics are valued for the university student-athlete, as indicated by the fact that team academic averages currently range between 2.13 and 2.73. A new position of academic coordinator was created at the suggestion of the Athletic council to monitor athlete's academic program, maintain an athletic study hall, and arrange for tutoring, when necessary.

Athletic Dircctor Lewis Mills expressed full sympathy with the foregoing. "Once a student-athlete gets here," he said, "we want to give him direction, we want him to get a degree. We would like to shoot for a 100 percent rate of graduation for our student athletes. You can't lower your standards to improve athletics."

Mills's contract was not renewed when it expired on June 30, 1986, and his ten-year incumbency as athletic director came to an end. President Ackell said in explanation: "I'm looking for a lot of improvement in the overall structure, image, and development of our athletic program. I know what a well-rounded athletic organization can do for a university. Unfortunately, we don't appear to have one right now." The basketball program underwent tremendous expansion under Mills, but his performance in other areas was not deemed satisfactory.

Dr. Richard L. Sander, assistant athletic director at Memphis State, was chosen to succeed Mills. "I see an awful lot of good things going on at VCU," he said, "and the school has the potential to do a lot more." Sander was said to be particularly effective as a fundraiser.

The university has serious problems with facilities for its sports activities. Facilities had to be rented from the city for women's field hockey and softball and men's soccer and baseball. Other equipment also is inadequate, with the result that VCU teams "have to travel more frequently and can host few events."

VCU initiated a weekend clinic in 1984 for the purpose of diagnosing, treating, and rehabilitating athletic injuries. The service is available to all athletes, but special attention is given to football players and other athletes from the Richmond area. The plan was conceived and developed by George Borden, VCU's sports medicine director. Dr. Thomas P. Loughran, member of the department of orthopedic surgery and former team physician for the Philadelphia Flyers of the National Hockey League, works with him on the program.

"Our goal is to have our patients treated, from start to finish, by people who are truly attuned to athletic injuries," Dr. Loughran stated. The clinic will not concern itself with drastic injuries, such as fractures or torn ligaments.

"The injury that forces you to carry the kid from the field on a stretcher . . . well, we're probably going to see that kid anyway," added Loughran. "The kid we're interested in is the one who has twisted his knee. He wakes up in the morning, it's sore, and he isn't sure how serious it is or what to do about it." Special equipment is available for the diagnosis and treatment of such injuries.

On another front, Billy Smith, who played center field and shortstop for the Rams in 1983, made such a superlative record that he was drafted by the New York Yankees, and sent to their farm system. Donnie Phillips, assistant coach and former star catcher for VCU, was invited to rookie camp by the world champion Detroit Tigers in 1985.

The VCU tennis team was exceptionally successful in 1984 and 1985, with an 18-12 record in the former year and 21-9 in the latter. Norm Schellenger, Jr., state collegiate champion, winner of the Sun Belt Conference tournament, and later men's state singles champion and a participant in international competition, was VCU's top player for 1984. Dave Hughes, ranked number two on the team, was Sun Belt runner-up.

In 1985 the team acquired three players from foreign lands and made the best record in VCU tennis history, defeating the University of Virginia 6-3, the first time UVA had lost to a state Division I team in five years. Kris Juliusson of West Germany was the no. one player, followed by Dave Hughes. Others in the first six were Spencer Kooshian, Scott Pennington, Jamie Hevron from Australia, and Fiesal Hassan from Zimbabwe. Hugh Waters IV, the coach who recruited most of these players, resigned in 1985 for personal reasons.

While the tennis record is exceptional, that of basketball in recent times has been even more so. During his six years as coach, ending in 1985, J. D. Barnett took his teams to the NCAA tournament by invitation five of those years, and compiled an overall record of 132 wins and 42 losses. His 1985 team had a 26-6 record, and ranked eleventh in the nation in both the Associated Press and United Press International polls. While VCU basketball teams had never had a losing season since 1968—before 1986—this national ranking is truly amazing, given the fact that VCU did not come into existence until 1968, and was completely unknown at that time. Barnett was chosen Sun Belt Coach of the Year twice.

During games, Coach Barnett seemed almost on the verge of apoplexy. "He's like a mad bee in a bottle," Lisa M. Antonelli wrote in the *Commonwealth* magazine. "He yells until his face is blue and his players' are red. . . . Watching him, you'd think that fitness and his relatively young forty years were the only obstacles between him and a massive coronary. . . . Barrett screams so ferociously that his daily diet includes a pack of Hall's Mento Lyptus drops in his throat."

Given Barnett's remarkable record in carrying VCU almost to the top of U.S. college basketball, it was to be expected that other institutions would seek his services. Some of them did, but he said several times that he had no intention of leaving. Then, all of a sudden, he announced in April 1985 that he had accepted an offer from the University of Tulsa. His six-year reign over VCU basketball was at an end.

Mike Pollio, who had served as assistant coach at VCU in 1973–75 under Chuck Noe, and was the highly successful head coach at Kentucky Wesleyan since 1979, was chosen to succeed Barnett. Pollio's teams won four Great Lakes Valley Conference championships, and in three of his last four years at Kentucky Wesleyan they were among the final four in the NCAA's Division II tournament. His overall record there was an impressive 117–35, and he was extremely popular.

The new VCU coach lost little time in making it known in no uncertain terms that he regarded the past academic showing of basketball players at the institution as "an embarrassment to the reputation of our school." Obviously speaking with the approval of President Ackell, he made it plain that there would be much more careful monitoring of basketball players' academic performance in the future.

Admitting that in the past he had been "as guilty as anyone," Pollio said "everything you read about academics among our student athletes is negative, negative, and I'm tired of it." He was particularly disturbed over publication in *USA Today* that from 1972 to 1982, VCU's percentage for graduation of basketball players was next to the lowest among the eight institutions in the Sun Belt Conference.

Pollio emphasized that new requirements had been laid down. In a two-page memorandum, approved by the administration, important provisions are as follows:

> Progress toward graduation: The NCAA requires a student-athlete to pass 24 hours a year. However, this does not give the athlete his required 126 hours toward graduation (from VCU). I will require any basketball player to pass 30 hours per year. If he has not passed these 30 hours by the end of the spring semester he will be required to attend summer school.
>
> Study hall: There will be mandatory study halls. They will be held in the library with an assistant coach in charge. Study hall will be open three nights a week. The following will be required to attend: all freshmen and anyone below a 2.0 [grade]—three nights; all transfers and anyone below 2.25—two nights; anyone between 2.25 and 2.5—one night.
>
> Evaluation forms: Every three weeks the players must present to their instructor an evaluation form which asks for their present grade and attendance record. The form will be returned to me.

The administration also has provided Pollio with a full-time director of academic counseling (Dr. Charles McLeod), and a standing faculty-administration-alumni committee (the VCU Intercollegiate Athletic Council), whose job is to formulate policy and ride herd on those responsible for carrying it out. These impressive and refreshing innovations should go far to make certain that conditions which prevailed under Coach Barnett will not be repeated.

In his first season as coach at VCU, Mike Pollio made a respectable showing. He was handicapped severely by the loss of three players from the previous year who went to the pros, and his team was relatively inexperienced. It got off to a discouraging start by losing three games in overtime and four by five or fewer points. But then it pulled itself together and did well. Pollio's future as a coach at VCU seemed bright.

Mike's modus operandi during games is on the wild side. Jennings Culley described it in the *Richmond News Leader:* "He leaps off the bench and punches the air with his fist. He jumps high and does a 360 degree pirouette faster than Mary Lou Retton. He falls on all fours and buries his head. He stomps the floor, then squats and slaps it with his hands . . . 'If I want my players to be at a sky-high level,' " says Pollio, 'I have to stay up there with them.' "

Some great basketball stars have played for Virginia Commonwealth University. Lorenza Watson blocked 135 shots during the 1977 season, a total that Coach Dana Kirk thought was a record for the whole country. Watson blocked 381 shots during his career at VCU and had 1,134 rebounds.

Gerald Henderson, a graduate of Richmond's Huguenot High School, ended his four years at VCU as a star of the first magnitude. He had an astonishing streak of sixty-three consecutive games in which he scored in double figures. Henderson graduated with a degree in health and physical education, and went to the Boston Celtics. He played on two Celtic teams that won the National Basketball Association championship, and was universally credited with making a clutch play in one of those games that was crucial to winning the title. In late 1984, nevertheless, he was traded to the Seattle Sonics, for reasons which few could understand, and which evidently had nothing to do with his ability.

Calvin Duncan is another VCU player for whom the sky would seem to be the virtual limit. Rich Radford wrote of him in the *Commonwealth Times:* "Calvin Duncan has the chance to become the best basketball player ever to come out of Virginia Commonwealth University. Better than Jesse Dark, better than Bernard Harris, better than Edmund Sherod, and maybe better than Gerald Henderson." He was "co-player of the year" for 1983 in the Sun Belt Conference, and in 1984 won a place on the all–Sun Belt first team, with Mike Schlegel and Michael Brown on the second team. In 1985 Rolando Lamb made the first team, Calvin Duncan the second team, and Mike Schlegel got honorable mention. Duncan received the first Sun Belt Conference Young Award for athletic, academic, and community endeavors.

The three stars of the 1985 team, Duncan, Lamb, and Schlegel, were all drafted by the pros. Duncan, with a 13.6 career scoring average, had played in ten tournaments and made the all-tournament team in nine of them. Lamb had a 17.3 average for his final season, and a 9.4 average for his career, with 550 assists. Schlegel, not notably tall or quick, made up for it with strength, drive, and determination. He had a career scoring average of 9.7 and 6.1 rebounds.

Virginia Commonwealth University had established itself by 1985 as nationally ranked in several branches of athletics. There were still deficiencies in facilities and equipment, but these had been upgraded. Proper attention was being paid to the scholastic performance of athletes, and President Ackell was determined to keep it that way. In less than two decades the university had made a place for itself as a strong competitor and a leading exemplar of clean athletics and superior sportsmanship.

79. Mike Pollio, coach of basketball, who made it plain on his arrival in 1985 that he would insist on adequate scholastic performance by his teams.

80. Gerald Henderson, one of the great basketball stars in VCU history, drafted by the Boston Celtics.

81. Calvin Duncan, one of the top performers in VCU basketball history, drafted by the pros, shown in action.

82. Mike Schlegel, another VCU basketball star who went to the pros.

83. Kelly Baker, a star of the championship women's volleyball team of 1986.

84. Idalis Otero, another star of the 1986 championship volleyball team.

85. Karen Craweley, also a star performer on the 1986 team.

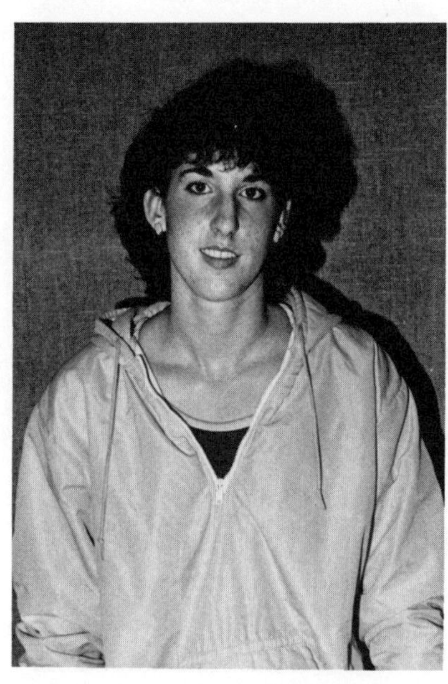

86. Nancy Hall, all-American swimmer in 1985, and holder of several VCU records.

87. Lewis B. Mills, director of athletics, 1976–86.

EIGHTEEN

A Forward Pace in Academe

ANNUAL FACULTY EVALUATION, even for tenured professors, was put into effect in 1984 by President Ackell, with the approval of the Board of Visitors. VCU is one of a minority of universities that have instituted this procedure. The subject was on the agenda of the Association of Governing Boards in 1984, and is being discussed nationwide.

"In essence," said Dr. Ackell in explaining the innovation, "the conclusions thus far indicate that the evaluation process should be developmental, rather than regulatory, and geared to improve and strengthen faculty performance. I believe our plan will meet these criteria."

A major criticism of tenure from outside the academic community is that it provides professors with a lifetime job, but with virtually no control over whether they perform well or poorly. Dr. Ackell emphasized that the plan strengthens tenure against these outside criticisms, since "we can and should have a reliable evaluation process."

The American Association of University Professors opposed this faculty appraisal as endangering academic freedom, but VCU went ahead anyway. As first outlined, the plan also met strong opposition from the faculty senate, but after modifications were introduced it was approved overwhelmingly. The annual evaluations are being conducted by departmental chairmen who make recommendations to the dean. A similar system is in effect at Virginia Polytechnic Institute and State University and at Radford University.

VPI and the University of Virginia are collaborating with VCU in an important cooperative graduate engineering program put into effect in the fall of 1983, and conducted via television. Courses in seven areas of engineering—chemical, civil, electrical, mechanical and systems engineering, industrial engineering and operations research, and materials science—are offered.

A long-standing void in the Richmond community is filled by this program, since it provides an opportunity for local engineers to obtain graduate instruction, and is an important factor in attracting new industry. Such Richmond-area companies as Philip Morris, Reynolds Metals, Virginia Power, DuPont, Allied Chemical, and Western Electric are taking advantage of the opportunity to give their staffs on-the-job training, when this is needed.

The program was launched under the direction of Dr. Thomas W. Haas. Students view the lectures, which are beamed live on color television by microwave from UVA and VPI. Audio communication between students and professors is made possible by highly directional microphones. The course is not limited to professional engineers; anyone with a proper educational background may enroll.

As early as 1930 the first two years of engineering were provided at RPI in a course that functioned in collaboration with VPI. Professor C. A. B. Foster was in charge of the program from 1942 to 1968. Then when VCU came into existence the course was called the curriculum in engineering. Students could attend for two years and then matriculate at VPI, UVA, or elsewhere for the last two years. Under President Warren Brandt it seemed desirable to expand the course to four years or to discontinue it. The decision was to discontinue. The course was not revived until 1983, when technical innovations made possible the present sophisticated offering.

Enthusiastic support for this graduate engineering project via television was expressed by T. Justin Moore, Jr., able utility executive and chairman of Governor Charles S. Robb's task force on science and technology in Virginia, charged with developing and promoting the highly significant Center for Innovative Technology.

The idea for such a center in Northern Virginia was primarily the result of suggestions from Moore and Robert E. R. Huntley, former president of Washington and Lee University, to Governor Robb. Aware of North Carolina's Industrial Triangle and other such centers, with their ability to attract industry, Moore and Huntley set out to develop something similar in Virginia. Governor Robb lent strong support at all points, and was instrumental in obtaining a $30 million appropriation from the state for the purpose.

This center in Northern Virginia is based largely on the scientific expertise of Virginia Commonwealth University, the University of Virginia, Virginia Polytechnic Institute, George Mason University, and Old Dominion University. Dr. John J. Salley, VCU vice provost for research and dean of graduate studies, was appointed vice president for administration and continuing education at the center. He served as interim director until a permanent director could be chosen from among the 240 applicants, of whom Dr. Salley was not one. He said he preferred to return to VCU on July 1, 1987.

A native Richmonder and alumnus of RPI, Dr. Salley took a degree in dentistry from MCV and a Ph.D. in pathology from the University of Rochester. He served as chairman of the department of oral pathology at MCV, and later as dean of the University of Maryland dental school and as a member of the Johns Hopkins University faculty. Salley went back to VCU in 1974 as vice president and dean. The following year Boston University conferred on him the honorary degree of Doctor of Science.

Dr. Robert H. Pry, a sixty-year-old retired research and electronics executive with Gould of Chicago, a large-scale manufacturer of advanced technology equipment and systems, was selected to head the facility in Northern Virginia. Nationally known as a scientist and administrator, Pry took over on January 1, 1985. "The people of Virginia pulled off quite a coup" in getting Dr. Pry, William Carey, executive director of the American Association for the Advancement of Science, said. President Frank L. Hereford, Jr., of the University of Virginia, himself an internationally known scientist, termed Pry "an absolutely first-rate scientist with a very impressive background in industry, and with many university associations in the country."

About a dozen of the nation's leading defense contractors, acting as a consortium, announced that they would locate on the center's thirty-five-acre tract near Dulles Airport. Among them are such tremendous operators as Boeing, General Dynamics, Lockheed, McDonnell Douglas, Rockwell International, and United Technologies.

Each of Virginia's participating universities will make a contribution to the operation consistent with its field of expertise. VCU will lead in biotechnology, with strong participation by UVA. Dr. Marino Martinez-Carrion, chairman of the department of biochemistry in VCU's school of basic sciences, will be in charge.

The project got off to a slow start. Dr. Pry, though an excellent scientist, apparently did not have the qualifications needed to promote and develop the center. He resigned in March 1986, and Dr. Ronald E. Carrier, the highly successful president of James Madison University, was named to succeed him. Carrier took a one-year leave of absence from James Madison.

With characteristic energy and initiative, Carrier got things moving, despite the difficulty of making plans for buildings on land held by two owners—eighteen acres in Fairfax County and seventeen in Loudoun. Financing also presented problems, but they were surmounted. Ground was broken on September 11 for the center's three-building, $24 million complex. Carrier was succeeded in 1987 by Dr. Edward M. Davis of IBM.

With the drastic change in student attitudes toward military training in the late 1970s and early 1980s, the army's Reserve Officer Training Corps was back in the good graces of the younger generation. VCU's ROTC classes were being taught at the University of Richmond, and later on the VCU campus. During the Vietnam war and the years immediately following, there had been nationwide demonstrations against the ROTC.

An ROTC course was not offered on campus at VCU until 1983. For several previous years there had been a collaborative arrangement with the University of Richmond, and VCU enrollees had to journey to that campus for the classes and drills. Commuting time and expense have been eliminated by the new plan. It also is said to enhance military career opportunities for VCU students, and to provide greater availability of scholarship aid.

Tuition, fees, and books, plus $100 a month for ten months, are provided for students in the ROTC. Also there is "a good chance for employment at $17,000 per year after graduation." In return, four years of active duty in the U.S. Army are required, after graduation as a second lieutenant. No fewer than 1,400 colleges and universities were expected to participate, of which 315 would train the cadets on campus, as at VCU.

On recommendation of President Ackell and with Board of Visitors' approval, a student was appointed to the visitors for the first time in 1982, but was not allowed to vote or attend executive sessions. Karen Fulper, an occupational therapy major, was the first appointee, with Ricky Mason, an economics and political science double major, as alternate. They were chosen by Ackell from lists submitted by the student governments on the two campuses. The student affairs committee recommended that one student be named to the board from each campus, but Ackell objected, saying that "this is one university", and there would be but one appointee.

Students also are represented on almost all the major policy-making committees, including those on tenure and promotion. Also, the university council has ten student members and the committee on student affairs eight. Students must apply for these appointments, and be recommended by the student appointments committee.

Surveys of freshman classes from 1973 to 1981, inclusive, showed that conservatism had grown during the period, since in 1973 only 7 percent described themselves as conservative, as against 17.3 percent in 1981. Similarly, in 1973 those calling themselves liberal totaled 44 percent, whereas the percentage had dwindled to 20.1 percent by 1981.

The freshmen gave three principal reasons why they chose VCU—academic reputation, availability of a particular major or degree program, and relatively low tuition cost. The poll also showed that approximately 40 percent of the freshman were in the top quarter of their high school classes.

About 12 percent of all students in 1982 were over thirty-five years of age. Two years later, 14.5 percent were black, the largest percentage in any largely white Virginia institution of higher learning. In the same year, 12 percent of VCU's 3,131 graduates were black, also the largest; University of Virginia had only 5.3 percent and VPI 2.4 percent.

The Rev. Curtis W. Harris, president of the Virginia branch of the Southern Christian Leadership Conference, complained that less than 10 percent of the faculty was black. Nevertheless, the State Council on Higher Education said that with thirty-eight black faculty in 1984–85, VCU led all the largely white state colleges and universities in the number of such teachers. Richmond City Councilman Henry Richardson, a black VCU graduate in planning, complained that his racial compatriots were not getting their due in the institution. Martin A. Miles, a black graduate student in policy analysis, said in a letter to the student newspaper that "we are now in the midst of a crisis situation at VCU." However, insofar as teaching staff is concerned, the basic problem at this and nearly all other universities is that the number of qualified black teachers is insufficient to satisfy the demand.

With almost all restrictions lifted with respect to visitation in the dormitories, a questionnaire distributed in 1983 to 150 students on the freshman floors of Johnson and Rhoads halls showed that 59.3 percent of the women and 19.04 percent of the men (a strange discrepancy), had had sex ten or more times in the preceding ten weeks. Results of the poll were published in the *Commonwealth Times.* Given the relaxed and permissive attitudes toward such behavior of many clergymen and religious teachers, the amount of sexual activity revealed by the questionnaire is hardly surprising. A poll in 1984 of 469 such persons in mainline Christian and Jewish congregations, as announced in *Psychology Today*, had it that 60 percent saw no objection to premarital sex, and 25 percent found adultery acceptable.

VCU police make many arrests on their rounds, but the vast majority of those arrested are not students. In 1982 and 1983 nearly 1,000 persons were taken into custody, but only 51 of these were enrolled at VCU. A VCU escort service is available as a protection for any student, faculty, or staff member. The service can be called on from 7 to 11 P.M., Monday through Thursday.

Fraternities are functioning freely at the university. There were eleven for males and six sororities for females in 1984, plus several auxiliary groups, with an overall total membership of about 400. Hazing is illegal, and most of these organizations require members to maintain a specific minimum grade point average,usually 2.5. Most also have certain hours set aside each day as library hours. A few are racially integrated.

"A lot of freshmen enter college wanting to join a fraternity because they think frats are like the ones in *Animal House*," Mike Carosi, of Kappa Sigma, said in an interview. "They think they'll be drinking beer and partying all the time, but when they get here they see it's not like that. We party together but we also work together."

The Greek letter organizations are active in promoting various public service projects, and this is especially true of the black fraternities and sororities. The blacks and whites work together, as in sponsoring Alcohol Awareness Week.

This is not to say, however, that all is sweetness and light in the domain of the Greeks. A fraternity was dropped from the official register in 1974 for failing to comply with the university's segregation policy. Then in 1983 members of Omega Psi Phi, a black fraternity with chapters at both VCU and Virginia Union University, got into a brawl with members of VCU's black Phi Beta Sigma. It occurred at a dance in the Franklin Street gym, and was quelled quickly by campus police and security personnel, according to an article in *Reflections in Ink*. But members of Omega Psi Phi then went looking for members of Phi Beta Sigma, both at the Wood Creek Apartments and at the university's new residence center. According to Kenneth L. Ender, director of VCU student activities, Omega Psi Phi was "obviously the aggressor". They did from $500 to $1,000 worth of damage to the apartment at Wood Creek, and then forced their way into the living quarters of Leslie

Rhodes at the residence center. "Several members assaulted him" and "he was hospitalized with minor injuries," Ender said. Ender withdrew the fraternity's official registration as a student organization.

Unbrotherly behavior toward one another by members of Sigma Phi Epsilon was noted in 1984 by Robert Benson in the *Commonwealth Times.* SPE, the largest fraternity on campus, is noted for "brothers fighting, brothers being thrown out of the frat, and even rumors of the whole frat being kicked off campus," Benson wrote. "Numerous fights have broken out at a local bar where SPE holds its weekly night activities every Thursday night." The fraternity's national charter was recently suspended, the article went on, and "to get it back they have had to hold 'a goal-setting retreat, structure a stronger brotherhood-development program, and work on their upkeep and maintenance of their fraternity house located at 1112 West Cary Street.' "

Academic dishonesty by students is dealt with on the east and west campuses by somewhat different means. The Self-Study of 1982–83 says on the point:

> Academic campus students are covered by the Academic Integrity Policy, approved in 1979. Following an examination of the case by the school coordinator (a faculty member), accused students are heard by an academic integrity board of four faculty members and two students; the board decides on guilt or innocence and sets penalties. The student has the right to appeal the decision. The MCV campus schools have long operated under an honor system, established in the constitution of the MCV student body. Accused students are heard by an honor council comprised of elected student representatives; the student has the right to appeal the decision.

The Self-Study went on to say that "these integrity policies have had some success." On the west campus, even though the faculty members have copies of the document setting forth the policy, "not all are fully aware of it yet." As for the MCV honor council, it "has had varying degrees of acceptance." Furthermore, 64 percent of faculty and 47 percent of students have either no knowledge of or no opinion regarding these systems, in spite of the wide publication."

Cheating was rampant on the academic campus in recent years, according to Jamie Sutphin, who wrote in the *Commonwealth Times* for April 3, 1984: "Getting away with cheating time and again, many students find it just another way to get a grade. . . . It's more fun than fear that students feel when they xerox old tests, open their notebooks, stare over shoulders and lean low on desks. I thought I was getting away from all that when I left high school, but if anything it's worse. . . . I've watched cheaters at VCU for three years. . . . It seems an understatement to say that it's unfair. As they cheat themselves, they cheat the entire campus."

Only two cases of cheating were brought before the academic integrity board on the west campus during the session of 1984–85. Neither student was expelled. As for the east campus, two cases have been brought before the honor council in recent years; one of these students was thrown out of the institution.

A plan to grant presidential scholarship awards to a limited group of topflight students, half freshmen and half transfers, became effective in September 1982, when the first twelve recipients entered the university. The awards are based on scholarship, statements of academic purpose, and supporting statements from high schools or colleges. The scholarship carries with it a cash award, access to honors courses and independent study courses, special summer orientation, library privileges, and first option to live in a privately owned apartment, usually available to upper class students only.

Additional special recognition for the gifted came the following year when an honors program was launched, with eighty-six students enrolled, ranging in age from seventeen to forty-five, and with women in the majority. A cumulative grade-point average of at least 3.5 is required. Those admitted to the program may take special classes, and they receive library, registration, and housing privileges denied the average undergraduate. There are also scholarships for the best-qualified students, and lectures by distinguished speakers, together with cultural enrichment activities. The program is coordinated by Dr. Thomas O. Hall, Jr., professor of philosophy and religious studies, who received the Distinguished Service Award at the 1986 convocation.

In an article in the *Richmond News Leader,* Dr. Hall explained that "the honors classes bring together outstanding students and enthusiastic professors who are carefully chosen because of scholarly ability, teaching expertise, and commitment to honors students." And he went on to say:

> Students and professors frequently comment that these small classes are always more challenging and more exciting. Students become intensely involved in the intellectual life as participants, not just recipients. Discussion stimulates the learning experience where students from various backgrounds interact with each other by exchanging information, ideas and values. . . . One of the most innovative features of the VCU Honors Program is a special linkage with five schools—including the school of medicine—on the MCV campus. Each year a group of carefully selected

honors students, who are still high school seniors, will be given early admission to various health sciences courses on the MCV campus. If these students maintain a 3.5 grade-point average, and fulfill other requirements, they need not make any further application for admission. This arrangement will encourage students preparing for health careers to broaden their education by taking more electives in the humanities and social sciences, which many leading universities and medical educators are now strongly advocating.

Membership in Phi Kappa Phi, the national honor society, is available to able students throughout the university. The chapter was founded in 1977, with its primary objective the recognition and encouragement of superior scholarship. Membership, by invitation only, is available to graduating seniors and advanced degree students in all disciplines who have demonstrated extraordinary academic achievement and are felt to be of good character. The first two distinguished member awards given by the national society to VCU faculty members went in 1985 to Dr. Wayne C. Hall, retired provost, and Dr. Lauren Woods, retired vice president for health sciences.

An application has been filed for membership in Phi Beta Kappa. The university authorities feel that the institution meets the requirements for membership in this prestigious scholarship society, and believe that their application will be granted in the near future.

Academic standards have been raised on the academic campus while preserving the heterogeneous nature of the student body. An average score in excess of 950 on the SAT is common for each entering freshman class. Applicants for the fine arts programs are judged more leniently as to SAT scores but rigorously with respect to artistic merit. The 200-odd students admitted annually under a particular dispensation for the disadvantaged are in a special category. And of course the thousands of working adults and other older students, mostly in the evening college, are also in a different category, although tests show them to be equal or superior to the regular students.

Undergraduates on the academic campus are required to maintain a cumulative grade-point average of at least 2.0, equivalent to a C, much like requirements of other colleges, according to Dr. Arnold P. Fleshood, associate vice president for academic affairs, now retired. This, he pointed out, applies to all work done, "not just work presented for graduation."

An $80,000 grant from the U.S. Department of Education to develop a minor in international studies made it possible for the university to join the International Student Exchange Program. Membership enables students to pursue their studies in approximately fifty universities in eighteen countries throughout the world. Students from all majors are eligible to apply, and several go overseas each year. The junior year is the preferred time and fluency in the native tongue is required where the language instruction is not in English. One year is the usual length of stay. Barbara Perrins is coordinator of the program.

Continuing education also is emphasized on both VCU campuses. Nearly 2,000 continuing education activities are offered by the division of continuing studies and public service, with an estimated 100,000 individuals involved. Dr. Howard L. Sparks, vice-provost for continuing studies and public service, is the responsible administrator. The university recently joined the experimental phase of the National University Teleconferencing Network, which, when fully implemented, will make a wider range and greater number of high quality continuing education programs available in the community.

Forty unique degree programs are offered at VCU, according to the State Council of Higher Education. These are courses offering an approved degree program that is provided by no other state-supported institution of higher learning in Virginia. These courses include seven doctoral, one first-professional, twenty masters, and twelve baccalaureate degrees.

A total of 3,261 degrees were awarded at the 1987 commencement. Applicants for these degrees are given an opportunity before graduation to confer with other graduates of VCU who are out in the workaday world, and thus to obtain first-hand, practical information concerning the various vocations and professions. This innovation was begun in 1984–85, and over six hundred alumni and alumnae signified a willingness to talk with potential graduates. The experiment was successful, according to Jean Yerian, who is in charge of the career planning and placement office. She said that among the participants "there was probably one of everything VCU has graduated since the 1930s." An amusing outcome of one of these conferences ocurred when a young man talked with a local lawyer concerning the legal profession, which he was thinking of entering. The alternative career was plumbing. After the lawyer told of overcrowding in the profession, overwork demanded, and overrated pay scales, the young man remarked, "I decided plumbing didn't sound so bad after all."

A score of companies are sending representatives to interview graduate business students each spring with a view to possible employment.

VCU's rehabilitation, research and training center is the only university-affiliated center in the United States whose major goal is to find jobs for the mentally retarded, and one of only three such centers devoted to research concerning these unfortunates. The organization helps between thirty and forty retarded citizens annually to find and hold jobs. Approximately ninety employers in the Richmond and Tidewater areas hire the retarded. The program, directed by Dr. Paul Wehman, is so highly regarded that it receives extremely large grants from the U.S. Department of Education.

VCU had a 20 percent increase in freshman applicants in 1986 as compared with 1985, and only 70 percent were accepted, as compared with 84 percent the previous year. The combined average of verbal and mathematics scores on the Scholastic Aptitude Test (SAT) of VCU freshmen admitted through the regular admissions process increased from 967 in 1985 to 974 for 1986. The national average is 906.

The number of faculty members in the academic division with doctorates has increased dramatically in recent years. Excluding the school of the arts, where the terminal degree is the M.A., the proportion holding doctorates increased from 45 to 78 percent between 1972 and 1983, the latest Self Study declares. In the Health Sciences Division, 77 percent hold doctorates, excluding the School of Allied Health Professions, where the terminal degree for most disciplines is the masters. Overall, 88 percent of the faculty in both the academic and health sciences divisions hold the highest academic degree appropriate to their fields.

Seventy-six percent of VCU faculty members with an opinion expressed themselves as "satisfied" as faculty members, when they responded to a questionnaire distributed by the Self-Study, and 86 percent said they were free to teach and conduct research, within the principles of academic freedom, and to participate in community affairs. On the other hand, 68 percent of the teaching force felt that they were not "appropriately involved in university governance," and 72 percent did not feel sufficiently involved in planning and budgeting.

Students were overwhelmingly favorable in nearly all of their responses, with 89 percent expressing themselves as "satisfied," and 91 percent saying that their professors were "prepared for class." Virtually the only unfavorable response was when 57 percent said they were "dissatisfied with student participation in institutional governance."

Salaries of faculty at VCU were found by the Self-Study to be about 10 percent below the average for a national group of peer universities.

The absence of a sabbatical program has caused various schools at VCU to explore "innovative ways of providing faculty with the opportunity to have blocks of time set aside for research or scholarship activity." Many such plans have come to fruition. The Self-Study of 1972 and that of 1982–83 recommended that a sabbatical leave policy be instituted.

The Distinguished Faculty Awards program was established in 1981 by the Board of Visitors, in order to recognize and honor faculty members with exceptional records in teaching, research, and service. These are the distinguished teacher award, distinguished scholar, or research, award, distinguished service award, and the university award of excellence. They are presented annually at the university convocation in October.

Inspirational and stimulating teaching is recognized by the first of the awards listed, and outstanding scholarship by the second, originally termed an award for achievement in research. The third recognizes uncommon service to the community or the university, while the fourth and highest award goes to "a truly exceptional recipient who has performed in a superior manner in teaching, scholarly activities, and service." Winners of these awards are listed in the appendixes to this volume.

The Wayne Medal, named for Edward A. Wayne, president of the Federal Reserve Bank of Richmond and of the Wayne Commission, which recommended the union of RPI and MCV in 1968 to form Virginia Commonwealth University, has been awarded to alumni and others who have served the university exceptionally well.

Four former members of the medical faculty have been accorded the greatly coveted designation of "master" by the American College of Physicians. This accolade goes only to those who are deemed to be among the top internists in the United States.

Dr. Charles M. Caravati, emeritus professor of medicine and former assistant dean of medicine in charge of continuing education, was the first member of the MCV family to receive this great honor. He was also the first to be given the Obici Award for outstanding contributions to medicine. He received the Distinguished Service Award of the Southern Medical Association, served as senior medical consultant for the McGuire VA Hospital, and is the author of *Medicine in Richmond 1900–1975*. The MCV Foundation, which Dr. Caravati served as president, and as chairman of the executive committee for five years, owes much to his indefatigable services over a long period. The department of medicine presented him with an engraved silver platter in 1970 in recognition of his forty-seven years of service to the department, and in 1985 he received the medical division's first Outstanding Alumnus Award. Caravati's conspicuously warm personality joins with his medical expertise to form a rare combination.

Dr. William Taliaferro Thompson, William Branch Porter professor emeritus of medicine and chairman of the department of internal medicine from 1959 to 1973, is another "master." "Tee" Thompson graduated from MCV in 1938 after leading his class each year. He was named chief of medical service at the McGuire VA Hospital in 1954. When he took over as chairman of the MCV department of medicine in 1959, it had twenty full-time faculty members. The number had trebled by the time he retired from the chairmanship nearly a decade and a half later. From 1976 to 1982 he edited the *Virginia Medical Monthly*, and the publication received two national awards during that time as the best in its field. Dr. Thompson served a term as president of the Richmond Academy, and was awarded a D.Sc. honorary degree by Davidson College, his alma mater. His portrait was presented to the health sciences division of VCU.

Dr. J. Morrison Hutcheson, MCV '09, and a member of the faculty for many years, was governor, regent, vice regent and master of the American College of Physicians. He served two five-year terms on the Judicial Council of the American Medical Association, and was president of the Richmond Academy, the Medical Society of Virginia, and the Medical College Alumni Association. Hutcheson served for thirty years on the board of Washington and Lee University, his alma mater, and was rector for several years. He was awarded the honorary degree of LL.D. by Hampden-Sydney College.

The fourth "master" designated from the MCV faculty by the American College of Physicians is Dr. Kinloch Nelson, former dean of medicine and recipient of many other distinctions, to which references have been made in previous chapters.

Town & Country magazine publishes periodically a much-discussed list of "The Best Medical Specialists in the U.S." The latest listing appeared in 1984, and included nine specialists from the health sciences division of VCU, as follows:

Surgical oncologist and gastrointestinal surgeon—Walter Lawrence, Jr.; gynecological cancer specialist—Leo J. Dunn; dermatologist—William P. Jordan, Jr.; kidney and liver transplantation specialist—H. M. Lee; urologists—Warren W. Koontz, Jr., and Robert Hackler; heart surgeon—Richard R. Lower; neuro-ophthalmologist—John Selhorst; gastroenterologist—John T. Farrar.

The health sciences division's first in vitro fertilization baby was born in

June 1985 to a Williamsburg couple, Ron and Mary Eimer. The "test-tube" infant was a boy weighing seven pounds eight ounces. The first such patients had been received at VCU about a year previously, and all became pregnant, but two of the three suffered miscarriages. In the fourth case there was a successful birth in Roanoke.

Dr. Sanford M. Rosenberg, director of the program, left the health sciences division to enter private practice soon after the successful birth of the Eimer baby. Dr. James M. East, director of the in vitro laboratory, also resigned, to join the staff of a local hospital. The in vitro program continues at the health sciences division with Dr. Kenneth A. Steingold as director, and Dr. Dennis W. Matt as head of the laboratory.

Mummies 8,000 years old—some 3,000 years older than those of ancient Egypt—from a people who fished and hunted along the coast of today's northern Chile, were studied intensively in June 1985 at the VCU health sciences division. Dr. Marvin J. Allison, a VCU pathologist, resigned in 1983 to join a team that was seeking to learn the secrets of about a hundred of these mummies, accidentally excavated in Chile. He returned to Richmond two years later to join with some thirty other pathologists from around the nation in studying these, "the oldest known artificially prepared bodies in the world." A symposium was conducted by Dr. Allison and Drs. Enrique Gerszten and Monique Fouant of the division's pathology department.

Apparently as part of a religious ritual, the bodies of these individuals of long ago were prepared elaborately. Dr. Allison stated that the skin, muscles, and organs were removed, along with the brain, and what remained was dried with hot coals. The legs, arms, and other parts of the skeleton were reinforced with straight sticks, so that the whole could be made to stand upright. It was covered with matting, smeared with clay, and painted black or red. A wig, fashioned from the deceased's hair, was placed on the skull. This apparition stood on its bony feet in the center of the village—a ritual that seems to have continued for some 4,000 years.

In a quite different area, Dr. Morton B. Gulak, associate professor of urban studies and planning and director until 1986 of Richmond's Revitalization Program, was reinforcing VCU's image as an urban university by taking a leading role in connection with ambitious plans for Shockoe Bottom. These revolve about Main Street Station, the Farmer's Market, and Tobacco Row, and cover the area bounded roughly by Grace, Main, 14th and 20th streets.

John A. Young Jr., downtown development coordinator for Richmond and executive assistant to the city manager, became the first full-time director of Richmond's Revitalization Program, succeeding Gulak. The latter had been part-time director of the program, and he relinquished the position to return to full-time teaching.

Two new scholarship programs were established in 1984 in honor of State Senator Edward E. Willey, an MCV pharmacy graduate of 1930, and for some thirty years a member of the General Assembly, in which he rose to a position of paramount influence. These are the Edward E. Willey Scholarship in Public Affairs and the Edward E. Willey Pharmacy Scholarship for Outstanding Scholarship and Leadership. Both carry a stipend. The late Senator Willey operated a drug store of his own for many years, and was president of both the Richmond and Virginia Pharmaceutical Associations. He was chosen pharmacist of the year by the latter association in 1956, and outstanding MCV pharmacy alumnus of 1982.

Senator Willey was one of numerous patients at the MCV hospitals who were having difficulty getting their bills in 1984. Others were getting them, but the bills were incorrect. The matter came up at a hearing before the General Assembly's Senate Finance Committee. President Ackell acknowledged the problem and said they were making every effort to solve it, but stated that a computer installed before he took over the presidency was seriously ineffective. New procedures had been introduced and definite improvement was noted, but it would take time to iron out all the kinks, he said.

"We've had a mess," Robert D. Shrock, health sciences finance director, said on another occasion. Straightening it out has been a priority for five years, and more automation is coming. The University of Virginia Hospital was having similar but somewhat less serious problems, Shrock declared.

W. Roy Smith, another eminent alumnus and distinguished pharmacist, served two years as rector of VCU and is a former president of the Medical College Alumni Association. He was one of the most influential members of the House of Delegates for decades, and served as chairman of the Appropriations Committee. He has also been potent in state politics.

After eleven terms in the House, Smith retired and joined A. H. Robins Company, where he headed the pharmaceutical division and became senior vice president. He resigned the post in 1982. A 1941 graduate in pharmacy from MCV, he worked in his father's drug store in Petersburg for a time. Roy Smith was president of the Virginia Pharmaceutical Association, was chosen pharmacist of the year in 1965 by the association, and was named outstanding pharmacy alumnus of MCV in 1984.

The Arnold P. Fleshood Fund was established in the School of Education in honor of Dr. Fleshood, the school's first dean, who retired in 1985 as associate vice president for academic affairs. The fund is to assist graduate students who wish to pursue a Master of Education degree designed to prepare them to become reading specialists.

Development, alumni affairs, and university relations at VCU were placed in charge of David W. Brown in 1984. He came to VCU from the Colonial Williamsburg Development Foundation, where he had been unusually successful as director of development. His title is vice president for advancement, a new position. He has overall supervision of VCU's four-year campaign for $52 million. Brown is a B.A. of Hiram College, Ohio, and has a master's degree in public administration from Syracuse University. From 1974 to 1980 he was director of corporate relations at Cornell.

Charles G. Thalhimer, retired vice chairman of Thalhimer Brothers, is in direct charge of the campaign for $52 million, which was formally launched on November 19, 1986. He announced then that $20 million already had been raised. The goal includes $22 million for endowment, $7.2 million for new program initiatives, $8.7 million in support of current academic programs, research, and student aid, and $14 million for capital improvements. James C. Wheat, Jr., heads the major gifts committee, Wallace Stettinius the corporate committee, and Dr. Wyatt S. Beazley III the campus campaign and physicians committee. G. Richard Wainwright, who had been named director of corporate relations for VCU some time previously, was working with Stettinius on the campaign.

Two major foundations have been extremely important in the development of MCV and RPI, and subsequently in that of VCU.

The Medical College of Virginia Foundation, established in 1949, with current assets of about $32 million, at market value, provides from $800,000 to $1 million annually for various worthy causes around the east campus. About 70 percent of the fund is restricted to certain purposes. For fiscal 1986 the MCV Foundation made total grants of $844,514. Of this, $786,000 went to the basic health sciences and the schools of medicine, dentistry, pharmacy, and allied health professions for faculty salaries, student scholarships, equipment, and research. Over $46,000 was contributed to the indigent care fund of the MCV hospitals. Exceptional leadership has been given the foundation over the years by the late Eppa Hunton IV, Dr.

Charles Caravati, and S. Douglas Fleet. David E. Bagby, Jr., is the current executive director.

The smaller Virginia Commonwealth University Fund, formerly the Richmond Professional Institute Foundation, has performed vital services over the years, as outlined in previous chapters. Whereas the MCV Foundation restricts its giving to institutions and departments on the east campus, the VCU Fund accepts gifts and owns property for the benefit of the entire university. Its holdings total approximately $18 million, at current market rates, and are largely restricted. The Alfred L. Blake chair of real estate is the principal beneficiary of the fund at this time. James R. Johnson, VCU's assistant vice president for financial affairs, is treasurer of the fund.

The VCU-MCV Women's Club has presented $10,000 to the university for the permanent establishment of a scholarship fund for women who need help in pursuing graduate degrees. It is named in honor of Jessie Hibbs (Mrs. Henry H. Hibbs), regarded as a pioneer in graduate education for women; and Dr. Marian Waller (later Mrs. Elam Toone, now deceased), MCV professor of medicine, who worked her way through graduate school as a laboratory technician, after putting her first husband through.

Dr. Francis J. Brooke, vice president for academic affairs and then provost of the academic campus, resigned in 1980, after a dozen years on the faculty, to accept the presidency of Columbus College, Columbus, Georgia. He had made important contributions to the building up of the west campus, especially in strengthening the faculty and raising academic standards.

Dr. Wayne C. Hall retired in 1985 as VCU provost and vice president for academic affairs. He had been second in command to President Ackell, and was in charge during the president's absences.

"We can thank Dr. Hall for his ability to recognize the need for change and his zeal to institute reform," Ackell said. "Among his finest achievements have been the strengthening of graduate studies, helping to establish the college of humanities and sciences, the cultivation of superior faculty, and a steady increase in overall academic quality." The Wayne C. Hall Research Award of $1,000, sponsored by Phi Kappa Phi, was established in his honor. It is an annual award for the best-written research proposal submitted by a graduate student or faculty member.

Myles P. Lash, executive director of the Medical College of Virginia Hospitals, resigned in 1985 to become national director of health care for the Arthur Young accounting firm. Dr. Alastair Connell, vice president for Health Sciences, stated that Lash had "brought the institution a long way" during his six years as executive director of the hospitals. "He is leaving it in a much stronger position than he found it," Dr. Connell declared. Myles Lash received the Young Hospital Administrator of the Year Award from the American College of Hospital Administrators. He is past president of the University Hospital Consortium. Carl Fischer, forty-six, executive director of clinical programs at the University of Arkansas for Medical Sciences, succeeded Lash in the spring of 1986.

VCU's Health Sciences Division has a collection in the basement of the Tompkins-McCaw Library that is unique in this part of the United States, if not over a much wider area. This is the remarkable series of medical and related artifacts, suitable for display, gathered almost singlehandedly by Dr. Peter N. Pastore (MCV '34) following his mandatory retirement from the faculty in 1976 at age seventy. It consisted originally of instruments, equipment, and other suitable material in otolaryngology, Pastore's specialty, and is being expanded to include representative exhibits in other segments of medicine.

Pastore, an exceptionally able and popular MCV student, who worked his way through by serving as night telephone operator for his last three years in medical school, began the collection during his freshman year. When he retired half a century later, and was able to devote a great deal of time to the enterprise, he launched it with about 650 items that he himself had assembled. He is enlarging the collection to demonstrate the progress of all branches of medicine through the development of medical instruments. In addition, antique medical books, papers on the history of medicine, and material from outstanding contributors to the profession are being sought, and brought together in the archives.

Some pieces of apparatus with weird-sounding names are on view—such as an intubation stent, bloodless tracheotome, bronchofibroscope, double cannula and flicker photometer. An early stethoscope is exhibited, and Pastore explains how the instrument happened to be invented. Something of the sort had to be devised, he said, because "the ladies in Victorian times objected to a doctor putting his ear on their chests."

"Pete" Pastore, who has been named "scholar-in-residence," not only devotes an enormous amount of time and thought to the collection, but he and Mrs. Pastore have made substantial financial contributions to it. They established the Peter N. and Julia R. Pastore Fund in 1947 with a gift of more than 50 milligrams of radium, especially for use in treating deafness in indigent outpatients during that period. Since then the fund has increased steadily through gifts from the Pastores and many other persons. The Pastores made a founding gift of $3,000 from the fund early in 1982 for support of the collection, and have contributed a total of $55,000 since that time to provide financial support for the employment of a curator or archival assistant.

Pastore served as chairman of the department of otolaryngology at MCV for thirty-five years, believed to be the longest geographical full-time otolaryngology chairmanship at any institution anywhere. He came in as department chairman in 1942 from the staff of the Mayo Clinic, where he was elected to Sigma Xi. Pastore also took an M.S. degree at the University of Minnesota. He got his A.B. in 1930, with Phi Beta Kappa, from the University of Richmond. He is a former president of the MCV Alumni Association and a member of the board of the MCV Foundation. Pastore received the distinguished service to medicine award at the 1985 VCU commencement. The following year he was invited to lecture in China and Brazil, and in 1987 he received the Presidential Medallion.

Virginia Commonwealth University has been unusually zealous in restoring and preserving the numerous historic structures on its grounds. The first annual preservation award of the Historic Richmond Foundation went to VCU in 1982 for its restoration of the two Putney houses, with their fine ironwork, on East Marshall Street.

Dr. Alastair Connell, vice president for health sciences, is highly conscious of the importance of creating an alluring ambience for the university, especially for the health sciences division. "I'm anxious to have a much more attractive atmosphere for the MCV campus," he has said. "I'd like to see a more campuslike atmosphere." As a native of Scotland, Connell comes from a country where ancient traditions are treasured, and storied structures are carefully preserved.

What is termed a Court End Consortium was organized in 1985 by the university in collaboration with the Museum of the Confederacy, the Valentine Museum, and the John Marshall House, all situated near one another in what was known as the "court end" of town a century and a half ago. The principal objective is to attract tourists, and the university is cooperating, although its buildings are not open to visitors.

On, or adjoining, the crowded east campus are a remarkable number of buildings with histories extending back into the early nineteenth century. In addition to those already mentioned there are Monumental Church, on the site of the terrible theater fire of 1811; the former First Baptist Church on Broad Street, built in the early 1940s in modified Greek Revival style; the Benjamin Watkins Leigh house, the home of a prominent U.S. senator from Virginia; the Maupin-Maury house, where Commodore Matthew Fontaine Maury, the "pathfinder of the seas," invented the torpedo that wrought so much devastation on Union warships in the Civil War; the Grant house, an early home of the Sheltering Arms Hospital; and First African Baptist, on the site of the original church of that name.

On the west campus, the three blocks extending along Franklin Street from Monroe Park to Ryland Street, were placed on the Virginia Landmarks Register and the National Register of Historic Places, as noted in chapter 9. The manner in which the handsome residences in this area have been treasured and used is an example to other institutions.

A titillating rumor concerning one of the notable Franklin Street dwelling places was circulated for years, and was picked up by a writer for a Richmond newspaper. It was to the effect that the Millhiser house at 916 West Franklin was connected by a tunnel under the street to some lady's boudoir on the opposite side. The writer made it fairly clear that he thought the whole thing was probably nonsense, but by publicizing it, he lent a certain amount of credence to the gossip. The supposed subterranean link to the gentleman's ladyfriend undoubtedly furnished grist for irresponsible chatter, but old-timers around the campus are emphatic in saying that no tunnel ever existed. The most authoritative denial came from Louis C. Saksen, assistant vice president for facilities management, who concluded after a thorough inquiry that the tunnel is a figment of somebody's fevered imagination.

A significant addition to the east campus came in 1985 when a marble bust of Hippocrates, who might be termed the patron saint of medicine, was presented to VCU, and placed in front of the Egyptian Building. Dr. Aristides Sismanis, associate professor of otolaryngology, spent almost two years planning and organizing the presentation of this gift to the university from Virginians of Greek ancestry. The Greek sculptor Menelaos Katafigiotis donated his time, skill, and materials to create the memorial, a duplicate of the bust in Athens. The original Hippocratic oath, dating from around 400 B.C., when Hippocrates lived, invokes the beneficence of Apollo and various other gods and goddesses, and is largely obsolete in its terminology and assumptions. A modern version of the oath is taken by students in nearly half of the medical schools in this country, although, paradoxically, not by those at VCU.

Six capital improvement projects for the east campus, costing $85.3 million, and planned for completion by the year 2000, were approved by the Board of Visitors in 1987. These are: a medical sciences building costing $33.5 million; ambulatory care expansion project, $11.7 million; limited renovation of the A.D. Williams Clinic and West Hospital, $8.2 million; renovation of second floor of the main hospital's supply and distribution building, $1.4 million; new hospital support facility, $20 million; renovation of McGuire Building and demolition of its annex, to provide new facilities for the schools of allied health professions and nursing, $10.5 million. Demolition of Dooley and East Hospitals is part of the overall plan. Half of the money for these projects is expected to come from private sources. No major new projects for the west campus are planned. The $13 million academic building on Main Street is nearing completion.

Affiliation of the Richmond Eye and Ear Hospital with adjacent VCU, in the form of a nonstock, nonprofit corporation, was agreed upon in late 1984, after years of discussion. Elimination of unnecessary duplication and furtherance of quality teaching, health care, and research in the areas of ophthalmology and otology, rhinology, and laryngology are to be given high priority. Continued development of a nationally recognized and academically oriented eye and ear institute is sought.

Many alumni who have achieved distinction have been mentioned previously. Two more deserve a special accolade.

Dr. Richard A. Michaux, an MCV graduate, now retired from the faculty, served on the Boards of Visitors of both the Medical College and VCU, and also on the board of Hampden-Sydney College, his other alma mater. The latter institution conferred on him the honorary degree of Doctor of Science. Michaux was president of the Richmond Academy of Medicine, the Medical College of Virginia Alumni Association, and the Richmond Surgical and Gynecological Society. He was also president of the Richmond German, served on the board of the Country Club of Virginia, and as senior warden of St. James Episcopal Church. As a captain overseas with General Hospital 45 in World War II he received the bronze star.

Dr. Percy Wootton, a 1957 M.D. of MCV and a member of the cardiology faculty, has served as president of the Richmond Academy, the Medical Society of Virginia, the Richmond and Virginia Heart associations, and the Richmond Society of Internal Medicine, and is a member of the council on legislation of the American Medical Association. He is said to be the youngest man ever elected president of the Medical Society of Virginia, and the youngest to receive its community service award. Dr. Wootton is a member of the Board of Trustees of Lynchburg College, his alma mater, and of the Science Museum of Virginia. He has been chief of medicine at Richmond Memorial Hospital, and is on the staffs of half-a-dozen other hospitals. He serves on numerous committees and boards, and is an elder of First Presbyterian Church. Wootton served two years in the U.S. Naval Reserve, and rose to the rank of lieutenant commander. He is married to the lovely and talented Jane Pendleton Wootton, who took her M.D. at MCV in 1965 and who returned to the practice of medicine at MCV some two decades later.

A Medical College graduate (1936) who has corrected facial deformities for some 6,000 children over a period of nearly half a century at Children's Hospital in Richmond, and has performed these operations without charge, is Dr. Leroy Smith. Now semiretired, he will continue his clinical work at Children's Hospital, which he describes as his "first love."

When he became a specialist in plastic surgery, Dr. Smith was the only physician in Virginia who limited his practice to that speciality. There are now eighty plastic surgeons in the state.

"The patient is always right," says Smith. "You don't ever blame them for anything. You always should be sympathetic to their needs and do your best to help. I think that's the secret of building good public relationships and certainly good practice of medicine."

He is described as a "warm, old-fashioned doctor who wants to help his patients; he exudes good will and warmth, and his patients certainly feel this."

Smith's alma mater, MCV, conferred on him the honorary degree of Doctor of Science in 1980. In addition to such private practice as he chooses to carry on in his partial retirement, he is serving as chairman of the Virginia Board of Rehabilitation Services.

The toll by death of prominent faculty members and graduates of MCV or the VCU health sciences division in the past two decades is staggering.

Dr. Samuel A. Anderson, Jr., a graduate of Washington and Lee and Johns Hopkins universities, was an eminent pediatrician on the clinical faculty of MCV for many years, until his retirement in 1965. In private practice in Richmond since 1928, Anderson was one of the organizers of the consultation and evaluation clinic at MCV, and its first director. In 1969 he received MCV's highest citation as "distinguished pediatrician." He died the following year.

Dr. Frederick B. Mandeville, who died in 1970, came to MCV from Stanford University in 1934, aged thirty-two, as a one-man department of radiology. He was said to be the youngest department chairman in any medical school at that time. "A brilliant man," declared the memorial committee, which deplored his death. "Dr. Mandeville devoted his time to the teaching of medical students and house officers. . . . Whenever he conducted a clinical pathological conference the auditorium overflowed with students and house officers, a testimony to his outstanding professional ability."

Nora S. Hamner, a 1914 graduate from the MCV school of nursing, crusaded against tuberculosis for more than half a century. Miss Hamner was the first woman named to MCV's Alumni Council and also the first to be named to the MCV Board of Visitors, to which she was appointed in 1953. She was awarded the honorary degree of Master of Science, the first woman to receive an honorary degree from the college. Miss Hamner was chosen executive secretary of the Richmond Area Tuberculosis Association in 1919 and she remained in that post for the next forty-three years. She died in 1971.

Two graduates of MCV lost their lives tragically, with their wives, in a hotel fire in Copenhagen, Denmark, in 1973. They were Dr. John P. Eastham, a 1937 graduate, and Dr. Carl Meador, who graduated in 1932. Dr. Meador had been president of the Richmond Academy and the Virginia Academy of General Practice.

Dr. Nathan Bloom, a graduate of the MCV school of pharmacy in 1925 and the medical school in 1932, served many years as a clinical professor and chief of the department of electrocardiography. He is described in the memorial after his death as "an effective and graphic teacher, beloved and respected by his students." Bloom wrote many articles for professional journals and was co-author of a textbook on electrocardiography.

Dr. T. Dewey Davis, professor emeritus of medicine at MCV, was drowned in 1977 while fishing on a pond near West Point. The boat flipped over when he lost his balance. He was seventy-eight years old. Dr. Davis was an MCV graduate, and served as president of the Richmond Academy, the Richmond Tuberculosis Association and the Medical College Alumni Association. He was also an elder in the Presbyterian Church.

Dr. Waverly Randolph Payne, a graduate of MCV in 1923, who practiced in Newport News, died in 1977 aged seventy-seven. He was president of the MCV Alumni Association, and represented the association on the MCV Board of Visitors. Dr. Payne was also on the board of the MCV Foundation, was past president of the Virginia State Board of Medical Examiners, and past president of the South Atlantic Association of Obstetricians and Gynecologists.

Dr. Carrington Williams, to whom previous references have been made, died in 1978, aged eighty-eight. He became professor of clinical surgery at MCV in 1939 and interim chairman of the department, 1955–57. The memorial, following his death, signed by Drs. William W. Martin, Jr., Carolyn McCue, and Hunter H. McGuire, Jr., said that "he declined the salary offered. . . . asking instead that the money be spent for operating his department." Dr. David Hume came to take over the department on a full-time basis, when full-time department heads were being named at MCV and almost everywhere else. "Nowhere was the transition more abrupt or charged with resentment than Richmond [as a result of Hume's methods], and no one could have been more sincerely distressed by the loss of mutual affection than Dr. Williams. . . . Subsequent restoration of friendship between MCV and Richmond was possible in large measure through Dr. Williams' careful leadership," said the committee. He contributed five chapters to the "classic textbook *Operative Surgery,* edited by J. S. Horsley and I. A. Bigger," and was "known not only for his skill and wisdom, but for the total recall and love of every patient he had ever seen." Williams was president of the Medical Society of Virginia, the Richmond Academy, the Southern Society of Clinical Surgeons, and the Southern Surgical Association. He was a delegate several times to the American Medical Association.

Dr. W. Linwood Ball, an MCV graduate in the class of 1927, died in 1979, aged seventy-five. He served as president of the Richmond Academy, the Virginia Council on Health and Medical Care, the Richmond Academy of Family Practice, and the Virginia Academy of Family Practice, and was a delegate to the American Medical Association for fifteen years. He was also vice president of the AMA and a member of its board of trustees. Ball served in the Virginia National Guard from 1928 to 1962 and retired as a brigadier general. In World War II he organized and commanded the Thirty-First Field Hospital, and from 1945 to 1946 was executive officer of Tripler General Hospital in Honolulu. Ball served on the staffs of three Virginia governors. "He was loved and respected by those who were privileged to know him," said the *Virginia Medical Monthly*.

Dr. Eugene Barbour Pendleton, a University College of Medicine graduate, class of 1908, who practiced for seventy years in Louisa and adjoining counties, and was believed to be the oldest and longest-practicing doctor in Virginia at the time of his death, died in 1981, aged ninety-five. Pendleton was the tenth man in his family to enter the practice of medicine, in a line going back to the early nineteenth century. His successor in that line, and the first woman in the family to become a physician, is Dr. Jane Pendleton Wootton. Dr. Eugene Pendleton delivered more than 2,000 babies during the course of his long practice. Those were the days when "house calls were made on horseback over dirt roads, or in the winter by sleigh."

Dr. J. Warrick Thomas, an internationally known allergist, and longtime clinical professor at the Medical College, died in 1982, aged seventy-three. He was named a Distinguished Fellow by the American College of Allergists at its congress in Paris in 1977. This award is not given every year, but only for "truly distinguished service to the practice of allergy." Dr. Thomas was president of the College of Allergists in 1952 and chairman of the board the following year. He was also a member of the board of the *Annals of Allergy*.

R. Reginald Rooke, a graduate of the MCV school of pharmacy, and former president of the National Association of Retail Druggists, with 36,000 members, died in 1984, aged eighty-six. He was also past president of the Medical College Alumni Association, and of the Richmond and Virginia Pharmaceutical associations. Mr. Rooke was rector of the MCV Board of Visitors for three years, and a member for eight. He also served on the Richmond City Board of Health. Chosen pharmacist of the year by the Virginia Pharmaceutical Association, he was given a gold cup and a portrait of himself. Rooke was awarded the honorary degree of Master of Pharmacy by the Medical College in 1952, the first person to be given this degree by the college.

Dr. Paul D. Camp, Jr., the first physician to establish a practice in Richmond limited to cardiology, and who practiced in the city from 1934 to 1978, died in 1984, aged eighty-one. He was on the clinical faculty at MCV, and director of the outpatient cardiac clinic, which he founded. Dr. Camp was governor for Virginia of the American College of Cardiology, and served as president of both the Richmond and Virginia Heart associations, as well as the Tri-State Medical Society. A graduate of the University of Virginia Medical School, he studied in London and Vienna, and under Dr. Paul Dudley White at Massachusetts General Hospital. The Medical Alumni Association of the University of Virginia conferred on Dr. Camp a certificate of appreciation for his leadership and outstanding contribution to cardiology. His sister and brother-in-law, Mr. and Mrs. Charles R. Younts of Atlanta, pledged $1 million for a Paul D. Camp, Jr., heart teaching center in the new University of Virginia Hospital. Camp was a founder and deacon of River Road Baptist Church, Richmond. An avid horseman, he served a term as president of the Deep Run Hunt Club.

Dr. Harold I. Nemuth, longtime clinical professor of preventive medicine, and vice rector of the VCU Board of Visitors, died in 1984, aged seventy-two, after a long and courageous battle with cancer. A graduate of MCV in 1932, Nemuth served as a medical officer with the navy in World War II, rising to the rank of commander. An accomplished jazz pianist, he entertained the navy men with his music. Dr. Nemuth's great concern for his patients was notable, "The most empathetic and dedicated physician I've ever known," one observer commented. He was a member of the governor's Council on Drug Abuse and Council on Aging, and from 1948 to 1966 he served as city police physician. The Virginia Military Institute made him an honorary alumnus, one of only five such alumni in the institution's long history. Nemuth was a member of Great Britain's Royal Society of Health, and the Richmond Bar Association voted him posthumously its Liberty Bell Award.

Dr. A. Ray Dawson, former professor and chairman of the department of physical medicine and rehabilitation at the VCU health sciences division from 1968 to 1973, and clinical professor there for many years, died in 1985, aged eighty-one. He was a 1929 graduate of MCV, and had post-residency training at the Mayo Clinic. From 1948 to 1965 he was chief of the physical medicine and rehabilitation service at the McGuire VA Medical Center. Dawson served as a flight surgeon with the U.S. Army Air Force in World War II, rising to the rank of lieutenant colonel. He opened convalescent rehabilitation hospitals along the East Coast for wounded soldiers, and was awarded the Legion of Merit. Named director of rehabilitation for the Virginia Department of Mental hygiene in 1966, Dawson was placed in charge of the department's geriatric services. In 1970 the Virginia Rehabilitation Association gave him an award for outstanding contributions to disabled Virginians. He served on the boards of numerous medical organizations and contributed to medical textbooks and journals.

Dr. Martin Markowitz died suddenly of a heart attack in 1985, aged sixty-five. A greatly admired surgeon, he graduated from the Medical College in 1944. As a captain in the U.S. Army medical corps he served as chief of surgery in three Japanese hospitals during the Korean War. Dr. Markowitz was clinical professor of surgery and clinical associate in gynecology at MCV, president of staff and chief of surgery at the old Sheltering Arms Hospital, and was on the staffs of several other Richmond hospitals. A specialist on cancer, he lectured to clubs and spoke over television and radio concerning cancer control. Markowitz was president of the Richmond unit of the American Cancer Society; he received a national award for that unit's public education project in 1965, and the Virginia division of the society's professional education award in 1983.

Another severe loss to medicine in Richmond occurred in 1985 with the death at age fifty-seven of Dr. V. Eric Kemp, Jr. He was pioneer in the field of coronary arteriography, and performed the first such procedure south of Johns Hopkins University. The technique calls for a coronary arteriogram, or coronary catheterization, by which the flow of blood in the heart and the amount of clogging in the arteries is studied. Kemp graduated from MCV in 1953, joined the U.S. Navy, attained the rank of commander, and served as battalion surgeon in Japan. He was a longtime member of the Medical College faculty, and served as director of the catheterization laboratory at Henrico Doctors' Hospital. Other positions held by Kemp included chief of cardiology at Richmond Metropolitan Hospital, and president of the Virginia Heart Association and its Richmond chapter.

In a separate category we lament the deaths of a dozen young graduates of MCV or the VCU health sciences division, all of whom died in their thirties and forties. Most of them served on the faculty, and several had attained a real measure of fame, although for some their careers had scarcely begun. One contemplates with great sadness this list of young lives cut short in their prime.

Dr. Frederick E. Vultee, Jr., was only thirty-seven when he died in 1963. Professor and chairman of the department of physical medicine and rehabilitation, he was said to have achieved already an international reputation. A graduate of the Yale medical school, he was "beloved by his students, his patients, and his associates," Dr. Richard G. Lester said in his memorial.

Dr. John H. Moon, a cancer specialist, died of that disease in 1972, aged forty-seven. A 1949 graduate of MCV, he entered the medical corps of the U.S. naval reserve. In the Korean War, Dr. Moon was in the terrible retreat in arctic weather from the Chosin Reservoir with the First Marine Division. On his return to MCV as a resident, he received several fellowships for cancer research. A small and seemingly superficial, but malignant, mole on his chest was removed, and he seemed in perfect health, but a decade later the cancer returned, and he died in three months. Dr. G. Watson James III was chairman of the memorial committee, which described Moon as beloved by his patients, and as a great entertainer, an authority on flowers, an outdoorsman, enthusiastic fisherman, member of several hunt clubs, and a history buff. An annual lecture in his memory was established at the college.

Dr. John W. Powell, who graduated from MCV in 1950, after taking his academic degree at Hampden-Sydney summa cum laude, died at age forty-three in 1965. His English professor at Hampden-Sydney said he was the most brilliant student he had ever taught, and, weighing only 150 to 155 pounds, he played center on the football team. "Jack" Powell served on the MCV faculty until his death. "Tireless in his devotion to his patients," the memorial committee declared, "a spell-binding raconteur . . . [with a] provocative wit and boundless store of anecdotes." And the committee went on to say: "How Almighty God in his infinite wisdom and mercy could take a man like this from his family and our community at the very height of his productivity will remain a mystery to the rest of us mortals."

Dr. Donald Lee Martin, who graduated from MCV in 1962, died ten years later, aged thirty-nine. On the obstetrics and gynecology faculty since 1966, Dr. Martin waged "an unbelievably courageous two-year battle" with sarcoma, which began with a simple cyst on his ankle. In his last illness "he was about the bravest person we ever met or heard of," said the memorial committee, headed by Dr. Philip L. Minor. Although his leg was amputated, "this didn't daunt him, and he was soon cheerfully learning how to use the artificial limb." But his "incredible courage" was not enough.

Dr. Tapan A. Hazra, chairman of radiation therapy and oncology for the VCU health sciences division, died in 1985, aged forty-eight. He came to Richmond from the faculty of Johns Hopkins University. Dr. Hazra, a medical graduate of the University of Bombay, India, was internationally known for his expertise in cancer of the prostate and breast. He was a fellow of the Royal College of Physicians, Edinburgh, a member of the Royal College of Radiology, London, and many other professional organizations. Hazra was a senior member of the Massey Cancer Center staff at VCU, and held a joint appointment as professor of pediatrics. He was the founder of the Susruta Society of Radiology, an organization of radiologists of Indian origin.

Dr. Christopher Lyon Wadsworth, assistant professor of dentistry, was found dead at his home in 1985, aged forty. He had suffered for years from multiple sclerosis, but in 1982 the students elected him professor of the year, and in 1984 chose him as best director of an extramural rotation. A graduate of Howard University, Wadsworth held a master's degree in public health from the University of North Carolina. He was the author of a number of scholarly articles, and only a month before his death, despite the disease that so gravely hampered his movements, he had completed studies of dental health facilities for the State Department of Health.

And this melancholy chronicle of those whose promising medical careers came to an abrupt close, concludes with the names of six other young graduates, several of whom were faculty members, who died between 1966 and 1979. They are Drs. Kenneth R. Baldwin, William Franklin Grigg, Jr., James Grayson Campbell, Carolyn Dale Candler, William C. Langdon, and William C. Williamson, Jr.

88. Dr. Stephen M. Ayres, who came in 1985 as dean of medicine, and is a nationally known author, editor, and specialist in pulmonary physiology.

89. Dr. Alastair Connell, a native of Scotland, came to VCU from the University of Nebraska as vice president for health sciences.

90. Dr. Peter N. Pastore, distinguished chairman of otolaryngology for 35 years, who, in his retirement, has assembled a remarkable collection of medical and related artifacts in the basement of the Tompkins-McCaw Library.

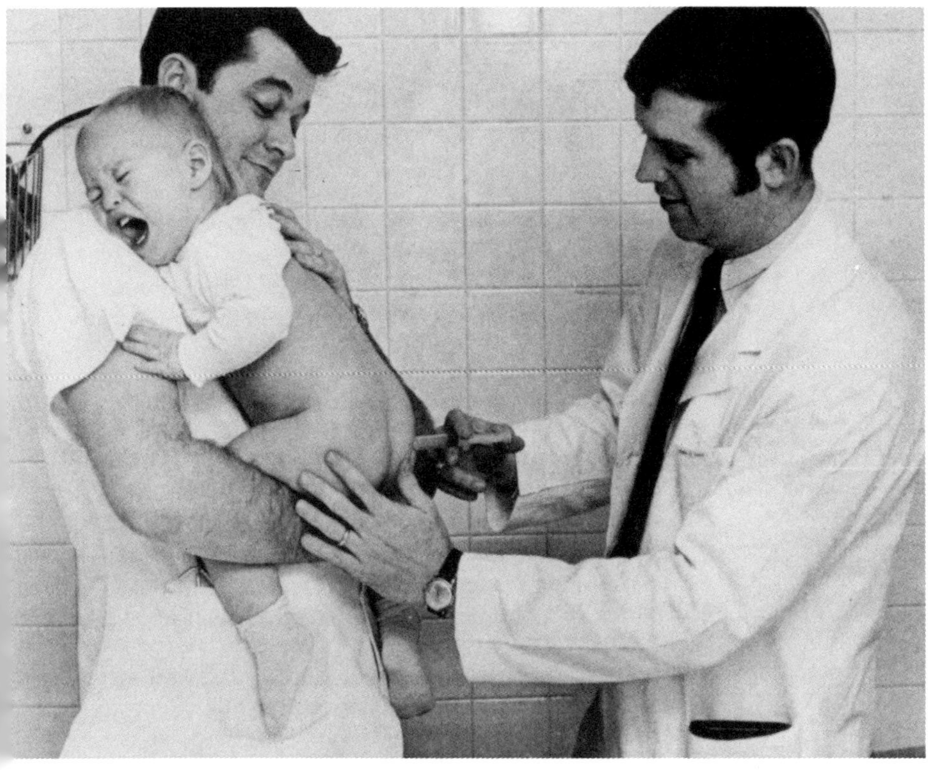

91. A youthful patient expresses himself in no uncertain terms.

92. Dr. W. Taliaferro Thompson, chairman of the department of medicine for fourteen years, editor of the *Virginia Medical Monthly*, and winner of several notable accolades.

93. Dr. Charles P. Ruch, provost and vice president for academic affairs, and former dean of the school of education.

94. Dr. Daniel T. Watts, first dean of the school of basic sciences, whose leadership was highly important in bringing the school to its present distinguished position.

95. Dr. H. St. George Tucker, Jr., internationally known specialist in diabetes, and winner of many awards.

96. Nell Blaine, famous artist, with one of her paintings. A graduate of VCU, she was awarded an honorary degree by the university.

NINETEEN

Moving Toward the Bicentennial

As Virginia Commonwealth University reaches its sesquicentennial year, and moves toward its bicentennial, the institution is able to point proudly to the excellence of many of its schools and departments. A number of them are unique in Virginia and even over a much wider area.

The Health Sciences Division has come a vast distance since 1838, when Hampden-Sydney College opened its medical department in what had been Richmond's Union Hotel at Nineteenth and Main Streets. Today the division boasts internationally known physicians and surgeons, pioneering in cardiac, kidney, and liver transplants, and celebrated scientists, especially in the biomedical disciplines. It operates a distinguished cancer center, a superlative pediatrics department, and a nationally recognized school of hospital administration, high-ranking schools of pharmacy, dentistry, and nursing, and a topflight School of Allied Health Professions, boasting one or more nationally or internationally ranked departments. And the 539-bed, $60 million ultramodern hospital gives the east campus a much-needed new dimension.

The academic division bears little or no resemblance today to the fledgling institution founded in 1917 on the third floor of a former residence, with only one full-time teacher. Excellent schools have been developed in the intervening years in several disciplines, and some are nationally recognized. These last include social work, the arts, business, mass communications, and urban services, and one of the largest and most complete evening programs in the United States. The urban mission of the institution is emphasized. The doctorate is offered in six subjects on the west campus, with psychology accounting for by far the largest share. Several badly needed buildings have been erected in the past decade and a half, supplementing the imposing mansions that have been carefully preserved and are still being used by the university.

The gratifying progress made over the years by RPI and MCV, and then by VCU, is due to the devoted labors of many persons whose contributions have been noted in previous chapters. They surmounted obstacles that would have daunted less dedicated men and women. Almost unbelievable brawls between prominent Richmond medical men, continuing for almost a hundred years off and on, threatened to damage the future of the Medical College irreparably, but it survived them all and went on to achieve national recognition. RPI did not face this particular type of obstacle, since its administration and faculty dwelt together in reasonable amity, but the total lack of any state funds for this state institution over a period of more than two decades came close to wrecking it. Only by virtue of amazing ingenuity was it able not only to survive but to progress.

The ferocious feuds among the city's doctors that rent the city for many generations are no longer prevalent. Rivalries still exist, of course, especially between groups attached to the various hospitals, some of which are suffering from lack of patients, but it would be unthinkable for doctors today to denounce one another savagely in the public prints, as occurred all too often in the late nineteenth and early twentieth centuries. The recent erection by several hospitals of annexes for doctors' offices does tend to split the local profession into factions once more, but there have been countervailing forces. For example, members of the various cliques were thrown together in MCV's overseas hospitals in the two world wars, and this tended greatly to lessen antagonisms. Men who had hardly spoken to one another before found themselves in close contact, enduring hardships and dangers together that caused them to appreciate one another's merits and to forget earlier animosities. Creation of Richmond Memorial Hospital following World War II in tribute to those who died in that conflict also brought the factions together. Something similar also happened with Sheltering Arms Hospital. And with the passing of several famous surgeons whose followers formed mutually hostile cliques, the nuclei for such cliques no longer existed. It would be absurd to claim that there are no keen rivalries or jealousies in Richmond's medical profession today, but certainly there are none comparable to those that prevailed at, say, the turn of this century.

It can also be said without fear of contradiction that animosities between the two campuses, so obvious when they were brought together by acts of the General Assembly in 1968, have declined drastically. The passage of time has contributed to this gratifying situation, since it has become increasingly clear that union was in the best interests of both parties. Then, too, many of the premier objectors among older alumni have passed to their reward in the intervening decades. The tremendous progress made by the west campus also has contributed to the lessening antagonism. Many at MCV were not charmed in 1968 by the prospect of joining with a much younger and less-prestigious academic institution, an institution, furthermore, whose students at that particular time seemed especially raffish and unkempt—although no more so than those at the Ivy League institutions in that particular era. One salutary recent step has been the merging of the two alumni associations, with benefit to both.

The Self-Study of 1982–83 is emphatic in declaring that practically nobody wants to revert to the time when the two schools were going their separate ways. "The last decade has brought so much progress," says the study, "not merely toward integration of the institution but in substantive improvement along so many lines, that hardly anyone could be found who could imagine going back to a separated existence, or would want to. Despite the enormous diversity within the university—of which physical separation is one but perhaps not the most important aspect—the merger is accepted and absorbed into our daily routines and thoughts about the future. We plan as one institution."

A few lingering and irrational evidences of hostility remain. For example, it was noted in the *Commonwealth Times* in 1985 that the movies shown on the east campus were closed to students from the west campus, and those on the west campus to students from the east. As time passes, such senseless prohibitions will be abandoned, and the two campuses will function as parts of a united institution.

Virginia Commonwealth University is ranked as a 1A center of learning, on the basis of the following criteria: (1) granting at least thirty doctoral level degrees, including first professional degrees, in three or more doctoral level and first professional program areas; (2) maintaining ten percent of enrollment in advanced graduate level programs, including first professional programs; and (3) ranking as one of the top one hundred research universities in the United States receiving federal funding.

Accreditation of VCU was reaffirmed at the annual meeting of the Southern Association of Colleges and Schools in December 1984, and this accreditation was remarkable for the fact that only two substantive recommendations were made, the best showing ever.

The university still evidences a strong urban thrust, but the emphasis is changing to some extent. The Self-Study of 1982–83 explained this:

> The original concept of an "urban" university, although still a powerful motivator, has proved too limiting for an institution whose state capital location encourages a statewide perspective, and whose professional schools seek to be nationwide leaders. But the alternative label of "comprehensive" is too vague, insufficiently descriptive of the particular mixture of program and perspective characterizing this institution at this time. High on the agenda for the future is work on a synthesizing statement of purpose and mission that will crystallize a more satisfying concept of who we are and what we wish to become.

VCU is obviously highly significant for the educational and cultural advancement of Richmond and Virginia. Its significance for the city's and the state's financial and business well-being is not so well known. The university has an annual budget of $358 million, and with 11,000 persons on the payroll is the largest employer in Richmond and the seventh largest in Virginia. It operates the fourth largest health sciences complex in the United States.

A few additional facts not mentioned previously are as follows: There were 1,965 full-time and 477 part-time faculty members on the staff of the university for the 1983–84 academic year, including 1,049 full-time faculty in the health sciences division, with house staff numbering 525 of whom 107 were interns and 418 full-time residents.

The VCU staff and faculty worked on approximately 350 sponsored research projects in the 1982–83 academic year.

VCU is ranked by the National Science Foundation as a major research and graduate university. It stands twenty-seventh among the 122 medical schools in the amount of funds received for research. Also the university stands forty-sixth nationally in medical science research and sixty-fifth in life science research. MCV hospitals were selected in 1985 as one of twenty of the nation's outstanding trauma centers by a panel of trauma experts.

About a dozen faculty members have received Fulbright grants since 1979.

President Edmund F. Ackell deserves a major share of the credit for the extraordinary progress made recently by Virginia Commonwealth University. His more than nine years in office (he took over in early 1978), have been highly productive in various directions.

Such is the view of the Board of Visitors, which has monitored his performance annually and reached highly favorable conclusions. Whereas a small minority of students and faculty members have been quoted in the student press as finding him "inaccessible," former Rectors Douglas Ludeman and Roy Smith do not regard these criticisms as valid. Both feel that he is doing "a fine job," and that the so-called lack of accessibility is no cause for serious concern. Dr. Ackell is a "no nonsense" type of executive with firm convictions. His management technique simply does not allow for unlimited access by professors and students. He meets regularly with representative faculty and student groups, and will see individuals when the occasion demands.

In a different area, Dr. Ackell has been expressing well-founded concern, if not alarm, for several years over the declining emphasis on the liberal arts in our centers of higher learning. In an unusually frank talk to the MCV Student Government Association in 1983, he declared that "the heart of the university has to be the liberal arts; they give us the ability to think." He pointed out that fewer than one-seventh of all students in this country are seeking liberal arts degrees, and that "this could be a travesty." In other words, the United States may be developing a surplus of graduates holding professional or business degrees, who have only a strictly limited knowledge of such subjects as history, English, philosophy, and foreign languages.

In his annual address to the faculty in 1984 the president made this sound observation: "The primary role of a university is to provide an education, not a job. A university is not simply a manpower training center. It is also a leadership development center and an ethical improvement center and an intellectual integrity center." On another occasion he declared his personal belief that "any educated person will have a strong sense of ethics, a clear sense of politics in the classical sense of that term, basic competency in problem-solving and reasoning, and competence in foreign language and communication skills." He added that a university-wide faculty committee was at work re-evaluating the VCU curriculum.

President Ackell's concern for the true values in college and university education is also reflected in his leadership role in efforts to curb the scandalous nationwide cheating and rule-breaking that has permeated intercollegiate athletics. He has been ahead of most university presidents in addressing this grave problem, since he advocated high standards for VCU in this area before the NCAA moved in on the situation.

"Ed" Ackell is not only a man of scholarly mind, with a clear vision of the true objectives of a college education; he is also a sociable human being, easy to know, outgoing in his social contacts. He and his charming wife Carole entertain attractively in their home at 4700 Charmian Road, Westmoreland Place.

Dr. Ackell's standing in the world of the higher learning is attested in various ways. He was one of seven university presidents from throughout the country who were invited in 1985 by the Israeli Embassy in Washington on behalf of the Israel Universities Study Group for Middle Eastern Affairs, to spend ten days in Israel studying the educational, political, social, and economic aspects of the country. The group made a report to the Israeli Parliament embodying their conclusions.

President Ackell has headed Virginia Commonwealth University long enough to have named appointees of his own choosing to all of the top administrative positions. Thus he has put his stamp on the institution, and has set it on the road to accomplishment in the direction he has laid out for it. That direction, as the university's first 150 years comes to a close, seems right for the school, the commonwealth and the world of education.

97. The R. Blackwell Smith pharmacy-pharmacology building, erected in memory of the former president of the Medical College at a cost of $12 million.

98. The great new Performing Arts Center on the west campus, with some of the finest facilities anywhere.

Appendixes

Bibliography

Index

APPENDIX A

Nobel Prize in Medicine and Physiology

1980 Dr. Baruj Benacerraf

APPENDIX B

The Presidential Medallion

1984 John A. Mapp
1984 Daniel T. Watts
1985 Dr. Kinloch Nelson
1986 Mr. and Mrs. Charles G. Thalhimer
1987 Dr. Peter N. Pastore
1987 Jewett Campbell

APPENDIX C

The Wayne Medal

1969 Edward A. Wayne, who received the die, or cast, rather than the medal
1971 Eppa Hunton IV
1978 Mr. and Mrs. E. Claiborne Robins
1978 H. I. Willett
1981 Dr. Wyndham B. Blanton, Jr.
1981 Dr. Harry M. Lyons
1983 Robert A. Wilson
1984 William E. Massey

APPENDIX D

Louise Obici Annual Award

(MCV graduates or faculty members)

1965 Dr. Charles M. Caravati

1968 Dr. Kinloch Nelson
1969 Dr. H. Hudnall Ware, Jr.
1979 Dr. Edwin L. Kendig, Jr.
1982 Dr. Henry St. George Tucker, Jr.
1983 Dr. Leo J. Dunn
1984 Dr. James Habel
1984 Dr. W. H. Chapman, Jr.

APPENDIX E

Medical Society of Virginia (Robins) Award
(MCV graduates or faculty members)

1963 Dr. John Wyatt Davis, Jr.
1970 Dr. Arthur L. Van Name, Jr.
1972 Dr. W. Linwood Ball
1977 Dr. Raymond S. Brown
1978 Dr. Harry J. Warthen, Jr.
1979 Dr. William J. Hagood, Jr.
1980 Dr. Cecil C. Hatfield
1981 Dr. Thomas W. Murrell, Jr.
1982 Dr. Paul C. Pearson
1983 Dr. Fay Ashton Carmines
1984 Dr. Percy Wootton
1986 Dr. Michael J. Moore

APPENDIX F

Distinguished Faculty Awards

1982

Teaching: Thomas P. Reinders
Scholar: Dr. Alexandre Fabiato
Service: Pratip Raychowdhury
Excellence: Marino Martinez-Carrion

1983

Teaching: John T. Povlishock
Research: Dr. Shaun Ruddy
Service: John V. Moeser
Excellence: William L. Dewey

1984
Teaching: A. Bryant Mangum
Research: Dr. Hermes A. Kontos
Service: Judith E. B. Collins
Excellence: Louis S. Harris
1985
Teaching: C. Williams Griffin
Research: George H. DeVries
Service: Iris A. Parham
Excellence: Dr. Walter E. Nance
1986
Teaching: Thomas V. McGovern
Scholar: David J. Smith
Service: Thomas O. Hall
Excellence: Dr. Harold M. Maurer

APPENDIX G

Dean's Award, School of Medicine

1976 Dr. Hunter H. McGuire, Jr.
1977 Dr. Richard H. Kirkland
1978 Dr. Gennaro J. Vasile
1979 Dr. Carolyn M. McCue
1980 Dr. Harry I. Lurie
1981 Dr. Harold J. Fallon
1981 Dr. Lazar J. Greenfield
1982 Dr. Shaun J. Ruddy
1983 Dr. Leo J. Dunn
1984 Dr. Jesse L. Steinfeld
1985 Dr. Harold I. Nemuth
1986 Dr. Harold M. Maurer

APPENDIX H

Distinguished Service to Medicine

1975 Charles P. Cardwell, Jr.
1976 Dr. Kinloch Nelson

1977 Eppa Hunton IV
1978 Dr. Miles E. Hench
1979 Dr. Randolph H. Hoge
1980 Dr. Elam C. Toone, Jr.
1981 Dr. Harold J. Fallon
1981 Dr. Lazar J. Greenfield
1982 Dr. Carolyn McCue
1983 Dr. Boyd W. Haynes, Jr.
1984 Dr. Henry St. George Tucker, Jr.
1985 Dr. Peter N. Pastore
1986 Dr. W. T. Thompson

APPENDIX I
Markle Scholars

Dr. Lazar J. Greenfield
Dr. G. Watson James III
Dr. Walter E. Nance
Dr. Leo J. Dunn
Dr. Hermes A. Kontos

APPENDIX J
Fulbright Scholars

Robert Armour
Daryle Dance
Richard Fine
C. Williams Griffin
M. Thomas Inge
Michael Miller
Richard Priebe
Howard Garner
James Hodges
Dr. Lyman M. Fisher
George Ferd

APPENDIX K
Guggenheim Fellows

Susan Kennedy
Dave Smith
Victor Kord

APPENDIX L
American Council of Learned Societies Fellowships

Boyd Berry
John Heil
Susan Kennedy

APPENDIX M
National Council for the Humanities Residential Fellowships

John Carstens
Susan Gohlman
Marguerite Harkness
James Kinney
Richard Mercer
Charlotte Morse

APPENDIX N
National Endowment for the Arts Individual Fellowships

Jack Earl
William Hammersley
Kent Ipsen
Susan Iverson
Curtis Ripley

APPENDIX O
Honorary Degree Recipients

1976

Eppa Hunton IV *Doctor of Laws*
Virginius Dabney *Doctor of Humane Letters*

1978

Theresa Pollak *Doctor of Humanities*

1979

Dr. Chapman H. Binford *Doctor of Science*

Paul G. Rogers *Doctor of Science*

1980

Dr. Richard C. Atkinson *Doctor of Science*

Dr. Leroy Smith *Doctor of Science*

1981

Dr. Baruj Benacerraf *Doctor of Science*

1983

Sydney Lewis *Doctor of Humanities*

Frances A. Lewis *Doctor of Humanities*

Tom Wolfe *Doctor of Humanities*

1984

T. Justin Moore, Jr. *Doctor of Laws*

1985

Father Timothy S. Healy *Doctor of Humanities*

Nell Blaine *Doctor of Fine Arts*

Justice Lewis F. Powell, Jr. *Doctor of Humane Letters*

1986

Floyd D. Gottwald, Jr. *Doctor of Humane Letters*

APPENDIX P

Rectors

1968–69 Virginius Dabney

1969–70 Eppa Hunton IV

1970–72 Robert A. Wilson

1972–80 Dr. Wyndham B. Blanton, Jr.

1980–81 Anne P. Satterfield

1981–84 Douglas H. Ludeman

1984–86 W. Roy Smith

1986 James B. Farinholt, Jr.

Bibliography

"Address to the Public in Regard to the Affairs of the Medical Department of Hampden-Sidney College." By Several Physicians of the City of Richmond. 1853.

Atlas, 1929–39.

"Attitude Survey of Former Patients at the Medical College of Virginia Hospitals." Summer 1983. Prepared by Professor J. David Kennamer.

Berthelot, M. "The Life and Works of Brown-Séquard." Annual Report. Smithsonian Institution. 1898.

Bimonthly Bulletin. University College of Medicine, 1896–97.

Blanton, Wyndham B. "Early American Medical Schools: The Medical College of Virginia." *Surgery, Gynecology and Obstetrics*, February 1933.

———. "Medicine." Chapter 12 in *Richmond: Capital of Virginia*. Richmond: Whittet and Shepperson, 1938.

———. *Medicine in Virginia in the Nineteenth Century*. Richmond: Garrett and Massie, 1933.

Bowers, Russell V. "Chimborazo Post (1862–1865)." *Scarab*, November 1962.

———."Civil War Days at the Medical College of Virginia." *Scarab*, August 1961.

———. "Our Faculty in Gray, Medical College of Virginia, 1860–1865." *Scarab*, February 1964.

Brashear, Alton D. *From Lee to Bari*. Richmond: Whittet and Shepperson, 1957.

Breedon, James O. "Body Snatchers and the Anatomy Professors." *Virginia Magazine of History and Biography*, July 1975.

Broders, Albert C. *Milestones in a Medical Career*. Privately published. N.d.

Bruce, Philip Alexander. *History of the University of Virginia, 1819–1919*. Vol. 2. New York: Macmillan, 1922.

Bryce, C. A. "Recollections of My Last Session at the Old Medical College of Virginia." *American Journal of Clinical Medicine,* vol. 29, 1922.

Bulletin. Medical College of Virginia, 1904–45, 1952–71.

Bulletin. Richmond Academy of Medicine, 1933–41.

Caravati, Charles M. Interviewed by Dr. Peter N. Pastore. Ms. Tompkins-McCaw Library.

———. *Medicine in Richmond, 1900–1975.* Richmond: Dietz Press, 1975.

Century of Virginia Pharmacy. Published by Virginia Pharmaceutical Association. Richmond, 1981.

Christian, W. Asbury. *Richmond, Her Past and Present.* Richmond: L. H. Jenkins, 1912.

Coburn, Randy Sue. "Tom Robbins: More Than a Pretty Face." *Richmond Times-Dispatch,* November 25, 1984.

Commonwealth Times, 1969–85.

Compton, A. Christian. "Telling the Time of Human Death by Statute." *Washington and Lee Law Review,* Fall 1974.

Converse, Ronald. "But When Did He Die? Tucker v. Lower and the Brain-Death Concept." *San Diego Law Review,* March 1975.

Deeming, Ralph. "Utter Stranger Equips Theatre." *Richmond* magazine, March 1929.

Dickinson, S. W. "Some Professional Recollections." *Virginia Medical Semi-Monthly,* March 9, 1917.

Dulaney, Paul S. *The Architecture of Historic Richmond.* Charlottesville: University Press of Virginia, 1968.

Elliott, M. C. "Shall the Medical Department of the University of Virginia Be Abandoned and Removed to Richmond?" N.d.

Epps, Garrett. "Impressions of a University." *VCU Magazine,* Summer 1983.

Epps, Rozanne Garrett. "Community of Interest—An Analysis of VCU's Evening College." M.A. thesis, VCU 1974.

"Fifteen-Year Development Program for Richmond Professional Institute, 1965–1980." Second draft.

Fifty Years in Richmond, 1898–1948. Richmond: Whittet and Shepperson, 1948.

First 125 Years, 1838–1963. MCV *Bulletin,* Fall 1963.

Flexner, Abraham. *Medical Education in the United States and Canada.* Arno Press and *New York Times,* 1972.

Futch, Ovid L. *History of Andersonville Prison.* 6th ed. Gainesville: University of Florida Press, 1978.

Geisinger, Joseph F., ed. *History of U.S. Army Base Hospital 45 in the Great War.* N.d.

George, William R. *The Image of Virginia Commonwealth University.* Published by marketing department, VCU, 1975.

Goldblum, Robert. "The 50,000-Watt Voice of Chuck Noe." *Style* magazine, April 23, 1985.

———. "Murry DePillars: High Energy." *Style* magazine, April 2, 1985.

Greenfield, Lazar J. "One Hundred and Forty-Five Years of Surgery at the Medical College of Virginia." Ms. Tompkins-McCaw Library.

Griggs, Walter S., Jr. "The Influence of Accreditation in the Development of the Medical College of Virginia into an Institution with University Affiliation." Ph.D. diss., William and Mary, 1979.

———. Interview with Ray Holmes on the above subject. Tompkins-McCaw Library.

Hibbs, Henry H. A *History of the Richmond Professional Institute.* Richmond: Whittet and Shepperson, 1973.

Historical Bulletin of Saint Philip School of Nursing and Alumnae. Published by Saint Philip Alumnae Association, Pinala W. Monroe, assistant historian. Richmond, 1978.

Hutcheson, J. Morrison. "George Ben Johnston, M.D., LL.D." *Annals of Medical History,* n.s., vol. 10, no. 1.

Johns, Frank S. "George Ben Johnston." *Southern Medicine and Surgery,* March 1944.

Johnston, George Ben. "Medical Education in the South." In vol. 10 of *The South in the Building of the Nation.* Richmond, 1909.

Larson, Paul S. "Brown-Séquard." MCV *Bulletin,* April 15, 1940.

"Legend of Chris Baker." *Scarab,* March 1954.

McCabe, W. Gordon. "George Ben Johnston, M.D., of Richmond, 1853–1916." From the President's Annual Report to the Virginia Historical Society, March 18, 1918.

McGuire, Hunter Holmes. Scrapbook kept concerning his confrontation with Dr. J. S. Wellford. In Tompkins-McCaw Library.

McGuire, Ruth Robertson. "The Nurses of Base Hospital 45." Address, February 27, 1932.

———. *Stuart McGuire.* Richmond: William Byrd Press, 1956.

McGuire, Stuart. "Hunter Holmes McGuire, M.D., LL.D." *Annals of Medical History,* 1938.

———. "A Protest against the Use of State Funds for Professional Education" before the Committee on Education of the Constitutional Convention of Virginia, 1901–2.

Maryland and Virginia Medical Journal, 1860–61.

Master Plan, VCU, vols. 1, 2, and 3, 1970.

MCV *News,* April 1951.

Meagher, Margaret L. *History of Education in Richmond.* Published under auspices of the WPA, 1939.

Medical Register, 1897–1900.

Medicovan, 1948–1973.

"Milestones, Marking the Achievements of the Past and the Opportunities of the Future." Published by MCV, 1926.

Milius, Helen C. "How Practitioners and Professors Reached a Truce." *Medical Economics,* Sept. 23, 1963.

Minutes, Board of Trustees and Executive Committee. University College of Medicine, 1904–13.

Minutes, Board of Visitors and Executive Committee. Medical College of Virginia, 1950–57.

Minutes, Executive Committee. Medical College of Virginia Faculty. 1928–38.

Minutes, Faculty. College of Physicians and Surgeons and University College of Medicine, 1893–1913.

Minutes, Faculty. Hampden-Sidney College Medical Department, 1847–54.

Minutes. Medical College of Virginia Board of Visitors Executive Committee, 1913–50.

Minutes. Medical College of Virginia Faculty, 1854–74, 1882–1926.

Minutes. Richmond Professional Institute Board of Visitors, 1962–68.

Minutes. Virginia Commonwealth University Board of Visitors Executive Committee, May 7, 1968–June 22, 1971; April 11, 1972–Dec. 8, 1972; May 29, 1974–Aug. 19, 1983.

Monumental Church Issue, MCV *Bulletin,* Summer 1961.

Moore, James T. "Battle for the Medical College." *Virginia Cavalcade,* Winter 1982.

Mordecai, Samuel. *Richmond in By-Gone Days.* Reprinted from 2nd ed., 1860. Richmond: Dietz Press, 1946.

Old Dominion Journal of Medicine and Surgery, 1902–16.

Olmsted, J. M. D. *Charles-Edouard Brown-Séquard.* Baltimore: Johns Hopkins University Press, 1946.

O'Neal, William B. *Architecture in Virginia.* New York: Walker and Company, 1968.

"Over a Century of Service to Virginia." MCV *Bulletin,* Spring 1953.

Pastore, Peter N., and Irby, Melissa L. "The Search for Invisible Space." Richmond Academy of Medicine *Antiques Show Magazine,* 1984.

Pollak, Theresa. *An Art School: Some Reminiscences.* 1969.

Powell, Hermie Wait. *The 100-Year History of Dentistry in Virginia.* Published by Virginia State Dental Association. Richmond, n.d.

Proscript, 1939–69.

Reflections in Ink, 1978–84.

Report of the Commission to Plan for the Establishment of a Proposed State-Supported University in the Richmond Metropolitan Area, Edward A. Wayne, chairman. 1967.

Report of the Higher Education Study Commission to the Governor and General Assembly of Virginia, Lloyd C. Bird, Chairman. 1965.
Report on Fatal Airplane Crash of Dr. David M. Hume, March 19, 1973. National Transport Safety Board.
Research in Action, 1975–85.
Response of the Board of Visitors of the Medical College of Virginia to the Invitation of the Commission on Medical Education in Virginia. Brief prepared by William R. Miller on behalf of the board. 1920.
Richmond, Capital of Virginia. By Various Hands. Richmond: Whittet and Shepperson, 1938.
Richmond and Louisville Medical Journal, 1868–79.
"Richmond Community Attitudes toward Virginia Commonwealth University." July 1983. Prepared by Prof. J. David Kennamer.
Richmond Medical Journal, 1866–67.
"Richmond Metro Area Attitude Survey, Medical College of Virginia Hospitals." Spring 1983. Prepared by Prof. J. David Kennamer.
"Richmond Professional Institute—An Evaluation of the Responsibilities and Future Role." March 1965.
"Richmond Professional Institute: An Urban College Growing in Service to Higher Education in Virginia." May 14, 1968.
"Richmond Professional Institute: Educational Program Development—Blueprint for Action, 1965–70."
Rogers, George W. "Richmond's Development into Medical Center Was Long-Term Process." *Richmond News Leader*, May 11, 1956.
RPI Handbook, 1959–60.
Rules and Procedures, VCU, 1972, 1978.
Sale, Marian Marsh. "The *Other* Most Urban College." *Commonwealth* magazine, May 1965.
Sanford, James K. *A Century of Commerce.* Richmond: Whittet and Shepperson, 1967.
Sanger, William T. *As I Remember.* Richmond: Dietz Press, 1972.
———. "Days Old and New." *MCV Quarterly*, Summer 1969.
———. *Medical College of Virginia Before 1925 and University College of Medicine, 1893–1913. Whittet and Shepperson, 1973.*
———. *Papers.*
Scarab, 1952–84.
School of Nursing at the Medical College of Virginia. Published on the 75th anniversary of the school, 1968.
"Scope and Mission of Richmond Professional Institute." June 1961.
Scott, Mary Wingfield. *Houses of Old Richmond.* Richmond: William Byrd Press, 1941.

Scrapbooks (three) on miscellaneous subjects. Tompkins-McCaw Library.

Scribner, Robert L. "The Medical College of Virginia." *Virginia Cavalcade*, Winter 1952.

Self-Study. VCU, 1972 and 1982–83.

Sheppard, L. Benjamin. "Reminiscences: 1930–1983." Ms. Tompkins-McCaw Library.

Shoemaker, Mary S. "Thomas Somerville Stewart, Architect and Engineer." M.A. thesis, University of Virginia, 1975.

Signpost: A Guide to Student Life, 1960–71.

Skull and Bones, 1915–18, 1923–45, 1948–52.

Southern Clinic, 1878–84, 1886–1919; numerous issues missing.

Spencer, Frederick J. "The Great Idealist: The Life and Times of Dr. Ennion G. Williams." *Virginia Medical Monthly*, Feb. 1968.

Spitler, Joann. *Encouraging Excellence.* Commemorating the 75th Anniversary of the School of Dentistry. Published by MCV. N.d.

Steele, Karen D. "The Egyptian Building: A Study." M.A. thesis, VCU, n.d.

Stethoscope and Virginia Medical Gazette, 1851–55.

Summers, Nancy G. "MCV—An Overview." N.d.

Taylor, William H. Article on, *The Messenger*, July 1944.

———. *The Book of Travels of a Doctor of Physic.* Philadelphia: Lippincott, 1871.

———. *De Quibus.* Richmond: Bell Book, 1908.

Tompkins, Christopher. "Forty-Three Years History." *Old Dominion Journal of Medicine and Surgery*, Aug. 1913.

Thompson, W. T. Jr., and Price, E. Randolph. "The Man of the Hour, 1862." *Scarab*, Nov. 1962.

Tucker, Beverley R. "Charles-Edouard Brown-Séquard." Address to History Section, Richmond Academy of Medicine, Apr. 13, 1937.

———. "Dr. William H. Taylor." MCV, *Bulletin*, April 15, 1940.

———. "George Ben Johnston: An Appreciation." MCV *Bulletin*, Sept. 1916.

"Two Groups Accuse Virginia Medical College of Stressing Research vs. Practice." *Medical Tribune*, Apr. 9, 1962.

VCU Today, 1972–85.

VCU Magazine, 1971–85.

Virginia Commonwealth University. President's Annual Report, 1982–83.

Virginia Medical and Surgical Journal, 1853–59.

Virginia Medical Monthly, 1874–96, 1918–84.

Virginia Medical Semi-Monthly, 1896–1917.

Warner, John Harley. "A Southern Medical Reform: The Meaning of the Antebellum Argument for Southern Education." *Bulletin of the History of Medicine*, Fall 1983.

Warthen, Harry J., Jr. "Medicine and Shockoe Hill." *Bulletin,* Richmond Academy of Medicine, Dec. 1936.

———. "The S.S. Arctic and Professor Johnson." *Virginia Medical Monthly,* July 1974.

———, and Williams, Carrington. "History of the Richmond Academy of Medicine, 1820–1960." *Virginia Medical Monthly,* Oct. 1962.

Wilson, Robert A. "The Public Relations Potential of a College Governing Board." Ph.D. diss. University of Arizona 1979.

Winthrop, Robert P. *Architecture in Downtown Richmond.* Richmond: Whittet and Shepperson, 1982.

Transcripts of oral interviews conducted by Alden G. Bigelow with the following: William E. Blake, Jr., Maurice Bonds, E. Allan Brown, Mrs. K. Chase, William O. Edwards, C. A. B. Foster, Jane Bell Gladding, Henry H. Hibbs, Jessie P. Hibbs, Raymond Hodges, Mary Kapp, Mary S. King, Rosamond McCanless, Theresa Pollak, Albert A. Rogers, and Lois Washer. Also an interview of Gilbert Baker by Sam Stage. All in James Branch Cabell Library.

Photo Credits

Dr. Kinloch Nelson, 56
Dr. Peter N. Pastore, 90
Richmond Newspapers, 40, 45, 52, 58, 60, 64, 68, 71, 73, 93
W. Ken Stevens, 81, 84
Dr. Weir Tucker, 29
VCU Archives, 1, 2, 3, 4, 5, 6, 7, 8, 9, 10, 11, 12, 13, 14, 15, 16, 17, 18, 19, 20, 21, 22, 23, 24, 25, 26, 27, 28, 30, 31, 32, 33, 34, 35, 36, 37, 38, 39, 42, 46, 47, 48, 49, 50, 51, 53, 54, 57, 59, 61, 63, 65, 67, 69, 72, 74, 75, 87, 88, 89, 91, 92, 94, 95, 97, 98
VCU Department of Athletics, 79, 80, 82, 83, 85, 86
VCU Office of University Relations, *Frontis.*, 41, 44, 55, 62, 66, 70, 76, 77, 78, 96
VCU Publications, 43

INDEX